ALSO BY JOSEPH J. ELLIS

His Excellency: George Washington

Founding Brothers: The Revolutionary Generation

American Sphinx: The Character of Thomas Jefferson

Passionate Sage: The Character and Legacy of John Adams

After the Revolution: Profiles of Early American Culture

School for Soldiers: West Point and the Profession of Arms (with Robert Moore)

The New England Mind in Transition

AMERICAN CREATION

AMERICAN CREATION

{ TRIUMPHS AND TRAGEDIES AT THE
FOUNDING OF THE REPUBLIC }

Joseph J. Ellis

Alfred A. Knopf · New York · 2007

THIS IS A BORZOI BOOK
PUBLISHED BY ALFRED A. KNOPF

Copyright © 2007 by Joseph J. Ellis
All rights reserved. Published in the United States by Alfred A. Knopf,
a division of Random House, Inc., New York,
and in Canada by Random House of Canada Limited, Toronto.

Knopf, Borzoi Books, and the colophon are
registered trademarks of Random House, Inc.

Some material in Chapter Six has been adapted from "The McGillivray Moment,"
originally published in *I Wish I'd Been There,* edited by Byron Hollingshead
(Doubleday, 2006).

ISBN-13: 978-0-7394-9509-4

Manufactured in the United States of America

To Alexander

CONTENTS

FOREWORD

The question that prompted this book first struck my mind in the fall of 2000. I was on a book tour for *Founding Brothers,* making presentations that happened to coincide with the presidential election and the subsequent vote-counting controversy in Florida. One question that came up at every stop concerned the Electoral College. How, in heaven's name, did the founders invent such a weird contraption? The other predictable question was more plaintive. Why must we choose between Al Gore and George W. Bush, whereas American voters two hundred years ago could choose between John Adams and Thomas Jefferson?

At least initially my answer to the second question was a model of scholarly prudence. The comparison between then and now, I explained, was inherently unfair. Those American statesmen "present at the creation" enjoyed the overwhelming advantage of being first, which conveyed a retrospective luster and iconic status that no one coming after could easily match. And once you learned something about the presidential election of 1800, which was one of the dirtiest and most controversial in American history, you would be less disposed to regard Adams and Jefferson as canonized political saints or the founding era as a pristine political paradise.

While historically correct, this answer proved wholly unsatisfying to most audiences, who seemed determined to regard the founding generation as the gold standard and our contemporary political leaders as a comparatively debased currency. Eventually I decided to play to their prejudices by paraphrasing a relevant observation from Henry Adams. If you reviewed all the American presidents panoramically, Adams joked, then you were obliged to conclude that Darwin got it exactly backward.

As a rhetorical tactic my response was a resounding success, ending the inquiry with a punch line that foreclosed further conversation. But intellectually my answer was only a clever finesse that provided no explanation whatsoever for the creative achievement of the founding generation except its privileged location at the start of the national story. And even though I was at pains to warn against any depiction of the founders as a group of demigods, my response permitted the mythical rendition of the founding era to persist as a once-upon-a-time location in the misty past sometime before the Fall.

Left unanswered, even unasked, was the obvious question: If you believed that the last quarter of the eighteenth century has stood the test of time as the most politically creative chapter in American history, and if you declared inadmissible any explanation for this creative moment that depended upon divine intervention, then what besides dumb luck can account for the achievement that was the American founding? Put simply, how did the American founding happen?

This book represents my attempt to answer that question. Early on, I decided that the answer was multisided, that no singular definition of political creativity could suffice, and that the biblical definition— to make something out of nothing—was entirely inappropriate. My approach, similar to that taken in *Founding Brothers,* was to assume that narrative is the highest form of historical analysis, that by inhabiting certain propitious moments and telling their stories, I stood the greatest chance of encountering and hunting down my quarry.

Later on, I discovered that some of the stories I had chosen to tell were as much about failure as success, in part because some of the problems facing the founders were insoluble, in part because some problems did not call out their fullest creative energies. Irony was also at work, meaning that impressive resolutions of some problems closed off options to solve others. By circumscribing federal power, especially at the executive level, for example, the founders placed the threat of despotism on the permanent defensive, but in so doing made it virtually impossible to end slavery or reach a just accommodation with the Native Americans.

This is a story, then, about tragedy as well as triumph, indeed about their mutual and inextricable coexistence. I come away from it still believing that the gathering of political talent at this historical moment is unlikely ever to be surpassed, which I suppose means that the Henry Adams quip, though wickedly mischievous, is not wholly unfair. But I also come away with a more chastened sense of celebration, periodically wishing that the founders had been demigods who could perform miracles. Then I catch myself and realize that, if flawless, they would have nothing to teach us. And they do.

AMERICAN CREATION

❧ The Founding ❧

DURING THE LAST QUARTER of the eighteenth century a former colony of Great Britain, generally regarded as a provincial and wholly peripheral outpost of Western Civilization, somehow managed to establish a set of ideas and institutions that, over the stretch of time, became the blueprint for political and economic success for the nation-state in the modern world. Over the course of the next two centuries these ideas and institutions—labeled "democracy" or "liberalism," though neither term would have been recognizable to the founding generation—replaced the monarchical dynasties of Europe in the nineteenth century, then defeated the totalitarian despotisms of Germany, Japan, and the Soviet Union in the twentieth.

Before we embark on the stories that follow, we need at least to glimpse the contours of the larger story, which is about the triumph of representative government bottomed on the principle of popular sovereignty, a market economy fueled by the energies of unfettered citizens, a secular state unaffiliated with any official religion, and the rule of law that presumed the equality of all citizens. What seemed so brazen and improbable at the time has become the accepted global formula for national success. The only alternative, apart from North Korea's and Cuba's last-stand versions of communism, is Islamic fundamentalism. And its essentially medieval values appear to be fighting a desperate rearguard action against modernity itself. The first enduring version of political modernity made its initial appearance in the United States during the revolutionary era.[1]

The most prominent revolutionary of all, George Washington, offered the first comprehensive explanation for this stunning achievement, and rather interestingly, he chose to emphasize the fortuitous conjunction of large-scale historical forces beyond human control rather than the actions or decisions of men. In Washington's formulation, written in 1783, even before the full story had played out, the American Revolution enjoyed two incalculable advantages: time—or perhaps timing—and space.

"The foundation of our Empire was not laid in the gloomy age of Ignorance and Suspicion," he wrote, "but at an Epoch when the rights of mankind were better understood and more clearly defined, than at any former period." Over the preceding two centuries, a number of English, Scottish, and French thinkers had generated a veritable treasure trove of political knowledge that undermined the medieval worldview about government, society, and even human nature itself. The American people were the beneficiaries of this accumulated wisdom—it had yet to be called the Enlightenment—which had its origins in Europe but was now destined to enjoy its fullest implementation in America. In effect, history had handed the American revolutionaries a blueprint for a new kind of political architecture that did not need to be discovered or invented, only applied. "At this auspicious period," Washington intoned, "the United States came into existence as a Nation, and if their Citizens should not be completely free and happy, the fault will be intirely their own."

The second providential advantage was space. Washington was not referring to the distance from predatory European powers provided by the Atlantic Ocean, though on other occasions he did describe that geographic fact as a priceless asset. He was referring, instead, to the almost limitless resources of the North American continent: "The Citizens of America, placed in the most enviable condition, as the sole Lords and Proprietors of a vast Tract of Continent, comprehending all the various soils and climates of the World, and abounding with all the necessaries and conveniences of life, are now by the late satisfactory pacification, acknowledged to be possessed of absolute freedom and Independency; They are, from this period, to be considered as the Actors on a most conspicuous Theatre, which seems to be peculiarly designated by Providence for the display of human greatness and felicity."[2]

It was a dazzlingly prophetic statement, especially since the western border at the time was the Mississippi, not the Pacific, and no one really knew what natural resources lay out there for future development and cultivation. But the key insight was that the American republic began with physical and economic assets as well as a rich intellectual legacy of enlightened ideas. It could afford to make mistakes, as it inevitably would, because the sheer potential of the continent would rescue and redeem blunders that would have proved fatal in a more constricted European context. (For example, the sale of western lands would bolster federal revenues sufficiently to make taxes unnecessary for the foreseeable future.) Though republican values were inherently opposed to all aristocratic legacies, the United States began with the largest trust fund of any emerging nation in recorded history.

Even Washington's explanation of the historical prerequisites for American political success acknowledged that the achievement, no matter how handsomely endowed, would depend on the adroit management of the advantages bestowed by history and geography. No matter how strong a hand had been dealt the revolutionary generation, it had to be played deftly. And if misplayed, all the advantages would collapse into a pile of humiliation and failure. This is what Abraham Lincoln meant eighty years later at Gettysburg when he said that no one was quite sure whether, in the absence of imaginative leadership, a government "so conceived and so dedicated can long endure."[3]

One of Washington's most distinguished contemporaries warned, however, that any shift in focus—from emphasizing the historical conditions underlying the American achievement to insisting on the decisive role of prominent personalities—ran major risks of distortion. John Adams sensed this shift happening in the first decade of the nineteenth century as he looked back at the history he had lived from his retirement perch at Quincy and compared his own memories with the histories already beginning to appear. In a characteristically candid and extraordinarily colorful correspondence with Benjamin Rush, his longtime friend and fellow revolutionary—a correspondence that even featured reports on their respective dreams—Adams warned that the emphasis on personalities and what historians now call "agency" was all wrong.[4]

Rush actually put it most succinctly: "I shall continue to believe that 'great men' are a lie," he observed, "and that there is very little difference in that superstition which leads us to believe in what the world calls 'great men' and in that which leads us to believe in witches and conjurors." Adams heartily concurred: "The feasts and funerals in honor of Washington is as corrupt a system as that by which saints were canonized and cardinals, popes, and whole hierarchical systems created." Adams had known and worked alongside Washington for twenty-five years, and could testify that His Excellency himself would object to "the pilgrimages to Mount Vernon as the new Mecca or Jerusalem." In an effort to display his own modesty—not a natural act for Adams—he made a point of objecting to his own sanctification: "It is become fashionable to call me 'The Venerable.' It makes me think of the venerable Bede . . . or the venerable Savannarola. . . . Don't call me 'Godlike Adams,' 'The Father of His Country,' 'The Founder of the American Republic,' or 'The Founder of the American Empire.' These titles belong to no man, but to the American people in general."[5]

Adams believed that the deification of the revolutionary leaders was transforming the true story of the American Revolution into a melodramatic romance: "It is a common observation in Europe that nothing is so false as modern history," Adams noted. "I should add that nothing is so false as modern history . . . except modern American history." In the Adams formulation, the true history was about chance, contingency, unintended consequences, about political leaders who were often improvising on the edge of catastrophe. Events, not men, were in the saddle, and all the founders were imperfect men rather than gods come down from Mount Olympus. "It was patched and piebald then," he wrote, "as it is now, ever was, and ever will be, world without end."[6]

When one young man tried to congratulate him for belonging to a truly heroic generation, Adams felt obliged to correct him: "I ought not to object to your reverence for your fathers, meaning those concerned with the direction of public affairs," he cautioned, "but to tell you a very great secret, as far as I am capable of comparing the merit of different periods, I have no reason to believe that we were better than you are." This was the note that Adams's grandson, Charles Francis Adams, chose to strike in the 1850s after editing his grandfather's papers: "We are beginning to forget that the patriots of former days were men like ourselves . . . and we are almost irresistibly led to ascribe to them in our imaginations certain gigantic proportions and superhuman qualities, without reflecting that this at once robs their character of consistency and their virtues of all merit."[7]

It is only fair to note that John Adams was particularly sensitive about the creation of a mythical American story line with a cast of demigods in part because he feared that he would not be given one of the starring roles. His critical assessments of Washington, Thomas Jefferson, and Benjamin Franklin, and even more his devastating denunciations of Alexander Hamilton and Thomas Paine, betrayed a throbbing obsession with his own place in the history books. In his old age he made himself into a one-man wrecking ball aimed at all the statues in the American temple, presumably concluding that if he was too palpably irreverent and too conspicuously imperfect to become an American icon, none of the other statues should be allowed to remain intact.[8]

Whatever his motives, Adams's prediction came true. The history of the American founding has become a conversation about the American founders, who have been mythologized and capitalized as Founding Fathers just as he feared they would. And until recently, Adams's fear that his own reputation would be eclipsed by Washington, Franklin, and Jefferson also proved prophetic. The operative question when discussing the American founding has become not "How did it happen?" but "How did they do it?"

BEFORE WE ENTER the electromagnetic field that continues to envelop both of those questions, a place where wildly extravagant claims and equally hyperbolic counterclaims seem to flourish more robustly than in any other area of American history, save perhaps the Civil War, we would be well advised to pause, get our historical bearings, and pose what is, at least on the face of it, a factual question: What, specifically, did the founding generation achieve? Why are they accorded such iconic status? What, in short, is all the fuss about? My own answer, offered with as much historical detachment as I can muster, is that there were five core achievements.

First, the revolutionary generation won the first successful war for colonial independence in the modern era, against all odds defeating the most powerful army and navy in the world. Washington liked to call the American victory "a standing miracle," a phrase that suggests some kind of supernatural intervention on America's side. As we shall see, the French were more important than the gods, and the strategic decisions that made victory possible also made miracles unnecessary. Nevertheless, Washington's phrase correctly captures the improbable character of the outcome as perceived by most informed observers at the outset of the war and the all-or-nothing gamble that the most prominent revolutionary leaders were prepared to take.[9]

Second, they established the first nation-sized republic. Until then it was presumed that republican governments based on the principle of popular consent could function only in small areas like Greek city-states or Swiss cantons, because the inherent weakness of republican government made it incapable of decisiveness or the management of a far-flung population. This presumption was proven wrong, and in the process the very definition of what it meant to govern a people was transformed forever in ways that put all coercive forms of political authority on the permanent defensive.

Third, they created the first wholly secular state. Before the American Revolution it was broadly assumed that shared religious convictions were the primary basis for the common values that linked together the people of any political community, indeed the ideological glue that made any sense of community possible. By insisting on the complete separation of church and state, the founders successfully overturned this long-standing presumption.

Fourth, they rejected the conventional wisdom, agreed upon since

Aristotle, that political sovereignty must reside in one agreed-upon location, that sovereignty was by definition singular and indivisible. The Constitution defied this assumption by creating multiple and overlapping sources of authority in which the blurring of jurisdiction between federal and state power became an asset rather than a liability, thereby making the very idea of sovereignty itself problematic and its rhetorical depository, "the people," an elusive and ever-shifting location.

Fifth, they created political parties as institutionalized channels for ongoing debate, which eventually permitted dissent to be regarded not as a treasonable act, but as a legitimate voice in an endless argument. Although British political parties foreshadowed the American party system, and although the founders themselves found it difficult to embrace the notion of a legitimate opposition, the framework they created allowed ongoing dialogue to become a hallmark of the modern liberal state.

Though not a separate achievement per se, a corollary triumph that merits mention is the ability to reconcile two competing and, in several respects, contradictory political impulses. There were really two founding moments: the first in 1776, which declared American independence, and the second in 1787–88, which declared American nationhood. The Declaration of Independence is the seminal document in the first instance, the Constitution in the second. The former is a radical document that locates sovereignty in the individual and depicts government as an alien force, making rebellion against it a natural act. The latter is a conservative document that locates sovereignty in that collective called "the people," makes government an essential protector of liberty rather than its enemy, and values social balance over personal liberation. It is extremely rare for the same political elite to straddle both occasions. Or, to put it differently, it is uncommon for the same men who make a revolution also to secure it.

These are considerable achievements that continue to glow even brighter with the passage of time, most especially as we witness the extreme difficulty many countries in Africa, Asia, and the Middle East experience in trying to re-create them. But while basking in the reflected glory of their glow, we also need to notice the shadows cast by the two most conspicuous failures of the revolutionary generation. In addition to asking "What did they do?," we need to ask "What did they fail to do?"

The darkest shadow is unquestionably slavery, the failure to end it, or at least to adopt a gradual emancipation scheme that put it on the road to extinction. Virtually all the most prominent founders recognized that slavery was an embarrassing contradiction that violated all the principles the American Revolution claimed to stand for. And virtually every American historian who has studied the matter has concluded that the persistence and eventual expansion of slavery made the Civil War almost inevitable. While there is plenty of room for honest disagreement over the viability of any emancipation policy in the revolutionary era, slavery remains a permanent stain on the legacy of the founders, as most of them knew it would.

The other shadow, almost as dark, was the failure to implement a just and generous settlement with the Native Americans. Again, what such a settlement might have looked like must remain an open question. (One of the stories that follows suggests an answer that was tried and found wanting.) But all the principal founders acknowledged that the indigenous people of North America had a legitimate claim to the soil and a moral claim on the conscience of the infant republic. This is another problem, like slavery, that either failed to engage the creative energies of the founders in their fullest form or was inherently insoluble.[10]

If this admittedly over-succinct summary is essentially correct, then the story of the founding is, at least at one level, an extraordinary tale of monumental achievement. The British philosopher and essayist Alfred North Whitehead was probably right to observe that there have been only two instances in the history of Western Civilization when the political leaders of an emerging nation behaved as well as anyone could reasonably expect. The first was Rome under Caesar Augustus and the second was America's revolutionary generation. The American historian Samuel Eliot Morison also thought the political creativity of the founders ranked at or near the top of any all-time list, though he cited the political ideas unleashed during the English Civil War as the only worthy competitor. Whatever the proper international comparison, there can be little doubt that the late eighteenth century was the most politically creative era in American history.[11]

But the triumph was also a tragedy of monumental proportions. For the founding left slavery intact south of the Potomac, a protected base from which it spread like a cancer into the territories of the southwest, thereby rendering any peaceful solution impossible as the slave population increased eightfold between 1776 and 1860. And the seeds of Indian extinction east of the Mississippi were indisputably sown in the late eighteenth century.

Taken together, these triumphal and tragic elements should constitute the ingredients for an epic historical narrative that defies all moralistic categories, a story line rooted in the coexistence of grace and sin, grandeur and failure, brilliance and blindness. No aspiring historian, or novelist, could wish for more. But that is not the way the story has been told. Instead, we have been asked to choose between two simplistic narratives of the founding, one featuring the founders as demigods who were permitted to glimpse the eternal truths, or, as Ralph Waldo Emerson once put it, "to see God face to face," the other crowded with a cast of villains who collectively comprise the deadest, whitest males in American history.[12]

It is an interpretive syndrome that Henry Adams once described as "infantile," but that might more accurately be labeled "adolescent." In the same way that teenagers display wild mood swings toward their parents—we go from omniscient seers to despicable idiots in the twinkling of an adolescent eye—the reputation of the founders over the past two centuries has oscillated in the same kind of swoonish arc between idolization and evisceration. The mindlessly celebratory and the naively judgmental responses to the founders are in fact complementary cartoons, the front and back sides of the same distorted picture that we periodically rotate, like a child fluctuating between the emotional imperatives of unconditional love and Oedipal hate.

Although the larger contours of this hyperbolic pattern continue to hold, over the last forty years most academic historians have essentially abandoned the founding and founders altogether in order to focus their scholarly attention on the inarticulate, peripheral, dispossessed Americans—women, slaves, and Indians. Ironically, this shift in focus, rooted in a conviction that mainstream politics is overworked terrain, has coincided with the publication of comprehensive editions of the papers of the most prominent founders that, taken together, constitute the most complete documentation of human endeavor by any political elite in recorded history.

But the currently hegemonic narrative within the groves of academe—race, class, and gender are the privileged categories of analysis—customarily labels (and libels) the founders as racists, classists, and sexists, a kind of rogues' gallery rather than a gallery of greats. Within this cloistered climate, in short, the Oedipal side of the adolescent interpretation holds sway, so that it is possible, in all seriousness, to argue that the American Revolution was an unmitigated calamity and the founding itself an abject failure because, as one historian put it, it "failed to free the slaves, failed to offer full political equality to women, failed to grant citizenship to Indians, failed to create an economic world in which all could compete on equal terms."[13]

Whether the founders are studiously ignored or condescendingly reviled within the academy, the effect on the larger public has been negligible, since the scholarly debates are in-house affairs, the books and articles written in language that the uninitiated find inaccessible and often incomprehensible. For whatever the reasons, historians dedicated to a recovery of the experience of ordinary Americans in the past have chosen to abandon ordinary readers in the present, preferring to communicate only with each other. This voluntary abdication by the academy, coupled with the availability of unprecedented documentary sources for all the major founders, has created a huge gap between what we actually know about the founding in all its messy splendor and what is known by most literate and educated Americans.

Starting about a dozen years ago, however, this gap began to be filled by writers, many not professional historians, who plundered the massive new collections of correspondence and documentation on the founding era to produce a flurry of books, mostly biographies, that became a publishing sensation because of their unforeseen popularity. Books on John

Adams, Benjamin Franklin, Alexander Hamilton, and George Washington, in addition to books about the drafting of the Declaration of Independence, Washington's crossing of the Delaware on Christmas night in 1776, and the founders as a self-conscious "band of brothers," enjoyed unprecedented commercial and critical success.

The source of this founders surge need not concern us here, though clearly there is an audience for serious history about our origins that the academy has largely ignored. The major point is that the founders and the founding are back, in a big way, as serious topics of public conversation. The long latent interest in our origins—the old "How did it happen?" question—has become relevant again. And, most importantly, the electromagnetic shield is breaking down. For one of the hallmarks of the recent founders surge is the emphasis on flawed greatness, the coexistence of intellectual depth and personal shallowness, the role of contingency and sheer accident instead of divine providence. The founding has at least begun to become the topic in an adult conversation rather than a juvenile melodrama populated only by heroes or villains. In a sense, we have reached the realistic place that John Adams wished us to occupy two hundred years ago.[14]

ALTHOUGH MOST professional historians of the revolutionary era have opted to avoid mainstream politics altogether in favor of less articulate and more marginalized groups—a rather bizarre choice as I see it, somewhat akin to showing up at Fenway Park with a lacrosse stick—there have been several attempts to answer the "How did they do it?" question in ways that carry us beyond the conventional cartoon. These attempts are not mutually exclusive but, quite the opposite, overlapping efforts at an explanation for the creative outburst of the founding era that carry us past vague suggestions that there was something special in the water back then.

The earliest of the recent efforts came from Douglass Adair, who focused attention on "the lust for fame" as a conspicuous thread that runs through the letters of all the founders. Fame as they understood it was not just popular recognition during their lifetimes; fame was forever. It meant living on in the memories of subsequent generations yet unborn. The only election result that counted for them, Adair argued, was posterity's judgment, and the only way to win that vote and achieve secular immortality was to conduct themselves according to a classical code that linked their personal ambitions, which were gargantuan, to the long-term interest of the nation-in-making. Only if the United States succeeded would cities, states, and mountains be named after them. (Washington's decision to free the slaves he owned in his will, for example, was in great part motivated by his realization that failure to do so would forever stain his reputation.) They were, in effect, always on their best behavior because they knew we would be watching, an idea we should find endearing because it makes us complicitous in their greatness.

The Adair argument certainly explains why any library of the founders' writings must bulge at the seams. They were compulsively fastidious about preserving every scrap of paper, Washington even requesting (and receiving) a team of secretaries to transcribe his wartime correspondence from a Continental Congress then unable even to clothe and feed his army. The obsession with posterity's judgment also explains why, in their old age, they often chose to retrospectively airbrush their youthful blunders out of the picture, as when Jefferson edited out his confident claim that the French Revolution would be a bloodless triumph. Especially toward the end, posing for posterity became an instinctive act, because posterity was the only afterlife of which most of them were certain. (Adams, colorfully irreverent to the end, declared that he was not sure if there was life after death, but "if it should be revealed or demonstrated that there is no future state, my advice to every man, woman, and child would be . . . to take opium.") The Adair interpretation does not attempt to offer a comprehensive explanation for the creative explosion at the founding, but it does help to explain why the founders came down to us as otherworldly icons.[15]

An altogether different explanation for the distinctive character of the founders' achievement comes from Gordon Wood, whose argument echoes the earliest observation by Washington that timing was crucial. As we have seen, Washington was referring to the availability of political ideas generated by the Enlightenment, which were abstract theories in Europe that became living ideas in the American laboratory. Wood endorses this explanation, but expands it considerably by describing the revolutionary era as a truly special moment that provided opportunities for political leadership and creativity never possible before and never achievable since.

It was simultaneously, Wood observes, a post-aristocratic and a pre-democratic age. The first condition meant that politics in America was open to a whole class of talented men—women were still unimaginable as public figures—who would have languished in obscurity throughout Europe because they lacked the proper bloodlines. Washington, for example, would have never risen beyond the rank of major in the British army. Adams would have become a mere country lawyer. Hamilton, who was literally a bastard, would have never enjoyed the opportunity to display his natural brilliance. To be sure, there was still a discernible social hierarchy in revolutionary America, but there was also unprecedented opportunity for movement from bottom to top (and vice versa). When the revolutionary crisis arrived, it could draw upon the latent talent of a segment of the population never before permitted access.

The pre-democratic side of the story, which Wood emphasizes, describes the founders as a self-conscious and unembarrassed political elite, what Jefferson called "a natural aristocracy," altogether contemptuous of being described as democrats. All of them regarded the act of campaigning for office as a formal confession that they were unworthy to serve, a statement that they were not statesmen but demagogues. While popular opinion was hardly irrelevant, it was regarded as flighty, undependable, shortsighted, and easily manipulated. The ultimate allegiance of the founders was not to "the people" but to "the public," which was the long-term interest of the citizenry that they, the founders, had been chosen to divine.

The founding generation, then, had the advantage of occupying a place in time that enjoyed the benefit of post-aristocratic access to latent talent without the liabilities of a fully egalitarian society in which an elitist sense of superiority was forbidden. Living between two worlds, without belonging completely to either, the founders maximized the advantages of both. In a sense, they were America's first and only Lost Generation, for, as Wood is at pains to show, they can never happen again. Or, as Mark Twain pronounced upon arriving at the Holy Land: "Christ been here once. Will never come again."[16]

A third explanation comes from Bernard Bailyn, who offers the disarmingly counterintuitive argument that the prescience of the founders was a function of their provincialism. Bailyn poses, more clearly than anyone else, the core question: How did this backwoods population of three to five million farmers, mechanics, and minor gentry, huddled on the distant edge of the British Empire, far removed from the epicenters of learning and culture in London and Paris, somehow produce thinkers and ideas that fundamentally transformed the landscape of modern politics?

His answer, at least as I read it, is that less was more. The American political conversation, in effect, could afford to range more widely because it was not weighed down by encrusted traditions, embedded institutions, and socially sanctioned inhibitions. Being on the periphery rather than at the cosmopolitan center carried a cultural stigma, to be sure, in which Britons described their American cousins as awkward bumpkins only one step removed from primitive savagery. (Proudly and slyly donning his coonskin hat in Paris, Franklin embraced the stigma and made it into a badge of honor.) But being far removed from the cultural metropolis, which was laden with what Jefferson liked to call "the dead hand of the past," the revolutionary generation was freer to question the old self-evident truths and invent their own without fear of offending established sources of power and authority because, in fact, there were none.[17]

Finally, and I hope not awkwardly, I have argued that the success of the founders was partially attributable to their ideological and even temperamental diversity. Although George Washington was primus inter pares, first among equals within the leadership class of the revolutionary generation, we speak of the founders in the plural for a reason. The American founding was a collective enterprise with multiple players who harbored fundamentally different beliefs about what the American Revolution meant. Adams and Jefferson went to their graves arguing with each other about what they had actually founded and how they had somehow done it. Unlike the French, Russian, and Chinese revolutions, or the scores of Third World revolutions in the twentieth century, the American Revolution never devolved into a one-man despotism— Napoleon, Lenin/Stalin, Mao—that became the sole face of the revolutionary project. The American founding was, and still is, a group portrait.

Political and personal diversity enhanced creativity by generating a dynamic chemistry that surfaced routinely in the form of competing convictions whenever a major crisis materialized. Every major decision— the ratification of the Constitution, the creation of the National Bank, the response to the French Revolution, the Jay Treaty—produced a bracing argument among founders of different persuasions about revolutionary principles. This not only enriched the intellectual ferment, but also replicated the checks and balances of the Constitution with a human version of the same principle.[18]

Despite their different points of emphasis, all four of these interpretations are welcome contributions, because they move us beyond the infamous electromagnetic field inhabited only by heroes and villains. And like the best of the recent entries in the founders sweepstakes, they contribute to a discernibly adult conversation about the sources and causes of the American founding as a significant political triumph. The stories that follow represent my effort to continue that conversation, and extend it so as to include the tragic dimension as well.

THE STORIES do not claim to offer either an exhaustive or a wholly comprehensive account of the founding era, here defined as the twenty-eight-year period between the start of the War for Independence (1775) and the Louisiana Purchase (1803). The repertory company of players has been assembled according to the Casablanca Principle, which is to say that I have rounded up the usual suspects, who have starring roles in some stories and make only cameo appearances in others. If four of the founders must be listed at the top of the bill, they would be, in alphabetical order, John Adams, Thomas Jefferson, James Madison, and George

Washington. Although each of the stories has been designed to stand on its own as a narrative of one significant moment of creative achievement or failure, taken together they feature several recurrent themes.

First, Adams was essentially correct in insisting that the major political decisions that shaped the founding were usually improvisational occasions. While there were a few cerebral epiphanies based on intense thinking, most creative choices were pragmatic responses to rapidly moving events beyond human control, on-the-run adaptations of classical texts to shifting contexts. The founders were, in fact, making it up as they went along, and any historical interpretation that emphasizes their otherworldly serenity or uncommon prescience in grasping how it would all turn out is a fundamental distortion of the way history happened.

Second, Washington was also correct in claiming that space was a priceless American asset. While that asset was an unsolicited geographic gift for which the founders could take no credit, recognizing its advantages provided the occasion for several of the most creative moments in the founding era. The scale of the American theater was unprecedented, especially when compared to tidier European spaces, and the most original political contributions made by the founders were offered in response to that unique condition.

Third, in terms of creativity, the control of pace was almost as impressive as the control of space. The founders opted for an evolutionary rather than revolutionary version of political and social change, preferring to delay delivery on the full promise of the American Revolution rather than risk implosion in the mode of the French Revolution. Although it is difficult for many modern-day critics to acknowledge the point, this deferral strategy, far from being a moral failure, was in fact a profound insight rooted in a realistic appraisal of how enduring social change best happens. But the exception to this rule, removing slavery from the political agenda on the grounds that it would die a natural death, proved a massive miscalculation.

Fourth, the successful management of space and pace was not matched when it came to race, which proved impervious to any imaginative response whatsoever. In the end, it was psychologically impossible for the founders to imagine the peaceful coexistence of whites and free African Americans in the same nation-state. (The same was not true for Native Americans.) Without any historical precedents to guide them, the founders could imagine a secular state and a large-scale republic, but they could not imagine a biracial society. As a result, whenever race entered the founding conversation, tragedy prevailed.

The sheer act of listing these themes suggests that an orderly set of conclusions resides inherently in the following stories, that generalizations can be neatly teased out of the separate tales, which then can levitate above the ground like distilled clouds of truth. But that is not really the way that stories work, or the way that historical truth, if there is such a thing, ought to be approached. Rather than float above the ground, we need to dive into the messy moments and do our best to listen as a finite number of long-dead men struggle to understand the historical currents of their rather propitious time. It is the spring of 1775, the War for Independence has just begun, but no one is quite sure what to do . . .

CHAPTER ONE

{ The Year }

IF PERMITTED the historical license to stretch the definition of a year, then the fifteen months between the shots fired at Lexington and Concord in April of 1775 and the adoption of the Declaration of Independence in July of 1776 can justifiably claim to be both the most consequential and the strangest year in American history. It was consequential because the rationale for American independence and the political agenda for an independent American republic first became explicit at this time. It was strange because while men were dying, whole towns being burned to the ground, women being raped, captured spies and traitors being executed, the official posture of what called itself "The United Colonies of North America" remained abiding loyalty to the British Crown.[1]

Whether the American colonists were living a lie, an illusion, or a calculated procrastination is a good question. But when Thomas Jefferson finally got around to drafting the Declaration of Independence in June of 1776, one sentence enjoyed special resonance as an accurate characterization of the past year: "Prudence, indeed, will dictate that governments long established should not be changed for light and transient causes; and accordingly all experience hath shown, that mankind are more disposed to suffer, while evils are sufferable, than to right themselves by abolishing the forms to which they are accustomed." This was Jefferson's lyrical way of describing the quite remarkable feat of making an explosion happen in slow motion.

After all, prudence does not ordinarily make its way onto any list of revolutionary virtues. The very idea of a cautious revolutionary would seem, on the face of it, a contradiction in terms. The standard story of most revolutions features a cast of desperate characters with impulsive temperaments, utopian visions, a surefire sense of where history is headed, and an unquenchable urge to get there fast. Indeed, tarrying along the way is usually regarded as counterrevolutionary.

If that is what the standard story of a revolution requires, then one of two conclusions about the American Revolution follows naturally: either it was not really a revolution at all but merely (or perhaps not so merely) a war for colonial independence, the first of its kind in the modern world, to be sure, but not a fundamental shift in the social order that left the world changed forever; or else it was a strange kind of revolution that did not fit the standard pattern because many of its most prominent leaders were convinced that the pace of change must be slowed down and the most radical of the revolutionary promises deferred. The result is another contradiction, or perhaps a paradox: namely, an evolutionary revolution.

In short, the decision to secede from the British Empire *was* accompanied by a truly revolutionary agenda for the infant American republic. But the most prominent leaders, John Adams chief among them, insisted on the deferral of the revolutionary agenda and, in some instances, its postponement into the distant future. Instead of regarding this gradualist approach as a moral and political failure, a conclusion that historians on the left regard as, shall we say, self-evident, the argument offered here is just the opposite. In my judgment the calculated decision to make the American Revolution happen in slow motion was a creative act of statesmanship that allowed the United States to avoid the bloody and chaotic fate of subsequent revolutionary movements in France, Russia, and China.

And so, within a very strange year of full-scale war occurring alongside political reticence, we find an equally strange pattern emerging that will establish the uniquely judicious framework within which the American Revolution proceeded. John Adams, the major figure in the Continental Congress, and George Washington, the commander in chief of the Continental Army, are the chief players in this unusual story. Thomas Paine, who fits the more conventional revolutionary pattern perfectly, turns out to be the exception rather than the rule, temporarily indispensable but ultimately disposable. The great creative achievement embodied in the leadership of Adams and Washington at this propitious moment was to assure that the American Revolution moved forward, to borrow a modern phrase, with all deliberate speed.

HINDSIGHTS

WHEN JOHN ADAMS looked back from retirement on his experience thirty years earlier in the Second Continental Congress, two recollections nudged out all the other memories. The first was a bit awkward to acknowledge publicly, but since Adams believed that truth should always trump modesty (especially false modesty), he laid down his personal marker on the proceedings: "I was incessantly employed through the Whole Fall, Winter and Spring of 1775 and 1776 during their Sittings and on Committees on mornings and Evenings," he recalled, "and unquestionably did more business than any other Member of that house."[2]

The second recollection had the effect of making the first impossible to verify. No true history of that fateful time would ever be written, Adams insisted, because the most important conversations occurred "out of doors" in local taverns and coffeehouses. What's more, the official record of the deliberations imposed a misleading gloss of coherence over the congressional proceedings, concealing the messy confusion that reigned supreme for all the delegates, himself included. Any coherent narrative of the deliberations must necessarily falsify the way it really was for all the participants, who were improvising without a script in a historical drama without a known conclusion.[3]

Adams was making a serious, perhaps even a profound, point: namely, that retrospective history—that is, history viewed with the benefit of hindsight—is invariably neater and tidier than history as experienced by those making it. But since hindsight is the only interpretive tool historians have at their disposal, we must run the risk of deploying it here, enjoying the clairvoyance that Adams and his fellow delegates were denied in order to establish the political context of the imperial crisis that they, albeit lacking our prescient perch, were confronting in the late spring and summer of 1775.

Why was there an imperial crisis? The answer of the moment was that British troops had gunned down ninety-five American patriots at Lexington and Concord. Adams was not sure whether this bloodletting would become the opening shot in a war for American independence. He was sure that it represented another escalation in what had become a twelve-year argument about the proper place of the American colonies within a reconfigured British Empire. The Adams version of that dispute was highly partisan. In effect, a corrupt British government had arbitrarily decided to impose new taxes and political restrictions on its loyal American subjects as part of a conspiratorial plot to deprive them of their traditional rights as Englishmen. The carnage at Lexington and Concord, then, was the logical and inevitable culmination of a conscious British scheme to transform loyal subjects into abject slaves.[4]

Hindsight permits a more detached and ultimately ironic version of the imperial story. In 1763, as a result of its stupendous victory in the French and Indian War, Great Britain found itself a newly arrived world power with a vast empire in the eastern third of North America. Previously, British governance of their thirteen coastal colonies had been a lackadaisical affair, with royal governors largely beholden to local legislatures, which controlled the power of the purse. Enforcement of the trade regulations purportedly required by the Navigation Acts was equally blithe in spirit. Now, however, the sheer scale of its recently acquired American empire, plus the sudden recognition that governance of its expanded domain required more management than a few secretaries and clerks in Whitehall could muster, forced a major overhaul of this accidental empire into something more appropriately imperial. What looked to Adams like a sinister plot to enslave the American colonists was viewed from London as a sensible plan to make the British Empire worthy of its name.[5]

There then ensued a decade of parliamentary legislation—the Sugar

Act, the Stamp Act, the Townshend Acts, the Coercive Acts—all designed to fold the colonies into the empire by placing them within the authority of Parliament, which represented the collective interests of all British citizens everywhere. The colonists, of course, contested that claim, Adams leading the way by arguing that American interests were not represented in Parliament, but rather in the respective colonial legislatures, which alone could justifiably speak for American interests because they alone were duly elected to do so.[6]

Knowing as we do the world-changing events about to transpire— a seven-and-a-half-year war in which more Americans were killed or wounded proportionally than in any subsequent conflict save the Civil War, in which the British lost their entire empire in North America except for Canada—it seems strange that such a massive movement of the historical templates could be caused by such a minor, merely constitutional, difference of opinion. In retrospect, the core problem blocking a sensible resolution was the British presumption—fully as self-evident to them as the truths that Jefferson was soon to hurl at "a candid world"—that imperial sovereignty must be singular. For George III and his chief minister, Lord North, it was akin to an axiom of political physics, a veritable Newtonian principle of political theory, that there must be one sovereign source of governance. To suggest otherwise was tantamount to arguing there was not one but many gods.

If they could only have jettisoned that assumption, a workable solution to the imperial crisis was staring them right in the face. Indeed, it was proposed by the First Continental Congress in 1774 and would be proposed several times again by the Second Continental Congress throughout 1775 and up to July of 1776. The solution was shared sovereignty, whereby the American colonies remained within the British Empire as loyal subjects of the Crown but retained control over their own domestic affairs. A version of this creative solution, called federalism, became the basis for the American constitutional settlement in 1787–88. A century later the same principle became the organizing feature of the British Commonwealth. Our dalliance with hindsight, then, ends with two overlapping conclusions: first, the American Revolution was eminently avoidable; second, the imaginative failure of the British ministry in 1775–76 constitutes perhaps the greatest blunder in the history of British statecraft.[7]

THE SUMMER OF 1775

THE SECOND Continental Congress convened in Philadelphia on May 10, 1775. It was the second because there had already been a first the previous year. The term "Continental" derived from the primary purpose of that earlier gathering, which was to establish a Continental Association charged with overseeing the nonimportation agreements adopted by the separate colonies in order to exert pressure on British merchants, and through them on the British government. The more obvious term "American" still carried lingering connotations of stigma, a word Londoners continued to use to describe low-life provincials on the periphery of the great metropolitan empire. "American" also implied a national identity and agenda that most colonists were not prepared to declare publicly, if at all.[8]

The man destined to dominate the sessions and eventually earn the title "Atlas of independence" did not look the part. At thirty-nine John Adams had already lost much of his hair, several of his teeth, and any semblance of a waistline. Though he had gained a reputation in the previous congress as an impressive orator, his diaries and letters reveal a man alternately vain and insecure, constantly measuring himself against his colleagues as a way of bolstering his own self-confidence. Edward Rutledge of South Carolina, for example, was "sprightly but not deep." Benjamin Rush of Pennsylvania, who eventually became a lifelong friend, was initially described as "Awkward as a junior Batchelor, or Sophomore." Adams seemed to regard the congress less as a legislature than as a theater, where he and the other delegates were trying out for the roles of Demosthenes or Cicero. "It is to be a School of Political Prophets, I suppose," he wrote to James Warren, then his closest friend, "a Nursery of American Statesmen." His highest aspiration was to be one of them.[9]

The chief Adams asset—apart from his almost painful earnestness, his Harvard degree, his deep reading of history, and his remarkable wife,

Abigail, who loved him unconditionally but confronted him candidly whenever his ego began to swell (e.g., "Down vanity!")—was a keen sense of where this political drama was destined to end. Just before leaving for Philadelphia he wrote Abigail, expressing his disdain for "Moody's Doctrine," named after an eccentric New England minister, Samuel Moody. The essence of Moody's Doctrine was that "When Men know not what to do, they ought not to do they know not what." Adams liked what he called "this oracular Jingle of Words," which made sense, he thought, for the majority of delegates in Philadelphia, who believed that a total rupture with Great Britain must be avoided at all costs. It did not, however, apply to him, since he believed the rupture had already occurred.[10]

Adams arrived at the Second Continental Congress as one of the avowed radicals, meaning one of the few delegates prepared to contemplate outright American independence. After the bloodletting at Lexington and Concord, to be sure, his radical posture no longer seemed so extreme, though the moderates in congress retained the balance of power. But Adams believed that the moderate agenda, despite its majority status, was already doomed. "We shall be convinced that the Cancer is too deeply rooted," he predicted, "and too far spread to be cured by anything short of cutting it out entirely." The moderates, he apprised Abigail, were "waiting for a Messiah . . . that will never come."[11]

But then, in almost the next breath, Adams sounded a more cautionary note that effectively outlined the two-pronged strategy that would define the agenda of the Second Continental Congress for the next year. The congress should move simultaneously on two parallel tracks, "the Sword in one Hand and the Olive Branch in the other—to proceed with Warlike Measures, and conciliatory Measures Pari Passu." Adams never seriously believed that conciliatory gestures possessed even a remote chance of succeeding. (This is why, many years later, when asked who did more than anyone else to promote American independence, he declined the honor in favor of George III.) On several occasions during the summer of 1775 he lost his composure and fired impertinent and ill-advised volleys at the moderate coalition in congress, which invariably got him into trouble. John Dickinson, the most prominent moderate

from Pennsylvania, he dismissed as "a certain great Fortune and pid-
dling Genius whose Fame has been trumpeted so loudly, [and] has given
a silly Cast to our whole Doings." When this remark made it into the
press, Dickinson and many of the other moderates ceased speaking to
Adams.[12]

But his abiding posture was patience. "We must have a Petition to
the King, and a delicate Proposal of Negociation & C. This Negociation
I dread like Death. But it must be proposed." He dreaded the effort
at political conciliation because, though only a chimera, it afforded a
golden opportunity for the British ministry to seize the political initiative by appearing open to a compromise, thus splitting the radical and
moderate coalitions in congress into wholly separate camps. (Fortunately, neither George III nor his chief ministers ever gave this obvious
strategy serious consideration until it was too late.) Despite his periodic
outbursts against moderates like Dickinson, Adams actually embraced
the two-track approach because it allowed the radical option of independence to ripen on the political vine: "We cannot force Events," he
explained. "We must Suffer People to make their own Way in many
Cases." Whether he was referring to the moderates in congress or the
much larger constituency out there in the American countryside was
not clear. But he believed that ideas needed to fester until both his fellow
delegates and his fellow Americans came to recognize, at their own
speed and in their own way, that what had initially seemed so improbable was in fact inevitable.[13]

In the meantime, the radicals and moderates in the congress could
work together, both sides acknowledging the complementary legitimacy
of the other. The hobbyhorse of the moderates was a compromise that
proposed an immediate cessation of hostilities and a recognition of royal
authority, but not parliamentary authority, over the colonies. The records
of the Second Continental Congress and the modern editions of the
collected letters of the delegates, on the other hand, are littered with
preparations for war: locating depositories of saltpeter for gunpowder
and lead for muskets or cannonballs; plans for an invasion of Canada;
the appointment of one of their own, George Washington, to assume
command of New England militia units outside Boston; opening Ameri-

can ports to foreign trade in brazen defiance of the Navigation Acts;
plans to create an American navy—Adams was the chief advocate and
architect of this scheme—with regulations modeled on the harsh but
effective code of the British navy.[14]

But, as Adams predicted, events rather than petitions would dictate
the direction of the outcome. On June 18, 1775, Abigail reported the first
salvo: "The battle began upon our intrenchments upon Bunker's Hill,
Saturday morning about three o'clock, and has not ceased yet, and it is
now three o'clock Sabbath afternoon. . . . How many have fallen, we
know not. The constant roar of the cannon is so distressing that we cannot eat, drink, or sleep. . . . I will add more as I hear further." She noted
that the Adams family physician, Joseph Warren, was a conspicuous
casualty who "fell gloriously fighting for his country." As casualty estimates trickled back to Philadelphia and London, it became clear that
the British had achieved a nearly ruinous victory, suffering over one
thousand killed and wounded out of an attacking force of less than
twenty-five hundred. Critics of George III's policy in London had a field
day, noting that a few more victories like this would result in the annihilation of the British army.[15]

Rather than cause George III and Lord North to reconsider their
policy, the Battle of Bunker Hill only hardened their resolve to crush the
American rebellion. They immediately began inquiries with Scottish
and German allies to recruit a mercenary army of twenty thousand
troops to supplement a British expeditionary force that would launch an
invasion of America the following spring or summer. For his part,
Adams interpreted the Battle of Bunker Hill as clear evidence that the
British army was not the unbeatable leviathan that had been advertised.
His resolve was also fortified a few months later upon receiving the news
that a British officer, James Drew, had walked over the battlefield the
day after the event and ordered his troops to summarily execute all the
wounded Americans. Drew himself also dug up the shallow grave of
Joseph Warren, spit on his body, then cut off his head. Gratuitous atroc-
ities of this sort only confirmed what Adams already knew: that there
was no turning back, that lines had been crossed that could never be
retraced. But Adams made no passionate speeches about Bunker Hill to

his fellow delegates in the congress. For once, he kept his mouth shut. Events spoke louder than words, and they were all headed his way.[16]

THE ENCAMPMENT

"I CAN NOW INFORM YOU," Adams wrote to Abigail in mid-June, "that the Congress have made choice of the modest and virtuous, the amiable, generous and brave General Washington, Esquire, to be General of the American army, and that he is to repair, as soon as possible, to the camp before Boston." While the newly appointed commander in chief was certainly virtuous and brave by any standard, very few candid observers would have called him modest or amiable. And the claim that there was an American army for him to command was, it turns out, a laughable exaggeration.[17]

When Adams recalled this moment in his memoirs many years later, he amplified his earlier inaccuracies, claiming that several other viable candidates were under serious consideration and that only his own strenuous effort on Washington's behalf assured his appointment. The simpler truth was that Washington alone possessed the core qualifications for the job: he was the most prominent American military hero during the French and Indian War; he was a Virginian, which was crucial in order to establish Virginia's solidarity with the ongoing conflict in Massachusetts; he was a fellow delegate sitting in the congress—the only one wearing a military uniform, by the way—and therefore one of their own. His selection was so foreordained that a story Adams liked to tell in old age actually captured a larger share of the truth: Washington was always chosen whenever American statesmen gathered because, Adams joked, at slightly over six foot three he was always a head taller than anyone else in the room.[18]

Temperamentally, at least on the face of it, Washington was the anti-Adams. If Adams was excitable, always on the verge of a volcanic eruption that threatened to overwhelm his opponents in a lava flow of words, Washington was preternaturally calm and almost obsessively self-controlled, a man accustomed to dominating any room by his sheer physical presence, to lead by listening while less secure men babbled on.

If Adams was a voracious reader with impeccable intellectual credentials as a lifelong student of politics and history, Washington's formal education had stopped at the grade-school level and his primal convictions about the world and how it worked had developed through experience rather than reading, chiefly as a young soldier on the Virginia frontier. (In effect, Adams had gone to Harvard and Washington had gone to war.) If Adams wore his ambitions and his heart on his sleeve, Washington's equally monumental ambitions were buried in a heart that no one was permitted to see, much less touch. If Adams conducted an ongoing conversation with himself in his diary, recording his doubts, impulses, vanities, even his dreams, Washington's introspections were invisible, thereby conveying the impression that they did not exist or that he regarded their expression as a wasteful self-indulgence. His diary entries were all about the weather, and when he recorded which way the wind was blowing, he was not being metaphorical.

On the other hand, Washington shared Adams's contempt for British presumptions of superiority. The fact that he had once been rejected for a commission in the British army did not strike Washington as a measure of his inferiority so much as a statement of their stupidity. In that sense, both men were self-confident and self-made; both deeply resented any imperial system that treated them as mere subjects. Finally, like Adams, Washington had come to the Second Continental Congress convinced that the prospect for a peaceful resolution of the imperial crisis was remote in the extreme. Despite their temperamental differences, then, in the crucible of this propitious moment they were kindred spirits politically, marching several steps ahead of public opinion.[19]

Even more than Adams, Washington harbored a realistic sense of the challenge posed by the British army, the finest and most professional force of its kind in the world. As he departed Philadelphia for Boston, Washington confessed to his brother-in-law, Burwell Bassett, that he might have committed himself to an impossible mission: "I am now Imbarked on a tempestuous ocean, from whence, perhaps, no friendly harbour is to be found. . . . I can answer but for three things, a firm belief in the justice of our Cause—close attention to the prosecution of it—and the strictest integrity—If these cannot supply the places of Ability & Experience, the Cause will suffer & more than probably my character along with it, as reputation derives its principal support from success." Compared to the cream of the British officer corps that he would encounter at Boston, Washington was a rank amateur who had never commanded more than a regiment in battle. He purchased several books on military organization and tactics on the way out of Philadelphia in the hope of giving himself a crash course on commanding an army.[20]

By the time Washington arrived at the outskirts of Boston on July 3, the smoke from Bunker Hill had cleared and the shape of the military engagement between American and British troops had already assumed the character of a marathon staring match. The American army, comprised entirely of New England militia, though soon to be reinforced by several companies of sharpshooters racing up from Virginia, Maryland, and Pennsylvania, occupied an eight-mile arc of breastworks and trenches encircling the town of Boston. Inside were seven thousand British regulars—Washington incorrectly believed they totaled over eleven thousand—under the command of Thomas Gage, soon to be replaced by William Howe. It was a recipe for stalemate, since the British had no intention of repeating the catastrophe of Bunker Hill, and the Americans lacked the tactical experience and proficiency to launch a successful offensive. As Washington put it a few months later: "Put them [his troops] behind a Parapet—a Breast Work—Stone Wall . . . and they will give a good Acct. . . . But they will not March boldly up to a work . . . or stand exposed on a plain." And so the Battle of Boston became the Boston Siege. "It seemed to be the principle employment of both armies," wrote one observer, "to look at each other with spyglasses."[21]

It also became clear very quickly that Washington had assumed command not of an army so much as of an insurgency. It was one thing to declare that a unified American army existed, and Washington did so immediately upon his arrival: "The Continental Congress having now taken all the troops of the several Colonies, which have been raised, or which may be hereafter raised for the support and defence of the liberties of America; into their Pay and Service. They are now the Troops of the United Provinces of North America; and it is hoped that all Distinctions of Colonies will be laid aside." But it was another thing altogether to translate that declaration from a hope into reality.[22]

New England farmers, artisans, and laborers had rallied to the cause in a glorious display of patriotism that, at its most primal level, was rooted in a stubborn and fiercely independent spirit. At its nub, that spirit resented and resisted anyone telling them what they must do. But that same independent spirit also recoiled at the imposition of military discipline as a violation of the very values they believed they were fighting for. Washington got himself into all kinds of political trouble by describing his New England soldiers as "an exceedingly dirty & nasty people" who are "by no means such troops, in any respect, as you are led to believe of them from the Accts which are published." They felt perfectly free to ignore the orders of their officers, whom they had elected and therefore regarded as chosen representatives rather than superiors. Leaving their posts for a few weeks to return home struck them not as desertion, but instead as a wholly sensible exercise of the very freedom they were defending.[23]

There are a few almost comical General Orders issued by Washington's headquarters, one demanding that soldiers cease randomly firing their muskets into the air, another that enlisted men refrain from relieving themselves wherever they felt the urge. Then there was this: "The General does not mean to discourage the practice of bathing . . . but he expressly forbids any person doing it at or near the Bridge in Cambridge, where it has been observed and complained of that many Men, lost to all sense of decency and common modesty, are running about naked upon the Bridge, whilst Passengers, and even ladies of the first fashion in the neighbourhood are passing over it, as if they meant to glory in their shame." Washington was just beginning to glimpse the paradox that would haunt his leadership of the Continental Army for the next seven years. In effect, the success of the army depended upon instilling a level of discipline that seemed, on the face of it, to defy the very values the American Revolution claimed to stand for.[24]

But this underlying and long-term problem—more finessed than ever really solved—paled in comparison to the immediate challenge, which was how to improvise an army. For over a century the British army had managed, by trial and error, to produce manuals and regulations providing routinized answers to the following questions: How are officers selected? What are the appropriate pay rates? Who controls the distribution of food, amenities, and clothing? Where should kitchens and latrines be located? To whom does the head of medical care report? These and a veritable litany of analogous organizational questions needed to be answered on the fly in the summer of 1775. Washington's experience as the master of Mount Vernon had accustomed him to manage a flood of details, but nothing could have prepared him for the daunting task of inventing an army de novo. "I have often thought how much happier I should have been," he admitted, "if instead of a command under such circumstances, I had taken my Musket upon my Shoulder & enterd the Ranks, or, if I could have justified the Measure to Posterity, & my own Conscience, had returned to the back Country, & liv'd in a Wig-wam."[25]

Washington's frustrations hint at the real story of the Boston Siege, which was not the bottling up of the British regulars, who eventually sailed off to Halifax to fight another day, but rather the haphazard creation of the Continental Army. Down in Philadelphia, Adams was attempting to manage a revolutionary conversation responsibly. Up in Boston, Washington was conducting a real-life experiment with the implications of that conversation for an army of citizen-soldiers.

For example, a core conviction of the day, sanctioned by revolutionary ideology and apparently confirmed by the bravery displayed at Bunker Hill, was that an army of American volunteers fighting for heartfelt principles could easily defeat an army of British professionals fighting for money. The orders emanating from Washington's headquarters gave frequent voice to this cherished conviction, usually in the form of a plea to make it come true: "Whilst we have men therefore who in every respect are superior to British Troops, that are fighting for *two pence or three pence a day:* Why cannot we in appearance also be superior to them, when we fight for Life, Liberty, Property and our Country?"[26]

But it soon became clear to Washington that this cherished conviction was really a seductive illusion. The voluntary principle, it turned out, was like an evanescent glow at daybreak, or the rapture of a new romance—marvelous while it lasted, but of limited duration. As Washington discovered, the initial enthusiasm of most militia units waned after a few weeks, so that "we find it impossible to detain men . . . in Service after they get a little tired of the Duties of it—& Homesick." As enlistments ran out in the fall and winter, Washington issued multiple pleas to remain in camp to defend "the Glorious Cause," but whole units saluted the cause while marching out of camp to their firesides, thereby forcing Washington to count on the arrival of fresh but inexperienced volunteers to replace them: "It is not in the pages of History," he observed, "to furnish a case like ours; to maintain a post within Musket Shot of the Enemy for Six Months . . . and at the same time to disband one Army and recruit another, within that distance of twenty odd British regiments."[27]

It all boded badly if the undeclared war should, as seemed almost certain to Washington, become a fully declared and protracted conflict. For in such a contest Washington believed the British army of committed professionals would enjoy a decided advantage over American volunteers. "To expect then the Same Service from Raw and undisciplined Recruits as from Veteran Soldiers," he warned, "is to expect what never did, and perhaps never will happen." Whether the ironies were lost on Washington is not clear, but his experience at the Boston encampment had forced him to conclude that in order to win a war for freedom, Americans must be coerced to fight, and the proper model for an effective fighting force was nothing less than the British army itself. In effect, the only way to defeat a standing army was to create one of your own.[28]

Fortunately, the very exigencies that forced Washington to reach such an unrevolutionary conclusion also had collateral consequences more in keeping with revolutionary principles. On both the racial and the class fronts, the pressures generated by the manpower demands of the Continental Army forced Washington to make decisions that, if only in retrospect, had revolutionary implications.

The first decision concerned African Americans. A sizable group of ex-slaves and slaves had joined the New England militia units that fought at Bunker Hill and then manned the breastworks encircling Boston. No one had seen fit to comment on their presence until the southern rifle-men arrived in camp and began to question serving alongside black troops. These complaints filtered their way up to headquarters, where Washington put the question to a Council of War consisting of all the general officers. The verdict was clear: "Agree unanimously to reject all slaves, & by a great Majority to reject Negroes altogether." The question came up again the following month during a discussion of the criteria for new enlistees: "Neither Negroes, Boys unable to bear arms, nor old men unfit to endure the fatigues of the campaign, are to be inlisted."[29]

But a month later, in December, as it became clear that the imminent departure of so many militia would leave the Continental Army seriously undermanned, Washington had a change of mind, if not a change of heart. "It has been represented to me that the free negroes who have Served in the Army, are very much dissatisfied at being discarded—and it is to be apprehended, that they may Seek employ in the ministerial Army—I have presumed to depart from the Resolution respecting them," he wrote to John Hancock, "& have given Licence for them being enlisted." He then apprised Hancock, who was serving as president of the Continental Congress, that "if this is disapproved by the Congress, I will put a Stop to it."[30]

Hancock, buried under an avalanche of paperwork, never responded. And so, in this backhanded, indeed grudging, fashion, Washington had inadvertently decided that the Continental Army would be racially integrated. Nor were black troops assigned only to segregated units. Though a few all-black units were added later in the war, most blacks served alongside whites and comprised, at any time, between 6 and 12 percent of the fighting force. Here was a stunning if silent social statement far ahead of popular opinion. The next time any American army would be so fully integrated was the Korean War.

Analogous movement occurred on the class front, again more out of necessity than choice. The awkward question this time was: Who should be appointed a general? In the British army the answer to this question was defined by aristocratic bloodlines and years of experience in the field. And in fact two of the generals Washington appointed to his staff, Charles Lee and Horatio Gates, were former British officers, though not generals, with greater military experience than Washington himself. But the two appointments that would shine with greater brilliance the longer the war lasted were Henry Knox and Nathanael Greene.

Knox was a portly Boston bookseller who could pass for a modern-day version of Santa Claus. Greene was an intense Rhode Island Quaker who had volunteered and served as a private in a local militia until after the outbreak of hostilities at Lexington and Concord. Neither man had any previous military experience, though both were serious students of military history. The very notion of either man serving as a British officer, much less a general, would have been preposterous. Over the course of the next seven years, however, both men displayed their natural talent for leadership, Knox as Washington's head of artillery, Greene most spectacularly during the Carolina campaign, when he bested the most accomplished British general, Lord Charles Cornwallis, on multiple occasions. Their latent talent would have remained latent, and therefore invisible, if Washington had not plucked them from the ranks in the first year of the war. And he did so because more obviously qualified candidates were simply unavailable. The careers of Knox and Greene serve as stellar examples of the dynamic role the American Revolution played in *creating* talent by providing it with an outlet impossible to imagine in any European nation at the time.[31]

Finally, there was one additional achievement locked into place at the Boston encampment, done so quietly and seamlessly that no one noticed it at the time—and very few have since. It was the routinized acceptance of civilian control over the military. Washington was the key figure. He simply took it for granted that he served at the pleasure of the Continental Congress and that the Continental Army, once that name started to stick, was the military arm of the delegates in Philadelphia. From the start, Washington deferred to the congress on questions of pay, the allotted size of the army, even final decisions about strategy. "I am not fond of stretching my powers," he explained, "and if Congress will say thus far & no farther you shall go, I will promise not to offend whilst I continue in their Service."[32]

The congress, for its part, avoided possible conflicts by routinely endorsing Washington's judgments as their own. In October a three-person congressional delegation, headed by Benjamin Franklin, traveled up to Boston to confer with the commander in chief on all the outstanding questions and ratified all his major recommendations. For his part, Washington went along with the official line that the British regulars ensconced in Boston were "ministerial troops," so that the ongoing war was officially not going on at all, because the king purportedly remained ignorant of the fighting. This allowed the minuet between radicals and moderates in congress to proceed apace with Washington's blessing. Not until April of 1776, when the siege had ended, did Washington express impatience with this functional piece of fancy, admitting that "I think it idle to keep up the distinction of Ministerial Troops." But by then, as we shall see, most members of congress concurred.[33]

Washington's supreme statement of civilian control, of course, would not occur until the end of the war, when he surrendered his sword to the president of congress and rode off into retirement as the American Cincinnatus. But his convictions on this score were present from the very start. It was typical of Washington: so simple, so essential, so unquestioned, yet so crucial.

Along the way, Washington's conspicuous deferral to the Continental Congress implicitly endorsed the unstated fact that the congress had assumed the status of a provisional national government empowered to speak for the American people as a collective whole. The congress never officially claimed that power outright, for to have done so would have surely provoked loud howls of protest from the emerging state governments. It had simply stepped forward in the midst of the imperial crisis, a political emergency if there ever was one, to coordinate the American response. But no matter how unstated and crisis-driven the causes, there were now two discernible projections of national unity—the Continental Congress and the Continental Army—even though no independent nation had yet declared its existence.

BIG BANG

THE TWO-PRONGED strategy of the Continental Congress—to pursue war and the possibility of reconciliation with Great Britain simultaneously—was a direct expression of the split between moderates and radicals in the congress. But there was also a third prong, a third perspective not represented in the congress at all, festering away "out of doors" throughout the nine months of the Boston Siege. It is difficult to know what to call this emerging constituency, since the term "radical" is already taken by the outright proponents of independence, and "radical revolutionaries" sounds like a verbal version of double exposure. Whatever we call this new political camp, its advocates interpreted the arguments hurled at Parliament's arbitrary power as more than a rationale for secession from the British Empire. Such arguments were also heard as a clarion call to topple all forms of arbitrary power in American society whatever their source. Here we first glimpse the revolutionary edge of the American Revolution.

Take, for example, the obvious anomaly of slavery. In June of 1775 Adams received an unsigned letter from a resident of Fredericksburg, Virginia, asking an awkward question: "Is it not incompatible with the glorious Struggle America is making for her own Liberty, to hold in absolute Slavery a Number of Wretches, who will be urged by Despair on one Side, and the most flattering Promises on the other, to become the most inveterate Enemies to the present Masters?" A few months later he received another letter signed "Humanity" that raised the same question in less literate but more poignant terms: "Whot has the negros the africans don to us that shuld tak them from thar own land and mak them sarve us to the da of thar deth . . . ? God forbit that it shuld be so anay longer. . . . I hear the gentleman that leads the army [i.e., Washington] holds 700 of them in bondeg." In point of fact, at the time Washington owned slightly more than a hundred slaves, but the discrepancy did nothing to blunt the force of the writer's question.[34]

Or take the question of women's rights. On this score Adams did not depend on unsolicited letters from anonymous authors. His own beloved Abigail lectured him in a series of letters during the spring of 1776. While her tone was playful, the banter had a discernibly serious purpose: "And, by the way, in the new code of laws which I suppose it will be necessary for you to make, I desire you will remember the ladies and be more generous and favorable to them than your ancestors. Do not put such unlimited power in the hands of husbands. Remember, all men would be tyrants if they could. If particular care and attention is not paid to the ladies, we are determined to foment a rebellion, and will not hold ourselves bound by any laws in which we have no voice or representation."[35]

Adams attempted to retaliate with mock disbelief, suggesting that women were the real tyrants within the household and that he had no intention of exchanging the tyranny of George III for "the despotism of the petticoat." But Abigail, determined to have the last word, concluded the exchange with a firm reiteration of her main point, which was that the very principles her husband was deploying to justify American independence had profound consequences for the status of women in an independent American republic: "But you must remember," she concluded, "that arbitrary power is like most other things which are very hard . . . and notwithstanding all your wise laws and maxims, we have it in our power, not only to free ourselves, but to subdue our masters, and, without violence, throw your natural and legal authority at your feet."[36]

Finally, there was that suddenly troubling phrase "the consent of the people," which was beginning to demonstrate alarmingly expansive tendencies. The favorite watering hole for delegates to the Continental Congress was City Tavern, where those unrecorded conversations that Adams predicted would never get into the history books happened every evening. The artisans, mechanics, and laboring class of Philadelphia exerted a discernible influence on those unofficial deliberations, an influence that reflected the important role these previously excluded groups had played since 1774 in running the committee structure that enforced the nonimportation agreements and, truth be told, dominated the politics of the city. An editorial in the *Pennsylvania Evening Post* conveys the flavor of the ongoing conversation:

Do not mechanics, and farmers constitute ninety-nine out of a hundred of the people of America? If these, by their occupations, are to be excluded from having any share in the choice of their rulers, or forms of government, would it not be best to acknowledge the jurisdiction of the British Parliament, which is composed entirely of GENTLEMEN? Is not half the property in the city owned by men who wear LEATHER APRONS? Does not the other half belong to men whose fathers or grandfathers wore LEATHER APRONS?[37]

More of the same came at Adams from Elbridge Gerry, an old Massachusetts friend, who forwarded his recent correspondence with James Sullivan, another New England stalwart for independence, who seemed to be undergoing a radical epiphany. As Sullivan put it:

Laws and Government are founded on the Consent of the people, and that consent should by each member of Society be given in proportion to his Right. Every member of Society has a Right to give his Consent to the Laws of the Community or he owes no obedience to them. This proposition will never be denied to him who has the least acquaintance with republican principles. . . . Why a man is supposed to consent to the acts of a Society of which in this respect he is an absolute Excommunicate, none but a lawyer well Labled in the feudal Sistem can tell.

Sullivan's major argument was that Massachusetts should abolish all property qualifications for the vote, but, as Adams pointed out to him, the implication of his argument destroyed *all* distinctions for citizenship: "There will be no end to it," Adams warned. "New Claims will rise. Women will demand a Vote. Lads from 12 to 21 will think their Rights not enough attended to, and every Man, who has not a Farthing, will demand an equal Voice with any other in all Acts of State." Why, followed to its logical conclusion, the Pandora's box Sullivan had opened dictated the establishment of unfettered democracy.[38]

Hindsight, our double-edged asset, again allows another prescient pronouncement at this stage of the story. To wit, it is no exaggeration to observe that between the summer of 1775 and the spring of 1776, the entire liberal agenda for the next century of American history made its appearance for the first time. Indeed, if one wished to push the evidence a bit, to include the civil rights and feminist movements, the next two centuries of political reform were previewed. But at the very least, the end of slavery, the recognition of women as citizens, and the expansion of the franchise to include the poor and propertyless were placed on the political table as inevitable consequences of the principles that the American Revolution claimed to embody.

The man who most passionately embraced this expanded agenda was Thomas Paine. Neither as tall as Washington nor as short as Adams, Paine was more improbable than either as a major figure. He was already thirty-seven years old when he arrived in Philadelphia in 1774, his only asset a letter of recommendation from Benjamin Franklin describing him as "an ingenious young man." Exactly what genius Franklin had detected in the not-so-young man can be divined only retrospectively, since his previous career in Lewes and London had featured a failed marriage, several failures as a shop owner and corset maker, and a knack for alienating himself from those in power. Beneath this disappointing veneer of a career, however, Paine had developed two talents that merited Franklin's description and that would bloom luxuriously in American soil: first, a deep sense of social justice that was rooted in the injustices he had witnessed and experienced within the urban working class of London; second, an uncommon ability to craft prose that expressed his political convictions in language that was simultaneously simple and dazzling. It soon became clear that he also possessed one additional gift, an exquisite sense of timing, for he was bringing his talents into a political environment primed to hear his unique voice and message. He became the prophet of the expansive American promise.[39]

In January of 1776 Paine burst onto the national scene with the publication of *Common Sense,* perhaps the most auspicious entrance in American journalistic history. Unlike most previous revolutionary pamphlets, which tended to dissect the legal tangles of Parliament's dubious claim to authority over the colonies in language most familiar to lawyers, *Common Sense* was true to its title and used the idiom of ordinary conversation. Whereas Adams had defended American claims to legal sovereignty over their own domestic affairs with conspicuous erudition in *Novanglus* (1774), Paine clinched the argument with the observation that an island could not rule a continent. Instead of tiptoeing around the sensitive question of royal authority, thereby endorsing the illusion that George III was some distant father figure anxious to undo the misguided travesties of his own ministers, Paine launched a frontal attack on George III and the very idea of monarchy itself.

Who in his right mind, Paine asked, still believed that kings enjoyed some unique access to God's will? No, the true history of the British monarchy was a sordid tale of corruption, criminal neglect, and institutionalized arrogance. The notion that George III cared a wit about his American subjects was a fairy tale for children, a sentimental dream from which all responsible citizens needed to awake. The myth of a kind and benevolent king was too good to be true, just as the diabolical demeanor of the real king was too true to be good.

In addition to its electric style, the sensational impact of *Common Sense*—it sold 150,000 copies within three months—was a function of its timing. It appeared just as news had leaked across the Atlantic of George III's speech to Parliament in October, which declared the colonies to be in a state of rebellion, rejected all diplomatic solutions, and requested authorization to dispatch a massive military expedition to smash the rebellion in one decisive blow. Whether the emperor had no clothes or was clad in a warrior's armor, Paine's point enjoyed the decisive advantage of an idea whose time had come.[40]

Ironically, Adams was initially presumed to be the author of all this. *Common Sense* had been unsigned, and Adams was well known as the most prominent critic of reconciliation in the congress. "I am as innocent of it as a Babe," Adams told his friends, adding that "I could not reach the Strength and Brevity of his style, Nor his elegant Simplicity, nor his piercing pathos." He then added a revealing caveat. The author of *Common Sense* had performed an invaluable role by ridiculing the futile strategy of the moderate faction in congress, but he was also a dangerous thinker who "has a better hand in pulling down than building."[41]

Adams was probably referring to Paine's proposal for an American government to replace Parliament and the king. It envisioned a unicameral National Assembly with elected representatives from all the states, no fewer than 390 delegates, that would meet once a year to pass all laws on the basis of a three-fifths majority. Though Paine never used the word "democracy" in *Common Sense,* presumably because he realized that the term carried negative connotations for most Americans as the rough equivalent of mob rule, his prescription for America's political future leaned in a discernibly democratic direction. And although Paine also refrained from mentioning slavery in *Common Sense,* presumably because he did not want to alienate readers south of the Potomac, he was on record elsewhere as making its abolition one of the first pieces of business in the independent American republic. And so, while Adams's nervous response to *Common Sense* can be attributed to envy at Paine's sudden emergence as the most visible spokesman for the radical cause of independence, the cause Adams regarded as his own special province, and while no explanation of Adams's behavior on such occasions should ever dismiss his throbbing sense of prideful insecurity, it also seems clear that his highly sensitive political antenna had correctly detected a new revolutionary presence in the radical camp.[42]

The clearest clue in *Common Sense* came near the end. "The cause of America is in a great measure the cause of all mankind," Paine had written. "We have it in our power to begin the world over again. The birthday of a new world is at hand." As Paine's subsequent career was to demonstrate beyond any doubt, these words provided a preview of coming attractions for Paine's mature vision of the American Revolution as the opening shot in a radical transformation of political institutions throughout the world. While Paine's working-class origins have made him a cult hero to historians and political activists with a Marxist bent, his revolutionary mentality had eighteenth-century origins that predated any Marxist scheme of class consciousness. Paine was a product of what came to be called the Enlightenment.

Like the French *philosophes,* primarily Diderot and Voltaire, Paine believed that a society of genuine equality and justice would materialize naturally once the last king was strangled with the entrails of the last priest. Once those despotic institutions imposed on mankind during the

Dark Ages were toppled, then the latent potential for self-government inside all human beings would flow forward to create a perfectly harmonious society requiring only a minimum of supervision. (Socialist utopias of the nineteenth century also featured this illusion.) One might also explain Paine's political vision as a projection of his own experience as a recent immigrant to America who discovered a comparatively open Philadelphia society where his own talents were not stymied by Old World barriers.

Whatever their origins, Paine's deepest political convictions were, as Adams correctly sensed, thoroughly visionary, blissfully utopian, completely confident that the laws of nature and history were on his side, and wholly contemptuous of any argument urging caution. Once the revolutionary energies were released, which in the current case meant once America renounced its ties with British monarchy, then the only proper course was to get out of the way, since the revolutionary agenda was self-enacting. Adams, of course, thought it needed to be carefully managed. From the Adams perspective, Paine was an indispensable ally in the cause of American independence. But the combination of his utopian convictions and his brilliant pen also made him the most dangerous man in America once independence was declared.[43]

THE SPRING OF 1776

"BY INTELLIGENCE hourly arriving from abroad," Adams observed in February of 1776, "we are more and more confirmed that a kind of Confederation will be formed among the Crowned Skulls, and numbskulls of Europe, against Human Nature." He was referring to the agreements the British ministry was negotiating with several Germanic principalities to provide mercenaries for the looming invasion of North America. News of the Prohibitory Act reached the Continental Congress about the same time, revealing that the king had declared the colonists beyond his protection, outlawed them as rebels, and confiscated all their property in Great Britain.[44]

If Adams himself had written the script for George III, he could have done no better at exposing the moderate faction's hope for conciliation as an utter fantasy. In fact, the moderate agenda in congress was effectively dead after the Prohibitory Act, since George III had not waited for his American subjects to declare their independence of his authority but had declared his independence of them. Ironically, this preemptive action created a major new dilemma for Adams, because it accelerated the political schedule on which he had been working. For the past year, of course, he had been pushing hard within the congress against the moderates, pleading the inescapable conclusion of American independence. Now that the inescapable conclusion was suddenly staring all the delegates in the face, Adams, instead of rejoicing, began worrying that events were moving faster than he or anyone else could manage. As he saw it, George III's precipitous action caused problems on two fronts.

First, out there in the countryside, beyond the corridors of congress, it was still unclear if the bulk of the citizenry were ready for a vote on American independence. What Adams called "the ripening" had proceeded apace, helped immeasurably by the magic of Paine's words in *Common Sense.* But whether the fruit was ripe enough for picking remained uncertain. The ordinary people out there in the farms and towns "are advancing by slow and steady steps to that Mighty Revolution which you and I expected for some time," he observed to James Warren, "but Forced Attempts to accelerate their Motions, would have been attended with Discontent and Convulsions." There were, of course, no modern-day polling experts to gauge popular opinion, but Adams's instincts told him that huge pockets of reluctance remained alive in key regions like New York and Pennsylvania.[45]

Second, it was by no means clear what forms of governance would replace those jettisoned once independence officially arrived. The Continental Congress had been functioning as a provisional national government for nearly a year. And a motley mixture of ad hoc provincial legislatures and extralegal committees had assumed emergency powers at the colony and local level. But how could these provisional improvisations be transformed into permanent institutions with some semblance of legitimacy? Abigail had raised that very question several months earlier in her own candid fashion: "If we separate from Great Britain, what code of laws will be established? How shall we be governed to retain our liberties? Can any government be free which is not administered by general stated laws? Who shall frame these laws? Who will give them force and energy? 'Tis true your resolutions [in the Continental Congress], as a body, have hitherto had the force of laws; but will they continue to have?"[46]

These were the kind of questions that Paine thought superfluous because he believed they would pretty much answer themselves. For Adams, however, they posed the quintessential problem for any statesman who happened to find himself in a revolutionary situation. In the Adams political universe, a revolution was more than an act of liberation from discredited authority; it was a transfer of authority from one corrupt regime to a more enlightened substitute that was achieved, if possible, with a minimum of trauma and a maximum of continuity. "I have ever thought it the most difficult and dangerous Part of the Business," he explained to Mercy Otis Warren, his other female confidante, "to contrive some method for the Colonies to glide insensibly, from under the old Government, into a peaceable and contented Submission to new ones. . . . There is danger of Convulsions. But I hope not great ones." He was that rarest of creatures, a conservative revolutionary.[47]

For the moment, there was nothing Adams could do to delay the revolutionary conversation that George III, of all people, had accelerated. So he chose to move on the other front in March of 1776. For several months his fellow delegates had been informally seeking his advice about the prospective shape of their respective colonial constitutions, which would obviously need major overhaul if not outright replacement if and when independence arrived. The delegations from New York, North Carolina, and Pennsylvania approached him more formally in March, deferring to his acknowledged authority as a student of government. After drafting several letters offering guidance, Adams decided to publish a single document that any or all colonies could consult. He gave it the modest title *Thoughts on Government,* and it appeared in the *Pennsylvania Packet* on April 22.[48]

Adams subsequently described *Thoughts* as a "poor scrap" and "mere sketch" that was "done in haste." This was typical Adams false humility. For our purposes, *Thoughts* is extremely revealing, since it provided the clearest statement to date of the principles that he believed essential in determining the shape of any American republic after independence. (The fact that it should be a republic was assumed by all.) Despite his modest posture and latter-day lamentations, Adams acknowledged the privileged opportunity he enjoyed, as he put it, "to have been sent into life, at a time when the greatest law-givers of antiquity would have wished to have." He was almost surely referring to *Thoughts* when he posed a confessional question to Abigail:

> Is it not a saying of Moses, "Who am I, that I should go in and out before this great people?" When I consider the great events which are passed, and the greater which are rapidly advancing, and that I may have been instrumental in touching some springs and turning some small wheels, which have had and will have such effects, I feel an awe upon my mind which is not easily described.[49]

Adams recommended a constitutional blueprint in which there were three branches of government—executive, legislative, and judicial—and in which the principles of separation of powers, an independent judiciary, and a bicameral legislature were the most salient features. Because these features eventually became hallowed harbingers of the federal Constitution, it has proved almost irresistible to view *Thoughts* through the window of 1787, as a shrewd prophecy of the core principles shaping the ultimate structure of the national government. Such forward-looking assessments, which Adams would surely have welcomed as acknowledgments of his prescience, invariably distort the historical significance of *Thoughts*, which was very much a creature of its own moment, the spring of 1776.

Most obviously, Adams was proposing an outline for republican government at the state, not the national, level. He was also careful not to describe *Thoughts* as a prescription that each colony should adopt wholesale. Instead, he urged the lawmakers in each colony to modify his model to fit their own experience. New England would want to insist on annual elections for all officeholders in keeping with its colonial charters, while most southern colonies would probably resist that feature as too popular and unfamiliar. Adams wanted the new constitutions to feel like adaptations of the old colonial governments rather than jarringly novel innovations. Given the traumatic impact of American independence, he emphasized the need for continuity with past political practices. Moreover, he openly acknowledged that different colonies would, indeed should, come up with different versions of republican government. A great experiment was being launched in the spring of 1776, and the colonies were a diverse collection of laboratories in which one should fully expect somewhat different results to emerge. In effect, America was just beginning a great conversation about what a republic should look like, a conversation that would almost surely continue for many years, perhaps decades, so it was naive to expect either uniformity or consensus about all the answers at the start.

Over the course of a long career Adams would make several contributions to that ongoing conversation. But here, at the very start, he insisted on the rejection of one premise that would haunt the conversation for decades to come, most especially when the dialogue developed a French accent. The premise was rooted in the assumption that once you removed the king as the sovereign source of authority, you needed to replace him with another equally sovereign authority. The republican alternative to a divinely inspired monarch, then, was an equally omniscient creature called "the people." And from that assumption flowed the premise that the essence of republican government was a single-house legislature or assembly where elected representatives would give voice to its new sovereign, "the people."

In contrast to Paine's plan, the distinguishing feature of the Adams republican framework, as described in *Thoughts*, was the notion that once you moved from a monarchy to a republic, you entered a new and thoroughly modern world bereft of absolutes and with multiple rather than singular sources of sovereignty. The belief in an omniscient entity called "the people," Adams suggested, was every bit as fictional as the belief in a divinely inspired king. One of the reasons Adams proposed a bicameral legislature—a core feature of his political thought that he kept harping on throughout his life—was that it created two arenas for the different versions of "the people." When asked, Adams would always concur that a republic was bottomed on the principle of popular sovereignty, but the political expression of that sovereignty in any government must be plural rather than singular because the interests of "the people" were diverse and often mutually exclusive. Hindsight again allows us to detect a truly modern idea entering the conversation in *Thoughts,* the idea of multiple or shared sovereignties. While Adams was a firm believer in making the American Revolution happen slowly in order to cushion the shock of abrupt change, this particular feature of his political thought represented a fundamental break with past wisdom that contained truly jarring implications for any singular definition of political authority.[50]

By May of 1776 Adams had developed a clear picture of how the orderly march toward independence should proceed: "The Colonies should all assume the Powers of Government in all its Branches first," he explained. "They should then confederate with each other, and define the Powers of Congress next. They should then endeavor to form an Alliance with some foreign State. When this is done, a public Declaration [of Independence] might be made." Over the next three months events would make a shambles of this neat scenario, but the scenario itself provides a revealing look at the conservative cast of Adams's revolutionary mentality. The formal break with Great Britain should come last, only after state and national governments were in place to responsibly manage the turbulence sure to accompany the rupture. As it turned out, only one part of the Adams vision, the creation of new state governments, played out as he intended.[51]

On May 10 the congress adopted a resolution recommending that every colony draft a new constitution to replace the existent British charters of governance. On May 15 Adams stepped forward to present a resolution that he had drafted, designed to serve as a preface to the congressional recommendation. It deserves to be quoted in full because it was a de facto declaration of independence, adopted only after a fierce debate occasioned by the clear realization of all the delegates that, with its passage, the die was cast:

Whereas his Brittanie Majesty, in conjunction with the Lords and Commons of Great-Britain, has, by a late Act of Parliament, excluded the inhabitants of these United Colonies from the protection of his crown: And whereas no answer whatever to the humble petitions of the Colonies for redress of grievances, and reconciliation with Great-Britain has been or is likely to be given; but the whole force of that kingdom, aided by foreign mercenaries, is to be exerted for the destruction of the good people of these Colonies; And whereas it appears absolutely irreconcilable to reason and good conscience, for the people of these Colonies now to take the oaths and affirmations necessary for the support of any government under the Crown of Great-Britain; and it is necessary that the exercise of every kind of authority under the said Crown should be totally suppressed, and all the powers of government exerted under the authority of the people of the Colonies for the preservation of internal peace, virtue, and good order; as well as for the defence of their lives, liberties and properties, against the hostile invasions and cruel depredations of their enemies: Therefore

RESOLVED, that it be recommended to the respective Assemblies and Conventions of the United Colonies, where no Government sufficient to the exigencies of their affairs has been hitherto established, to adopt such Governments as shall in the opinion of the Representatives of the People best conduce to the happiness and safety of their Constituents in particular, and Americans in general.

Adams immediately described these words to a friend as "the most important Revolution that ever was taken in America" and went to his grave fifty years later insisting that he, not Thomas Jefferson, drafted the real declaration of American independence.[52]

One collateral consequence of the resolution was to prompt a widespread series of public meetings throughout the colonies at several levels—colony, county, town, village—to debate and decide on the congressional recommendation. This was the ultimate revolutionary moment for Adams, the occasion to discover whether the fruit of independence had sufficiently ripened within the people at large to permit a harvest. In a sense, Adams dreaded this moment most of all, fearing he might discover that he had been leading a parade that only a precious few chose to join. While he knew in his heart he was right, he also knew in his head that popular opinion should never be trusted to know the right. But he also knew in his soul that, at this dramatic moment, it *must* be trusted, for this was the acid test of the entire republican experiment. George III had made a fatal decision in a monarchical way, imposing his policy to subdue the American rebellion by force rather than resolve it by diplomacy, despite huge pockets of opposition throughout the British nation, most especially in London. Now an equivalent decision on the American side needed to be made in a republican way, bottom up rather than top down. All a true republican believer could do in a situation like this, even one as dubious about the omniscience of "the people" as Adams, was to hold his breath and wait for ordinary citizens to speak.

It was like an election that lasted for several months, though early returns in the initial weeks made the final verdict abundantly clear. Despite lingering pools of reticence in New York and Pennsylvania, what we now call "the grass roots" came out overwhelmingly for independence, often adopting the language of Adams's resolution of May 15 to justify their regretful but resolute decision. The fruit of independence essentially declared itself ready for picking. Almost as important, the multiple state, county, and local manifestos tended to subordinate the controversial questions about the political agenda of an independent American republic to the more pressing requirement of national union. Inherently divisive issues like slavery, voting qualifications, and women's rights were postponed to the future, lest they complicate and contaminate the major message, which was separation from the British Empire. The Adams strategy was, in effect, fully vindicated. The revolutionary implications of the republican argument were suppressed—this was the dog that did not bark—in deference to the more compelling need to rally around what was now almost universally described as "The Cause."[53]

IMPORTANT EPILOGUE

As IF IN A STORM, the lightning struck in May of 1776 and did its work, but it took another six weeks for the thunder to sound in the form of the Declaration of Independence. During that time critical events proceeded apace on three separate tracks: the ongoing referendum in the American countryside continued to register a popular mandate for independence; a British expeditionary force of more than 100 ships and 32,000 troops began its voyage across the Atlantic with orders to nip the incipient American rebellion in the bud; Washington's ragtag version of an army marched out of Boston toward New York, 12,000 amateur soldiers that Washington somehow hoped could hold their own against a vastly superior and more experienced British force.

By the early summer of 1776, then, all the essential political and military questions that had been lingering in limbo for over a year had been resolved. The outcome of the American Revolution, of course, remained undecided. And it would take over seven years of desperate fighting, the near dissolution of the Continental Army, multiple humiliations at the hands of British regulars and the despised Hessian mercenaries, a veritable roller-coaster ride for Washington from hope to despair and back again, before the British eventually decided that the whole bloody business had been a terrible mistake that could and should have been avoided. But the arrival of that realization came too late to prevent the loss of Britain's North American empire. The lessons learned from that painful experience were profound, and became the basis for governing the second British Empire the following century and for making it the most successful imperial power in world history. But that, as they say, is another story.[54]

The end of this story, at least the version of it that Adams liked to tell in his old age, has always had a discernibly self-serving tone and the distinctive odor of jealousy. In the Adams version, the drafting of the Declaration of Independence was merely an ornamental afterthought. The real declaration had already happened in May, when the congress, guided by his resolution, had ordered the states to draft new constitutions. No one in the Continental Congress, Adams argued, regarded the formal declaration in July as anything more than a ceremonial culmination, an epilogue, if you will, to the main story, where he had been the central character.

Somehow, Adams complained, an alternative story line had found its way into the history books, a narrative that featured the Declaration of Independence as the decisive event and Thomas Jefferson as the major figure. "Was there ever a Coup de Theatre, that had so great an effect as Jefferson's Penmanship of the Declaration of Independence?" Adams asked incredulously. The Declaration was merely "a theatrical side show . . . Jefferson ran away with the stage effect—and all the glory of it."[55]

Should we take Adams at his obviously self-serving word? Here are the unadorned facts of the matter. On June 7, Richard Henry Lee of Virginia moved the resolution "that these United Colonies are, and of right ought to be, free and independent States." The congress decided to delay a vote on Lee's resolution until July 1 in deference to several delegations that were legally bound to confer with their constituents before casting a vote for independence. In the meantime, the congress appointed a five-person committee—Adams, Jefferson, Benjamin Franklin, Robert Livingston, and Roger Sherman—to draft a document implementing Lee's resolution, so that, presuming the resolution passed, the congress could proceed without pause to announce the decision to the world.

Acting as informal chair of the committee, Adams first asked Franklin to draft the document, but he declined, citing as reasons a bad case of gout and a lifelong aversion to writing anything that would be edited by a committee. At the time, Adams had just assumed the duties as chair of the newly created Board of War and Ordnance, duties he considered his top priority given the looming British invasion at New York. So he delegated the drafting to Jefferson, who performed the task promptly—Adams later claimed it took him only "a day or two." After making a few minor revisions in Jefferson's draft, the committee placed the document before the full congress on June 28.[56]

Thus far, the facts tend to align themselves with the Adams version of the story. The deep sense of significance that later generations would ascribe to the Declaration of Independence did not exist for most delegates in the congress, who were preoccupied with more pressing military and strategic priorities. Adams was also historically correct to insist that the key decisions had already been made, both in the congress and in the towns and hamlets throughout the land. Weeks before Jefferson penned his famous words, independence had become a foregone conclusion and the main arena had shifted from Philadelphia to New York, where all the finely wrought arguments about colonial rights were about to be put to the ultimate test on the battlefield.

One piece of evidence, however, does not fit Adams's interpretive pattern, ironically provided by none other than Adams himself. On July 2, after two days of debate, the congress passed Lee's resolution. The next day Adams wrote the following words to Abigail:

> Yesterday the greatest question was decided which ever was debated in America, and a greater, perhaps never has nor will be decided among men. A Resolution was passed without one dissenting Colony, "that these United Colonies are, and of right ought to be, independent States . . ." The second day of July, 1776, will be the most memorable epocha in the history of America. I am apt to believe that it will be celebrated by succeeding generations as the great anniversary festival. . . . It ought to be solemnized with pomp and parade, with shows, games, sports, guns, bonfires and illuminations from one end of this continent to the other, from this time forward forevermore.[57]

Adams got everything right about the anniversary of independence, even down to the obligatory fireworks, everything except the date itself. True enough, he thought the passage of the Lee resolution more significant than the passage of the Declaration itself. But his own words at the moment convey an excited recognition that the formal vote on independence, no matter how foreshadowed, was still a major event. If only an epilogue, it was nonetheless a rather important epilogue.

That still begs the question of the wording of the Declaration itself. After voting on the Lee resolution, the congress moved immediately to a consideration of Jefferson's draft. In committee-of-the-whole format the delegates spent two days making editorial changes that revised or deleted about 20 percent of the text. They found Jefferson a bit wordy for their taste, some of his language too florid or sentimental, and insisted on removing any reference to the slave trade or slavery itself, even when Jefferson blamed it all on George III. Mostly they focused on the latter two-thirds of the document, the lengthy list of grievances against the king. They cared most about that section because the whole point of the Declaration was to justify independence, which depended upon demonstrating in one conclusive indictment that George III had betrayed their trust. Different colonies had also experienced imperial oppression in different ways over the past fifteen years, and each delegation wanted its own experience reflected in the text.[58]

It is difficult to imagine any modern-day legislature performing an editing task of this magnitude and scope, and it is impossible to imagine it being done as well. While Jefferson went to his grave thinking that the delegates had "mangled" his draft, the overwhelming opinion of scholars is that they improved it considerably. All of which seems to further erode the Adams version of history. The obvious interest the delegates demonstrated in the content and language of the Declaration seems to indicate that they regarded it as more than a mere afterthought.

Finally, there is one more consideration that escaped everyone's notice at the time but has since become the singular focus of attention almost to the exclusion of all else. The delegates made very few changes in the early section of the Declaration that preceded the litany of grievances against the king. The following words, as far as we can tell, occasioned little if any comment:

> We hold these truths to be self-evident, that all men are created equal, that they are endowed by their Creator with certain unalienable rights, that among these are Life, Liberty, and the pursuit of Happiness. That to secure these rights, Governments are instituted among Men, deriving their just powers from the consent of the governed.

Apparently regarded by all the delegates at the time as a mere rhetorical flourish designed to introduce the more serious business, these fifty-five words would grow in meaning to become the seminal statement of the American creed. With these words, Jefferson had smuggled the revolutionary agenda into the founding document, casually and almost inadvertently planting the seeds that would grow into the expanding mandate for individual rights that eventually ended slavery, made women's suffrage inevitable, and sanctioned the civil rights of all minorities. No less a figure than Abraham Lincoln, who could rival Jefferson in his way with words, put it most poignantly in 1858: "All honor to Jefferson—to the man who, in the concrete pressure of a struggle for national independence by a single people, had the coolness, forecast, and capacity to introduce into a merely revolutionary document, an abstract truth, applicable to all men and all times, and so to embalm it there, that to-day, and in all coming days, it shall be a rebuke and a stumbling block to the very harbingers of the re-appearing tyranny and oppression."[59]

To repeat, no one noticed it at the time. And there is no evidence that Jefferson himself had any inkling that he had written the seminal statement of the American promise. Nevertheless, Lincoln was right. There they were, the magic words of American history, buried in the text, lying dormant until subsequent generations awakened to their implications, an awakening process that, truth be told, continues into the twenty-first century. At first blush it might seem extravagant to make so much of fifty-five words composed in solitude by a junior member of the Virginia delegation who just happened to be a genius with language, hastily approved by very busy men who were too preoccupied with present challenges to focus on the future implications of Jefferson's words. But in this particular instance we can say with considerable confidence that these were destined to become the most potent and consequential words in American history, perhaps in modern history. They became the political fountainhead for all the liberal reforms that would seep out and over the nation, and eventually much of the world.[60]

A year filled with desperate improvisations, then, ended with a culminating moment of creativity that has turned out to be the most brilliant improvisation of all. In that sense, though Adams had been proven right at each stage of the yearlong march toward independence, he was proven wrong about the final chapter. For the draft of the Declaration of Independence, sent out to the world on July 4, 1776, assured that the War for Independence would be more than just that. If only latently and surreptitiously, it deserved to be called the American Revolution.

CHAPTER TWO

{ The Winter }

LOOKING BACK at the moment of triumph in 1783, no less an authority than George Washington observed that the American victory in the War for Independence defied all logic, indeed was quite likely to defy the capacities of future historians to explain it at all.

> If Historiographers should be hardy enough to fill the page of History with the advantages that have been gained with unequal numbers (on the part of America) in the course of this contest, and attempt to relate the distressing circumstances under which they have been obtained, it is more than probable that Posterity will bestow on their labors the epithet and marks of fiction; for it will not be believed, that such a force as Great Britain has employed for eight years in Country could be baffled in their plan of Subjugating it by numbers infinitely less, composed of Men oftentimes half-starved; always in Rags, without pay, and experiencing, at times every species of distress which human nature is capable of undergoing.[1]

Washington's endorsement of the war's successful outcome as a highly improbable and almost incredulous achievement was rooted in the assumption that it was primarily a contest between two armies. And from that perspective incredulity is wholly justified, since the British army was unquestionably the most proficient fighting force in the world, as the French had discovered to their shock and horror on the

Plains of Abraham at Quebec in 1759, and would discover again at Waterloo in 1815. Indeed, the chief reason the sun never set on the British Empire in the nineteenth century is largely attributable to the invincible combination of its army and navy, which remained the supreme military power in the world until hollowed out by the grinding depravities on the Western Front in World War I. Within the panoramic span of more than a century and a half of British imperial hegemony, then, the defeat in North America stands out as an exception to the dominant pattern, a providential accident that verges on a miracle, which is pretty much what Washington claimed.

Since supernatural explanations are not customarily considered either permissible or persuasive by most historians, it seems obvious that there is something wrong with the assumption that the war was primarily or exclusively a contest between armies. In terms of logic, the Continental Army, especially after it was bolstered by the French army and navy in 1778, was a necessary but not a sufficient cause of the American victory. Some additional ingredient must have played a crucial role in the military chemistry, something that offset and eventually eroded the professional advantage enjoyed by the all-powerful British leviathan.

Recent American experience in Iraq, and our earlier experience in Southeast Asia, should help to identify the missing variable in the equation by allowing us to grasp the strategic dilemma confronting British policy-makers in London and Whitehall more empathetically than was previously possible. The earliest articulation of this strategic dilemma appeared in the House of Lords in 1775, when the Earl of Camden, attempting to question the wisdom of George III and Lord North in imposing a military solution on the American rebellion, delivered a prescient warning: "To conquer a great continent of 1,800 miles, containing three millions of people, all indissolubly United on the great Whig bottom of liberty and justice, seems an undertaking not to be rashly engaged in. . . . It is obvious, my lords, that you cannot furnish armies, or treasure, competent to the mighty purpose of subduing America."[2]

The Earl of Camden was not correct in describing the American colonists as "indissolubly United" behind the principles of the American Revolution. There were hefty pockets of loyalist sentiment throughout the middle colonies and the Carolinas. And, more significantly, there was a substantial portion of the American populace, probably a statistical majority, that wanted to get on with their own lives without worrying about declaring their allegiance to one side or the other. But the good earl was absolutely correct in recognizing that the vast scale of the American theater posed potentially intractable problems of control for any army of occupation.

Winning battles was important, but not decisive. The ultimate battle-field was popular opinion in that elusive and extended arena called "the countryside," where allegiance ebbed and flowed according to the sustained presence of British or American troops on the ground. Given the limited number of British troops, and the nearly unlimited geographic space they needed to control, the British army faced an insurmountable problem in Lord Camden's assessment. For their vaunted battlefield prowess would eventually dissipate its energies marching hither and yon through the vast American theater, searching for the strategic center of the rebellion, which in fact had no geographic location.

From the very outset of the war, then, there were two competing scenarios for its conduct, each of which led to near-certain but contradictory conclusions. On the one hand, if the war became a conventional contest between armies along the lines of the French and Indian War, the Americans could not hope to win. On the other hand, if it became a protracted conflict for the hearts and minds of the American populace, the British would almost surely lose. Or, perhaps more accurately, the British would be forced to recognize that winning came at a cost in troops and treasure that they were unprepared to pay.

The pivotal moment in the war, when the second scenario replaced the first, occurred in the winter of 1777–78. The locale for this decisive strategic shift was a previously obscure hamlet twenty miles northwest of Philadelphia named Valley Forge, a place enshrined in mythology ever since as a kind of American Gethsemane, where Washington, the American Christ, kneels in prayer amidst bloodstained snow beseeching the Lord for deliverance. The real story of Valley Forge is both more and less dramatic than the mythological stereotype. While the sheer survival of the Continental Army was at stake that winter, the real story of Valley

Forge went far beyond questions of suffering and survival. The very character of the War for Independence changed at this moment from a clash between armies to a competition for control of the countryside. It moved from a war the Americans could not win to a struggle they were unlikely to lose.[3]

While there were no epiphanies at Valley Forge that made it into the historical record—the image of Washington kneeling in prayer amidst the snowdrifts is a complete fabrication—lessons were learned, gradually and grudgingly as it turned out, that altered the strategy of the Continental Army for the remainder of the war. The key insight, which went against all of Washington's personal instincts, was that both space and time were on the American side, so that the only way to lose the war was to try to win it.

The major player in this story is Washington, with Nathanael Greene cast in an important supporting role. A very young John Marshall makes a cameo appearance, glimpsing for the first time why the political goals as well as the military strategy of the War for Independence needed to change, from a confederated republic to a consolidated nation-state. In several senses, then, the winter at Valley Forge became the decisive moment both in the war and in the very meaning of the American Revolution.

WINTRY SCENES

GIVEN THE HISTORICAL haze that has settled over Valley Forge as the quintessential symbol of stoic survival amidst the snow, best to begin with the unadorned facts about the place itself, then the firsthand testimony of witnesses present on the ground at the time, uncorrupted by any subsequent sentimentalism.

Valley Forge was a rural village in southeastern Pennsylvania, about two thousand acres of wooded hills dotted by occasional clearings, surrounding farmhouses, and outlying buildings. Far from a vacant wilderness, at fifty residents per square mile it was one of the more densely populated farming regions in Pennsylvania. Neither deserted nor a desert, the fertile land produced more wheat, grain, and livestock for sale in the markets of Philadelphia and beyond than any similarly sized area in North America. In fact, one of the reasons Washington had selected Valley Forge as a site for his winter encampment was its abundant food supply, which he wanted to deny the British army ensconced in nearby Philadelphia and claim for his own troops. The central irony of the "starving time" that afflicted the army at Valley Forge was that it occurred squarely in the middle of the richest and most productive agrarian community on the Atlantic coast.[4]

What about the ordinary troops—Washington called them "the soldiery"—of the Continental Army that inhabited those log huts at Valley Forge? Our best guess is that there were approximately twelve thousand of them. But all records of troop strength are snapshots in a moving picture. Because of desertions, expiring enlistments, and new arrivals, the Continental Army was an ever-shifting aggregate, part turnstile and part accordion. By the time of Valley Forge the enlisted veterans, what we might call the core of the corps, were not typical yeoman farmers of the sort that fought at Bunker Hill or the Boston Siege. They were, instead, indentured servants, recently arrived immigrants from Ireland or Scotland, emancipated slaves, landless sons from New England, mechanics from Philadelphia. They represented the poorest strata of American society, there because, truth be known, they had no brighter prospects. The more representative, property-owning citizenry had gravitated to the state militias, where the obligations were less open-ended and the discipline less demanding. One of the likely reasons the ordinary soldiers suffered so silently and patiently at Valley Forge was that the harsh conditions only replicated the difficult experiences of their earlier lives as the dregs of society.[5]

It is also wrong to think of these men all clumped together within the Valley Forge hamlet. The headquarters of the Continental Army was located there, to be sure, but the army itself was deployed in a wide arc, stretching from northern Delaware up through Valley Forge, then around to southern New Jersey. This crescent-shaped deployment provided a more secure defensive perimeter, afforded greater range for foraging expeditions in the countryside, and provided multiple avenues of escape to the interior if General William Howe, for some inexplicable reason, decided to abandon his comfortable quarters in Philadelphia and launch a winter campaign. Just as the Continental Army was the name for an ever-changing congregation, Valley Forge was the name for the center of a broadly diffused deployment.[6]

If these historical facts complicate and confuse the mythical picture of Valley Forge, virtually all of the firsthand accounts tend to confirm the desperate character of the conditions experienced by the Continental Army at the onset of the Valley Forge winter. An army surgeon, Albigence Waldo, described a soldier named Will upon arrival in camp. He was without shoes, his breeches were tattered and his shirt in strings, his hair was lice-infested and disheveled, his body covered with sores. Exhausted by hunger and exposure, he kept repeating the lamentation "I fail fast. Soon I shall be no more." No less an authority than Washington himself confirmed the scenes of "blood on the snow": "To see men without Cloathes to cover their nakedness, without blankets to lay on, without Shoes, by which their Marches might be traced by the Blood from their feet—and almost as often without Provisions as with; Marching through frost & Snow . . . is a mark of patience and obedience which in my opinion can scarce be parallel'd."[7]

Statistical evidence only reinforces the firsthand anecdotal evidence. The hospital records reveal that, on average, only 3,000 to 4,000 of the 12,000 troops were fit for duty. About 2,000 were unavailable for lack of clothes or shoes, 3,500 were "sick present," meaning confined to their huts but too weak to fight, and 2,500 were "sick absent," meaning in hospital. Benjamin Rush, who supervised all the hospitals, warned Washington that they were all laboratories for contagious diseases like dysentery, typhus, and smallpox: "There cannot be greater clamity for such men to come into our hospitals *at this season* of the year," Rush observed. "I assert that *the great majority* of those who die under our hands perish with diseases caught in our hospitals."[8]

Only a week after arriving at Valley Forge, Washington wrote Henry Laurens, the new president of the Continental Congress, describing the prevailing miseries of his troops, "which must be seen to be believed" and which "it is neither in my power to relieve or prevent." He concluded with an ominous warning that some historians have speculated was excessive and melodramatic: "I am now convinced beyond a doubt, that unless some great and capital change suddenly takes place . . . this Army must inevitably be reduced to one or the other of these three things: Starve—dissolve—or disperse."

In his monumental biography of Washington, John Marshall, who was present at Valley Forge as a junior officer in Daniel Morgan's elite unit of Virginia riflemen, made a point of endorsing Washington's dire appraisal to Laurens. "The representations made in this letter," Marshall observed, "were not exaggerated." In addition to the statistical and anecdotal evidence, there are also brief glimpses of desperation in the official record, as when the troops were forbidden to cut up their tents as they moved into log huts, even though they were using the shredded canvas as wraps for their bare feet in lieu of shoes. The Continental Army, it seems abundantly clear, was on the verge of collapse.[9]

The immediate cause of the crisis was the sudden disintegration of the quartermaster department and its operational arm, the commissary system. Thomas Mifflin, a prominent Philadelphia Quaker of some ability and greater ambition, had been serving as quartermaster general for nearly two years, capably managing an ad hoc collection of commissary agents, maintaining at least a measure of control over the inevitable graft and corruption that came with sizable government contracts. When Mifflin abruptly resigned his post in the fall of 1777, his replacement proved incompetent and the entire supply system collapsed into a heap of administrative chaos and profiteering. To be fair, the outright criminal negligence was accompanied by a dramatic plunge in the purchasing power of the wildly inflated Continental currency, which many American farmers regarded as virtually worthless. The net result was that the pipeline of food and clothing stopped flowing and then dried up altogether just when the Continental Army arrived at Valley Forge.

Washington's initial response was to explode in a fury of frustration, peppering his letters to derelict commissary agents with curse words (e.g., "Dam it"). His aides attempted to cast the verbal indiscretions in a positive light. "This is language that His Excellency is by no means accustom'd to use," they explained to one agent, "and you may judge of the provocation when he is oblig'd to adopt it." Washington's eventual solution to the problem was to appoint Nathanael Greene, his ablest and most trusted lieutenant, as quartermaster general. Given Greene's rank and status as a field commander, this decision, which Greene initially resisted, signaled Washington's newfound recognition that the supply problem constituted the most serious threat, more serious than Howe's army, to the army's survival. But before Greene could begin to work his customary magic, the empty stores and magazines meant that food, clothing, blankets, and shoes were simply unavailable when the snow started.[10]

February of 1778 was probably the worst month, as shortages forced the entire garrison to survive on half rations and visitors described soldiers crying, "Famine! Famine!" While precise numbers are impossible to calculate, the best educated guess is that about two thousand troops died of some combination of disease, malnutrition, and exposure throughout the winter. Ironically, despite supply lines that stretched over two thousand miles across the Atlantic, the British army at Philadelphia spent the winter nestled in the bosom of comparative health and serenity.[11]

THE SINEWS OF WAR

THE SUPPLY PROBLEM, while catastrophic in its immediate consequences, was eminently solvable. (Indeed, Greene eventually solved it.) But the deeper problems afflicting the Continental Army all flowed from the fact that the war, now in its third year, had gone on longer than anyone expected at the start. As Greene put it to Washington, "Every body expected a short and speedy issue to the unhappy dispute, and every one felt a perfect freedom to make the necessary sacrifices to bring about a proper reconciliation." But now, after three grueling campaigns and with no end in sight, the bloom was off the patriotic rose: "People begin to think coolly, they compare their condition in the field with that at home—the situation of their families, & their future prospects grow into objects of importance. . . . Every officer sais he is willing to bear a part of the common burden, but a very few have resolution to engage under such a hopeless prospect as the present institution exhibits to the view of every one in the service."

In effect, the Continental Army, which had been built around the principle of voluntary sacrifice to "The Cause," had never been designed to fight a protracted war of attrition. Expecting a sprint, it now found itself engaged in a marathon. And in that kind of contest, the superior resources of the British army would gradually grind down whatever remnant of dedicated patriots that emerged from those makeshift huts in the spring. If Greene was right, two of the conventional assumptions that had shaped American thinking about the conduct of the war were turned on their heads: first, a group of virtuous volunteers could not defeat an army of professionals; second, in a protracted war, time was on the British, not the American, side. "It is almost an established maxim in European Politics," Greene observed, that in a lengthy war "the longest purse will remain masters of the field," for in such a contest "money is the sinews of war."[12]

These were not the kind of conclusions calculated to buoy the spirits of the starving soldiers shivering in those huts. But Greene's strategic assessment provided just the kind of candid appraisal that Washington had requested, in fact ordered, from all the general officers in camp. Their written opinions were designed to inform Washington as he prepared for a crucial conference with a civilian delegation from the Continental Congress that convened at Valley Forge in January of 1778. Washington synthesized their uniformly pessimistic judgments to draft his own report to what was called the Camp Committee. (Actually, Washington delegated the drafting to a precocious aide-de-camp by the name of Alexander Hamilton.)[13]

This deliberative process itself merits at least a passing comment, since it is difficult to imagine the senior officers of any European army being consulted so fully or responding so candidly, especially when the news being delivered to the commander in chief was all bad. The overwhelming consensus, on the other hand, confirmed Washington's early diagnosis: namely, the Continental Army as currently constituted was on the verge of dissolution.[14]

In fact, the report that Washington delivered to the Camp Committee contained a message that defied the central assumption on which the entire military effort had rested until now, an assumption hallowed by its association with the republican values that the American Revolution purportedly embodied. This cherished assumption, Washington was at pains to explain, was in fact a sentimental illusion:

> Men may speculate as they will—they may talk of patriotism—they may draw a few examples from ancient stories of great achievements performed by its influence; but, whoever builds upon it, as a sufficient basis, for conducting a long and bloody War, will find themselves deceived in the end. We must take the passions of Men, as nature has given them, and those principles as a guide. . . . I do not mean to exclude altogether the idea of patriotism. I know it exists, and I know it has done much in the present contest. But I will venture to assert that a great and lasting War can never be supported on this principle alone. . . . For a time it may, of itself, push men to action—to bear much—to encounter difficulties; but it will not endure unassisted by interest.[15]

The report proposed a litany of organizational reforms for a "new model" army: consolidating the number of undermanned battalions; upgrading the status of the cavalry; regularizing the criteria for promotion. But there were two essential recommendations on which all the other reforms depended: first, all officers who signed up for the duration should receive pensions of half pay for life, and, if they are permanently disabled or killed, their wives and children should be compensated; second, mandatory quotas, in effect a draft, should be imposed on each state in order to assure that the fighting strength of the Continental Army reached its full complement of slightly more than forty thousand troops. Washington recognized that both requests (i.e., creating a standing army of professionals and replacing voluntarism with coercion) violated the very principles the American Revolution purportedly embodied. But it was the only way to win the war. And defeat rendered all the republican principles irrelevant.[16]

While the Camp Committee planned to take that painfully paradoxical message back to congress, where the reception could be expected to be some combination of incredulity and stunned silence, there appeared in camp a one-man answer to one of Washington's military problems, a former Prussian officer who styled himself Baron von Steuben. The title was a complete fabrication, as were Steuben's claims of intimacy with Frederick the Great and the rank of general. (He had never gotten beyond captain.) In that sense Steuben looked much like those other European officers who kept showing up at Valley Forge with inflated credentials and equally inflated egos, demanding high rank and quickly exposing themselves as insufferable nuisances.[17]

Steuben, it turned out, was different. Though a fraud, he proved himself a lovable character and a highly competent officer with a special knack for drilling soldiers on the parade ground. Soon after his arrival in late February he could be seen every morning barking commands in his imperfect English, studded with German profanities, maneuvering troops from column to line and back again with increasing precision, shouting orders to platoons, then companies, then entire regiments. Within weeks his appearance on the parade ground became the major attraction of the day for all visitors to the camp, and Steuben himself became the self-styled maestro of military orchestrations.

But Steuben's daily performance was more than an amusing show that broke the boredom of camp. To be sure, modern soldiers justifiably regard marching exercises as tiresome routines designed to occupy time with no direct connection to their combat effectiveness. On the eighteenth-century battlefield, however, the tactical deployment of troops in disciplined formations often made the crucial difference in adjusting to shifts in the direction of flanking assaults, massing firepower at the point of attack, or maintaining unit cohesion during a strategic retreat. Rather incredibly, prior to Steuben's arrival there had been no uniform standards of march and maneuver at all in the Continental Army. (Different units had their own tactical rules, just as they had their own uniforms.) During two recent battles, at Brandywine and Germantown, despite spirited efforts and excellent marksmanship that impressed several British officers, the inability of American troops to move in disciplined formations amidst the smoke and confusion had a decisive impact on the outcome. What Steuben had to teach, then, the

Continental Army had a considerable need to learn if they ever hoped to match the prowess of the British army on a conventional battlefield.[18]

Just as Greene had been Washington's answer to the supply problem, Steuben became his answer to the discipline problem. Washington appointed him inspector general toward the end of the Valley Forge encampment. No equivalently simple solution existed for what we might call the turnstile problem, the transitory character and ever-shifting composition of the Continental Army, now a problem rendered more acute by a prolonged war that had outlived its glory phase. The only person who could solve that problem was a magician who could wave his magic wand and re-create in the population at large the patriotic ethos already being referred to nostalgically as "the spirit of '76." No one of that description showed up at Valley Forge, so from Washington's perspective, still fixated on the conventional assumption that it was a mano a mano contest between his army and Howe's, the future seemed as bleak as the Valley Forge weather.

FLUTTERINGS

THE SOCIAL STRUCTURE of the Valley Forge encampment was a perfect pyramid built out of the classic Aristotelian categories: the one, the few, and the many. The one, of course, was Washington, whose lodgings at the Isaac Potts farmhouse became operational headquarters from which he rode out each day to inspect the troops in much the manner that he inspected the slaves and fields of his Mount Vernon plantation. The many were the ordinary soldiers huddled in their huts, by all accounts bearing their deplorable conditions with remarkable patience, sometimes singing a patriotic ditty entitled "War and Washington" as the commander in chief rode past. The few were the officers, whose demeanor, at least as reflected in the official records, comes across as sufficiently strange to merit our attention.

Two overlapping patterns of behavior within the officer corps catch the eye. First, the records reveal an obsessive concern with rank, to include minute distinctions of seniority that often required courts-martial to resolve. While the enlisted men were suffering silently, the officers seemed to be perpetually engaged in petty arguments about their relative status in the military hierarchy, at times resembling, as Adams put it, apes scrambling for nuts. Second, minor arguments around the campfires (e.g., Did you bring your troops up fast enough at Brandywine? Whose horse should be allowed to feed first?) quickly escalated to major matters of honor, which often required adjudications before they escalated again to personal challenges and even duels. While the ordinary soldiers shivered stoically, their officers seemed fixated on a kind of juvenile competition about their respective reputations.[19]

All these fragile and throbbing egos could be attributed to stress, but the more plausible explanation is that the officer corps at Valley Forge had come to regard itself as an indigenous American aristocracy. Looking ahead to the postwar years, the seeds of the Society of the Cincinnati were planted at this moment, rooted in the conviction that the officer corps was the elite "band of brothers" that remained true to "The Cause" just when it seemed to be lost and when the idealism of 1775–76 was dying out in the population at large.

In the British army, one was an officer because one was an aristocrat. In the Continental Army, one was an aristocrat because one was an officer. And because elite status depended upon negotiable calculations of merit rather than clear bloodlines or established fortunes, the persistent bickering within the officer corps, the excessive laments about "mortification" and "indignity," were expressions of a thin-skinned uncertainty about where one stood in the pecking order. The American officers clearly regarded themselves as an American meritocracy. But merit in this new American context proved incessantly negotiable and contentious once unmoored from European guidelines and forced to invent its own criteria.

With all the advantages of hindsight, one can also detect a new idea emerging within the officer corps at Valley Forge about the political goals of the American Revolution. Peeking ahead to the 1780s and 1790s, it is no accident that the leadership of the Federalist Party—to include Washington, Alexander Hamilton, and John Marshall—shared the sufferings of the Valley Forge winter, and internalized in those dire conditions a palpable sense that a fully empowered central government was necessary to win the war and oversee the peace.

The Continental Congress, which had functioned as a de facto central government throughout the first year of the war, had surrendered that mandate in the summer of 1776. More accurately, it had been wrestled away by the states, which became the sovereign units of an American confederation rather than the junior partners in an American nation. By 1777 Washington had begun the practice of drafting an annual Circular to the States, and his correspondence at Valley Forge was littered with letters to the respective governors of Pennsylvania, New Jersey, Virginia, Connecticut, and New York, each one acknowledging that the states, not the Continental Congress, had the final say on all crucial questions of manpower and money.[20]

This made eminent ideological sense, since the state legislatures could justifiably claim that the constitutional crisis which prompted secession from the British Empire had rejected Parliament's authority in favor of the colonial assemblies, which were just as unwilling to subordinate themselves to a domestic version of Parliament in Philadelphia. While ideologically correct, this political arrangement was a fiscal and military nightmare, for the diffusion of authority from one to thirteen autonomous sources wreaked havoc with any coherent process of planning or policy. It was like surveying the battlefield not with binoculars but with a kaleidoscope.

As a result, the seeds of a truly national vision were planted at Valley Forge for the first time. The war was still about American independence, to be sure, but unless a consolidated nation-state with powers to make domestic and foreign policy for all the states emerged after independence, all the wartime sacrifices would be for naught, because the infant American republic would most probably dissolve into a collection of state and regional sovereignties. At least the germ of this nationalistic perspective began to congeal within the officer corps at this time, alongside the belief that the Continental Army, not the state-centered Continental Congress, was the only surviving national institution that represented the American people as a whole. During the first third of the nineteenth century the most articulate and influential advocate for a truly national interpretation of the American Revolution was John Marshall, who in his capacity as chief justice of the Supreme Court enjoyed a privileged perch from which to exercise his influence. Valley Forge was the place where his animating idea was born, for it was the place where the inherent inadequacy of a state-based confederation first materialized and the linkage between independence and nationhood first entered the political conversation.[21]

Alongside the flutterings of a proud but insecure officer corps, the surviving records contain analogous flutterings about challenges to the previously impregnable status of the commander in chief himself. During the military campaign of 1777 Washington had failed to prevent Howe's army from occupying the American capital at Philadelphia, despite heroic but futile efforts at Brandywine and Germantown. The singular American military victory had occurred at Saratoga in October, when Horatio Gates had managed to defeat and force the surrender of General John Burgoyne's entire army, about seven thousand troops, in large part because the New England militia had rallied in impressive numbers to surround and subdue Burgoyne's marooned force. The contrast between Washington's failure and Gates's success prompted a whispering campaign within the Continental Congress and beyond about the wisdom of replacing Washington with Gates.[22]

Nothing much came of this ill-managed scheme, which included the publication of letters—all forgeries—purporting to reveal that Washington was really a British spy who had been poised to sell out his countrymen for money from the start of the war, much in the manner of Benedict Arnold two years later, though the opportunity never quite presented itself. The identities of the major schemers—Thomas Mifflin, Benjamin Rush, and a previously obscure foreign officer named Thomas Conway—were quickly exposed. For his part, Washington maintained a calm public front, leaking to the press this bravado statement: "Whenever the public gets dissatisfied with my services, or a person is found better qualified to answer her expectation, I shall quit the helm with as much satisfaction, and retire to private life with as much content, as ever the wearied pilgrim felt upon his safe arrival in the Holy-Land."[23]

Knowing as we do how this little episode turned out, most historians have sensibly concluded that Washington's survival as commander in chief was never seriously threatened, and therefore the subject deserves only a quick glance before moving on to more important matters. But within the Valley Forge encampment the conclusion of the story was unclear, so the scheme to replace Washington fueled the gossip engines throughout the winter, producing a sustained surge of support for Washington within the officer corps and several challenges to duel with anyone failing to demonstrate sufficient levels of loyalty to his leadership. In the same way that the officers of the Continental Army closed ranks around their own superior virtue at Valley Forge, they also closed ranks around Washington as their only and irreplaceable commander in chief. "I wish you Could know as well as myself," wrote Lafayette, "what difference there is Between You and Any other man Upon the Continent. . . . If you were lost for America, there is no Body who could keep the army and the Revolution for Six Months."[24]

In the longer sweep of history, the ill-fated scheme to replace Washington marked the start of an unbroken pattern. Throughout the remainder of his public life, anyone who went up against Washington frontally was soon the recipient of a one-way ticket to oblivion. Within the briefer compass of the Valley Forge encampment, Washington's status as "the singular figure," the only man to command the Continental Army enjoying the complete confidence of his soldiers and officers, hardened into another self-evident truth of the American Revolution, which, like "The Cause" itself, must never again be questioned.

THE COUNTRYSIDE

AT LEAST ON THE FACE of it, two unquestioned facts about the conditions at Valley Forge appear irreconcilable. On the one hand, the chronic food shortages of December and January became a full-fledged famine in February. Several officers commented on the deplorable situation, describing troops on the verge of both starvation and desertion, horses dying for lack of forage, their decaying bodies filling the air with a sickening stench. On the other hand, the arc of the army's deployment ran directly across the most fertile and productive farming region in the country. Gouverneur Morris, one of the delegates on the Camp Committee, put it most succinctly: "An American Army in the Bosom of America is about to disband for the want of something to eat." In effect, the Continental Army was starving to death while located squarely in the middle of America's most bountiful breadbasket. How could that possibly be?[25]

The short answer is that the bulk of the local farmers preferred to sell their crops to the British army in Philadelphia. "I can assure Your Excellency," explained one officer on patrol duty, "not less Flour than is sufficient to maintain Eight or Ten Thousand men goes daily to Philadelphia . . . and scarcely a day passes but a Number gets into that Place by the different roads on this side of the Schuylkill." A veritable caravan of grain and livestock flowed from the countryside into the city to feed British troops, the wagons often driven by women and children in order to minimize the likelihood of arrest if stopped by American patrols. "I am the more chagrined at the want of provisions to which I am informed your Army is reduced," wrote William Livingston, the governor of New Jersey, "as I believe it is partly owing to the boundless Avarice of some of our Farmers, who would rather see us ingulphed in eternal Bondage, than sell their produce at a reasonable price."[26]

Actually, at least from the point of view of the farmers, price was the problem, because the Continental Army purchased supplies with certificates whose value was tied to the vastly inflated Continental currency, making the certificates nearly worthless. The British paid in pounds sterling, a much more reliable medium of exchange. And so their decision to sell to the British army was not so much a political statement as it was a wholly rational economic calculation based on self-interest.[27]

But even that explanation oversimplifies a more complicated question of allegiance throughout the countryside surrounding Valley Forge. For it implies that the bulk of the populace identified with the patriot cause, but were forced to put their patriotism aside in order to feed their own families. The social and political reality, in truth, was much messier. If we could draw a map of the adjoining counties and color the pro-British areas red and the pro-American areas blue, the result would resemble a random pattern of red and blue patches, but the largest area would need to be colored purple, reflecting a population that remained equivocal: Quakers who were conscience-bound to a posture of neutrality; lukewarm patriots or loyalists whose allegiance shifted in accord with the military balance of power in their neighborhoods; and a substantial segment of indifferent citizens who just wanted the war to go somewhere else and allow them to get on with their lives.[28]

Such a map exposes the utter inadequacy of two political assumptions prevalent at the time and resonant in the history books ever since. The first assumption claimed that the vast majority of the American citizenry supported the war. That was probably true in 1775–76, but it was no longer true by 1777–78. The second assumption claimed that the two political camps, labeled Whig and Tory or patriot and loyalist, were clearly delineated and permanent categories. That was never true, and the longer the war went on, the more fluid and dynamic these categories became, and the larger the population became that did not fit neatly into either political camp. In effect, the countryside around Valley Forge constituted a microcosm of the increasingly muddled allegiances that a protracted war had created in those middle states where the conflict had generated its greatest havoc.

And the worse the famine within the Valley Forge encampment became, the worse the muddle and the havoc became for the local residents. With the army facing starvation, Washington felt obliged to order a "Grand Forage," sending Greene with a detachment of nearly a thousand troops to forcibly purchase, which meant to confiscate, all the cattle, horses, and grain that remained in the region. The ever-resourceful Greene vowed to do his duty, despite the distasteful business of watching whole families collapse in sorrow and desperation as his soldiers carried away everything they owned. Greene reported that the scenes could break your heart, but also that the pickings were surprisingly slim because British foraging expeditions out of Philadelphia had already picked the country clean. "We take all the Horses and Cattle, Hogs and Sheep fit for our use," he explained, "but the Country has been so gleaned that there is but little left in it." Most of the local farmers tried to hide whatever crops and livestock not already sold to the British in nearby swamps in order to feed themselves during the remainder of the winter. And it was almost impossible to get reliable intelligence on these hidden caches, because, as Greene explained, "Whigs here are afraid to give any information respecting the Tories for fear that when we are gone they will be carried prisoners into Philadelphia."[29]

Indeed, the war in the countryside had become a series of foraging fights between the two armies, with the local residents trapped in between. One farmer, who claimed allegiance to the cause of American independence, described the vicious cycle that resulted from the ever-shifting situation on the ground: "That we can neither stay at our Houses, go out nor come in with Safety. That we can neither plough, plant, sow, reap nor gather. That we are fast falling into Poverty, Distress, and into the Hands of our Enemy." And farmers of a loyalist persuasion suffered the same fate whenever the Continental Army was in the area. Those attempting to avoid recriminations by claiming neutrality quickly discovered that no such thing existed.[30]

If the local residents were trapped between the unpredictable arrivals of two marauding armies, Washington was caught between two equivalently incompatible courses: confiscating the food that prevented the starvation of his soldiers, which understandably alienated the very people the American Revolution was intending to defend, or maintaining his revolutionary principles while watching his army dissolve. This was never a difficult choice, though Washington preserved his conscience by insisting that all confiscated crops must be paid for in certificates. While worthless, they provided a moral balm. As for the women and children driving supplies into Philadelphia, they should not be physically harmed, but their horses and wagons should be confiscated. And those men identified as ringleaders in this illicit traffic should be arrested and hanged in public executions designed to make a statement. He did not reverse a request from the commander of one patrol outside Philadelphia to fire on all men carrying food into the city, then leave their bodies on the road as warnings to those similarly disposed. He drew the line, however, short of what we now call "pacification." When presented with a proposal to deny Howe's army access to the farms within a ten-mile radius of Philadelphia by forcibly removing all the inhabitants to more distant locations, he rejected the suggestion as a solution that was worse than the problem it solved, concluding that "the horror of depopulating a whole district . . . would forbid the measure."[31]

These sorrowful scenes and difficult choices exposed a major new development in the strategic chemistry of the war. In the countryside around Valley Forge it became clear for the first time that the American Revolution, while still and always a struggle for independence, was also now a civil war for the hearts and minds of the American people. And the two contests were closely connected.

Until now, Washington had viewed the war as a conventional contest between two armies. His whole effort had focused on sustaining a fighting force in the field that could match and eventually defeat the British army. While he never entirely abandoned that conventional conviction, the foraging fights around Valley Forge forced him to confront the unconventional dimensions of the emerging conflict. Greene had warned him that "the longest purse" usually won a protracted war, a viewpoint that made an eventual British victory, like the added sums of an accountant's ledger, almost a mathematical certainty. Now, however, the volatile political chemistry of the countryside changed the terms of the equation, for the new variable was not money but allegiance. Even the longest purse could not defeat the deepest resistance.

A new term entered Washington's military vocabulary, "cover the country," signaling the recognition that deployment of the Continental Army and local militia units as a kind of roving police force that controlled the countryside was a crucial new mission, in many ways more important than set-piece battles with the British army. This was a new way of thinking for Washington, not easy for him to embrace given his honor-driven sense of battle as much like a summons to duel. Nor did it arrive in his mind as lightning flash or epiphany. (Temperamentally, Washington was incapable of epiphanies, and indisposed to trust them in others.) But as the snows at Valley Forge began to melt, he was gradually coming to grasp the wisdom of a defensive strategy designed to make control of the countryside as crucial as winning battles.[32]

RITES OF SPRING

ONE OF THE BEGUILINGLY quaint customs of eighteenth-century warfare was the agreed-upon understanding that armies do not fight in winter. If Howe had chosen to defy that custom in the winter of 1777–78 (and the same argument would apply to the previous winter encampment at Morristown), he would almost surely have destroyed the Continental Army during its season of wholesale comings and goings, when it was completely vulnerable. But the idea of waging a decisive winter campaign, so obvious to us schooled in the relentless character of modern warfare, never even occurred to Howe, for the same reason that it never occurred to regular troops in either army to lie down in the prone position on the battlefield when the enemy prepared to fire a volley. The mentality of the age was closer chronologically to the chivalric world of medieval jousts than it was to the more lethal landscape of the modern battlefield after World War I. This despite the fact that most combat casualties on the American side during the American Revolution occurred at extremely close quarters, at the point of a bayonet in the most grisly and gruesome fashion imaginable. There were no rules of civility at that horrific moment, but there were unspoken and unbreakable rules of engagement that commanders of armies honored as gentlemen, and one of them was that war did not happen in winter.

But that also meant that the arrival of spring foreshadowed preparations for the next campaign. As Washington began those preparations, his major problem was knowing how large a force he would command. About two hundred officers had resigned their commissions in the course of the winter. Expiring enlistments, desertions, debilitating wounds, and deaths had reduced the enlisted troops to less than five thousand men—exact numbers are impossible to calculate—and therefore made all planning dependent on the number of new recruits who would show up for the next campaign. In late March Washington apprised Henry Laurens and the Continental Congress that "our present situation at this advanced Season is truly alarming, and to me highly distressing, as I am convinced that we shall be plunged into the campaign before our new arrangements are made and the Army properly organized."[33]

Strictly speaking, there was nothing new about this predicament. The accordion-like contraction, then expansion, of the Continental Army had become, like the campaign season itself, another rite of spring. During the previous winter encampment at Morristown, troop strength had actually dropped lower than the bottom point reached at Valley Forge. But Washington's major argument to the Camp Committee, and through it to the congress, had been based on the proposition that such annual ups and downs could not continue. At some point, and Washington had warned that Valley Forge might very well mark that point, the ranks would not refill and the Continental Army would simply disappear.[34]

As new enlistees began to trickle into camp in March and April it became clear that nothing so dramatic would occur this season. But it also became clear that nothing so robust as Washington had envisioned in his report to the Camp Committee—a total force of over forty thousand—was even remotely possible. By the time the new complement of troops from Virginia arrived in camp—they were late because of delays forced by undergoing mandatory inoculation for smallpox—the newly constituted army numbered about twelve thousand. In effect, the army that marched out of Valley Forge would be the same size as the army that marched in, though many of the men filling the ranks would be different.[35]

Where would they be marching to? That was the question Washington put to all his general officers in April, the same solicitation of opinion from his chief lieutenants that he had requested earlier before drafting his report to the Camp Committee. As Washington saw it, there were three strategic options: attack Howe's army in Philadelphia; assault the British garrison in New York and occupy the city, a notorious haven for loyalists; or assume a defensive posture and fight a "war of posts" in which direct engagement with the British army should be avoided except under the most favorable conditions.[36]

All the general officers responded within a matter of days, leaving a written record that affords a clear window into the strategic thinking of the leadership within the Continental Army at this most propitious moment. Most of the officers were still thinking of the war in conventional terms as a contest between armies. Most favored one of the two offensive choices, though one aggressive officer, Lord Stirling, recommended simultaneous attacks on both Philadelphia and New York. The clear consensus was that the Continental Army needed to deliver a decisive blow against Howe's army along the lines that Gates had delivered against Burgoyne at Saratoga. This was a matter of honor, as they saw it, as well as the only way to win the war.

In retrospect, there were two fault lines running through their recommendations: first, they continued to assume that the more protracted the war, the greater the British advantage, in effect that time was on the side of the British army; second, they were proposing an aggressive strategy that, by their own calculations, would require between 25,000 and 35,000 troops to succeed, yet the current strength of the Continental Army was less than half that level. The very idea of a defensive strategy seemed dishonorable, almost cowardly, though one officer, William Maxwell, observed that Washington's third option made no sense to him "unless it should be our designs to beat the Enemy by protracting the War to a length that they could no [longer] prosecute it, which I believe is not our Intention."[37]

Three officers dissented from the majority view. Steuben was somewhat equivocal, preferring an attack on either New York or Philadelphia, but also worrying about any strategy that put the survival of the Continental Army at risk. "In the present Situation of American Affairs," he explained, "I could never determine myself to vote for general actions, upon which the fate of the nation might depend."[38]

The most outspoken endorsement of a wholly defensive strategy came from a French engineering officer, Antoine-Jean-Louis Duportail, who dismissed the offensive options as suicidal and the men who advocated them as juvenile romantics obsessed with honor and glory, therefore blind to the obvious strategic reality—namely, that it was the British and not the American army that needed to win the war. Duportail offered the clearest and most prescient analysis of the advantages that would accrue to the American cause over time, and of the folly of discarding that advantage by seeking a decisive battle against a superior British army. The key strategic question, he noted, was not even being posed. All prospective engagements, wherever they occurred, should be evaluated according to the geographic availability of escape routes for the Continental Army if it was defeated. In that sense, the only strategy that mattered was an exit strategy.[39]

The most imaginative and prophetic advice came from Greene, in part because he had spent the winter at Valley Forge reconnoitering the countryside, in part because he had read widely in the military history of the Roman Empire and therefore was more keenly attuned to the intrinsic difficulties faced by any army of occupation, no matter how formidable its military prowess. "The only hope that the Enemy can ever have of subjugating this Country," Greene observed, "is by possessing themselves of our Capital Cities, distressing our trade—destroying our stores, and debauching one part of the Community to lend their Aid to subjugate the other." Over the past two years the British army had demonstrated its capability to accomplish most of the initial goals, as their current occupation of both New York and Philadelphia clearly demonstrated. But the latter goals, which required them to consolidate their conquests, that is, to convince the population to accept as permanent their supremacy, were a much more daunting task, requiring the abiding deployment of more troops than Great Britain could ever afford to provide. "The great difficulty the Enemy labour under," Green concluded, "is to continue *and secure* their conquests at the same time." He went on to predict, correctly it turned out, that the British would launch a southern campaign aimed at the Carolinas and Virginia, hoping that military victories in that region would break the spirit of the rebellion by convincing the majority of southerners that resistance was doomed. In Greene's analysis the two armies were primarily pawns in a struggle for the hearts and minds of ordinary citizens in the countryside, the ultimate battlefield where the conflict would be decided. The New York versus Philadelphia question that Washington posed, he argued, should be resolved within that larger strategic context.[40]

It would be lovely if we were writing a story about Washington's capacity to recognize wisdom when it was offered. At later moments in his military and political career that story would be true. But in this instance he digested the written recommendations from all his general officers and decided he could not make a decision. His response, written out as "Thoughts Upon a Plan of Operation for Campaign, 1778," simply summarized the competing pieces of advice without indicating a preference. Indeed, like most of his senior officers, he seemed disposed toward an offensive strategy. All his personal instincts pointed him in that direction. What held him back was not recognition of the strategic insights provided by Steuben, Duportail, or Greene, but rather the more practical recognition that he lacked the troops to mount an offensive campaign against either Philadelphia or New York. He was not by nature an indecisive man, but in this situation he opted to "wait on events," a backhanded way of adopting the defensive option, at least for the time being.[41]

EVENTS AND ARCS

WHILE WASHINGTON brooded, those events on which he was waiting began to arrive at Valley Forge faster than the new recruits. The major event, long anticipated but stunning in its impact, was the news that France had signed a treaty of alliance with the United States. This was the equivalent of an international earthquake that shook all the capitals of Europe, none more so than London, where the North ministry now found it necessary to reassess its military commitment in North America within a larger global struggle against its most formidable European rival. Washington announced the splendid news to the army on May 5, and the following day Steuben staged a grand parade of the entire Continental Army that featured a demonstration of "running fire" up and down the line, salvos from thirteen cannons, and spirited shouts of "huzzah" from all the assembled troops. A huge table was set up in the middle of camp, where all the officers were invited to join the commander in chief to sample "a profusion of fat meat, strong wine and other liquors." The celebratory mood was an appropriate way to declare the end of the Valley Forge winter and to anticipate the imminent assistance of the French army, coming to the rescue like cavalry from across the Atlantic.[42]

Another piece of foreign news with strategic implications carried a more mixed message. In late April Washington learned that the British ministry, probably anticipating America's French connection, had proposed new conciliatory terms and appointed a peace commission to negotiate an end to the conflict. In truth, the terms being proposed were not new, but were essentially identical to those offered by the Continental Congress two years earlier. In effect, Parliament would agree not to tax the colonies, recognizing the right of each colonial assembly to do so, and the colonists would pledge their allegiance to the king and remain economic partners within a reconfigured British Empire.

From a British perspective this was an idea whose time had come, but from Washington's perspective it was an idea whose time had come and gone. He interpreted the peace initiative as another British plot that was "founded in principles of the most wicked and diabolical baseness, meant to poison the minds of the people." The real British goal, he believed, was to divide the American people, who "are pretty generally weary of the present war," therefore vulnerable to any apparently sensible political compromise that ended the suffering. But it was too late for compromise. Too much blood had been spilled, the pains and losses were "so great and so many, that they can never be forgotten." The British were now prepared to offer America everything except independence, but, as Washington put it to Laurens, "Nothing short of Independence . . . can possibly do." Laurens concurred, reading the new British proposal as a tacit acknowledgment that their army was mired down in a war without end against "a country that cannot be subjugated."[43]

Unbeknownst to either Laurens or Washington, another message from Lord North's ministry was being delivered to Howe in Philadelphia at about this time. Sir William had bested Washington on almost every battlefield, but he had not found a way to win the war. So he had fallen out of favor with the powers that be in London and was being recalled. He was to be succeeded by Henry Clinton, who would soon receive new instructions from George Germain, the minister of war and chief architect of British strategy. These instructions reflected the sea change in British thinking produced by the anticipated French alliance and, more generally, the eroding public support for an increasingly expensive quagmire. Given these new developments, "the war must be prosecuted upon a different plan from that which it has hitherto been carried on." Clinton should "relinquish the idea of carrying on offensive operations against the rebels within land." More specifically, he should evacuate Philadelphia, consolidate his main army in New York, and abandon any effort to crush the Continental Army with one decisive blow. Meanwhile, a sizable British force would be deployed in the Carolinas, where robust loyalist sentiment was presumed to exist.[44]

It was a strategic decision made in a much more imperial, top-down fashion than the messier and more consensual process followed by Washington. And it left little discretion to Clinton—or Howe for that matter—whereas Washington himself enjoyed near-dictatorial powers on all questions involving the deployment of the Continental Army. But despite the stark difference in style, and despite Washington's wait-and-see version of a decision, both sides were committing themselves to a defensive strategy north of the Potomac for at least the foreseeable future. It was a recipe for an even more protracted war in which dueling armies gave way to the much murkier competition for hearts and minds.

And so, as Washington led the Continental Army out of Valley Forge on June 18, 1778, one chapter in the War for Independence ended and a new one began. Most elementally, the Continental Army had survived a near-death experience to fight another day, so the subsequent mythological renderings—Gethsemane, Christ in the desert, the winter of discontent—contain more than a grain of truth. It truly was a close call, and if the army had not survived, the story of American independence would have ended abruptly, then had to wait another century or so to reappear as a more evolutionary than revolutionary tale, along the lines of a Canada or an Australia. The strategic center of the rebellion was not a place, it was the Continental Army itself. By marching out of Valley Forge with approximately the same number of troops that marched in, Washington was essentially declaring that the soul of the American Revolution remained alive and well.

But Valley Forge was also pivotal for another reason. During the next three years the Continental Army would fight only one major battle. That was at Monmouth Court House soon after decamping from Valley Forge, when plans to harass Clinton's rear guard as it marched toward New York accidentally escalated into a full-fledged conventional battle. Otherwise, there were no set-piece battles at all within the crucial corridor running from eastern Pennsylvania up to western Connecticut, where all the major engagements had previously occurred. There the character of the conflict shifted from winning battles to controlling the countryside.

Washington grasped, but only partially, the implications of these altered conditions. The conventional strain in his thinking remained dominant, as he kept waiting for the arrival of the French army and navy that would allow him to smash the British army at New York in one decisive war-ending battle. (Eventually he got his wish, though at Yorktown rather than New York.) In truth, the only reason he avoided a major engagement for so long was that he lacked the manpower. If all his recommendations to the Continental Congress had been implemented, and if the Continental Army had therefore doubled in size with a permanent core of well-supplied veteran troops, Washington would have surely acted differently and more aggressively. But that never happened.

Instead, he was forced to keep the Continental Army in a defensive posture. And in doing so he demonstrated that he did grasp the new strategic conditions that first revealed themselves at Valley Forge. The key piece of evidence on this score was his deployment of the Continental Army. For three years it was stretched in a long arc that started in Philadelphia, moved up through New Jersey, around New York into the Hudson Highlands, then down into the hill country of western Connecticut. This represented a macroscopic version of the microscopic deployment at Valley Forge, offering accessible avenues of escape to the west if confronted by a superior British force and, more importantly, assuring American control of the countryside where the bulk of the civilian population resided.[45]

Even when the British adopted a southern strategy in 1780 and dispatched their main army under Charles Cornwallis into the Carolinas, Washington refused to budge from his strategic perimeter. (He made Greene his one-man solution again, sending him with a small "flying army" to bedevil Cornwallis, which he proceeded to do with his customary brilliance.) In spite of his instinctive urge to defeat the British army, Washington realized that the most crucial battlefield was elsewhere, out there on that psychological terrain where ordinary Americans were calculating their interests and allegiances. By controlling that terrain he assured victory in the most decisive battle of the war. Yorktown thus became a gift from the gods that satisfied Washington's fondest dream, but Valley Forge was the pivotal moment when he first glimpsed the strategic reality that made a Yorktown of some sort inevitable.

CHAPTER THREE

⟨ The Argument ⟩

Iₙ 1783, the year the War for Independence officially ended, Washington wrote his last Circular to the States. His prose was uncharacteristically lyrical; indeed, the letter contained the most poetical passages that Washington ever wrote. And his message was equally uplifting—nothing less than a visionary version of just what the recent American victory actually meant. "The Citizens of America," Washington wrote,

> placed in the most enviable condition, as the sole Lords and Proprietors of a vast Tract of Continent, comprehending all the various soils and climates of the World, and abounding with all the necessaries and conveniences of life, are now by the late satisfactory pacification, acknowledged to be possessed of absolute freedom and Independency; They are, from this period, to be considered as the Actors on a most conspicuous Theatre, which seems to be designated by Providence for the display of human greatness and felicity.[1]

In short, the American victory not only meant independence from the British Empire, it also meant the creation of an American empire in its stead as the dominant power on the continent. The American Revolution, as Washington saw it, was a continuation of the French and Indian War for control of the eastern third of North America. The Peace of Paris (1763) had eliminated France from contention. Now the Treaty of Paris (1783) had eliminated Great Britain. There was now no one left, save the disparate Indian tribes, to contest American supremacy east of the Mississippi.

When Lafayette proposed a grand tour of the European capitals as a kind of victory parade, Washington countered with a proposal for an American tour of the "New Empire," starting in Detroit, sailing down the Mississippi River to New Orleans, then heading back through modern-day Mississippi and Alabama to Savannah. It was a breathtaking imperial vision, which more than half a century later would be given the name "manifest destiny." "We have indeed so plain a road before us," wrote Washington, "that it must be worse than ignorance if we miss it."[2]

Not everyone agreed. The very fact that Washington's Circular was directed at the respective state governments constituted an implicit recognition that they, and not the Confederation Congress (i.e., the government under the Articles of Confederation), were the true sovereign sources of political power in the infant American republic. Meanwhile, down in Philadelphia, the Treaty of Paris could not be approved for several weeks because not enough delegates cared enough to show up to constitute a quorum. Instead of a powerful nation-state with imperial pretensions, the government established under the Articles of Confederation was not really much of a government at all, but rather a diplomatic conference where the sovereign states, each of which regarded itself as an autonomous nation, met to coordinate a domestic version of foreign policy. It was, in effect, designed to be weak, and lacked altogether the authority to manage a burgeoning empire.

Given the subsequent history of the United States, which confirmed Washington's imperial vision by consolidating its power on the continent in the course of the nineteenth century, then emerged in the twentieth century as the dominant economic and military power in the world, it is essential to remember that the term "United States" began as a plural rather than singular noun, more like the modern-day European Union than a latter-day Roman Empire. Allegiances remained primarily local; they then clustered into state-based loyalties, then periodically enlarged to regional affinities and interests. (Just before Jefferson sat down to write the Declaration of Independence, he bemoaned his exile in Philadelphia, far away from the bosom of "my country," by which he meant Virginia.) The dominant view of most prominent and ordinary American colonists in 1776 was that they were joining together in common cause to defeat the British leviathan, but this union was a temporary necessity, less a marriage than a forced friendship. The only thing that had held the colonies together was their mutual membership in the British Empire. The only thing that had held the states together, and only barely, was their mutual opposition to the authority of the British Empire. Now that the war was won, the states began to go their separate ways.

If Washington was right, the burgeoning American empire required a fully empowered central government to manage its inevitable expansion across the continent. But such a national government contradicted the most cherished political values the American Revolution claimed to stand for. From Washington's perspective the Confederation Congress appeared "little more than an empty sound" or "a Nugatory body" destined to "sink into contempt in the eyes of Europe." From the perspective of the vast majority of American citizens, however, the inherent weakness of the Articles of Confederation was a shining example of republican principles, since a strong central government replicated the distant and despotic political power against which they had recently rebelled.[3]

The gap between these two political camps was an unbridgeable chasm separated by a fundamental difference of opinion over the true meaning of the American Revolution. The outright nationalists, of whom Washington and most officers in the Continental Army were the most outspoken advocates, were a decided minority at war's end. The staunch confederationists, on the other hand, were a clear majority who also enjoyed the incalculable ideological advantage of knowing that a powerful American nation-state violated the hallowed political principles embodied in "the spirit of '76."

How that chasm was bridged, how a dedicated minority of nationalists managed to redefine "the spirit of '76," which then became "the spirit of '87," is the story we try to tell here. It is, of course, an oft-told tale, and the ground we will be traversing is littered with the dead bodies of many previous historians, who have thereby, if inadvertently, marked the trail. Unfortunately, their respective versions of the story tend to align themselves either with the nationalists, who regarded the Constitution as the culmination of the American Revolution, or with the confederationists, who regarded it as a betrayal. As a result, the historical dialogue has been trapped within the political framework the original participants established in the 1780s, essentially repeating, over and over again, the partisan arguments of each side or, on occasion, attempting to fashion a split-the-difference compromise that still remained hostage to the original formulation.[4]

As I have argued elsewhere, taking sides in this debate is like choosing between the words and music of the American Revolution. Both sides had legitimate claims to historical truth. Both sides harbored the sincere conviction that they spoke for the deepest impulses of the American Revolution. That awkward fact should serve as the bipartisan starting point for any genuinely detached effort at grasping the messy and shifting meanings of the American Revolution after independence was won.[5]

Our focus, the two-year period from 1786 to 1788, can make a plausible claim to being the most creative moment in all of American political history. The climax of the story is not the Constitutional Convention in the summer of 1787, but rather the Virginia Ratifying Convention in the summer of 1788, where the contested terms of the debate between the two sides are most fully exposed. The main character in the story is James Madison, a diminutive, paralyzingly shy Virginian who emerged at this dramatic moment as America's most profound political thinker. The star-studded supporting cast features George Washington, Alexander Hamilton, George Mason, and, perhaps most poignantly, Patrick Henry. Ironically, none of these players believed wholeheartedly in the constitutional settlement proposed in 1787 and ratified in 1788, which was more the product of painful compromise and elegant improvisation than any pure and sustained argument about political theory.

The argument that eventually won out, which was a new and wholly unprecedented version of federalism, emerged from the messy political process itself rather than from the mind of any single thinker. In essence, the argument that triumphed defied logic and the accumulated wisdom of the entire European political tradition, for it made argument itself the answer by creating a framework in which federal and state authority engaged in an ongoing negotiation for supremacy, thereby making the Constitution, like history itself, an argument without end.

AN AMERICAN EUROPE

By 1786, only three years after his panoramic prophecy of an emerging American empire, George Washington had grown convinced that his beloved American republic was not on the verge of greatness but rather at the edge of anarchy. Multiple letters poured out from Mount Vernon, warning that the government established under the Articles of Confederation had proved itself "a rope of sand" and was now lurching from mere incompetence to complete dissolution: "Without some alteration in our political creed, the superstructure we have been seven years raising at the expense of much blood and treasure must fall. We are fast verging to anarchy & confusion."[6]

The fear that the infant nation would not fulfill its vast promise was almost more than he could bear: "No morn ever dawned more favourable than ours did—and no day was ever more clouded than the present. . . . Thirteen sovereignties pulling against each other, and all tugging at the foederal head, will soon bring ruin on the whole." The solution was simultaneously obvious and, at least within the current framework, impossible: "I do not conceive we can exist long as a nation," he lamented to John Jay, "without having lodged somewhere a power which will pervade the whole Union in as energetic a manner, as the authority of the different state governments extends over the several States." The time was fast approaching when responsible statesmen needed to make a fundamental choice: "We are either a United people, or we are not. If the former, let us, in all matters of general concern act as a nation, which have national objects to promote and a National character to support—If we are not, let us no longer act a farce by pretending to it."[7]

Therein lay the rub. For the vast majority of Americans regarded the Confederation Congress as some distant irrelevancy and their local and

state governments as their only meaningful sources of political authority. Washington's broader nationalistic perspective was exceptional rather
than typical, having developed in the crucible of a long war in which the
inability of the Continental Congress to coerce the states, and the recal-
citrance of the states to provide men and money on a reliable basis,
nearly cost America its glorious victory. Or so thought the former commander in chief, for whom American independence had become syn-
onymous with the creation of American nationhood.[8]

His lamentations after the war, then, were merely reiterations of his
complaints during the war about the absence of a fully empowered central government, then to win the war, now to manage the peace, which
included the consolidation of the continent over the course of the next
century. The bulk of the populace did not share this perspective for two
elemental reasons: first, the political arguments against Parliament's
authority located sovereignty in the states and stigmatized any American
version of Parliament as an equivalent threat to the very liberties won in
the war; second, no positive national ethos existed in the minds and
hearts of ordinary Americans to maintain some semblance of unity once
the British troops sailed away. As a result, the weak federal government
established under the Articles of Confederation accurately reflected
both the ideology that justified the American Revolution as well as the
mentality and experience of most American citizens, for whom grand
visions of a powerful nation-state with imperial pretensions floated far
above their daily lives.

The result was a prevailing indifference toward the obvious inadequacies of the Confederation Congress. Considerable debate had accompanied the creation of the respective state constitutions, most of which
adopted some version of the Adams model proposed in *Thoughts on Government:* an elected executive, a bicameral legislature, and an independent judiciary. Nothing comparable occurred when the government was
established under the Articles of Confederation, in part because it was
designed and ratified while the war still raged, in part because it was not
really supposed to be a national government at all.[9]

As a result, when the Confederation Congress shifted its location
from Philadelphia to Princeton, then to Annapolis, then to Trenton,

then to New York, no one objected to the appearance of impermanence. Indeed, impermanence was somewhat reassuring. So was the abject failure to retire the swelling national debt, loosely estimated at $150 million, though no one was really sure. After all, federal taxes or duties smacked of Parliament's ill-begotten efforts two decades earlier, which of course had started all the trouble. Finally, the fact that many delegates refused to show up, or, when they did, chose to leave as soon as their own business was finished, only confirmed the appropriately ephemeral status of any faraway central authority. Critics of the inherent weakness of this fly-by-night arrangement failed to grasp that weakness was what most Americans wanted.[10]

James Madison was one of the critics who did grasp this frustrating fact: "The question whether it is possible and worthwhile to preserve the Union of the States," he warned in 1786, "must be speedily decided one way or other. Those who are indifferent to the preservation would do well to look forward to the consequences of its extinction." The word that Madison, along with most critics of the current confederation, used to describe the consequences of inaction was "anarchy," a term suggesting utter chaos, widespread violence, possible civil war between or among the states, and the likely intervention of several European powers eager to exploit the political disarray for their own imperial purposes.[11]

While we can never know for sure, since history veered sharply in another direction at the end of the decade, the most likely outcome if the Articles of Confederation collapsed was not anarchy but dismemberment into two or three separate confederacies. Madison himself acknowledged that the gossip mills in both Europe and America were predicting that the imminent dissolution of the Articles would probably lead to "a partition of the states into two or more Confederacies." An article in the *Boston Independent Chronicle* envisioned a regional union of five New England states, leaving "the rest of the continent to pursue their own imbecilic and disjointed plans." The most probable scenario was a tripartite division of regional alliances that created an American version of Europe. New England would be like Scandinavia, the middle Atlantic states like western Europe, the states south of the Potomac like the Mediterranean countries. How this new American trinity would have fared over the ensuing decades is anybody's guess. Whether it would have become a mere way station on the road to civil war and foreign invasion or a stable set of independent republics that coexisted peacefully and prosperously is impossible to know. But separate confederacies, not outright anarchy, appeared the most likely alternative if and when the Articles dissolved.[12]

Madison had come to the same conclusion as Washington: namely, that the full promise of the American Revolution could be secured only by a stable and wholly consolidated nation-state. But he had reached that conclusion by a very different route. His fragile constitution made service in the Continental Army or Virginia militia impossible to contemplate, so he never shared Washington's wartime frustrations at serving thirteen different masters or watching men die of starvation at Valley Forge. Madison's frustrations took shape in the political arena, more specifically in the Virginia legislature and Confederation Congress, where he watched a bewildering collection of interest groups and political factions conspire to block essential legislation and conceal their narrowly partisan agendas behind a veil of popular rhetoric. In Virginia, these insidious efforts took the form of fearmongering the Anglican clergy in order to block Jefferson's bill for religious freedom, paper money schemes designed to swindle creditors by permitting debts to be paid off in wildly inflated currency, or candidates for office irresponsibly promising to eliminate all taxes upon election. In the Confederation Congress they took the form of persistent absenteeism, utter disregard for the mounting national debt, Rhode Island's reliably obstructionist stance toward all money bills, and sectional scheming that distorted any coherent conversation about foreign policy. In effect, Madison encountered the early manifestation of a wild-and-woolly democratic political culture in the states, with all its attendant excesses and shenanigans, topped off by a federal government that was not really a government in any meaningful sense of the term.[13]

In August of 1786 Madison apprised Thomas Jefferson, then serving as America's minister in Paris, of a recent proposal floating around the delegations at the Confederation Congress. The proposal recommended the calling of a "Plenipotentiary Convention" to amend the Articles of Confederation in ways that were left unspecified: "Though my wishes are in favor of such an event," Madison explained to Jefferson, "yet I despair so much of its accomplishment at the present crisis that I do not extend my views beyond a Commercial Reform. To speak the truth, I almost despair even of this." Madison was reflecting the prevailing opinion within the small circle of nationalists, which recognized that their sense of urgency was not shared by the population at large and that a premature effort at serious reform would almost surely fail, a victim of the very gridlock it sought to remedy. Or worse, a convention called at this time might very well vote to dismember the union altogether in favor of regional confederacies in the European mode.[14]

Four developments in the fall of 1786 converged to convince Madison that, whether or not the time was ripe, further delay ran even greater risks than a bold gamble against the odds. The first development concerned navigation rights on the Mississippi River, which prompted a political crisis that had been brewing since the previous spring. John Jay, who had primary responsibility for foreign policy in the Confederation Congress, proposed the surrender of American rights to use the Mississippi for twenty-five or thirty years in return for a generous commercial agreement with Spain. All the northeast states had voted in favor of the proposal, primarily because they stood most to gain from expanded trade with Spain.

But Jay's initiative set off alarm bells throughout Virginia and settlements on the western frontier, where the entire Mississippi Question was linked to the prospects for westward expansion. Jay's proposal conjured up the specter of a northeastern conspiracy to sell out western interests for eastern profits. Madison regarded Jay's initiative as "alarming proof of the predominance of temporary and partial interests over those just and extended maxims of policy . . . which alone can effectuate the durable prosperity of the Union." Up to now, the one major issue the Confederation Congress had managed to handle with some measure of effectiveness was the rival claims of the various states to western lands, chiefly because the largest claimants, especially Virginia, had ceded authority to congress as the appropriate arbiter. Now, however,

Jay's proposed treaty threatened to undermine the consensus that the western lands were a national treasure of benefit to all, what Madison described as "a bountiful Gift of Nature to the United States . . . secured to them by the event of the late Revolution."

Instead, the development of western lands was becoming a partisan issue in a sectional competition for dominance, which Madison described as "a flagrant violation of Justice, a direct contravention of the end for which the federal government was instituted and an alarming innovation of the System of the Union." The crisis also boded badly for peaceful coexistence among putative American confederacies, for it suggested that sectional conflicts over the western lands possessed the potential to produce civil war if and when the sections went their separate ways.[15]

The second development that influenced Madison's thinking about the precarious state of the union was an insurrection of farmers in western Massachusetts who were protesting the new taxes and mortgage foreclosures by the state legislature in Boston. The initial reports received by Madison vastly exaggerated the scope and scale of the insurrection (eventually called Shays's Rebellion after Daniel Shays, one of the rebel leaders); they described an enormous army of twelve thousand aggrieved farmers, many veterans of the militia and Continental Army, poised to capture weaponry at the Springfield Armory and then roll east like a relentless tidal wave, gathering momentum and supporters as they attempted to overthrow the government in Boston, all the while shouting slogans against the Massachusetts governor that echoed the arguments against George III.

In fact, there were only twelve hundred rebels, who were easily routed at Springfield by a force of over four thousand Massachusetts militia under the command of Benjamin Lincoln. They were then hunted down and sent flying to the winds, after which the Massachusetts government relaxed the restrictive legislation that had prompted the uprising in the first place. Madison regarded the episode as a harbinger of imminent anarchy and claimed, without any evidence, that British agents had instigated the insurrection and that, again against the grain of the evidence, the failure of the Confederation Congress to send federal troops to assist the Massachusetts militia represented a failure of national will that endangered the very survival of the American republic. However misguided, these were sincere convictions on Madison's part, rooted as they were in the genuine belief that "the spirit of '76," with its reflexive resistance to any coercive expression of governmental authority, was incompatible with any viable national union.[16]

The third development was a hopeful gesture toward moderate reform that failed miserably. The Virginia legislature had endorsed a convention of delegates from the respective states at Annapolis to remove long-standing impediments to interstate commerce. Only five states showed up at the convention in September of 1786, which put all the delegates, including Madison, in the embarrassing posture of preachers without a congregation. In the ironic way that history often happens, the failure of the Annapolis Convention caused Madison to conclude that since modest efforts at reform of the Articles of Confederation were politically impossible, there was really nothing to lose by attempting a more radical solution. If the Annapolis Convention had succeeded, Madison would probably have remained committed to incremental change in the Articles. Its failure emboldened him to go for broke and endorse a proposal from an equally agitated New York delegate named Alexander Hamilton, destined to be his greatest collaborator and then his most awesome enemy. Hamilton urged another convention in Philadelphia the following spring to address the root causes of the problems affecting the confederation. It was as if a bloodied boxer, reeling from a flurry of damaging blows, resolved to go for a knockout in the last round.[17]

The fourth and last development was less complicated, in fact involved only a single person. But that person was none other than George Washington, who happened to be the only man in America whose sheer prestige instantly transformed a lost cause into a viable contender. In late October of 1786 Madison spent three days visiting with Washington at Mount Vernon. They quickly discovered a mutuality of interests that would work its magic over the ensuing months. Madison found that Washington agreed completely with his dire diagnosis of the existent confederation, whose imminent collapse threatened to destroy all that he had fought for. Washington discovered a youthful fellow Virginian, young enough to be his son, with brilliant political instincts, plus savvy beyond his years. Washington did not recognize it at first, but he was being courted, and eventually manipulated, out of retirement and back to center stage.[18]

The only way to assure that the convention scheduled for the spring did not meet the same ludicrous fate as the Annapolis Convention was to elect state delegations comprised of the most prominent figures, whose reputations guaranteed that reform of the Articles would be taken seriously. In this recruitment process Washington was the ultimate prize. In November of 1786 Madison apprised Washington that the Virginia legislature had unanimously voted to place his name at the head of the list of seven delegates to the convention. Washington was taken aback by this news, since he had not given his permission for such an appointment, in fact had made it quite clear to Madison that his attendance was utterly impossible. After all, he had effectively promised the American people that he would never return to public life when he stepped down as commander in chief. He was the American Cincinnatus, permanently ensconced under his vine and fig trees at Mount Vernon. What's more, he had already declined an invitation to attend the annual meeting of the Society of the Cincinnati, which was scheduled in Philadelphia at the same time. Finally, it was not at all clear that the Philadelphia Convention would enjoy any greater success than the aborted Annapolis Convention, and at this stage of his illustrious career Washington was not in the habit of risking his reputation for questionable causes.[19]

Madison's response to this litany of protestations was the political equivalent of guerrilla war. Of course Washington himself must have the final say on this matter, but in the meantime it would be extremely helpful to the larger cause if he allowed his name to remain on the list of Virginia's delegates, since that was sure to inspire prominent figures in other states to step forward; plus, "having your name at the front of the appointments" would serve "as a mark of the earnestness of Virginia." In the meantime, Washington's silence would permit the possibility "that at least a door could be kept open for your acceptance hereafter, in case the gathering clouds should become so dark and menacing as to supersede every consideration, but that of our national existence or safety." The outgoing governor of Virginia, Edmund Randolph, joined in Madison's shrewd recruitment campaign, reminding Washington that he was, once again, America's most indispensable figure: "For the gloomy prospect still admits one ray of hope," wrote Randolph, "that those who began, carried on & consummated the revolution, can yet rescue America from impending ruin."[20]

For four excruciating months Washington attempted to wiggle away, but Madison had set the hook firmly in their October conversations, when Washington had acknowledged that he, like Madison, believed that the American experiment with republicanism had reached the edge of the abyss and that widespread popular apathy should not deter responsible statesmen from attempting a desperate last-minute rescue. Madison would never let him forget that fundamental assessment, which left Washington with no clear escape route other than to claim that he was no longer a responsible statesman, an obvious absurdity. Left unsaid was the equally obvious fact that Washington's own legacy was at stake.

His tortured machinations ended in March of 1787, when he agreed to serve. He immediately wrote Madison to declare that, now that he was committed to the cause, there was no sense in proposing halfway measures which merely patched over the structural problems of the existent but expiring confederation of states. As he began to think about the agenda for the looming convention, Washington was firmly convinced that it should "adopt no temporizing expedient, but probe the defects of the Constitution to the bottom, and provide radical cures, whether they are agreed to or not." The Articles of Confederation did not need to be revised, they needed to be completely replaced with a fully empowered national government that possessed a clear mandate to coerce the states in both foreign and domestic policy. As it turned out, Madison had also reached exactly the same conclusion.[21]

MADISON'S MIND

ALTHOUGH HE HAD no way of knowing it at the time, in the spring of 1787 Madison was poised to launch the most creative phase of a thirty-year public career at or near the epicenter of national politics, from which he would emerge as one of the giants of an age not lacking for worthy rivals. How anyone who stood about five foot four and weighed 130 pounds could become an American giant is obviously a story about intellectual rather than physical prowess. The story is further complicated by the fact that Madison was also an inordinately shy man, the kind who drifted to the dark corners of a room on most social occasions, whose voice was so weak that stenographers would later lament that they could not hear what he was saying in speeches or debates. His fellow classmates at Princeton (class of 1771) had marveled at the powers of his mind but worried that those powers would never survive long enough to attract notice, because they were encased in a body so frail and sickly that he would never reach his prime. As it turned out, he outlived everyone in his class and died in 1836, brandishing the title "The Last of the Founders."[22]

Washington had obviously spotted something special in the young man, an affinity on the larger question of radical reform of the Articles, to be sure, but also an instinctive willingness to put his considerable mental talent at the disposal of others without claiming credit for himself. He seemed to lack a personal agenda because he seemed to lack a personality. Or perhaps it was because he was so preternaturally serene, so comfortable with himself, that matters of personal credit never occurred to him.

Whatever the cause, within the oversized egos and flamboyant oratorical styles of the Virginia dynasty, Madison stood out by being self-consciously inconspicuous. His style, in effect, was not to have one. As a result, his arguments during debates tended to arrive without rhetorical frills or partisan edges, but rather with the naked power of pure thought. Like the man himself, they seemed all mind and no matter.

And yet, for a man so discernibly cerebral, Madison was stunningly adroit at the hurly-burly of practical politics, which usually boiled down to twisting arms and counting noses. Washington could certainly attest to his skill on the former score, for he had begun his negotiations with Governor Randolph and Madison adamantly refusing to reenter public life, then had found himself—how had it happened?—fully committed to lead the Virginia delegation at Philadelphia. On the latter score, Madison had created a network of contacts in all the states that provided essential information on the delegates being selected for the looming convention.

His running tabulation revealed that the Philadelphia Convention would not repeat the fiasco at Annapolis. There would be a clear majority of delegates committed to a major overhaul of the Articles. Most of those favoring the status quo had boycotted the selection process. This piece of political homework led Madison to the surprising conclusion that there was at least a fighting chance to rescue the fragile American republic from dissolution. Washington's recruitment to the cause gave the gamble legitimacy. News about the prospective delegates gave it plausibility.[23]

Between March and May of 1787 Madison launched a two-pronged campaign designed to prepare himself for the summer debates in Philadelphia. This was characteristically Madisonian behavior, since he habitually compensated for his deficiencies as an orator by always being the most fully prepared participant, the kind of frustrating opponent who always had more relevant information at his fingertips and who also somehow understood the logical implications of your argument better than you did. One campaign looked outward to the prevailing opinion in the respective state delegations, a wholly practical effort to determine how far in reforming the current confederation most delegates were prepared to go. The other campaign looked inward to his own convictions, a wholly introspective effort, aided by reading in the "literary cargo" of books on history and political theory that Jefferson had recently sent him from Paris.

Writing from Richmond, Edmund Randolph apprised him that the Virginia electorate would tolerate no more than a modest revision of the Articles, primarily some enhancement of the powers of the Confederation Congress to raise revenue and regulate trade. Any effort at more radical reform would run against the grain of public opinion and almost surely lose. Writing from Paris, Jefferson concurred, though for different reasons. The existent government, Jefferson observed, was like a fabric that needed to be patched but not discarded. The hole that needed patching concerned federal sovereignty over foreign affairs, but all domestic policy ought to remain the exclusive province of the states. On the other side stood a small coterie of ultra-nationalists, who had formed around Washington as a trusted group of political consultants, to include Henry Knox, John Jay, and Alexander Hamilton, all of whom thought the Articles were beyond redemption and must be completely replaced. The more Madison thought about it, the more he too concluded that only root-and-branch reform would suffice.[24]

He admitted to Randolph that his preference for a go-for-broke strategy might seem, as he put it, "if not extravagent, absolutely unattainable and unworthy of being attempted." But he had grown convinced that "unless the Union be organized efficiently & on Republican Principles," the inevitable result would be eventual dissolution and "the partition of the Empire into regional & hostile confederacies." As he read the political context, Madison concluded that halfway measures were worse than nothing at all, for they would only prolong the agony and thereby delay a timely decision until the hopeless end.[25]

Moreover, the outline of a truly efficacious answer was abundantly clear to him. Instead of a single-house legislature representing the states, there should be a bicameral legislature representing and proportional to the population in the states. There should also be an executive branch with expanded powers over foreign policy. Whatever document emerged from the convention should also be ratified by special state conventions instead of state legislatures in order to demonstrate that it was the will of the people rather than a compact among the states. Finally, and most decisively, the newly created federal government ought to possess veto power over all state laws "in all cases whatsoever."

Madison realized that this last proposal, and the language he used to describe it, was inflammatory, for it echoed precisely the words Parliament had used to justify its authority over the colonial assemblies in the Declaratory Act of 1766. In that sense, Madison was arguing that a more energetic federal government needed to possess the same sovereign power over the states that the rebellious colonies had regarded as tyrannical two decades earlier. His insistence on a federal veto even put him a half step ahead of the other ultra-nationalists like Jay, Knox, and Hamilton, though all of them agreed that sovereignty must be shifted from the states to the national level.[26]

Madison had in fact reached these radical conclusions by March of 1787, so that the intensive reading and thinking that he did throughout the spring was not an open-ended intellectual odyssey so much as a focused effort to marshal evidence for a preordained conclusion. Though he had the demeanor and disposition of a scholar, he had the mentality of a lawyer defending a client, which in this case was a fully empowered American nation-state. He understood his task as a partisan exercise in which he amplified evidence that supported his case and prepared to rebut evidence from the other side. Historians who have described Madison's preparation for the Constitutional Convention as a brilliant philosophical probe into the deepest complexities of republican government misconstrue the cast of Madison's mind, which mobilized its fullest energies when the preferred verdict was already known beforehand.

For example, his "Notes on Ancient and Modern Confederacies" was not a detached appraisal of the checkered history of Greek, Italian, Germanic, and Dutch confederations, but rather a concerted effort to demonstrate that all confederations were inherently weak political alliances, usually created to provide defense against a common enemy, that eventually dissolved because of a joint refusal to surrender sovereignty to a central source. Time and time again, Madison observed, the same thing happened for the same reasons. It was almost a mathematical axiom. Confederations were an inherently transitory political configuration headed either toward dissolution, which was the usual outcome, or toward unity, the rare but obviously preferred destination. The political lessons that history provided, then, were unambiguous. Either the confederated republic of the United States came together as one nation or it suffered the sad fate of its European predecessors, which was some combination of civil war, anarchy, and political oblivion.[27]

Similarly, his "Vices of the Political System of the United States" reads like an indictment of the Confederation Congress prepared by a relentless special prosecutor hell-bent on obtaining a conviction. The case against the Articles was easy to make, since the cardinal conviction that sovereignty resided in the states made all federal legislation merely advisory and all cooperation among the states wholly voluntary, the fatal weakness Madison had already demonstrated in meticulous detail throughout European history. But he wanted to assemble a full catalogue of specific failures as a kind of handy reference work that he could then draw upon during the looming debates in Philadelphia.

Thus the lengthy list of political vices, which might also be read as a latter-day version of Jefferson's lengthy indictment against George III in 1776: the states had failed to honor their tax obligations during the war and their promise to fund veterans' pensions after the war; they had refused to cooperate on internal improvements like roads and canals and had blocked efforts to facilitate interstate trade; they had encroached on federal authority by signing separate peace treaties with various Indian tribes; they had refused to abide by provisions in the Treaty of Paris that required payment of back debts to British creditors (Virginia was the chief culprit on this score); they had created a bewildering variety of state laws that made any uniform system of justice impossible. And so on.[28]

Then, near the end of the litany, Madison made a distinctively different point. Thus far his catalogue of vices had emphasized the failure of the states to meet their federal responsibilities. Now, however, he shifted his focus to failures *within* the states to act in the public interest. Local demagogues, claiming to be tribunes of the people, had learned how to make "sophisticated arguments with the glowing colours of popular eloquence." He was probably thinking of Patrick Henry's recent effort to mobilize the Virginia clergy against Jefferson's own bill for religious freedom. But his larger point emerged from a more sweeping diagnosis of the state governments since the end of the war. As we have seen, John Adams had glimpsed the point earlier in his *Thoughts on Government,* when he warned against embracing the seductive illusion that there was a stable and homogenous entity called "the people" that could be represented in a single-house legislature. But in the Adams formulation a bicameral legislature solved the problem because Adams continued to think within the classical categories of the few and the many, whose different interests could be safely housed in two legislative branches.

Madison took the next theoretical step, exploding the few and the many into a collage of competing factions and interest groups, all waving the hallowed banner of "the people" to sanction their self-interested agendas. He was particularly offended by the power of fleeting majorities to ride roughshod over the rights of minorities, though he was not thinking so much of protecting the civil rights of the poor and propertyless, but rather the rights of creditors from paper money schemes that allowed debts to be repaid with nearly worthless currency. His major point was that the experience of the state governments since the end of the war clearly demonstrated the folly of any simple or singular expression of the popular will, and that there was a glaring gap between what advertised itself as the will of the people and the abiding interest of the public.[29]

Then Madison took yet another theoretical step, generally regarded by most historians and constitutional scholars as his most brilliant contribution to modern political science. The conventional assumption, most famously articulated by Montesquieu, held that republics worked best in small geographic areas, where elected representatives remained close to the interests of the citizens who elected them. This prevailing assumption had in fact shaped the argument against parliamentary authority during the pre-revolutionary debates over British taxation and was the major reason why control of the purse was vested in the colonial, then state, assemblies. But Madison had just spent many pages in "Vices" demonstrating that proximity to the electorate had not produced responsible political behavior by state legislators. Quite the opposite: the overwhelming evidence, as Madison read it, revealed a discernible pattern of gross irresponsibility, a cacophony of shrill voices, a veritable kaleidoscope of local interests with no collective cohesion whatsoever.

So Madison reversed the conventional logic. Small republics, like the states, were actually more vulnerable to factional squabbling and sectarian divisions than large republics, because the larger scale of the enterprise vastly increased the number of competing factions, thereby producing "a greater variety of interests, of pursuits, of passions, which check each other. . . . So an extensive Republic meliorates the administration of a small Republic." It was not just that a fully empowered national government was likely to attract a better class of statesmen more capable of resisting local pressures, though Madison believed that was true too. More fundamentally, an extended American republic, contrary to the prevailing wisdom, made space an asset rather than a liability.[30]

Here was the germ of the idea that Madison would develop more fully in *Federalist 10* and that twentieth-century political scientists would identify as the earliest formulation of the pluralist conception of politics. As a result, a veritable legion of scholars has descended upon this moment to locate the source of Madison's inspiration. The "literary cargo" of books Jefferson had sent from Paris included the histories of David Hume, which contained an embryonic version of the idea that Madison might have picked up. Another possible source is Adam Smith's *Wealth of Nations* (1776), where Smith's analysis of the synergistic balance of the marketplace, surely familiar to Madison, provided an economic version of the idea that Madison might have transposed to the political arena. Madison's leadership in behalf of the Virginia statute for religious freedom also exposed him to the unique religious history of the American colonies, whereby the sheer proliferation of different sects and denominations led eventually to the principle of religious toleration because no single church or creed could achieve dominance. This too might have struck Madison's mind.[31]

A more prosaic interpretation, which is also more attuned to the lawyerlike thinking he was engaged in at this time, is that Madison recognized that the size argument was a mainstay of those defending the Articles and the status quo. It was surely going to be shouted at him in Philadelphia by those opposing radical reform. He therefore needed to have a rebuttal ready, needed in effect a new weapon in his intellectual arsenal to counter their anticipated attack on this vulnerable front. Wherever the idea came from, in short, he grasped it so firmly because he was looking for it and knew he needed it. As we shall see, the very novelty of the idea, which essentially turned a core assumption of revolutionary ideology on its head, limited its influence in the Constitutional Convention and the crucial ratifying conventions. In a sense it was an idea so far ahead of its time that no one could fully appreciate its originality. But at the time of its actual birth in the spring of 1787, the idea was effectively forced upon Madison, or perhaps the urgent need for just such an idea primed his mind to grasp for it.

THE SPIRIT OF '87

MADISON ARRIVED in Philadelphia on May 5, 1787, with a clear sense of the political challenge he faced and an equally clear vision of the proper shape a truly national government needed to assume. On the first score, his canvass of the various state delegations showed that the convention would be almost equally divided between moderates, who wished to reform the Articles, and radicals like himself, who regarded the Articles as beyond repair and wished to replace them altogether. Taken as a whole, then, the delegates gathering in Philadelphia represented only one side of the broad spectrum of popular opinion in the country at large, for those vehemently opposed to any change in the Articles had chosen to boycott the convention, and those who found the whole question of political reform irrelevant to their daily lives, probably a statistical majority of the American people, were wholly oblivious to some distant conclave in Philadelphia.[32]

On the latter score—the proper shape of the new government— Madison harbored no doubts. To be sure, there were still many highly specific and even technical questions that would require answers. But Madison knew he was more fully armed to fight these political skirmishes than anyone else. (If God were in the details, so the saying went, Madison would be present to greet Him upon arrival.) The larger contours of a truly national American republic were what mattered most, and Madison saw them clearly in his mind's eye.

First, the new government needed to benefit from the accumulated wisdom generated in drafting the state constitutions, where the proper political recipe dictated three separate branches—executive, judicial, and legislative—each with clearly prescribed powers and overlapping jurisdictions. Second, the legislative branch should be bicameral and, most crucially, both branches should be proportional according to population, thereby decisively shifting the core definition of representation from states to the citizenry itself. Third, and Madison regarded this as his most controversial but nonnegotiable proposal, all state laws must be subject to approval at the federal level in order to leave no doubt where sovereignty now resided. Finally, the new constitution must be ratified by special state conventions elected for that exclusive purpose rather than by the state legislatures, thereby making a clear statement that it was a creature of the people at large and not a compact among the states.[33]

Although Madison spoke over two hundred times during the course of the ensuing summer, his most important contribution to the Constitutional Convention occurred before it officially convened. Because a quorum could not be reached until late May, Madison enjoyed about two weeks in which to lobby his fellow delegates from Virginia. Washington required little lobbying, in fact had already extracted a promise from Madison that nothing less than "radical remedies" should be proposed regardless of the political risks they ran. "The situation of the General Government (if it can be called a government) is shaken to its foundations," Washington observed upon arrival in Philadelphia. "In a word, it is at an end, and unless a remedy is soon applied, anarchy & confusion will inevitably ensue."[34]

Other members of the Virginia delegation, chiefly Edmund Randolph and George Mason, were more disposed to go for half a loaf rather than risk total failure. But in several unrecorded meetings of the Virginia delegation in mid-May the ultra-national agenda favored by Madison and Washington won out and became the basis for the initial negotiating position of the entire delegation. The result was the fifteen-point Virginia Plan, which embodied all of Madison's major proposals with the exception of the federal veto over state laws, which Randolph and Mason insisted on softening with more ambiguous language.[35]

As a result, when a quorum was reached and the Constitutional Convention officially assembled on May 29, all of Madison's pre-convention homework bore immediate fruit in the form of the Virginia Plan, which established radical reform as the initial agenda defining the terms of the debates. No one on the moderate side of the argument had come with equivalently clear alternative proposals, so the ultra-national agenda as embodied in the Virginia Plan commanded the field by default. For those defenders of the status quo who regarded the Convention itself as an orchestrated coup d'état, or at least as a gathering of dubious legitimacy, insult was now added to injury. For, as they saw it, the calling of the Constitutional Convention had represented a hijacking of the political debate about the Articles by an organized minority of alarmists, and now the Convention itself had been captured by a radical minority of the delegates.

From Madison's perspective, events were flowing in a perfect pattern. The radical agenda was in the proverbial saddle, poised to ride forward to victory. And George Washington was selected to occupy the chair as presiding officer over all deliberations, the ultimate trump card against all who questioned the legitimacy of the Convention itself. One could hardly have hoped for more.[36]

Most of June was taken up with the composition of the new congress, which according to the Virginia Plan should be bicameral, with representation in both houses proportioned to population. On June 6 Madison unveiled his theory of the extended republic for the first time as part of his argument for direct election to the House of Representatives. Given the originality of the idea that a larger-scale republic would prove more stable and less coercive than a smaller one, the virtual silence greeting the idea seems strange. (Perhaps the novel idea was so novel that no one quite understood it.) At any rate, by mid-June the moderate delegates, who had been unprepared for the radical initiative of the Virginia Plan, recovered their balance with an initiative of their own. Called the New Jersey Plan after the home state of its chief advocate, William Paterson, its distinctive feature was a proposal to merely amend the Articles and to insist on retaining representation by state in the congress. The fat was now in the fire, since the core issue at stake—whether sovereignty should reside at the state or federal level—had been raised in the all-important context of congressional representation.[37]

The eventual resolution, which has come to be called "The Great Compromise," effectively set the political agenda for the remainder of the Convention and defined the abidingly ambiguous meaning of the constitutional sentiment ever after. By making representation proportional to population in the House and by state in the Senate, "The Great Compromise" essentially declared the theoretical question of state versus federal sovereignty politically unresolvable except by a split-the-difference structure that neither camp found satisfactory. The only workable solution was to leave the sovereignty question unclear.

Both Madison and Washington interpreted the compromise as a devastating defeat. Washington thought it was a death knell for the national cause he had left retirement to champion and expressed his deep regret "at having any agency in this business." Madison was too dogged a political warrior to give up, but he was forced to concede that his radical vision of a nation-state that was much more than a loose confederation of states was politically impossible at this time. Allegiances remained encased in local and state-based compartments that simply could not be ignored or discarded. The clinching evidence for this realistic conclusion arrived in the form of three separate votes on his proposal for a federal veto of state legislation, each presented in somewhat different versions but all failing by a decisive majority. With their defeat, the Madisonian project of radical reform was essentially dead.[38]

Though it might seem somewhat sacrilegious to suggest it, the remaining debates in August and early September over the judicial and executive branches were really an extended epilogue. The members were tired, the weather was hot, and the chasm between moderate and radical camps was obviously unbridgeable. Madison threw his best energies into these debates, determined to rescue some sliver of federal power. But the language describing the judiciary was purposely vague and open-ended, creating a Supreme Court that was anything but supreme. The more extensive debates over the executive branch produced several frustrating moments, as the delegates argued endlessly over how to elect and impeach a president, while studiously avoiding any clear mandate for what he should actually do.

Even before the final draft of the document was completed, Madison wrote in code to Jefferson, lest any prying eyes read his pessimistic assessment. Madison believed that he had lost the big battles, which were his arguments for a federal veto of all state legislation and for proportional representation in both branches of the legislature. The principle of state sovereignty had been qualified but not killed, as he believed it should be. "I hazard an opinion," he informed Jefferson, "that the plan should it be adopted will neither effectually answer the national object nor prevent the local mischiefs which everywhere excite disgust agst the state governments." The sovereignty question had not been faced squarely and answered in nationalistic terms, as he wished, but had in effect been finessed and left purposely ambiguous.[39]

Washington was only slightly more positive. In a letter to his beloved Lafayette, he seemed to say that the final draft of the Constitution struck him as an inherently equivocal document that almost invited contradictory interpretations: "It is now a child of fortune, to be fostered by some and buffeted by others. What will be the General opinion on, or the reception of it, is not for me to decide, nor shall I say anything for or against it." Given the diversity of opinions present in the Convention, however, it was probably "the best that could be obtained at this time."[40]

Over a month later, in October of 1787, Madison wrote a long and quite remarkable letter to Jefferson that provided his more considered thoughts on what the Convention had achieved and failed to achieve. All the delegates had been required to take an oath of confidentiality throughout the summer sessions. So this letter represented Madison's first opportunity to inform Jefferson about his version of the deliberations. Given the fact that Jefferson was on record as believing that only modest reforms of the Articles were required, and given the fact that Madison had just led a failed effort to replace the Articles with a fully empowered national government, Madison crafted his lengthy letter as both a diplomatic and an educational document, a gentle but firm letter to his former political mentor, essentially apprising him that the crisis was much worse than anyone in Paris could possibly fathom.

On the one hand, there was an impressive consensus at the Convention that the union must be preserved. No one, Madison reported, argued "in favor of a partition of the Empire into two or more confederacies." The worst possibility, in effect, had not happened. In the same positive vein, the decision to make representation proportional in the

House of Representatives implied a fundamental change that "embraced the alternative of a Government which instead of operating on the States, should operate without their intervention on the individuals comprising them." This was a major improvement. The net result was "to draw a line of demarkation which would give to the General Government every power requisite for general purposes, and to leave to the states every power which might be most beneficial to them." What Madison did not say was that the delegates had been unable to agree where that line was drawn and had returned to their different states with fundamentally different interpretations of where the balance of power in the Constitution actually resided.

If the delegates had only embraced his proposal for a federal veto over state legislation, Madison explained, this ambiguity would have been resolved. But rejection of his proposal left a huge question mark hanging over the new government, "for without such a check in the whole over the parts, our system involves the evil of imperia in imperio," in other words an almost deliberate blurring of the crucial sovereignty question. An alternative solution was to vest authority in the federal judiciary and thereby "keep the States within the proper limits, and supply the place of a negative on their laws." But the powers accorded the judiciary under the proposed Constitution were extremely vague and wholly inadequate to the task.[41]

Lurking beneath the unresolved conflict between state versus federal sovereignty, Madison explained, lay a fundamental difference of opinion over who "the people" actually were. Madison almost surely knew that Jefferson himself needed to be educated on this point, so there was nearly a lecturish tone to his analysis:

Those who contend for a simple Democracy, or a pure republic, actuated by the sense of the majority, and operating within narrow limits, assume or suppose a case which is altogether fictitious. They found their reasoning on the idea . . . that they all have precisely the same interests, and the same feelings in every respect. . . . We know however that no Society ever did or can consist of so homogenous a mass of Citizens. . . . In all civilized Societies, distinctions are variable and unavoidable. . . . There will be rich and poor; creditors and debtors; a landed interest, a monied interest, a mercantile interest, a manufacturing interest. Those classes may again be subdivided according to the different productions of different situations of commerce and manufactures.[42]

Madison then unfurled his counterintuitive idea that the only remedy for this toxic social chemistry was to expand the size of the area and population over which the government operated: "In a large Society," Madison argued, "the people are broken into so many interests and parties, that a common sentiment is less likely to be felt. . . . Divide et impera, the reprobated maxim of tyranny, is under certain qualifications, the only policy by which a republic can be administered on just principles." Contrary to all conventional wisdom about republican government, in order to avoid its generic weaknesses "it must operate not within a small but an extensive sphere." Here, in the letter to Jefferson, Madison offered the clearest and fullest formulation to date of his novel argument about republican size and scale, so there is some reason to believe that Jefferson grasped the point more readily than the delegates in Philadelphia.[43]

But Madison's major point was that the new Constitution, while a significant improvement over the anemic Articles and therefore deserving of Jefferson's support, was itself fatally flawed because of its failure to resolve the sovereignty question. Madison was still reeling from his multiple defeats at the Convention, so his quite brilliant exegesis of the debates and the document that emerged from them reflected his own throbbing disappointment.

Over the ensuing months, however, as he observed the ratification debates in the other states and prepared for the all-important debate in Virginia, Madison began to change his mind. What he initially regarded as the fatal weakness of the Constitution gradually grew into its greatest strength.

THE DEBATE

DURING THE TEN MONTHS after the Constitutional Convention the most far-ranging and consequential political debate in American history raged throughout every state in the union. As it was nearing conclusion, Washington described the fullness and openness of the debate as another "standing miracle," equivalent to the victory over the British army. "We exhibit at present the novel & astounding spectacle of a whole people deliberating calmly on what form of government will be most conducive to their happiness, and deciding with an unexpected degree of unanimity in favour of a system which they conceive calculated to answer the purpose." In truth, there was nothing like unanimity in the final verdict, which remained in doubt until the very end, and the votes in the three most crucial states—Massachusetts, Virginia, and New York—were extremely close.[44]

Unlike the debates in the Constitutional Convention, which occurred behind closed doors and between two sides—moderates and radicals—who agreed that the existent government required revision, the ratification debates were open to the public and covered by the press. (Virginia even provided stenographers to produce transcripts of the full debate.) Most importantly, the two sides differed over the fundamental question of revision or retention of the Articles. This was the reason why, late in his life, Madison argued that any judgment about the "original intentions" of the framers must be based on the ratification debates rather than the debates at the Constitutional Convention.

All attempts to explain the debates in primarily or exclusively economic terms have been discredited by modern scholars. The messy truth is that there was a maddening variety of voting patterns from state to state, and within states from county to county, that defied any single explanation, economic or otherwise. The labels affixed to the two sides also defied logic, for both sides were federalists, meaning that they advocated a confederated republic, but disagreed over the relative power of the states and the central government in the confederation. In the same way that the Virginia delegation had seized the political initiative at Philadelphia, the pro-ratification side stole the rhetorical march by calling themselves Federalists. This left the opponents of ratification in the awkward posture of accepting the wholly negative connotation of Antifederalists. Even before the state-by-state debates had begun, the Federalists had won the preliminary round.

The newly named Federalists also enjoyed two additional strategic advantages. First, the opponents of ratification lacked any alternative to the Constitution other than the Articles. Although most Antifederalists probably preferred a moderate revision of the Articles, that option was not available. Madison was convinced from the start that "the question on which the proposed Constitution must turn is the simple one whether the Union shall or shall not be continued." As he put it, "There is no middle ground to be taken." Those delegates who found the Constitution excessively nationalistic and the Articles hopelessly inadequate had nowhere to go. It was a take-it-or-leave-it decision that the Federalists could plausibly characterize as a choice between union and dissolution.[45]

Second, the Virginia and New York conventions were scheduled at the end of the ratifying sequence, which meant that political pressure would gather momentum on these, the most crucial and problematic states, to ratify or risk being left isolated after nine states, the minimum required for approval of the Constitution, had already voted. As Madison put it, "It is generally believed that nine of the states at least will embrace the plan, and consequently the tardy remainder must be reduced to the dilemma of either shifting for themselves, or coming in without any credit for it." Taken together, the misleading labels, the limited pro or con options, and the political calendar all worked to the Federalist advantage.[46]

On the other hand, the Antifederalists enjoyed advantages of their own, primarily the quite potent claim that they spoke for the true "spirit of '76." The Antifederalist argument was anchored in the revolutionary ideology that regarded any powerful central government as a domestic version of the very British government they had supposedly repudiated forever. If the watchword for the Federalists was "anarchy," the watchword for the Antifederalists was "consolidation," meaning a nefarious clustering of political power in secretive conclaves (like the Constitutional Convention itself), where courtiers and politicians plotted to cheat ordinary Americans of their liberty and the rightful rewards of their daily toil. "Consolidation" conjured up the specter of a political monster devouring the rights purportedly guaranteed by the hallowed, indeed sacred, War for Independence. One historian has called the Antifederalists "men of little faith," but the Antifederalist rebuttal embraced that very label as a badge of honor, conveying a well-placed distrust toward any government far removed from the citizens it claimed to represent. The worst thing about a consolidated government, so the most passionate argued, was that, once in place, its relentless expansion of arbitrary power was unstoppable, its tendency toward corruption was inevitable, and its appetite for despotism was unquenchable.[47]

The Antifederalists also enjoyed the rhetorical advantage of representing the preference of a clear majority of the populace. Although there is no way to know for sure, it seems highly probable that a popular referendum would have produced a negative vote on the proposed Constitution. In Virginia, for example, John Marshall, a staunch Federalist, acknowledged that the population at large opposed ratification, but the ratifying convention itself was evenly split because voters had chosen the most prominent state and local leaders regardless of their position on ratification. The Antifederalists could therefore claim, with considerable plausibility, to speak for the majority of "the people." Of course Madison claimed that no such creature existed and that mere majorities were often misguided. Nevertheless, the Antifederalists could and did argue that they were protecting ordinary Americans from a hostile takeover of the American Revolution by an elite minority who had themselves lost the true republican faith.[48]

The chief goal of *The Federalist* was to contest that claim and offer a coherent rebuttal that made the Constitution a rescue rather than a betrayal of the principles of the American Revolution. Writing under the pseudonym "Publius," Madison and Alexander Hamilton, with a modest assist from an ailing John Jay, turned out eighty-five essays between November of 1787 and March of 1788. When Hamilton presented his former commander in chief with a bound copy of the entire collection, Washington pronounced it an instant political classic: "When the transient circumstances and fugitive performances which attended the crisis shall have disappeared," he predicted, "that work will merit the notice of Posterity." Posterity has tended to confirm Washington's judgment, as twentieth-century historians and constitutional scholars have made *The Federalist* the seminal source for interpreting the original intentions of the framers and the most profound deliberation ever on the American experiment with republican government.[49]

As prescient as Washington proved, our semi-sacred sense of *The Federalist* somewhat distorts an accurate understanding of its role while the ratification debates raged. First, the great deliberation on republican government was composed hurriedly, without much time for deliberation at all. Rather than serene political philosophers, both Hamilton and Madison conducted themselves like harried journalists turning out copy on a deadline, or perhaps like beleaguered lawyers producing briefs for a crucial client. Second, as an embodiment of "original intent," *The Federalist* represented only one side of the argument, an avowedly partisan case for ratification that made no pretense of detachment. Third, there is reason to believe that *The Federalist* has exerted more influence on modern-day constitutional arguments than on the eighteenth-century debates that occasioned it. Its distribution beyond New York was spotty; with a few exceptions, the language of the essays was inaccessible to ordinary readers; and its greatest impact was to galvanize support among Federalist delegates already committed to ratification.[50]

What's more, both Hamilton and Madison were forced by the political exigencies of the moment to frame their argument on behalf of the Constitution around a core idea that they had both strenuously opposed at the Philadelphia Convention. As we have seen, Madison had argued for the clear supremacy of the federal government and for the resolution of the sovereignty question at the national rather than state level. If anything, Hamilton was more of an outright nationalist, preferring that the states disappear altogether. Both men had regarded the more blurred resolution reached at Philadelphia as a terrible defeat that left the all-important question of sovereignty undecided. Now, however, they embraced the very ambiguity they had condemned as a fatal weakness of the Constitution as its central strength.

Madison's conversion did not occur because of intellectual conviction—he still preferred a sovereign nation-state—but rather because he now realized that if he had won the argument at Philadelphia and produced a constitution with an unambiguously sovereign central government, it would have enjoyed no chance at ratification. Like a politician who must accommodate himself to unwelcomed evidence about public opinion, Madison shifted his ground to become the chief advocate for the very argument he had opposed in Philadelphia: namely, that the Constitution institutionalized a unique form of shared sovereignty.

He came to this conclusion gradually and grudgingly. His earliest Publius essays, written in November and December of 1787, reiterated the arguments he had made in Philadelphia: confederacies were inherently unstable forms of government, a conclusion documented by a rather tedious review of virtually all the confederacies in European history; then the more original argument about the greater stability of an extended republic, rendered public for the first time in *Federalist 10*. Both of these arguments were in accord with his strongly nationalistic convictions.[51]

Starting in January of 1788, his message began to change, most probably in response to the obviously effective Antifederalist charge that the Constitution created a consolidated federal government. It was no such thing, Madison now insisted, for the Constitution vested the central government with only those enumerated powers essential for preservation of the union. All residual powers remained with the states. The persistent potency of the state governments thereby assured that the bogeyman depicted by the Antifederalists was a complete fabrication, and the clearly delineated and separate powers of the three federal branches provided added assurance that no full-blooded consolidation could occur at the national level.

The Antifederalists seemed to believe that sovereignty needed to reside in one location, which in fact was the very mistake the British had made when insisting on parliamentary sovereignty (and, conveniently forgotten, Madison himself had insisted on it at the Constitutional Convention). But the political architecture of the new government defied the old orthodoxy of singular sovereignty by creating a unique diffusion of power. Whatever one wanted to call this new version of federalism, the one thing it clearly was not was a consolidation. In what amounted to a cross-examination of the Antifederalist side, Madison had discovered the beauty of ambiguity, or perhaps shifting sovereignties. Though driven to this novel argument by necessity rather than choice, Madison had, willy-nilly, come upon an agreement just as original as his counterintuitive case for an extended republic.[52]

By the spring of 1788 it had become clear that the decisive battle in that larger fight would occur in Virginia. Madison had hoped that the magic number—nine states—would have ratified before the Virginia Convention assembled in June. But both New Hampshire and North Carolina decided to defer their votes, presumably waiting for Virginia and New York to point the way. And Rhode Island, true to its maverick reputation, chose to boycott the entire ratification process, just as it had boycotted the Convention. As a result, the Federalist side in Virginia would not enjoy the incalculable advantage of debating a fait accompli.

In April Madison abandoned his more theoretical role as Publius— the *Federalist* essays were complete—and reverted to his practical identity as the assiduous vote counter, working the numbers to tally the delegates selected for the convention in Richmond. After an initial burst of optimism, apprising both Jefferson and Washington that the Federalists had a clear majority, he became more circumspect. It was going to be extremely close, he concluded, with the delegates from the northern part of the state firmly for ratification, the Tidewater counties firmly against, and the balance of power belonging to the western delegates and the delegates from the Kentucky district, still part of Virginia.[53]

The wild card that upset any rational calculation of the outcome was Patrick Henry, who had refused to serve on the Virginia delegation to the Philadelphia Convention, ominously observing, "I smell a rat." Madison somewhat caustically apprised Washington that Henry's absence in Philadelphia "proceeded from a wish to leave his conduct unfettered on another theatre, where the result of the [Virginia] Convention will receive its destiny from his omnipotence." Washington knew that Henry intended to oppose ratification because Henry had already expressed his deep regret that he found himself on the other side of the one man for whom he had "the greatest Reverence." Apart from Washington, Henry was not only the most popular figure in Virginia, but also the most famous and formidable orator in America, forever enshrined in the American pantheon for hurling his verbal thunderbolts at George III over a decade before independence was declared.[54]

Madison had been on the receiving end of Henry's eloquence on several occasions, most painfully when Henry blocked passage for several years of the bill for religious freedom drafted by Jefferson and defended by Madison. Jefferson was especially irritated by Henry's mesmerizing way with the spoken word, which he regarded as a crudely emotional appeal that ought not defeat his own lyrical and logical prose. But so often it did. Jefferson explained to Madison that Henry's oratorical power was an inexplicable and unpredictable force of nature, like a hurricane, and the only thing to do when confronted by it was to "devoutly pray for his imminent death." Not only had such prayers gone unanswered, but Henry was now poised to work his magic as the leading voice against ratification of the Constitution in the debate destined to determine its fate. Even more than the Lincoln-Douglas debate over slavery, or the Darrow-Bryan debate over evolution, the Henry-Madison debate in June of 1788 can lay plausible claim to being the most consequential debate in American history.[55]

Despite Madison's diminutive size, it was a clash of titans with diametrically different personalities and styles. Henry was animated, passionate, spoke without notes, and combined the appearance of an actor on the stage and an evangelical minister at the pulpit. Madison spoke calmly, in a voice so low that the stenographer complained he could not catch his every word. He held his hat in one hand, which contained notes that he consulted like a professor delivering an academic lecture. But as a result his arguments arrived without flourish or affectation, in a sense the more impressive because of their austerity. As John Marshall put it, "Mr. Henry had without doubt the greatest power to persuade," while "Mr. Madison had the greatest power to convince."[56]

In his maiden speech on June 5, Henry fired a full salvo aimed to strike every premise in the Federalist case for ratification. First, where did the alarmist notion come from that America was on the verge of anarchy and the Articles were about to expire? As far as Henry could tell, the Virginia economy was humming along nicely, the people were going about their business and their lives with conspicuous serenity. It was almost a perfect example of Jefferson's famous phrase about the "pursuit of happiness." And arguments that the government under the Articles was inadequate to the task flew in the face of all the evidence: "The Confederation . . . carried us through a long and dangerous war. It rendered us victorious in that bloody conflict with a powerful nation. It has secured us a territory greater than any European monarch possesses. And shall a Government this strong and vigorous be accused of imbecility for want of energy?"[57]

Second, by what elusive authority did the delegates at Philadelphia justify the phrase "We, the people"? This apparently innocent expression fully exposed the truly radical character of this new Constitution, which dispensed with the states and claimed to operate directly on the citizenry: "Have they said, 'we, the states'? Have they made a proposal of a compact between States? If they had, this would be a confederation. It is otherwise, most clearly a consolidated government. The question turns, Sir, on that poor little thing—the expression 'We, the people,' instead of the States of America." It seemed transparently clear, then, that Virginians were being asked to approve an exact replica of the British leviathan that patriotic Americans had sacrificed so much blood and treasure to escape. Consider, for example, the all-important issue of taxation: "Suppose every delegate from Virginia opposes a law levying a tax. What shall it avail? So . . . you are taxed not by your own consent, but by people who have no connection with you." The echoes of '76 were unmistakable.[58]

Third, given the alarmist justifications and the patently radical recommendations, what was the unspoken agenda that guided those secret sessions in Philadelphia? Was it not abundantly clear that Great Britain had become our new model and that we now proclaimed our desire to become a powerful nation-state with imperial pretensions of our own?

Some way or other we must be a great and mighty empire; we must have an army, and a navy, and a number of things. When the American spirit was in its youth, the language of America was different. Liberty, Sir, was the primary object. . . . You make the citizens of this country agree to become the subjects of one great consolidated empire of America. . . . When I come to examine these features, Sir, they appear to me horribly frightful. Among other deformities it has an awful squinting; it squints toward monarchy.[59]

Finally, Henry objected to the claim that Virginia's deliberations were merely an irrelevant epilogue to a story with a foregone conclusion. "It is said that eight States have already adopted the plan," which makes eventual ratification virtually certain. But if this is so, Henry asked rhetorically, why are we gathered here? Is it not an insult to the largest and most powerful state in the union? "I declare," Henry concluded, "that if twelve States and a half had adopted it, I would with manly firmness, and in spite of an erring world, reject it."[60]

Over the next two days Madison delivered two lengthy speeches that took the form of a point-by-point rebuttal of Henry's presentation. During the course of the Convention there would be multiple speakers on both sides—Edmund Randolph and John Marshall most prominently for the Federalists, George Mason for the Antifederalists—but the undisputed champions of each side were Henry and Madison. As a result, when Madison rose to speak, he fully realized that Henry's prowess and prestige made him the central target and the proper focus for all the finely tuned, well-rehearsed arguments Madison had developed over the past two years. In this dramatic, all-important venue, his meticulous homework paid off.

Madison found Henry's glowing description of the government under the Articles to be the kind of incredulous remarks made by someone living on another planet. During the war the states had failed to pass taxes or meet troop quotas, and after the war the Confederation Congress and the state legislatures had only continued the pattern of fiscal irresponsibility. All the European markets and bankers regarded the American government as wholly untrustworthy. Madison then unfurled, once again, his argument about the systemic weakness of all previous confederacies, unloading his research on the Achaean League, the German system, the Swiss and Dutch confederations, then asking rhetorically: "Does not the history of these confederacies coincide with the lessons drawn from our own experience?" He then answered his own question with the obvious conclusion: "A Government which relies on thirteen independent sovereignties for the means of its existence is a solecism in theory, and a mere nullity in practice." Far from being alarmists, critics of the Articles were in fact historically informed realists.[61]

Next came Henry's argument that the Constitution created a consolidated government that essentially annihilated state power in favor of an omnipotent federal government. If Henry were to read the Constitution carefully, Madison observed, his fears would quickly evaporate, for he would discover that it was truly a unique creation: "It is in a manner unprecedented. . . . It stands by itself. In some respects it is a Government of a federal nature; in others it is of a consolidated nature." This hybrid creature rendered Henry's flamboyant accusations irrelevant because "We, the people" did not refer to "the people as composing one great body—but the people as composing thirteen separate sovereignties." Apparently Mr. Henry needed to be reminded of the abiding significance the states would have in the new order. The Senate represented states and was elected by the state legislatures. The states appointed the electors who chose the president. All subsequent constitutional amendments must be ratified by the states. Thus the proposed Constitution "is of a complicated nature," concluded Madison, "and this complication, I trust, will be found to exclude the evils of absolute consolidation, as well of a mere confederacy." As for the fact that eight states had already ratified, instead of regarding this fact as unsolicited political pressure on Virginia to comply, perhaps it should be seen as a measure of wisdom on the part of our fellow Americans from which we should learn.[62]

The genius of Madison's argument for a version of sovereignty that was at once shared and divided raised the wholly pragmatic and politically painful compromises reached at the Constitutional Convention to the level of a novel political discovery: to wit, the notion that government was not about providing answers, but rather about providing a framework in which the salient questions could continue to be debated.

Much like his extended republic idea, Madison's argument about the efficacy of argument turned an orthodox assumption on its head.

To be sure, at the rhetorical level several prominent Federalists, including Hamilton and Madison in *The Federalist* and James Wilson at the Pennsylvania ratifying convention, had argued that the Constitution had in fact located ultimate authority in one source, which was that hallowed collective called "the people," even though Madison was on record privately as believing that no such entity existed. At the practical level, however, the Constitution had created a political framework in which state versus federal sovereignty was an ongoing negotiation to be resolved on a case-by-case basis. Embedded in the document, as Madison now read it, was an argument about the political efficacy of argument itself. Instead of a fatal weakness, the deliberate blurring of sovereignty was an abiding strength. In that sense Henry and his Antifederalist colleagues were being invited to hop aboard this more modern, capacious, and exciting political train and continue the debate. But the trip itself was the true destination.

This proved to be the clinching argument and the true genius of the Constitution in the long run. At the Virginia Convention, however, it is unclear if it, or any argument, made the decisive difference. Most of the delegates, after all, had arrived in Richmond already knowing how they would vote. And in Virginia, as in all the state ratifying conventions, very specific and highly localized concerns tended to trump theoretical arguments. The Tidewater delegates, for example, were most concerned that ratification would require them to honor the provisions of the Treaty of Paris to pay outstanding debts to British creditors. The western and Kentucky delegates voted in accord with their expectations about the posture of a newly empowered federal government on the Mississippi Question and the pace of westward expansion. The conversion of Edmund Randolph to the Federalist cause—he had attended the Constitutional Convention but refused to sign—might have influenced some delegates. But the beauty of Madison's argument, and what made it so powerful, is that it made the ongoing clash of all such interests the operative principle, so in a sense the conflicting interests within the Virginia Convention embodied the new Madisonian theory.

Sensing defeat, Henry transformed the latter days of the convention into a debate about the essential addition of a Bill of Rights, crafted to more clearly limit the powers of the federal government and leave the bulk of domestic policy to the states. Madison regarded Henry's efforts on this score as a tactical ploy designed to confuse undecided delegates. His response was to accept *recommended* amendments but not *binding* conditions to ratification. Thus the warp and woof of the convention debates near the end focused on desperate political maneuverings that ignored Madison's larger argument.[63]

Henry's final speech, on June 29, in which he proposed forty amendments to the Constitution, was halted by an intense thunderstorm, suggesting that even the gods wished to hear no more arguments against ratification. The final vote was close but decisive (89–79). When the Antifederalists caucused afterward to consider drafting a challenge to the verdict, Henry summarily rejected the proposal. He had done his best, he said; they had all done their best. But they had lost, and now "they had all better go home." With all its faults, the Constitution was clearly destined to become the law of the land.[64]

Not that Henry's argument on behalf of sovereign states ever completely died. In what must be one of the richest ironies in American history, over the next decade the man who most forcefully advocated Henry's position was none other than Madison himself. Even later, long after Henry was gone, the Confederate States of America adopted his argument as the central rationale for secession from the union. The ultimate resolution of the argument did not occur in the political arena but on the battlefields of the Civil War, where both of Madison's ingenious arguments—about the stability of an extensive republic and an institutionalized forum for everlasting debate—became casualties in the bloodiest war in American history.

It would be inappropriate to offer a last word on this story, since the whole point of Madison's most insightful argument for the new Constitution was that it enshrined an argumentative process in which no such thing as a last word would ever be uttered. But since Washington proved, in so many different contexts, to be the exception that proved the rule, perhaps there is some basis for giving him the last word here.

After the vote in the Virginia Convention made ratification assured, Washington, in an uncharacteristically philosophical mood, observed that history worked in strange ways. "A multiplicity of circumstances . . . appear to have cooperated in bringing about the happy resolution," he mused, citing Shays's Rebellion as a near calamity that nevertheless prompted the Philadelphia Convention, which then "ushered us towards permanent national felicity." A few months earlier, when the victory was still in doubt, he offered a different version of the same ironic point. The very potency of the Antifederalist argument, as misguided as Washington regarded it to be, served a useful purpose. For it called forth, in opposition, "abilities which would otherwise not perhaps been exerted that have thrown new lights upon the science of Government, that have given the rights of man a full and fair discussion." No man was better equipped to understand the irony of it all than James Madison.[65]

CHAPTER FOUR

{ The Treaty }

O N THE FACE of it, the biggest loser in the American War for Independence was Great Britain, which lost most of its North American empire. But Great Britain rebounded from this devastating defeat to become the dominant world power for the following century and a half. Before history finally happened to the British Empire, its projection of imperial power around the globe enjoyed a level of success not seen since the headiest days of Rome. In that sense, the American Revolution was only a disappointing first act, followed by unparalleled British ascendancy.

There was no second act for the Native American population. For the roughly 100,000 Indians living between the Appalachians and the Mississippi, the American victory in 1783 proved an unmitigated calamity from which history would provide no rescue, unless forced removal to land west of the Mississippi can be regarded as such. The British defeat triggered a tidal wave of western migration on the part of settlers who understood the phrase "pursuit of happiness" to mean owning their own land. This demographic surge into Indian Country proved relentless and ultimately unstoppable. If only in retrospect, after the American Revolution the Indian population east of the Mississippi was fighting a holding action against the odds—ultimately it was a matter of numbers—in which the tragic conclusion seems inevitable.[1]

But the clairvoyance of hindsight actually obscures the choices perceived by the participants caught in the moment. On the Indian side, it never occurred to most tribal chiefs that the scratch of a pen in Paris had dispossessed them of lands they had controlled for centuries. The British intruders had now been replaced by the American intruders, to be sure, but there seemed no reason to believe that this change would mean that the future would be dramatically different from the past. The exception, and a major one, was the Iroquois Confederation, called the Six Nations, whose alliance with Great Britain had cost them dearly during the war, a devastating experience that allowed them to glimpse the inexorable power building to the east. For the more western tribes, on the other hand, in that vast expanse stretching south from the Ohio Valley through what is now Tennessee, Alabama, and Mississippi, the war between the whites remained a distant event of little consequence for their daily lives. Until the front edge of the looming American invasion reached their tribal lands, most Indian leaders presumed, quite plausibly, that what one Shawnee chief called "our island" was both safe and impregnable. Nothing in their previous experience equipped them to regard themselves as tragic victims.[2]

Meanwhile, on the American side, the leadership of the new national government created by the recently ratified Constitution declared its determination to avoid a policy of Indian removal at almost any cost. Under the Articles of Confederation Indian policy had been an incoherent blend of federal and state jurisdictions, with a gloss of reassuring rhetoric that covered a crude reality of outright confiscation. Now, for the first time, the power to implement a coherent national policy toward the Indian tribes east of the Mississippi was vested in the federal government and, more specifically, in the executive branch. This effectively placed control of policy in the hands of three people: President George Washington, Secretary of State Thomas Jefferson, and Secretary of War Henry Knox. All three agreed on two fundamental principles: first, Indian policy was a branch of foreign policy, or, as Knox put it, "the independent tribes of indians ought to be considered as foreign nations, not as the subjects of any particular state," a position that sanctioned federal authority over the states and executive authority over policymaking; second, as sovereign nations the Indian tribes possessed legitimate rights that must be respected. Again, Knox put it most succinctly:

"Indians being the prior occupants of the rights of the soil. . . . To dispossess them . . . would be a gross violation of the fundamental Laws of Nature and of that distributive Justice which is the glory of a nation."[3]

In short, as the apparently inevitable tragedy so clear to us began to unfold, neither side regarded it as inevitable. Washington went so far as to declare that a truly just Indian policy was one of his highest priorities, that failure on this score would damage his reputation and "stain the nation." No man in American history was more accustomed to getting his way than Washington, especially when he invested his personal prestige in the cause. The fate of the Native American population proved the exception to that rule, a case where his own efforts proved inadequate for reasons that not even he could control.[4]

This, then, is a story about failure. Next to the failure to end slavery, or at least put it on the road to extinction, the inability to reach a just accommodation with the Native Americans was the greatest failure of the revolutionary generation. And they knew it. Here the creative response to a daunting challenge, which had risen to the occasion in earlier crises, proved inadequate to the task at hand. Perhaps the problem was insoluble. But then harnessing the radical impulses of the Revolution, defeating the most powerful military force in the world, and forging a union among thirteen sovereignties had all appeared insoluble as well. And some combination of imagination, vigorous commitment, pragmatic adjustments, and dumb luck had won the day. Not so on this occasion.

Why is an intriguing question, rendered even more interesting because all the major white players in the story—Washington, Jefferson, and Knox—believed that a solution was quite clear, at least theoretically. But the real star of the story was a charismatic, mixed-blood Creek chief named Alexander McGillivray, who became the one-man embodiment of the answer to the entire dilemma. McGillivray's designation as the singular solution was, at least in retrospect, an act of desperation for which he should not be judged accountable. Despite being the most talented Indian statesman of his time, McGillivray lacked the power to avert the tragic outcome. And as Washington eventually discovered, he lacked the power as well. The power did not reside in political leaders or even in government itself. Ultimate power lay with those white settlers streaming over the Appalachians into Indian Country, a relentless tide that swept all treaties, promises, excellent intentions, and moral considerations to the far banks of history. This, then, is a story about irony, in which the triumph of the American people made an American tragedy inevitable for the first Americans. In the end, demography trumped diplomacy.[5]

AN IMPERIAL REPUBLIC

THERE WERE NO Indians present for the negotiation of the Treaty of Paris. On the one hand, this was wholly understandable, since the multiple Indian tribes were not nation-states in the manner of Great Britain, France, and the United States, so it is difficult to imagine which tribes or confederation of tribes deserved a place at the table. On the other hand, the treaty shifted control over the eastern third of North America from Britain to the United States, a landmass stretching from the Atlantic to the Mississippi and the Great Lakes to the Gulf of Mexico. Three-quarters of that huge area remained Indian Country, with a resident population of approximately thirty tribes long accustomed to regarding the land as their gift from the Great Spirit. It never occurred to them that this expansive region could be owned by any mortal, much less that control over land could shift because mere men an ocean away, who had never hunted or walked upon its ground, had written their names on a piece of parchment.

In truth, it also never occurred to the diplomats in Paris to invite Indian representatives to the negotiations. Throughout the colonial period all the European powers presumed that the entire Western Hemisphere could be carved up among themselves based on decisions made in London, Paris, and Madrid, which in turn were based on previous explorations, subsequently rendered legal by kingly proclamations. For example, the French based their claim to the entire Mississippi Valley on La Salle's sail down the river in the seventeenth century. (They later buried lead plates along the banks registering their claim.) The British based their claim to the Ohio Country and beyond on the Virginia Charter of 1606, which had conveniently left the western border of the colony undefined, leaving lawyers to decide whether the proper boundary was the Mississippi or the Pacific Ocean.

The arrogance of this Eurocentric approach was matched only by its ignorance, since most of the European diplomats would be hard-pressed to distinguish the Appalachians from the Rockies or the Mississippi from the Potomac. But arrogance and ignorance aside, this imperious mode of defining empire enjoyed the incalculable advantage of being the unquestioned way of doing business within all the European capitals and courts. It was what being an empire was all about. Whether they realized it or not, by signing the Treaty of Paris the newly created American republic was announcing its arrival as the youngest member of the imperial family and the successor to France and Great Britain as the sovereign power over all the people south of Canada and north of Florida.

This new imperial status raised for the first time a disquieting question that has haunted American foreign policy ever since. Put simply, how could a republic be an empire? More specifically, how could a government founded on the principles articulated in the Declaration of Independence, which stigmatized the arbitrary and coercive policies of the British Empire, then proceed to behave just as imperiously toward the original occupants of American soil as the British had acted toward them? More tellingly, did not the treatment of the Indian population constitute an obvious acid test of the republican values the American Revolution claimed to stand for?

Initially, from 1783 to 1786, the Confederation Congress and the commissioners they appointed to negotiate treaties with several Indian tribes preferred not to notice the contradiction. Treaties signed with the Six Nations at Fort Stanwix, with the Ohio tribes at Fort McIntosh, and with the Cherokees at Hopewell were blatantly imperialistic affairs in which the American negotiators argued that the Indians were "a conquered people" who should be grateful to be consulted at all: "You are mistaken in supposing that . . . you are become a free and independent nation," explained one American negotiator, "and can make what terms as you please. It is not so. You are a subdued people."[6]

As the Americans saw the situation, after the Treaty of Paris there was no such thing as Indian Country, since all the land from the Atlantic to the Mississippi belonged to the United States by right of conquest. When the chiefs of the Ohio tribes expressed their willingness to negotiate concerning lands south of the Ohio River, the American commissioners corrected them: "We claim the country by conquest; and are to give not to receive." It was a take-it-or-leave-it proposition in which the Indians surrendered a portion of their tribal lands or faced war with the United States and certain annihilation.[7]

From the very start, however, this explicit expression of American power struck some observers as too conspicuously coercive. Not only did the conquest theory make the United States appear to be just another imperial power in the European mode, it almost surely entailed a series of Indian wars on the frontier that would prove expensive in blood and treasure. (And events were to demonstrate that the Ohio tribes were a much more formidable enemy than anyone had initially imagined.) An alternative approach was first proposed by Philip Schuyler, a former general in the Continental Army and prominent New York land baron who had extensive experience dealing with the Six Nations during the war.

Schuyler's proposal, which was immediately endorsed by Washington as the preferred course, envisioned a more gradual and indirect form of American imperialism. Rather than take the eastern third of the continent in one gulp, he recommended a series of smaller bites, a staged expansion driven by the front edge of American settlements. "As our settlements approach their country," Schuyler explained, "they [Indians] must, from the scarcity of game, retire further back, and dispose of their lands, until they dwindle comparatively to nothing, as all savages have done . . . when compelled to live in the vicinity of civilized people." The end would be the same—eventual Indian removal east of the Mississippi—but the means would be less violent and blatant because demography would do the work of armies. In the Schuyler scheme the Americans could afford to be patient and gracious at each stage, knowing full well that every treaty was merely a temporary halt on the inexorable march westward. From a republican point of view the great advantage of this strategy was to replace outright coercion with some semblance of mutual consent. One might call it veiled imperialism, or perhaps imperialism without an imperious edge. It was a more cost-effective and palatable version of genocide that permitted republican principles to coexist, albeit uneasily, alongside Indian extinction.[8]

There were a few dissenting voices. Benjamin Hawkins, an Indian commissioner and future senator from North Carolina, observed that the architects of American Indian policy would have a lot of explaining to do when they reached the pearly gates of heaven and had to account for their treatment of the aborigines. The kind of poignant evidence Hawkins had in mind came from one Cherokee chief who effectively and quite lyrically suggested that the boundary lines agreed to at the Treaty of Hopewell, now being systematically violated by white settlers, were never intended to be permanent, but only the first step in a series of subsequent encroachments consciously designed to exterminate the Cherokee Nation in slow motion:

> At our last treaty . . . we gave up to our white brothers all our land we could any how spare, and have but little left, to raise our women and children upon, and we hope you wont let any people take any more from us without our consent. We are neither Birds nor fish; we can neither fly in the air nor live under water, therefore we hope that pity will be extended to us. We are made by the same hand and in the same shape with yourselves.[9]

Within the Confederation Congress there was little dissent about the proper direction of Indian policy—staged removal—but considerable confusion about who should manage it. Congress enacted an ordinance in August of 1786 giving itself "the sole and exclusive right . . . of regulating the trade and managing the affairs with the Indians, not members of any states." This seemed clear enough, and sanctioned a congressional provision creating northern and southern departments of Indian affairs above and below the Ohio River that reported to the secretary of war, an ominous sign that diplomacy would probably not suffice. But in the same ordinance the Confederation Congress qualified its own claim to jurisdiction by declaring that federal authority only obtained "provided that the legislative right of any state within its own limits be not infringed or violated." This language seemed to sanction the separate treaties that New York, North Carolina, and Georgia were negotiating with Indian tribes within their borders, creating constitutional confusion about who was really in charge.[10]

A different kind of mixed message was sent in the Northwest Ordinance of 1787. On the one hand, the ordinance defined the terms for establishing territories and soon-to-be states in the region stretching from the Ohio River to the Mississippi. The clear implication of this landmark legislation was that any Indian presence in the northwest was presumed to be temporary, this despite treaty obligations with the Ohio tribes that said otherwise. On the other hand, the ordinance also contained a reassuring promise that American policy toward the Indians would always be conducted according to the purest version of republican principles:

> The utmost good faith shall always be observed towards the Indians; their lands and property shall never be taken from them without their consent; and in their property, rights, and liberty, they shall never be invaded or disturbed, unless by just and lawful wars authorized by Congress; but laws founded on justice and humanity shall, from time to time, be made, for preventing wrongs being done to them.

Whether this rhetorical flourish was designed to mislead the Indians, or to soothe the consciences of its American authors, or some subtle combination of the two is impossible to know. Given the relentless reality of the ongoing removal policy, however, it is difficult to avoid the conclusion that such promises of justice constituted a republican cloak over an imperialistic agenda.[11]

THE SUMMER OF 1789

JUST A FEW MONTHS after he assumed office as president, George Washington received a rather remarkable letter from Henry Knox, his recently appointed secretary of war. Federal authority over Indian policy needed to be clarified, Knox argued, in order to rescue it from the jurisdictional confusion that had prevailed under the Articles of Confederation. The best way to achieve the necessary clarity, Knox suggested, was to insist that "the independent tribes of indians ought to be considered as foreign nations, not as the subjects of any particular state." Although the recently ratified Constitution had very little to say about Indians or Indian policy, one phrase (Article 1, Section 8) authorized Congress "to regulate commerce with foreign nations, and among the several states, and with the Indian tribes." This language provided ample grounds for claiming federal sovereignty over the states, and by insisting that all Indian tribes were foreign nations, all treaties with them fell under the authority of the executive branch to make treaties "with the advice and consent of the Senate" (Article 2, Section 2). The ink on the Constitution was barely dry, but Knox was engaging in a pioneering effort—the effort continues apace today—to interpret the meaning of its words. In this instance, the goal was to lodge control over Indian policy squarely in the executive branch of the federal government.[12]

But Knox was just getting started. Once the executive branch achieved jurisdiction, Knox argued that virtually all the premises on which Indian policy had previously been conducted required review. The conquest theory, which presumed that all Indians east of the Mississippi were mere "tenants at will," struck Knox as a gross violation of the republican principles that he and Washington had fought for in the late war. "It would reflect honor on the new government," Knox observed, "were a declarative Law to be passed that the Indian tribes possess the right of the soil of all lands . . . and that they are not to be divested thereof but in consequence of fair and bona fide purchases, made under the authority, or with the express approbation of the United States." There were matters of principle at stake here with long-term implications for both the fate of the Indians and the fate of the republican experiment itself. As the chief symbol and custodian of the revolutionary legacy, Washington needed to recognize that his own place in history would be considerably influenced by his management of this crucial issue at this most propitious moment.[13]

What, for example, might posterity say if "instead of exterminating a part of the human race by our modes of population," which is to say the demographic strategy of Indian removal, "we had preserved through all difficulties and at last had imparted our Knowledge of cultivation, and the arts, to the Aboriginals of the Country?" What, on the other hand, would posterity say if we persist in the current policy, which is in truth to assure that "in a short period the Idea of the Indian on this side of the Mississippi will only be found in the pages of the historian?"[14]

Knox was recommending a wholesale reversal of American Indian policy, in effect arguing that a genuine republic could not function in the manner of European empires. Not only did the conquest theory violate republican principles, but the demographic strategy of removal was only an oblique version of imperialism, a more gradual and palatable version of removal. Knox was challenging the legality and morality of removal itself, the fundamental assumption of American Indian policy no matter how achieved. This was a stunning suggestion, rendered even more radical by the fact that no government official to date had dared even to mention an alternative scenario. Indeed, only a few months earlier the congressional instructions to American commissioners negotiating the Treaty of Fort Harmer with the Ohio tribes had urged them to seize "any opportunity that may offer of extinguishing the Indian rights to the Westward as far as the River Mississippi." Knox was arguing that the prevailing policy of the United States toward Native Americans was nothing less than a direct repudiation of the values embodied in the American Revolution.[15]

How had Knox reached this disquieting conclusion? The immediate answer is that he had spent the late spring and early summer of 1789 reviewing all the treaties negotiated with Indian tribes under the Articles and concluded that the question of federal versus state jurisdiction required resolution. Beyond the jurisdictional issue, however, Knox had spent the preceding three years as de facto secretary of war under the Articles and was therefore at the center of the wind tunnel for all correspondence on Indian affairs. As such, he was in a position to read the most plaintive pleas from various Indian chiefs at the receiving end of American policy and to know that virtually every treaty was violated by state governments and white settlers almost immediately upon signing. Even more distressing, the promises the governments were making to the tribes were never even intended to be kept. They were willful and duplicitous misrepresentations (i.e., lies) designed to establish only temporary borders with Indian Country that would steadily recede until they reached the Mississippi. Knox realized that he was complicitous in a massive and wholly disingenuous deception.[16]

For the deeper sources of Knox's disquietude one has to look further back. He had begun his career as a Boston bookseller who was plucked from obscurity by Washington and, more generally, by the exigencies of the War for Independence. Despite lacking any military experience whatsoever, Knox was appointed head of artillery in the Continental Army in 1776 during the Boston Siege. For the next eight years Knox was constantly at Washington's side and became, next to Nathanael Greene, his most trusted lieutenant. This was the defining chapter in Knox's life, when he lived the struggles and the crises at the primal level and internalized the revolutionary principles at stake, as well as the sense that he and the other members of the officer corps embodied those principles most palpably.[17]

His wartime experience gave Knox impeccable revolutionary credentials and a deeply felt conviction that those credentials provided instant credibility as a custodian of the revolutionary legacy. As a charter member of the "band of brothers," he also felt honor-bound to register his criticism whenever that legacy was defied. As Knox saw it, to abandon that responsibility in order to accommodate the ongoing travesties against Native Americans constituted a betrayal of both the Revolution and his own integrity. Though he did not look the part—as a portly figure whose horses swayed under his weight and who tottered rather than swaggered to his place in American history—Knox was fully prepared to play the role of conscience of the American Revolution. He also possessed the influence, earned in eight long years of wartime camaraderie, to apprise Washington himself that duty called him to the same role.

Speaking of wartime experience, Knox had also earned a reputation as a highly realistic advisor, calculating the probable costs and benefits of engaging the British army in prospective battles throughout the War for Independence. His more pragmatic argument for transforming America's Indian policy followed in this vein, predicting that a policy of outright confiscation would provoke Indian wars up and down the entire western frontier that would cost the United States at least $15 million a year. Given the size of the national debt inherited from the Confederation Congress, this cost was prohibitive. Knox made it clear that moral considerations were paramount, that "injustice would stain the character of the nation beyond all pecuniary considerations," but that this was a case where ideals and interests coincided. Throughout the summer of 1789 Knox lobbied Washington to make reform of American Indian policy a priority of his presidency.[18]

It is difficult to know which of Knox's arguments—the moral, the economic, or the fate of Washington's own reputation—had the greatest impact. It is clear that Knox managed to capture Washington's attention and persuade him to rethink his earlier position on Indian policy, which had presumed the inevitability and desirability of removal. This itself was a major achievement, since Washington was simultaneously preoccupied with appointments to his cabinet, defining the intentionally vague powers of his office as described in the Constitution, delegating fiscal policy to Alexander Hamilton, supervising passage of the Bill of Rights, and in general launching the first large-scale experiment in republican government in all history. For Washington to decide that Indian affairs merited his personal attention amidst this cacophony of political and constitutional pressures was a testimony to Knox's influence and to Washington's recognition that the issue at stake was too important to be delegated to others.

Knox and Washington hammered out the shape of a new Indian policy for the United States in the late summer of 1789. Strictly speaking, once the Indian tribes were defined as foreign nations, Indian policy should have become a branch of foreign policy under the authority of the secretary of state. But Thomas Jefferson, recently appointed to that office, was on the way home from Paris, and domestic affairs—the marriage of his eldest daughter—would delay his arrival in the capital at New York until the following spring. But since Knox had essentially been doing the job for the past three years anyway, had all the relevant information at his fingertips, and in fact was the primary advocate for a basic change in American policy, Jefferson's absence made little difference and might actually have helped the cause, since it would have taken time to bring Jefferson up to speed.

The presumptive inequality inherent in the conquest theory would be replaced by treaties between equals negotiated "on principles consistent with the national justice and dignity of the United States." Coercion, the imperial way of doing business, would be replaced by mutual consent, the republican way. The terms of all treaties would be binding on both parties in perpetuity and both the power and the honor of the federal government would be pledged to their enforcement. The demographic version of Indian removal would be strenuously opposed, if necessary by American troops garrisoned on the borders of Indian Country to block white migration and evict any settlers who managed to elude their surveillance. All treaties would also contain a provision whereby the tribes would be provided with tools and instruction in husbandry so that they could make a gradual transition from hunting and gathering to agricultural economies, which would simultaneously allow Indian culture to evolve from a savage to a more civilized status and reduce the size of the territory necessary for Indian survival.

What Knox and Washington envisioned as the outcome of the new policy was a series of Indian enclaves or homelands east of the Mississippi whose political and geographic integrity would be protected by federal law. The wave of white settlements would be required to bypass these Indian enclaves, leaving several Indian territories east of the Mississippi that would eventually, over the course of the next century, be assimilated as new states. It was a vision in which the westward expansion of an American empire coexisted alongside the preservation of the original Americans.[19]

But would it work? The only way to find out was to try it out, the only question being what tribe or confederation of tribes to select as the ideal test case. Knox, in fact, had already made that decision. In July of 1789 he began sending Washington extensive reports on the Creek Nation, whose hunting grounds extended from western Georgia to northern Florida and across modern Alabama into eastern Mississippi. The Creeks were a southern version of the Iroquois, in the sense that they exercised considerable influence over adjoining tribes, to include the Cherokees to the north and the Chickasaws and Choctaws to the south and west, so that a treaty with the Creeks had broader implications for the entire southern department. What's more, the Creeks were already well on their way to developing an agricultural economy, one reason they and their tribal neighbors were referred to as the "Civilized Tribes." Their economy had become dependent on obtaining supplies (tools, clothing, blankets, weapons) from British agents in Pensacola and Spanish agents in New Orleans. If the United States could displace the British and Spanish as their major trading partner, political allegiance was sure to follow. Finally, there was a dominant chief in the Creek Nation by the name of Alexander McGillivray, who exercised near-dictatorial authority over all Creek tribal councils. Unlike the Ohio tribes, where authority was divided among several warrior-chiefs, the Creeks had an acknowledged leader who could speak for the Creek Nation and enforce the terms of a treaty dependably. All in all, if the experimental American Indian policy required a laboratory, the Creeks seemed to present the optimal opportunity for success.[20]

By late August of 1789 Knox had persuaded Washington to make a diplomatic initiative toward the Creeks with a model treaty based on the new approach. Because this would be the first treaty with a foreign power negotiated since the ratification of the Constitution, it forced Washington to interpret the constitutional requirement to obtain "the advice and consent of the Senate" for the first time. Washington believed that the phrase required him to consult with the Senate in person, so he scheduled a meeting in the Senate for August 22, accompanied by Knox.

The result was part fiasco, part comedy. Because this was a precedent-setting occasion, the Senate spent most of the previous day debating parliamentary etiquette, including where the president should sit and whether or not to applaud his entrance. The following day Washington presented the case for sending a commission to the Creeks with treaty terms designed "to attach them firmly to the United States" and put an end to the sporadic violence on the southern frontier. Washington blamed the bulk of the violence on the Georgians rather than the Creeks, claiming that the borders established by previous treaties "have been entirely violated by the disorderly white people on the frontiers." But regardless of the question of culpability, it was now time to reach a new and just accommodation with the southern tribes, and the proposed treaty with the Creeks would begin that important diplomatic process. If the members of the Senate had any specific questions, Secretary of War Knox would be pleased to answer them.[21]

Then the farce began. Several senators declared that they could not possibly provide their advice and consent until they had seen all the relevant documents. Knox's explanations were surely accurate, but hardly adequate; they needed to see for themselves. Other senators suggested that, given the need to review the documents, perhaps the best way to proceed was to refer the matter to a committee. One senator, William Maclay of Pennsylvania, reported that Washington became visibly irritated and was heard to mutter: "This defeats every purpose of my coming here." Once the senators realized that they had given offense to the president, they became reluctant to speak, producing several awkward silences. Washington eventually got up, motioned toward Knox to follow him, and strode out of the Senate "with a discontented air" and vowing under his breath never to return.[22]

He broke that vow two days later. This time he provided the Senate with three written-out questions beforehand. There was no debate. The Senate, properly embarrassed at the awkwardness of the previous session, endorsed the appointment of a special commission to negotiate a treaty with the Creeks. Washington thanked the Senate, walked out briskly, never returned, and from that moment to the present day "the advice and consent of the Senate" ceased to mean direct presidential consultation.

The instructions to the commissioners, drafted by Knox, urged them "by a just and liberal system of policy to conciliate and attach them [i.e., the Creeks] to the Interests of the union." If any of the previous treaties were found to be faulty, the commissioners were instructed to renegotiate them and pay compensation for past misunderstandings. They should promise to place the Creek Nation "under the protection of the United States of America," to include a line of military posts to guarantee the new borders against white encroachments. Finally, the commissioners should establish a bond of trust with Alexander McGillivray, who "was reputed to possess great abilities and unlimited influence over the Creek nation and part of the Cherokees." Winning over McGillivray was the highest priority, and, in order to "attach him warmly to the United States," they were permitted to offer him military rank in the American army with its attendant salary in return for an oath of loyalty. This thinly veiled bribe should do the trick, they thought. They had no way of knowing that they were dealing with the Talleyrand of the southern frontier.[23]

THE McGILLIVRAY FACTOR

THE COMMISSION SENT to offer McGillivray the opportunity to launch a new chapter in Indian-American relations on the Knox model was headed by Benjamin Lincoln, one of Washington's favorite generals during the Revolutionary War. Lincoln was accompanied by David Humphreys, a former aide-de-camp to Washington with a degree from Yale, the ambition to become a major American poet, diplomatic experience in Europe, and bottomless confidence in his own significance. Knox had stacked the commission with men of stature whom he and Washington knew personally. The negotiations designed to establish a fundamentally new direction in American Indian policy were scheduled for late September at a frontier outpost named Rock Landing, which was located in what is now central Georgia on disputed land between the Ogeechee and Oconee rivers. McGillivray, leaving nothing to chance, arrived accompanied by an entourage of nine hundred Creek warriors and chiefs.

All descriptions of McGillivray that have survived agree on two points: he was very light-skinned, and he was physically unimpressive.

The light skin was a function of his mixed ancestry. His father was a well-to-do Scotsman who had sided with the British in the late war, had his estate confiscated along with other loyalists, then had sailed home to Scotland, never to return. His mother was half French and half Creek, making McGillivray only one-quarter Indian. But because Creek society was matrilineal and his mother was descended from a prominent Creek family, McGillivray was regarded by all the Creeks as a full-blooded member of the Creek Nation.[24]

On the physical front, he was a walking bundle of ailments. He suffered from migraine headaches and acute rheumatism that often incapacitated him for weeks at a time. He also labored under several self-inflicted diseases, including chronic alcoholism and syphilis sufficiently severe that his fingernails kept falling out. Unlike most Indian chiefs, McGillivray's stature did not depend on his conspicuous bravery in battle. He himself acknowledged that he was not much of a warrior and that in his first engagement he had hidden behind a bush during the fighting, then crawled out at night to take the scalp of a dead American soldier.

His prowess as a Creek leader derived from his intellectual rather than his physical strengths. His father had sent him to Charleston to receive a classical education in Latin and Greek. McGillivray was fluent in English, Spanish, and Creek and well read in British and European history. When most Indian chiefs were confronted with the conquest explanation for their loss of standing after the Treaty of Paris, they could respond only with a mixture of confusion and disbelief. McGillivray denounced the conquest theory as a violation of international law:

> We do in the most solemn manner protest against any title claim or demand the American Congress may set up for our lands, Settlements, and hunting Grounds in Consequence of the Said treaty of peace between the King of Great Brittain and the States of America, declaring that we were not partys, it being a Notorious fact known to the Americans, known to every person who is in any ways conversant in, or acquainted with American affairs, that his Brittanick Majesty was never possessed either by session purchase or by right of Conquest of our Territorys and which the Said treaty gives away.

In short, no one, neither the British nor the Americans, had ever conquered the Creeks, so the entire conquest argument was really a transparent rationale for outright thievery.[25]

McGillivray's control over the Upper Creek and Lower Creek tribes, as well as his influence over their Cherokee, Chickasaw, and Choctaw neighbors, was rooted in his literacy in English and Spanish and his impressive negotiating skills with British and Spanish traders, who provided tools, clothing, weaponry, and amenities to all the southern tribes. All licenses to trade with the various tribes required his authorization, for which he collected a fee. He was also part owner of the major trading post in Pensacola, which earned him a handsome annual profit and allowed him to amass the wealth of an Indian-styled southern aristocrat. He owned a log mansion, fifty to sixty slaves, and several hundred horses and cattle in Little Tallassee, near present-day Montgomery, Alabama. He also owned a smaller plantation with another wife and family in Mobile.

He defied all the stereotypes: part Indian, part white; part defender of Creek rights, part southern slave-owner; part statesman, part corrupt power broker. He was an early American version of those modern-day Third World dictators during the Cold War who skillfully played off the major powers against one another to preserve both their own prominence and the independence of their own people while enriching themselves in the process. An unalloyed realist, McGillivray regarded that building wave of white settlers on his eastern borders as the greatest threat. For that reason, and also because of Georgia's confiscation of his father's estate, amidst all his multiple identities, he was resolutely anti-American.

As a result, McGillivray was extremely reluctant to attend the conference at Rock Landing. As he saw it, the balance of power in the region belonged to the Creek Nation and its allies. He could deploy over five thousand warriors at a moment's notice, a force more than sufficient to defeat any attack by Georgia's militia. And the puny American army was tied down in ongoing battles with the Ohio tribes. As long as Spanish supplies flowed freely to his warriors, Creek Country was impregnable. What's more, he did not trust the word of the Americans. His contacts with the Six Nations and the Ohio tribes made him fully aware that all treaties with the Americans establishing secure borders had almost immediately been violated. And his own experience with the state governments of South Carolina and Georgia only reinforced his skepticism: "We have received friendly talks and replies, it is true," he observed, "but while they are addressing us by the flattering appellations of Friends and Brothers, they are stripping us of our natural rights by depriving us of that inheritance which belonged to our ancestors and hath descended from them to us Since the beginning of time."[26]

He was persuaded to attend the conference with the Americans, ironically, by Esteban Miró, the Spanish governor in New Orleans. Miró obviously did not want McGillivray to sign a treaty with the Americans, but he feared that an unwillingness to negotiate would lead to a full-scale war on the southern frontier. McGillivray believed that the Creeks could win such a war, but Miró was less confident and feared that an American victory would lead to Spain's loss of all of Florida, which at the time included the entire Gulf Coast. McGillivray could not afford to alienate his Spanish allies, so he agreed to show up at Rock Landing. The diplomatic chemistry was therefore poisoned from the start. The American commissioners believed that they were launching a new era in Indian affairs destined to establish a precedent for Indian-white coexistence east of the Mississippi. McGillivray believed that he was jumping through the proverbial hoops, appeasing the American negotiators, pretending to be pliable, drawing out the inevitable confrontation.

Humphreys, who did the bulk of the negotiating on the American side, had a somewhat mixed first impression of McGillivray: "His countenance has nothing liberal and open in it—it has however sufficient marks of understanding. In short, he appears to have the good sense of an American, the shrewdness of a Scotchman & the cunning of an Indian. . . . His influence is probably as great as we have understood it was." Meanwhile, McGillivray's first impression of Humphreys was totally negative. He described Humphreys as "that puppy" and "a great boaster of his political knowledge," a mere babe in the woods whose presumptive tone and condescending style were almost too much to bear.[27]

The treaty terms Humphreys proposed were also a problem. From Humphreys's perspective, he was offering the Creeks the most generous terms ever made to any Indian tribe, a guarantee of almost all their tribal land and a promise of protection by the federal government against white encroachments. From McGillivray's perspective, the proposed treaty required the Creeks to surrender their claim to the land between the Ogeechee and Oconee rivers, where several hundred white families were already settled. When Humphreys pointed out that the disputed land had already been surrendered to Georgia in a previous treaty, McGillivray argued that he never had agreed and never would agree to give up any Creek land, that the Georgians had found some "Indian vagabond" who lacked any authority to sign that treaty, which was clearly illegal. As for the American promise of protection, the Creek Nation did not require protection. It could perfectly well take care of itself and had no desire to become an American colony. And why should he trust American promises, given the undeniable record of broken promises with the Six Nations and the Ohio tribes?

Humphreys's version of what happened next emphasized McGillivray's obstinacy, fueled by huge consumptions of whiskey. "He got very much intoxicated," Humphreys reported, though he also observed that McGillivray "seemed to retain his recollection and reason beyond what I had ever seen in a person, when in the same condition." McGillivray's version took pride in his intransigence: "The arts of flattery, ambition and intimidation were exhausted in vain. I at least told him that by G-d I would not have such a Treaty cram'd down my throat . . . so I remained obstinate in my purpose and came on." By "came on" McGillivray meant that he gathered together his nine hundred warriors and rode out of Rock Landing.[28]

In his report to Washington, Humphreys observed that McGillivray, who was supposed to be the singular solution, was in fact the primary problem: "I believe that no room for doubt was left in the mind of everyone present," Humphreys asserted, "that, if a Peace shall not be concluded, the fault will rest with McGillivray alone. . . . It is a melancholy consideration to reflect that a Whole Nation must sometimes perish for the sins of one man." Humphreys speculated, correctly it turned out, that McGillivray had never intended to negotiate in good faith, that his whole purpose was to extract concessions that he would then use to obtain better terms from his Spanish friends.[29]

McGillivray left Rock Landing with spirits soaring. He had upheld the honor of the Creek people against the implicit coercion of the American government, which had the audacity to send a mere child-man to intimidate the chief of the Creek Nation. What stories he could now tell around the council campfires of American desperation and weakness. On the ride home he encountered a group of Georgia settlers who requested his permission to carve out a colony of their own within Creek Country under his protection. McGillivray observed:

Although I am not a sorcerer, I could manage them as I pleased. They are extremely ignorant and unpolished; each sentence that came from my mouth, they took as pure gospel. They got it into their heads that I was going to establish a new state, and 1500 families were ready to present me with petitions to become my subjects. I amused myself and juggled with them until we parted.

If they did attempt to settle on Creek land, he would order his warriors to drive them away and, if they refused, to kill every one of them.[30]

Knox apprised Washington that their best effort to forge a new Indian policy had failed miserably: "We have the Mortification to inform you that the Parties have separated without a Treaty. The terms which were offered . . . were not agreeable to Mr. McGillivray." Washington had just returned from a monthlong tour of New England and faced a backlog of pressing decisions, to include appointments to the newly created federal judiciary, preliminary discussions with Alexander Hamilton about the size of the national debt and the proper outlines for American fiscal policy, plus a steady barrage of letters from job applicants, many former veterans courting favor. But he pushed aside all these important chores to immerse himself completely in the correspondence and documents relating to the Creek problem. The entire future of American Indian policy was at stake. The northern frontier was on the verge of open warfare with the Ohio tribes. Now the southern frontier threatened to explode as well. This was an issue that required his individual attention.[31]

What had begun as an initiative by Knox driven by a clear moral imperative—the preservation of Indian culture east of the Mississippi—was now transformed into a strategic dilemma driven by economic considerations. How many warriors could McGillivray deploy, how many federal troops would be required to defeat him, and what would the campaign cost? What was the likelihood of an alliance of all the southern tribes under McGillivray? And then, the nightmare scenario, what was the possibility of a pan-Indian alliance of all the northern and southern tribes with McGillivray playing the leadership role that Pontiac, the great pan-Indian chief of the 1760s, had played earlier?[32]

The answers that Knox provided were not encouraging. An all-out war against the southern tribes would cost at least $15 million, based on the estimate that McGillivray could call upon five thousand warriors, more if the Cherokees, Choctaws, and Chickasaws joined the campaign. Presuming that the Ohio tribes mounted an organized resistance that required a military response, the United States would be forced to fight a two-front war, the cost of which in men and money would defy the imagination.[33]

Throughout the War for Independence Washington and Knox had engaged in countless conversations of this sort, gauging the prospects of military action against the British army in multiple contexts, always balancing the strategic stakes against the limited resources of the Continental Army. On the basis of this truly searing experience, both men had learned to think together in a thoroughly realistic fashion. Indeed, one could argue that they had eventually won the war by prudently deciding when to decline risky battles.

When they brought the same cost-effective calculus to the combustible situation on the southern frontier, the conclusion was crystal clear. As McGillivray himself had apparently known from the start, a military campaign against the Creeks was politically and economically impossible to justify. Only a diplomatic solution made sense. And that meant that McGillivray must be appeased, not because doing so was morally right, but because it was now strategically necessary.

Meanwhile, down in Creek Country, McGillivray was relishing his humiliation of "that puppy Humphries" and apprising his Spanish contacts in St. Augustine and New Orleans that he was fully prepared, with their support, to repel any American invasion. Not only could he count on the assistance from the neighboring southern tribes, he had been cultivating diplomatic relations with the northern tribes for over two years. In that sense, Washington's concerns about a pan-Indian confederation were not far-fetched. Ironically, at the same time that state delegations were meeting at Philadelphia in the summer of 1787 to form "a more perfect union," all the Indian tribes south of the Great Lakes, to include the Iroquois, Hurons, Mohawks, Wyandots, Oneidas, and Shawnees, had convened with the Creeks and Cherokees to create an Indian alliance, their Native American version of the Constitutional Convention.

The negotiating position of the Americans had always been a diplomatic version of the proverbial iron fist in the velvet glove. In effect, either accept our terms or suffer the consequences. McGillivray was immune to such veiled threats because he believed, with considerable evidence to support his stance, that he enjoyed a more potent iron fist than the Americans. The American presumption of invincibility, in short, was both a bluff and a fiction. The Americans needed him more than he needed them.[34]

Then a new ingredient entered the strategic chemistry, an ingredient equally worrisome to McGillivray and the Washington-Knox tandem. In January of 1790 the Georgia legislature announced the sale of twenty-four million acres of land to three private companies, collectively called the Yazoo Companies, which claimed control over a vast region now comprising the states of Tennessee, Alabama, and Mississippi—in other words, all of Creek Country. The legal rationale for this sale was the original Georgia charter, which placed the western border of the then colony at the Mississippi River. This inflated claim made perfect sense to most members of the Georgia legislature, who owned shares in this speculative bonanza, making it a thoroughly corrupt and breathtakingly brazen scheme from the start.[35]

From the perspective of Knox and Washington, this Yazoo initiative was a blatant assertion of state sovereignty that defied both the principle of federal control over Indian affairs and the prevailing presumption that Indian policy was a branch of American foreign policy. If allowed to stand, it made any treaty with the Creek Nation inherently worthless. From McGillivray's perspective, the Yazoo Companies threatened to release a gigantic new wave of white settlers into Creek Country, a demographic occupation more formidable than a conventional military invasion. He was confident he could defeat an American army, but endless waves of settlers posed the threat of an endless war on the southern frontier that even McGillivray could not be sure to win.

Because McGillivray had a well-earned reputation for unscrupulous behavior and had also demonstrated that he did not mind cutting deals that lined his own pockets on occasion, a delegation of Georgia stockholders in Yazoo attempted to bribe him by offering him shares in the lucrative venture in return for his cooperation. But McGillivray was unscrupulous only when it served the greater interest of the Creek Nation. He rejected the bribe and interpreted the offer as further evidence of his critical role as the dominant power broker on the southern frontier. He took even greater satisfaction in his obvious importance when he learned that, having failed to bribe him, several anonymous Georgia legislators had put out a contract to have him assassinated.[36]

This new Yazoo ingredient altered the political chemistry. Prior to Yazoo, McGillivray would have almost surely rejected any offer from Knox and Washington to renew negotiations, convinced as he was that the Creeks and their Indian allies, handsomely supplied by Spain, controlled the balance of power in the region. Now, however, the resumption of negotiations would allow McGillivray to sign a treaty with the federal government that reaffirmed federal control over Indian policy and thereby undercut Georgia's preposterous claims of sovereignty. On this crucial point, his agenda and the Knox-Washington agenda were perfectly aligned.

Beyond that common point, however, McGillivray harbored no illusions. "All the eagerness which Washington shows to treat with me on such liberal terms," McGillivray observed, "is not based, I am persuaded, on principles of Justice and humanity." The Americans were already stretched too thin because of the ongoing war on the northern frontier and lacked sufficient manpower and money to mount a viable military campaign in the south. Their menacing threats on that score were only a bluff that he was fully prepared to call. But if he could negotiate a treaty that aligned the federal government with the Creek Nation against the Georgians, the Yazoo threat was then likely to disappear.[37]

The new offer was hand-delivered by a former officer in the Continental Army named Marinus Willet. Knox and Washington had decided to pull out all the stops. All matters, including the disputed land between the Ogeechee and Oconee rivers, were on the table for negotiation. More significantly, McGillivray would not be required to deal with inferior underlings like Humphreys. This time the two great leaders, Washington and McGillivray, would meet at the summit. McGillivray and a delegation of lesser Creek chiefs were invited to the American capital at New York for an extended visit that would permit promises to be made face-to-face in the best tradition of the Indian council fires.[38]

McGillivray found Willet more candid than Humphreys, a man of parts who might have made an excellent Creek warrior. Though McGillivray was immune to all forms of flattery and did not enjoy the prospects of a long and tiring trip, especially given his somewhat questionable physical stamina, this was an offer he could not refuse. "A treaty concluded at New York, ratified with the signature of Washington and McGillivray," he noted with obvious pride in the co-equal status, "would be the bond of Long Peace and revered by Americans to a distant period." Preparations for the seven-hundred-mile excursion began in May of 1790.[39]

THE SUMMIT

IT WAS QUITE A SCENE. McGillivray rode in a coach with his American escort, Marinus Willet, followed by twenty-seven Creek chiefs on horseback, all fully feathered and resplendent in Indian dress as they traveled toward the white man's capital. Along the roads in Georgia and the Carolinas, witnesses were stunned, claiming they had never seen so many warriors whose intentions were entirely peaceful. In Virginia there were mandatory stops in Richmond and Fredericksburg, where local dignitaries hosted lavish dinners, complete with multiple toasts to "the Creek Washington." Philadelphia was an even greater extravaganza of celebration. By the time the procession reached the outskirts of New York, so many peace pipes had been smoked and so many glasses had been lifted that the diplomatic negotiations themselves seemed a ceremonial afterthought. The cheering crowds signaled the start of a new era of peace on the southern frontier.

As they were ferried across from New Jersey to Manhattan, McGillivray and his entourage were welcomed like European royalty. One New York newspaper claimed that they had seen nothing like it since Washington's inauguration. Ships in the harbor fired salutary salvos. Officers from the St. Tammany Society greeted them at the wharf, clad in Indian bonnets as a statement of their fraternal fellowship. Then there was a parade past Federal Hall, where all the members of Congress came out to cheer while the Creek chiefs broke out in song that interpreters described as a tribute to brotherhood. The festive procession then moved to Knox's house, where Knox invited McGillivray to reside during his stay in New York and McGillivray announced that he would deposit his nephew to the care of the Knox family for his education and upbringing, which symbolized the union of the two families. Then it was on to the presidential mansion, where Washington offered his official welcome. The extravaganza ended at City Tavern with a sumptuous dinner and more toasts, all punctuated by Creek songs and shouts that gave the occasion an exotic flavor by blending Indian and white versions of etiquette. It was what we might call a major multicultural event.[40]

Coverage in the New York press concurred that no European diplomats had been welcomed so royally. As Knox and Washington saw it, this made perfect sense, since winning over McGillivray was more strategically crucial than solidifying a diplomatic relationship with any European power. While avoiding a costly war on the southern frontier was obviously the primary priority, the prospect of initiating a wholly new direction in American policy toward the Indians made the occasion even more significant. A treaty with the Creeks that recognized their legitimate claim to a large slice of land east of the Mississippi guaranteed by the federal government would serve as a model for all subsequent negotiations with the eastern tribes. Appearances were also important because McGillivray, surely influenced by his extensive correspondence with British and Spanish allies, regarded the American republic as a highly problematic experiment destined to dissolve like all republics before it. While the core of his confidence in the supremacy of Creek power was military—his warriors would outnumber and outfight any American army sent against them—there was also a political dimension to his confidence. Namely, he believed that the American republic was a fragile and ephemeral union likely to be short-lived. From McGillivray's perspective, the centuries-old Creek Nation was sure to outlast this American upstart. Knox and Washington had planned the conspicuous display of political and military prowess in the national capital to show McGillivray that this republican experiment, unlike its European predecessors, was here to stay.[41]

The Creek delegation remained in New York for nearly a month. Most days were devoted to diplomatic negotiations, while the evenings were occupied by ceremonial celebrations, though the nightly convivialities helped to establish a spirit of mutual trust that lubricated the daily sessions. There is some telltale evidence that McGillivray's evening lubrications left him with frequent hangovers the next day, but it is also possible that his periodic incapacitation was a result of his chronic ill health.

One of the highlights on the ceremonial side was the viewing of a new portrait of Washington by John Trumbull, one of America's most prominent artists, who had also expressed a desire to paint a group portrait of the Creek chiefs, whose intrinsic nobility he compared to classical depictions of Roman senators. At the viewing of the Washington portrait, however, the Creeks shrieked with amazement and disbelief, because they had never before seen a picture that conveyed dimension on a flat surface. They accused Trumbull of practicing "magic" and refused to sit for him lest they fall victim to his spell.[42]

No record of the daily negotiations has survived, for the simple reason that no record was ever made. We do know that Knox assumed primary responsibility for the negotiations with McGillivray and that he was joined by Thomas Jefferson, the recently arrived secretary of state, who brought his long-standing interest in Native American history and languages to the task. In his later career as president, Jefferson would oversee the process of gradual Indian removal that culminated in the Indian Removal Act (1830) under Andrew Jackson. But at this earlier stage of his career Jefferson aligned himself squarely behind the Knox-Washington initiative to preserve Indian enclaves east of the Mississippi.[43]

One of his first acts as secretary of state was to draft a memorandum arguing that all the claims of the Yazoo Companies were illegal because Georgia had ceded all its western lands to the federal government upon joining the union. At Knox's request, he also drafted another legal opinion, arguing that the Creeks, like all Indian tribes, should be regarded as foreign nations. This in turn meant that all treaty provisions signed by the president and ratified by two-thirds of the Senate, to include all trade provisions, immediately became the law of the land and therefore invulnerable to legal challenge by any state or private company. Though he subsequently reversed himself on the latter score, regretting his endorsement of such unrestrained executive authority, at this moment Jefferson believed his highest duty as secretary of state was to support the policy of his president, and he marshaled the evidence to support the new-model treaty with the Creek Nation like a dedicated lawyer serving his client.[44]

At a deeper and less legislative level, moreover, Jefferson brought the most fully articulated sense of the underlying moral issue at stake at this defining moment in the shaping of American policy toward the Native Americans. He had written the most compelling defense of Indian culture by any American of his time. In his *Notes on the State of Virginia* Jefferson had devoted an entire section to "Aborigines," which attempted to recover the influence of Virginia's Indian tribes in shaping the history of the Old Dominion. More to the point, he had mounted a full-scale defense of Indian intelligence, courage, and integrity against the derogatory claims to the contrary by the eminent French scientist Count Buffon, who had argued that the American Indians were a biologically and mentally inferior collection of savages unworthy of comparison with white Europeans.[45]

Jefferson politely but firmly argued that Buffon, Europe's most renowned natural scientist, did not know what he was talking about. On the basis of personal observation and considerable study, Jefferson refuted each of Buffon's charges, offering dramatic evidence of Indian eloquence, physical bravery, and deeply ingrained sense of honor. All of which led to the conclusion that the Native Americans "are formed, in mind as well as in body, on the same model as Homo sapiens Europaeus." Whatever differences existed between Indians and whites were a function of the primitive conditions within which Indian culture currently found itself. (And Jefferson thought that, at least in some respects, Indian culture was actually superior; witness the numbers of white captives who preferred to live out their lives as Indians.) In the short term this meant that no enlightened American or European could in good conscience dismiss Native Americans as savages in order to justify their dispersion and removal. And in the long term it meant that the eventual assimilation of the Indian and Anglo-Saxon peoples of North America would benefit both races, a conclusion that Jefferson was unable to embrace with regard to the African Americans.[46]

Though it is likely that both Knox and Washington shared Jefferson's basic convictions about the integrity of Indian culture, neither of them had ever expressed themselves so fully or so publicly on the issue. So Jefferson's addition to the diplomatic mix gave the unrecorded conversations of late July and early August 1790 a clearer moral foundation than they would otherwise have had. For different reasons, all three men had reached the same conclusion. Namely, the current negotiations with McGillivray and the Creeks offered the opportunity to place American Indian policy on a path that avoided the unjust and tragic fate toward which it was currently headed. And posterity would ultimately judge them on how they conducted themselves at this decisive moment.

McGillivray cared not a wit about posterity's judgment. His sole goal was to protect the Creek Nation from the demographic avalanche building to the east. His most pressing priority, then, was to block the claims of the Yazoo Companies by enlisting federal support against the expansive pretensions of Georgia. He apparently extracted a personal promise from Knox that the United States government would do just that, for he later claimed that his major achievement during the negotiations was "to have signed the death sentence of the Company of the Yazoo."[47]

The core proposal in the American negotiating position was a federal guarantee, which in the end meant the deployment of troops, to maintain secure borders for the newly defined Creek Nation. But nothing in McGillivray's mentality permitted the fate of the Creeks to depend on trust in the word of any person or government. He saw himself engaged in a four-sided diplomatic game, simultaneously playing the United States government against the state of Georgia and the Americans against the Spanish. Any commitment he made to the Americans was temporary and conditional. It would expire if and when the American republic collapsed, which he thought to be imminent despite the conspicuous display of political permanence designed to impress him. Or it would be disowned whenever the Spanish made him a better offer. Or whichever came first. What became known as the Treaty of New York passed the Senate on August 7, 1790, by a vote of 15–4. Both Georgia senators voted in the negative, and one Georgia congressman, James Jackson, complained that the treaty gave away three million acres of Georgia's land to "a savage of the Creek nation," presumably McGillivray, who had "been caressed in a most extraordinary manner, and sent home loaded with favors."[48]

The preamble to the treaty declared that it was designed to produce "peace and prosperity to our southern frontier" and to attach "the Creeks and the neighboring Tribes to the interests of the United States." In effect, the United States would displace Spain as the major ally and trading partner of the Creek Nation, which was now "under the protection of the United States of America and no other sovereign whatsoever." The eastern border of Creek Country was set at the Oconee River, about thirty miles west of McGillivray's preference on the Ogeechee, because so many white families had already settled in the disputed territory that removing them would be extremely difficult. The western border was left purposely ambiguous, allowing McGillivray to claim it was the Mississippi and the Americans to claim it did not quite stretch that far. A reasonable estimate of the new Indian protectorate would include modern-day western Georgia, eastern Tennessee, northern Florida, all of Alabama, and eastern Mississippi. By any standard, it was a huge domain.[49]

Another provision implied, albeit discreetly, that the Creek homeland was supposed to shrink over time. "That the Creek Nation may be led to a greater degree of civilization," the treaty read, "and to become herdsmen and cultivators, instead of remaining in a state of hunters, the United States will from time to time furnish gratuitously the said nation with useful domestic animals and implements of husbandry." These apparently innocent words carried a hidden meaning that McGillivray surely recognized. The Creeks, who already practiced some farming, were being urged to make a complete transition to an agricultural economy, which would require much less land than a hunting and gathering economy. Left unsaid was that subsequent treaties would reduce the huge size of the current Creek Country. By how much was also left unspecified.[50]

Just as huge as the geographic area being defined, at least for the present, as Creek Country was the promise being made by the American government: "The United States solemnly guarantee to the Creek Nation, all their lands within the limits of the United States to the westward and southward of the boundary described in the preceding article." No matter how ambiguous the current borders of the Creek Nation, and no matter how much they were likely to shrink in the future, the word of the national government was pledged to protect Creek Country from all encroachments by state governments and white settlers. This was a colossal commitment, which Knox regarded as morally essential for his entire enclave strategy and economically preferable to a drawn-out series of Indian wars on the frontier.[51]

There were two secret articles not included in the treaty but shared with the members of the Senate before their vote. First, the United States agreed to establish a trading partnership with their new Creek allies, starting at $60,000 worth of goods a year. McGillivray insisted on a two-year delay in the implementation of this policy, putatively to work out the details of its operation, probably to use the time to see if he could get a better offer from the Spanish. Second, McGillivray was made a brigadier general in the American army at an annual salary of $1,200. Lesser Creek chiefs would receive lesser amounts. This obvious bribe was intended to replace the annual stipend McGillivray already received from the Spanish. Though such arrangements were too crassly exploitive to be mentioned in the treaty itself, McGillivray had made it known that he regarded them as common practice in all such negotiations and would be personally offended if the Americans failed to reward him for his service.[52]

The signing ceremony occurred August 13 at Federal Hall with the entire Congress in attendance. As befitted his new rank, McGillivray wore a military uniform of blue faced with red. The other Creek chiefs wore their most resplendent native costumes, entering the room shouting and shrieking words that one newspaper reporter described as eerily like war yells. The treaty was read aloud and an interpreter provided a simultaneous translation for the Creeks. Washington then delivered a solemn address, pronouncing the Treaty of New York a mutually beneficial agreement between two great peoples. McGillivray responded in kind and thanked the people of New York for their gracious hospitality and Washington for his gift of beads and tobacco. All the chiefs then shook hands with Washington Indian-style, locking arms while grasping elbows. The Creeks then formed themselves into a chorus and sang a final song. The interpreter explained that it was about perpetual peace.[53]

EPILOGUES AND AFTERTHOUGHTS

ECHOES OF THE CREEK chorus had hardly died before the prospects for peace of any duration met the same fate. The unmanageable problem was demographic. Settlers on the Georgia frontier kept pouring across the newly established Creek borders by the thousands, blissfully oblivious to any geographic line drawn on the maps by some faraway government, cheered forward every step by the Georgia legislature, which saw them as foot soldiers in the Yazoo campaign for control of the southern frontier. Knox sent a detachment of federal troops to police the borders, but it was like stopping a flood with a bucket of sponges. Washington recognized the strategic dilemma right away. "Unless we can restrain the turbulence and disorderly conduct of our own borders," he observed, "it will be in vain to expect peace with the Indians—or that they will govern their own people better than we do ours." In his opinion, the white settlers and their promoters were the chief culprits, and it infuriated him that "a lawless set of unprincipled wretches . . . can infringe the most solemn treaties, without receiving the punishment they so richly deserve." Washington eventually concluded that "scarcely anything short of a Chinese wall will restrain the Land jobbers and the encroachment of settlers upon the Indian Country." He took the failure personally, believing that his signature on the Treaty of New York was his pledge of honor as well as the solemn word of the United States government. Both were now being exposed as worthless.[54]

McGillivray did not think in terms of promises and honor so much as interests and power. Once the enormous scale of the American invasion became abundantly clear in 1791, he decided it was time to switch sides again, this time from the Americans to the Spanish. When the Spanish expressed their skepticism about his reliability, given the recent betrayal of his Spanish alliance for the Americans, McGillivray denied that there had ever been a betrayal, arguing that the Treaty of New York had never aligned the Creeks with the Americans. This was a barefaced lie, and the Spanish recognized it as such, but they had no viable alternative to McGillivray as the only leader who could mobilize Indian resistance to the Americans. So they welcomed him back, embraced the fiction that he had never left, and even increased his annual stipend to $2,000 in order to best the American bribe.[55]

McGillivray made the conversion complete by traveling to New Orleans in July of 1792 to negotiate a new treaty with Spain. There was nothing like the ceremonial splendor of the New York negotiations— no grand parades, no lavish dinners, no ingratiating toasts, no Creek chorus—only a private meeting between McGillivray and the new Spanish governor, at which McGillivray vowed "that it was never my intention to be on good terms with the Americans." He then, somewhat in contradiction, expressed his deep regret at accepting "the least dependence on a people I know to be the National & determined enemy of all the Indian Nations & whom it is incumbent upon as to resist." The Treaty of New Orleans reaffirmed the Creek alliance with Spain and their mutual commitment to expel all the American intruders from Creek Country. McGillivray also held out the hope that the Spanish-Creek coalition would be joined by Indian tribes from the Ohio Country, the forever alluring vision of a pan-Indian alliance: "I have reason to suspect," he told the Spanish governor, "a deputation from the Northern tribes of Indians in here in the ensuing Spring for the purpose of animating the Southern tribes to exert themselves in the Common Cause."[56]

In effect, less than two years after the passage of the Treaty of New York all the hopes and peaceful prospects it embodied had evaporated. The relentless and apparently inexhaustible reservoir of white settlers continued to roll westward, making a mockery of all plans for an enduring Creek homeland. McGillivray had gone back to the Spanish, who supplied the weapons for the resumption of vicious fighting across the entire southern frontier. Whatever opportunity had ever existed for a new direction in Indian policy that preserved a tribal presence east of the Mississippi was lost forever.

The rest, as they say, is history. The pan-Indian alliance never materialized and the Spanish-Creek alliance proved just as incapable of blocking the white demographic surge as the American government had been. McGillivray did not live to witness the end of the story. He died on February 17, 1793, of complications from his multiple ailments. Witnesses said that he appeared to be fifty years of age, though he was only thirty-four. An obituary in *Gentlemen's Magazine* in London predicted, correctly it turned out, that the Creek Nation would not see his like again.[57]

Over the course of the next fifty years Creek Country became Slave Country, the cradle of the deep south, and the most racially conscious region in the nation. But the division was white versus black, not white versus red, for the Creeks had virtually disappeared as a people and a nation. During the final stages of Indian removal they did not present a major problem, like the more resilient Cherokees, because they had almost ceased to exist.[58]

Given the enormous issues at stake for the future of American society, and given the truly tragic conclusion, there is an almost irresistible urge to wonder if the story could have turned out differently. But if the tale told here is essentially correct, the answer must be a dispiriting but firm no.

What stands out is the exceptional quality of leadership on both sides at this defining moment. Knox and Washington, with an assist from Jefferson, chose to defy the odds and transform American policy toward the Native Americans. They did not do so because it was politically expedient, quite the opposite. They did so because the revolutionary fires still burned inside them and they knew, deep down, that Indian removal was incompatible with the republican values they cherished. They inherited an Indian policy headed inexorably toward the extermination of Indian Country east of the Mississippi and they attempted to turn it around. Their respective revolutionary credentials allowed them to argue, with complete confidence, that principle needed to take precedence over popular opinion. For, make no mistake, a referendum among the white citizenry would have produced an overwhelming majority for Indian removal. They made a heroic effort and they failed, though it is difficult to imagine what they might have done differently to change the outcome.

On the Indian side, it is also difficult to imagine a more capable and shrewd leader than McGillivray. He played the cards that were dealt him as deftly as possible. Though unscrupulous in the realpolitik sense of the term, he was incorruptible whenever the fate of the Creek Nation was at stake, and his combination of pure intelligence, diplomatic agility, and sheer audacity made him the most effective Indian leader of his time. Looking back with all the advantages of hindsight, McGillivray remains the most impressive Indian leader we might have handpicked to avert the tragedy. Yet he too failed.

Why such failure amidst such leadership? Part of the answer was sheer numbers. The white American population was doubling every twenty to twenty-five years at the same time the Indian population was declining at roughly the same rate. By the last decade of the eighteenth century an ongoing demographic explosion was radiating out from the eastern rim of North America, and the Indian population opposing it was simply outnumbered and overwhelmed. No political effort to contain or control this explosion stood much chance of success.

Whatever chance did exist depended upon the capacity of the recently launched federal government to impose its will on the state of Georgia and the white population stretched across the southern frontier. In order to honor its promise of protection to the Creeks, the United States government needed to assume control over the eastern border of Creek Country, a roughly five-hundred-mile arc stretching from what is now eastern Tennessee to the Florida panhandle. That in turn would have required a string of forts permanently garrisoned by at least ten thousand federal troops, this at a time when the entire American army was slightly more than one-tenth that size. At virtually every level— logistical, economic, political—there was not the most remote chance of implementing such a plan.[59]

Ironically, the problem that Washington faced was almost identical to the problem the British had faced after the Proclamation of 1763, when George III declared the land west of the Alleghenies a vast Indian reservation off-limits to American colonists. And, double irony, on that occasion Washington had angrily protested the British policy and taken considerable satisfaction in observing that it was inherently unenforceable. In 1790 he found himself cast in the role of George III, with results equally ineffectual.

Given this obvious historical precedent, why did Washington and Knox think they could succeed where the British, with considerably greater power at their disposal, had failed? Why did they not recognize from the start that they lacked the resources to enforce their treaty obligations? How could they not realize that they were making promises they could not keep?

Part of the answer is that both Knox and Washington, and in a different way Jefferson as well, saw themselves as custodians of the true meaning of the American Revolution. And they harbored no doubts that the peaceful coexistence of Indians and whites on the North American continent was in keeping with revolutionary principles, just as Indian removal was a betrayal of them. All three men were accustomed to taking great risks against all odds in defense of those principles. As Jefferson so lyrically put it, they had on multiple occasions chosen to risk "their Lives, their Fortunes, and their sacred Honor," and on each occasion had watched history prove them right. Indeed, whenever Washington had invested himself in a major cause of dubious prospects, whether it was defeating the British army or siding with the nationalists at the Constitutional Convention, he had never lost. As long as the revolutionary winds were at their backs, and they certainly were in the effort to revise Indian policy, they had reason to believe they could win all wagers regardless of the odds. And who in his right mind was going to bet against Washington?

But the truth was that there were revolutionary winds blowing in the opposite direction as well. The Knox-Washington initiative had been a top-down affair conceived and planned in the executive branch with little if any consultation with Congress except for the Senate ratification vote, which had itself happened awkwardly, even comically. Washington was able to argue successfully that, because Indian tribes should be treated as foreign nations, jurisdiction over Indian policy was properly lodged in the executive branch. From Washington's perspective, only a bold assertion of executive power could put American Indian policy on a republican course. But in the minds of many observers in the Congress and out, such a conspicuous projection of executive power itself violated republican principles and conveyed the distinct odor of monarchy. Merely to mention that word was to ring all the revolutionary bells and to conjure up Jefferson's sweeping indictment of monarchical power in the Declaration of Independence. At this point in the tender life of the embryonic American republic, no policy that depended completely on the stark assertion of executive power was politically sustainable.

Faced with the problem two hundred years later, the president would have nationalized the Georgia militia and ordered them to enforce the law defining the Creek borders, and the Supreme Court would have ruled that such actions were constitutional. None of these options were available to Washington because the political institutions and legal precedents to make them possible were still aborning. In their absence, ultimate authority resided outside of government altogether, with those ordinary American citizens seeking a better life and a parcel of land to the west. In that sense, Indian removal was the inevitable consequence of unbridled democracy in action.

CHAPTER FIVE

❧ The Conspiracy ❧

THE ATTEMPT to create a just Indian policy failed despite the best efforts of America's most prominent political leaders to make it happen. The creation of a two-party system succeeded despite entrenched resistance by virtually all the founders to its very existence. As the most perceptive student of the origin of political parties so nicely put it: "The Fathers hoped to create not a system of party government under the Constitution but rather a Constitutional government that would check and control parties." And the man who, as much as anyone else, created the first organized opposition party in the United States also uttered the most concise condemnation of his very creation: "If I could not go to heaven but with a party," proclaimed Thomas Jefferson, "I would not go there at all."[1]

From our modern-day perch it is easy to see the indispensable role that organized political parties came to play later on in channeling the combustible energies of a wild-and-woolly democratic culture into a coherent and disciplined framework. It is also possible to discern the invaluable contribution that the two-party system made in providing a safe and structured location for ongoing dissent, in effect creating a routinized and institutionalized outlet for argument in lieu of the guillotine or the firing-squad wall. Yet if we were somehow able to dial up Jefferson in the hereafter and apprise him that he might well have listed the two-party system on his tombstone as one of his most lasting legacies, on a par with his Virginia statute for religious freedom, he would have regarded the suggestion as a preposterous joke.

At first glance, the founders' hostility to political parties seems strange, since the core idea that partisanship can serve the public interest was very much in the air throughout the late eighteenth century. Edmund Burke had written a much-discussed treatise on the subject in 1770, arguing that political parties not only were unavoidable products of representative government, but also performed valuable functions in orchestrating debate, much in the way that the adversarial system worked in legal trials. Adam Smith's *Wealth of Nations* (1776) described the unhindered collision of selfish and ambitious interest groups as the dynamic—if dirty—secret of the capitalistic marketplace. And, as we have seen, borrowing in part from Smith's free market idea, James Madison had argued in *Federalist 10* that the collision of political factions in an extended republic would produce greater stability, making size an asset rather than a liability. One could also argue that the contrived compromises reached at the Constitutional Convention, especially on the extent of executive power and the blurry line separating state and federal jurisdiction, created an inherently argumentative context that made the emergence of political parties of some kind virtually inevitable. And that, of course, is precisely what happened.[2]

So why were the founders, pretty much to a man, so resistant to the inevitable, especially when the creation of the first functioning two-party system in world history turned out to be perhaps their most lasting contribution to modern political thought? Why did they have to be dragged—kicking, screaming, and, perhaps most interestingly, denying what they were quite obviously doing?

The full answer to those questions lies within the folds of the story told in the pages that follow. The two major players are James Madison and Thomas Jefferson, early on dubbed "the General" and "the Generalissimo" of the emerging Republican Party. A major supporting role goes to Alexander Hamilton, the most flamboyantly brilliant member of the cast, who nearly steals the show but whose chief purpose here is to serve as the fixed object against which Madison and Jefferson do their political version of isometric exercises. Minor roles belong to two men most accustomed to heading the bill, George Washington and John Adams, neither of whom could quite fathom the partisan bickering that shaped their respective presidencies as anything more than dissonant noise that drowned out the classical harmonies.

Washington and Adams, in fact, were representative American statesmen who understood the terms "party" or "faction" as epithets that conveyed a disreputable commitment to a narrow and usually private agenda at the expense of the public interest. (The closest approximation in our modern political vocabulary is "lobbyist.") Their role model was the Patriot King, first described by Henry St. John, Viscount Bolingbroke, a British opposition thinker much admired by America's revolutionary generation for his endorsement of disinterested virtue as the hallmark of statesmanship, floating above factional squabbles and misguided popular surges to act in the long-term interest of the nation regardless of the political cost at the moment. It was psychologically impossible for either Adams or Washington to regard himself as the leader of a political party. Indeed, Washington was the ultimate Patriot King of all time. And Adams took considerable delight in committing political suicide by refusing to fight a popular war with France in 1799, a decision that led to his defeat in 1800 but that he forever regarded as the finest moment of his presidency.[3]

Modern American journalists and politicians still pay rhetorical homage to this inveterate disdain for polls, popularity, and partisanship, which is one of the chief reasons the founders enjoy such iconic reputations as the gold standard for our diluted political currency. The truth is that Washington and Adams were the last of a classical breed, and Jefferson was the first president to point the way to modernity as the avowed—though he was extremely reluctant to admit it—leader of a political party.

In a sense the problem was a matter of language. There was no neutral vocabulary available to talk about political parties, just as there was no way to discuss executive power without referring to kings and courts. Although the notion that economic interest groups or political factions could play a positive role in the marketplace or the political arena was generally understood, being regarded as a party leader remained a major stigma. It was one thing to recognize the clash of interests as a permanent feature of political life. It was quite another to embrace self-consciously and openly the role of party advocate and partisan, which on the face of it came across as a confession of corruption and moral deficiency that automatically disqualified such a person for national office. Even campaigning for office was considered a declaration of unworthiness.

Given the political framework created by the constitutional settlement of 1788, which made the establishment of an ongoing political dialogue of some sort inevitable, and given the stigma that surrounded organized political parties, a premium was put on a distinctive form of intelligence that could adroitly navigate between the two imperatives. Crudely put, this meant creating a political party while claiming, in all sincerity, that you were doing nothing of the sort. As it turned out, this was a talent that Jefferson possessed in abundance.

At certain points in the story the distinction between Jefferson's genuine self-deception and outright duplicity is impossible to identify with any certainty. But this is the phase of Jefferson's career that, as his most devoted biographer has acknowledged, defies customary notions of truth and candor, a time when Jefferson "frequently seems to be out of character." In order to put the best face on his multiple misrepresentations, Jefferson's ablest defenders have attributed them to his visceral urge to avoid all explicit forms of conflict: "The boldness of his mind," so Dumas Malone argued, "was sheathed in a scabbard of politeness. . . . It would have been surprising if such a man did not occasionally cross the thin line between courtesy and deception."[4]

Less devoted defenders of Jefferson have speculated that Jefferson's psychological agility during this formative phase of his political career was in fact the rule rather than the exception. Charles Francis Adams, grandson of John, put it this way: "More ardent in his imagination than his affections, he [Jefferson] did not always speak exactly as he felt towards friends and enemies. As a consequence, he has left hanging over a part of his public life a vapor of duplicity, or, to say the least, of indiscretion, the presence of which is generally felt more than it is seen."[5]

From our perspective, however, positive or negative assessments of

Jefferson's integrity at this historical moment are beside the point. If you begin with the assumption that the invention of the two-party system was a major achievement, and that seems beyond contention, and if you acknowledge that the political culture of the age threw huge obstacles on the path of that very invention, then anyone with the mental agility to leap over these obstacles must invariably violate the principles of the past in order to make possible the politics of the future.

For one of the ultimate implications of the two-party system that was so hard for most of the founders to accept was the realization that different versions of truth could coexist alongside one another and both claim, with considerable plausibility, to be true. Unlike mathematics, in politics there was no agreed-upon solution reached by sheer brainpower and logic, but rather an ongoing and never-ending struggle between contested versions of the truth. (The proper model, in effect, was not the Newtonian universe but the Darwinian jungle.) Only someone with a deep affinity for what we might call multiplicity, someone accustomed to negotiating his many-chambered personality, playing hide-and-seek within himself, was psychologically prepared to function within this modern world of party politics. And Thomas Jefferson fit this description more perfectly than anyone else.

Henry Adams captured the inherent elusiveness of Jefferson most eloquently in his magisterial *History:* "Almost every other American statesman might be described in a parenthesis. . . . A few broad strokes of the brush would paint the portraits of all the early Presidents with this exception . . . but Jefferson could be painted only touch by touch, with a fine pencil, and the perfection of the likeness depending upon the shifting and uncertain flicker of its semi-transcendent shadows."[6]

THE CRUISE AND THE CONSPIRACY

THE STORY BEGINS with Jefferson and Madison enjoying a leisurely cruise up the Hudson River in May of 1791. Jefferson described it as a "botanical excursion," and all the correspondence that has survived supports that innocent characterization. Letters home reported on the azaleas, blackberries, and white pines encountered on the trip. Lake

George was a magnificent surprise, but Lake Champlain was a disappointment, and the battlefields at Saratoga and Ticonderoga could speak only if you knew how to listen to the ghosts of the fallen. In general, Jefferson reported to his daughter, New England springs were bland and tepid compared to the explosion of color in Virginia at this season. After traversing Vermont to the headwaters of the Connecticut River, the two Virginians sailed down western New England like tourists soaking up the sights, smells, and sounds of a foreign country.[7]

But this apparently innocent adventure was not what it seemed. While their botanical explorations were sincere, in between the conversations about flora and fauna the two men found time to discuss politics. Madison later acknowledged that their discussions ambled from the destructive effects of the dreaded Hessian fly to the equally disastrous law creating the Bank of the United States, just passed by the Congress and signed by the president. Jefferson and Madison shared their mutual chagrin at—these are their words—the "stockjobbers," "Tories," and "monocrats" who had triumphed with the passage of the bank bill. All such despicable creatures, observed Madison, "dabbled in federal filth," presumably suggesting that all private investors in the bank were determined to make a private fortune at public expense. It was like the biblical scene when the money changers took over the temple.[8]

The conversations that occurred on the cruise, then, were less botanical than political. And they were political in a distinctly hyperbolic style. If you accept their rhetoric at face value, the deepest impulses of the American Revolution, the true "spirit of '76," were being hijacked by a conspiracy of northern bankers and "paper-men" who composed a "speculative phalanx" moving forward behind the satanic leadership of Alexander Hamilton. Though these men represented a tiny minority within the overall populace, they had somehow managed to engineer a hostile takeover of the fledgling American republic and were now poised to consolidate their control to the detriment of all the ordinary citizens, mostly farmers, the true lifeblood of the nation. The ultimate goal of this Federalist faction was to undermine the republican government and replace it with a monarchical state in which the presidency became a hereditary rather than an elective office and "money-men" became the new American aristocracy.

Given the depth and breadth of this mounting conspiracy, they warned, the true friends of pure republican principles needed to organize an opposition that would restore the uncorrupted republican faith. The first step in that direction required a newspaper to expose the Federalist plot and enlighten the public about the hovering political threat. Jefferson and Madison chose Philip Freneau, a New Jersey journalist and sometime poet, to launch the *National Gazette* as the official voice of what became the Republican Party. Jefferson promised to pay him a salary as a translator in the State Department, though his real job would be to promulgate "the ancient Whig doctrine." Freneau would be given exclusive access to all foreign intelligence passing through Jefferson's office and "the publication of all proclamations and other public notices within my department."[9]

There is no question that Jefferson and Madison were sincere; their personal correspondence confirms the heartfelt conviction that a Federalist plot was afoot. There is also no question that Jefferson and Madison were wholly sane and thoroughly rational men. The question then becomes: How did they develop such a quasi-paranoid image of the Federalist agenda, an image that would cause one of the primary authors of *The Federalist* to repudiate all his previous arguments on behalf of a sovereign federal government and make Jefferson, a member of Washington's cabinet, believe that his highest duty was to subvert the very government he was allegedly serving?

By any neutral standard, the picture that Jefferson and Madison saw in their heads was a preposterous distortion. How could two men who had never fired a shot in anger during the war suggest that Washington and Hamilton, both military heroes, were in any sense of the word "Tories"? How could John Adams, the acknowledged "Atlas of independence," be tarred with that same brush? As for monarchical ambitions, Washington had already demonstrated his immunity to all such ambitions by rejecting the crown at the end of the war, and his efforts to define the powers of the presidency all operated within a framework of republican presumptions. To be sure, Washington could appear quite regal at ceremonial occasions or riding around the capital like God on horseback, but he could not help being physically majestic.

Finally, the Hamilton financial program, topped off by the bank, represented an effort to restore fiscal stability to an American economy burdened by debt and previously incapable of doing much about it. The enrichment of a few investors was an extraneous by-product of an economic policy rather brilliantly designed to persuade the international market-makers that the United States was not, in modern parlance, a banana republic. How, in heaven's name, could fiscal responsibility be seen as an unmitigated evil?[10]

One obvious answer to these overlapping questions is that the conspiratorial mentality that Jefferson and Madison were imposing on the Federalists represented a domestic version of the arguments made against George III and Parliament in the 1760s and 1770s. The conviction that malevolent forces were gathering in the shadowy alleys of Whitehall and the smoke-filled coffeehouses of London, where British officials were plotting the enslavement of the American colonists, became a centerpiece of revolutionary ideology. To raise any question about the rational character of this depiction was to risk being labeled a Tory, and the ideology enjoyed a hallowed status once the movement for American independence succeeded. Jefferson and Madison were simply moving this time-honored ideological lens, through which the colonists had viewed British imperial policy, training it on the Federalists, and seeing the same sinister conspiracy at work on American soil.[11]

But in two respects this shift of focus posed credibility problems not encountered when the British were the villains. First, the potency of revolutionary ideology depended upon distance. The alleged British plotters were an ocean away, faceless creatures vulnerable to conspiratorial stereotypes in large part because of their complete invisibility. On the other hand, all the villains in the purported Federalist plot were intimate acquaintances of Jefferson and Madison, colleagues who had a history of working together (e.g., Madison and Hamilton on *The Federalist*). This should have made them much more difficult to demonize.

Yet somehow Jefferson managed to do it. He went to his grave insisting that Hamilton, who sat next to him at all cabinet meetings, "was not only a monarchist, but for a monarchy bottomed on corruption," while his old friend Adams had lost the revolutionary faith and "been taken up by the monarchical federalists." Late in life he could still claim to recall dinner parties in New York when he was secretary of state and found himself the only true republican amidst "a general prevalence of monarchical sentiments." It would seem that monarchists, like the communists of a later time, were everywhere. To repeat, there is little question that Jefferson was sincere and believed what he said. There is also little question that what he saw owed a great deal to his own fertile imagination.[12]

Turning the Federalists into an updated version of British conspirators faced an even larger problem. The core constitutional argument against the British ministry and Parliament was that because the American colonists were not represented in Parliament, all taxes or restrictive laws were being imposed on them without their consent. Take away that core argument and the plausibility of the conspiratorial charge became much more difficult to sustain. But all the Federalist plotters were duly elected or appointed officials chosen by the citizenry in accord with the rules prescribed by the very Constitution that Madison had done so much to shape. The Federalists, then, were a very strange kind of cabal, an elected government freely chosen by a substantial majority of American voters.

These obstacles posed a serious challenge to any domestic deployment of the revolutionary ideology. One advantage that Jefferson and Madison enjoyed and used to overcome these obstacles was their Virginia base, which gave them a safe haven to develop their conspiratorial conversation and a supportive constituency already primed to understand the coded vocabulary about "stockjobbers," "money-men," "monocrats," and "the fiscal party" without any extended explanations. If you used this vocabulary in New York or Philadelphia, you ran the risk of being misunderstood or judged slightly insane. In Virginia, however, it was part of the mainstream vernacular because it made perfect sense when delivered with a southern accent, since it provided a convenient explanation for the catastrophic decline of the tobacco economy and the mounting indebtedness of the planter class in the Old Dominion. Henry Adams subsequently labeled it the "Virginia-write-large" version of the American Revolution.[13]

Madison's turnabout was very much a symptom and consequence of the realignment of political power in Virginia after the narrow victory by the Federalists in the ratifying convention of 1788. The shift occurred in response to the debate over Hamilton's financial plan in 1790–91, chiefly the federal assumption of state debts and the establishment of a national bank. These developments forced the planter class of Virginia to realize, for the first time, that their days as America's premier political elite were numbered, soon to be replaced by the commercial and financial elite of New York and New England. One of the distinguishing features of most conspiracy theories is the tendency to personalize what are, in truth, impersonal forces of unwelcomed change. Hamilton and his banking cronies thus became the personification of the reasons for Virginia's economic decline, felt most sharply by the Tidewater planters, who also happened to be the long-standing nucleus of Virginia's political elite.

It did not help, though it blended nicely with the old revolutionary ideology, that Hamilton and his henchmen were eerily reminiscent of the British and Scottish creditors who were bleeding the Virginia planter class to death with such diabolical concepts as compound interest rates. Bankruptcy often arrived as a complete surprise on many Virginia plantations, a product of accounting legerdemain that many planters took considerable pride in not comprehending. (Both Jefferson and Madison would die bankrupt.) Hamilton's financial plan for fiscal solvency galvanized all their pent-up frustrations, which were rendered even more passionate because, truth be known, the planters had not the dimmest understanding of what Hamilton was talking about.

Finally, there was yet another distinctly southern ingredient in the Republican ideological recipe, though it was unspoken. Whether one regards slavery as the proverbial elephant in the center of the room or the ever-hovering ghost at the banquet, the etiquette of political conversation in Virginia forbade any candid discussion of the subject. The correspondence between Jefferson and Madison embodied this etiquette of silence. Their letters, much like the text of the Constitution, never mentioned slavery as a factor in their indictment of the Federalist agenda, not because it was unworthy of notice, but because it was like a piece of inadmissible evidence with explosive implications capable of blowing up their entire case. Their orchestrated silence on the slavery issue provides one of those rare occasions when the very absence of evidence is the most important piece of evidence of all. Perhaps this was what John Quincy Adams was referring to when he described the seamless but unspoken character of the Jefferson-Madison partnership as "a phenomenon, like the invisible and mysterious movements of the magnet in the physical world."[14]

What, then, was being left unsaid? Many years later Nathaniel Macon, a prominent Virginia Republican, blurted it out: "Tell me if Congress can establish banks, make roads and canals, whether they cannot free all the Slaves in the United States." The fiscal program of Hamilton, most graphically embodied in the bank, surely did conjure up the dreaded menace of a northern commercial elite as vampires sucking the blood out of the agrarian south. But Hamilton's program was also the fullest projection of federal sovereignty over the states, the kind of undiluted statement of a wholly national ethos that Madison had not so long ago advocated just as strenuously as Hamilton. By 1791 Madison's mind had changed on this score, as had the minds of many formerly staunch Virginia Federalists. And one of the reasons for the shift, floating silently above the explicit demonization of a "phalanx of bankers," was the sudden realization that, once the federal government assumed control over domestic policy, slavery was doomed.[15]

The specific incident that exposed this dreaded possibility occurred in the spring of 1790, when two Quaker petitions, one signed by none other than Benjamin Franklin, urged the Congress to take up the question of the slave trade as well as the persistence of slavery itself in any self-respecting American republic. Franklin's stature made it impossible to ignore or table the petitions, which produced the first open and fully recorded debate over slavery in the history of the United States. Madison led the floor fight in the House to block any extension of federal authority over slavery, arguing that the Constitution specifically forbade any congressional limitation on the slave trade for twenty years and implicitly relegated any and all legislation regarding slavery itself to the state governments. Madison also drafted the committee report that affirmed this strict interpretation of the Constitution, breathing a sigh of relief that "the wave had passed safely under the ship."[16]

As much as any man in America, however, Madison knew there would be other waves, because the Constitution had drawn a very blurry line between federal and state jurisdictions, a line that was sure to move back and forth on a case-by-case basis during the formative years of the infant nation. And this is where the creation of a national bank intersected in alarming fashion with the slavery question. For in the debate over the bank that raged throughout February of 1791, its opponents, to include both Jefferson and Madison, based their opposition on its unconstitutionality, arguing that Congress possessed only certain enumerated powers, that the power to create a corporation (i.e., the bank) was not one of them, so the bank violated the Tenth Amendment, which reserved all powers to the states not specifically delegated to the federal government. But the winning argument proved to be Hamilton's, which cited the "necessary and proper" clause of the Constitution (Article 1, Section 8) to sanction congressional authority as one of the implied powers inherent in the Constitution. Hamilton quoted, almost verbatim, the argument made in *Federalist 44*, which everyone presumed he had written: "No axiom is more clearly established in law, or in reason, than that wherever a general power to do a thing is given, every particular power necessary for doing it, is included."[17]

This argument not only won the day, but also established an expansive precedent for federal power with almost limitless implications and applications. Madison must have cringed as Hamilton's argument was read out loud in the House, because he, not Hamilton, was the author of *Federalist 44*. His earlier incarnation as an unbridled nationalist was now being thrown in his face.

It was not just the bank itself, then, that terrified Madison and his fellow Virginians, though that source of dread was real enough. It was the open-ended definition of federal power on which the bank was authorized, which in effect gave the federal government a roving mandate to extend its authority wherever it wished, to include the thoroughly vulnerable issue of slavery. In the Republican vision of the current political situation, most especially its distinctive Virginia version, corrupt "money-men" were making fortunes by shuffling pieces of paper while whispering insulting jokes about the unknowing yeoman farmers they were fleecing. But neither Jefferson nor Madison was really a farmer. (Neither man ever did a full day's work in the fields.) They and the Virginia constituency they represented were planters, and the labor source on which the plantation economy rested, ever so precariously it turned out, was slavery.

So the whisperings they detected among the Federalist conspirators made perfect sense because they mirrored their own whisperings about the subject that could not be talked about openly. Indeed, apart from its obvious economic and moral significance, the slavery issue created an environment conducive to a conspiratorial mentality, a political world in which the unspoken was all-important, secrecy was an essential attribute for success, suspicion was wholly justified, mutual trust was foolishly naive, and one's deepest motives were presumed to be hidden. In that sense, the Republican view of the Federalists enjoyed such credibility in Virginia because it was a projection onto their enemies of a deceptive agenda with which they had a deep and intimate experience.

CULTIVATING THE COVERT

Explaining Madison's conversion to the Republican camp is a tricky business, in part because Madison's thought process was always more serpentine than simple, in part because the switch was almost breathtakingly dramatic, from the leader of the ultra-nationalists at the Constitutional Convention and the Virginia ratifying convention to the leader of the opposition that challenged the legitimacy of everything he had previously advocated. One obvious explanation is Jefferson's influence. Upon Jefferson's return from France, so the story goes, Madison resumed his customary position as acolyte to his Monticello mentor, a subordinate posture in which he remained perfectly comfortable for the next thirty years, even during his own presidency, ending only with Jefferson's death.

This explanation fits the folds of Madison's personality, which instinctively recoiled from the glare at center stage, relished performing the essential behind-the-scenes tasks for which others received the credit, and genuinely worshipped the ground that Jefferson walked on. On the other hand, the explanation is not only too neat and simple, it is historically, or at least chronologically, incorrect. For Madison's conversion began in the winter and spring of 1790, before Jefferson arrived on the scene in New York.

A second explanation, not wholly incompatible with the first, is that Hamilton's *Report on Public Credit* (1790) truly stunned Madison with its aggressive projection of federal control over fiscal policy, for this was not a version of the national ethos that Madison had in mind two years earlier. A corollary to this explanation, which surfaced most explicitly during the debate over the Quaker petitions against slavery, is that he felt obliged to represent the interests of his Virginia constituents, for whom control over what he called "that species of property" was not a negotiable issue. Here he had to choose between being a Virginian or an American, and he went with the electorate that put him in office.

A third explanation, admittedly more speculative, is that Madison had fully internalized the argumentative framework established by the Constitution as an ongoing dialogue between federal and state sovereignty. He understood, perhaps more deeply and profoundly than any man of his time, that the survival of the republican experiment depended on a balanced conversation between advocates of federal and state sovereignty. That conversation could continue productively only if both sides enjoyed roughly equal claims to legitimacy. From this perspective, the Hamiltonian initiative had drastically unbalanced the political equation and thereby threatened to terminate the conversation when it had barely begun. Madison's highest duty, then, was to jump on the other side of the political seesaw to restore the balance and thereby sustain the ongoing dialogue. (He switched sides again near the end of his life during the Nullification Crisis.) If correct, his conversion to the Republican cause was not really a partisan act, but one of the shrewdest nonpartisan decisions imaginable.

Whatever Madison's motive, he became the political point man for the Republican opposition. (It was awkward for Jefferson to play any public role, given his position as secretary of state in the Washington administration.) Between November of 1791 and December of 1792 Madison wrote eighteen essays for Freneau's *National Gazette* that effectively announced the arrival of the Republican Party as a viable alternative to the Federalists. Though virtually everything done in these initial years of the American republic set a precedent, Madison's essays, all done anonymously, were especially unprecedented because they declared the presence of an opposition party as a new feature on the American political landscape.[18]

In one of his early essays Madison came close to articulating the modern rationale for a two-party system: "In every political society, parties are unavoidable," Madison wrote. "The great object should be to combat the evil . . . by making one party a check on the other. . . . If this is not the language of reason, it is that of republicanism." This approximated the modern notion of two permanent parties, forever disagreeing and routinely rotating into power and out. But it soon became clear that Madison remained an important increment away from the full-blooded acceptance of two equally legitimate political parties dueling for the favor of the citizenry. For in Madison's formulation the duly elected government, which he did not call Federalists but "anti-republicans," was illegitimate. (The "anti-republican" label, like the "Antifederalist" label in the ratification debate, was designed to put the enemy on the defensive.) The political conflict was not a collision of co-equals, but a war between the forces of light and the forces of darkness in which the Republicans represented the soul of the American Revolution and the Federalists its betrayal.[19]

In an essay entitled "A Candid State of Parties" Madison linked the emerging struggle between Federalists and Republicans with the ageless conflict between the few and the many, which took the form of "the Court versus the Country" in Georgian England, then "the Tories and the Whigs" in the American Revolution. Here Madison was at least temporarily abandoning his previous claim in *Federalist 10* that the extended size of the American republic would produce multiple factions, whose interaction would prevent the kind of two-sided division now being trumpeted as the timeless political pattern. The virtue of this simpler vision, which was really more Jeffersonian than Madisonian, is that it cast the Federalists in the role of recognizable villains in a patriotic story line that everybody knew by heart, an updated version of the song entitled "The Spirit of '76" with lyrics provided by Jefferson's uplifting rendition of liberty versus power in the Declaration of Independence.[20]

As Madison knew better than anyone else, the story line did not fit the 1780s, that is, unless one wanted to argue that the Antifederalists were the true heirs of the revolutionary legacy and the Federalists its enemies. While it was possible for Jefferson to embrace that conclusion, since he was in Paris and played no role in either the Constitutional Convention or the ratification debate, that was not true of Madison. Given his role as the most prominent Federalist of all in 1787–88, for him to recognize the Antifederalists as the heroic predecessors of the Republicans was akin to having Martin Luther declare his ultimate allegiance to the Vatican.

His solution, which was somewhat strained, was to argue that the Federalists had always harbored a minority of "closet monarchists" and "secret tories," and this very faction had somehow managed to seize control of government at the federal level and in several of the states. This coup d'état had occurred because of the disproportionate power wielded by "the men of influence, particularly the moneyed interest," who also enjoyed the advantage of physical proximity because "they all live in cities." The vast majority of Americans, on the other hand, were farmers, who were spread out and too busy tilling the soil to pay much attention to politics.

In one essay Madison praised the simple virtues of the agrarian life—another decidedly Jeffersonian theme—which contrasted completely with the inherently corrupt world of urban bankers and speculators. There was no question, then, that a sinister minority had temporarily wrested control of the government from the silent majority. "The Republican party, as it may be termed, conscious that the mass of people in every part of the union . . . must at bottom be with them," Madison concluded, should remain confident that this Federalist ascendance was an aberration, that "the issue in the present instance should be reversed, and the government be administered in the spirit and form approved by the great body of the people."[21]

While this was highly questionable as history—"the great body of the people" had recently elected Washington almost by acclamation—it was extremely shrewd as propaganda. For Madison had transformed the quite real clash of economic and political interests between the planter class of the southern states and the commercial class of the northern states into an ideological struggle between two different versions of the American Revolution, a struggle in which the rhetorical advantage belonged to the Republicans. Like a skilled lawyer who had switched clients, he proved himself supremely capable of moving from the most adroit defender of the Federalists to the most able prosecutor of the Federalist agenda. And in so doing, Madison provided the outline of the Republican agenda for the remainder of the decade.

If, for whatever reasons, Madison had changed his mind, his former collaborator on *The Federalist* had not. Alexander Hamilton had assumed his duties as secretary of the treasury with the clear sense that "the spirit of '87" had trumped "the spirit of '76," which in effect meant that sovereignty now resided in the federal government and his efforts to create a coherent fiscal policy for the nation should operate from that assumption.

Only slightly taller than the diminutive Madison, Hamilton projected a sense of stature at odds with his size, a kind of "little giant" who dominated the center of any room in which Madison drifted to the darkened corners. He also defied the understated Virginia style by being conspicuously and outspokenly brilliant, the kind of man who not only needed to win every argument but also needed to demonstrate that you had lost. As far as Hamilton was concerned, those people now styling themselves Republicans either had been asleep for the last four years or were collectively non compos mentis, for the duly ratified Constitution had dispensed with the state-based government of the Articles in favor of a fully empowered national government in which control over fiscal policy was a clearly delineated federal responsibility.[22]

Never one to long remain on the defensive, Hamilton launched an assault on the Republican camp in the fall of 1792, writing a series of essays for *The Gazette of the United States* under the pseudonym "Catullus." In response to the charge that the Federalists were plotting a conspiracy to undermine the republican principles of the American Revolution, Hamilton countered that the Republicans were the real conspirators, and he made Jefferson the most villainous conspirator of all. Though Madison had become the point man for the Republicans, Hamilton identified Jefferson as the mastermind of the opposition and "the most intriguing man in the United States," whose behind-the-scenes skulduggery required exposure in the public papers.

In the Hamiltonian account, Jefferson had always harbored reservations about the dramatic shift away from the state-centered focus of the Articles and remained at best a lukewarm supporter of the Constitution. His decision to hire Philip Freneau as a translator in the State Department was a transparently conspiratorial plot to launch a political assault on the very administration he allegedly served, thereby making him a Trojan horse and "the Catiline of the American republic" all rolled into one. (Most educated Americans recognized Catiline as the treacherous conspirator who almost destroyed the Roman Republic and whose vile character inspired Cicero's famous oration in behalf of virtue as the quintessential quality for a republic statesman.)[23]

While Hamilton's conclusions were thoroughly partisan, the evidence on which they were based was factually accurate. Jefferson's views of the Constitution and his conduct with Freneau were pretty much as Hamilton described. When asked about the Freneau connection, Jefferson, somewhat lamely, argued that Freneau was not his puppet, but was free to write anything he wished. This was a disingenuous defense that stopped just short of being an outright lie.

Hamilton's exposure of Jefferson's covert role in the Republican plotting prompted a series of Federalist assaults on his character that drew selectively on his previous career to document his shallowness and lack of integrity: as governor of Virginia he had fled ignominiously before invading British troops; as minister to France he had failed to comprehend the bloody consequences of the French Revolution, insisting that all would turn out well because he clung tenaciously to "theoretical principles fit only for Utopia"; as the author of *Notes on the State of Virginia* he had declared "the inherent inferiority of Blacks to Whites, because they are more unsavory and secrete more by the kidneys"; as a mathematician he kept shifting his theorems as he twirled away in his specially designed pivot chair, which became a favorite symbol of Jefferson's endemic rotations and vacillations. He was, in the Federalist demonology, a misguided, duplicitous, dangerous dreamer whose sublimated ambition would never be satisfied until he became president of the United States.[24]

Jefferson never responded to these charges, though he did permit his surrogates, chiefly Freneau, Madison, and James Monroe, to do so. He remained reticent for personal and political reasons. On the personal level, he loathed open controversy, regarding it as dissonant noise that interrupted the natural harmonies he heard in his head. On the political level, he could ill afford to become a conspicuous participant in the broadsides against the Federalists as long as he was serving in Washington's cabinet. By remaining silent on the Freneau connection while allowing others to deny it in the press, he avoided having to tell a lie and kept his fingerprints off all incriminating evidence.

In Jefferson's case, however, it is difficult to know where deception ended and self-deception began. After an especially partisan attack on Washington by Freneau, Jefferson wrote plaintively to Madison: "The President is not well. . . . He is extremely affected by the attacks made . . . on him in the public papers. I think he feels these things more than any person I have ever met with. I am sincerely sorry to see them." Yet this apparently genuine expression of regret came from the very man who was subsidizing Freneau to inflict the pain. His thoughts seemed to run on two separate and parallel tracks that never intersected, thus making him simultaneously incapable of either candor or hypocrisy.[25]

This bimodal style allowed Jefferson to orchestrate state-by-state schemes for Republican electoral victories with Madison, who always had the numbers at his fingertips, then join Washington the same day and work together with great affinity on the design of the projected capital on the Potomac. The only subject capable of upsetting this psychological balancing act was Hamilton. On several occasions while meeting with Washington, when Hamilton's name came up, Jefferson erupted. Hamilton, he blurted, was "a tissue of machinations against the liberty of the country which has not only received and given him bread, but heaped its honors upon his head." In another outburst Jefferson described the Hamilton fiscal policy as "designed to prepare a change from the present republican form of government, to that of a monarchy." This was mainstream Republican rhetoric, a maxim within the planter class of Virginia, but when uttered in Washington's presence it provoked the sober assessment that Hamilton, like he, favored a strong executive, but neither Hamilton nor anyone else in his administration wished to restore the monarchy, and that anyone who believed such nonsense had thereby provided "a proof of their insanity." Jefferson never unburdened himself with Washington again, and from that moment onward began to take notes documenting Washington's creeping senility, spreading gossip that the once great man was now past his prime.[26]

The whispering campaign against Washington made strategic sense, since any direct criticism of the greatest hero of the age was likely to backfire, and by insinuating that Washington was oblivious to Hamilton's machinations behind the screen the Republicans could focus their fire on more vulnerable targets, chiefly Hamilton and his banker friends.

The bank, indeed, was the perfect target, and in language eerily prophetic of Andrew Jackson's diatribes forty years later, Jefferson urged Madison to depict the bank as the satanic symbol of the dreaded "consolidation," a nefarious aggregation of arbitrary power that rolled over the interests of ordinary Americans. Jefferson had reached the conclusion that the bank was not just unconstitutional, it was actually treasonable. "For any person to recognize a foreign legislature in a case belonging to the state itself," he apprised Madison, "is an act of *treason* against the state." This was the first explicit expression of a view that Jefferson would expand upon more broadly seven years later in the Kentucky Resolutions. Namely, control over all domestic legislation rested within the states, so any federal legislation objectionable to a state was an illegal intrusion by what was in fact a foreign government.[27]

This was a rather extreme position that moved the blurry and shifting line separating federal and state jurisdiction about as far back as any die-hard Antifederalist could wish. Perhaps sensing that this was not the kind of constitutional position he should advertise, Jefferson urged Madison to keep it confidential. Shortly thereafter, the two Republican leaders decided to draft all future letters to each other in code, using the cipher first deployed when Jefferson was abroad. (In August of 1792 Madison regretfully reported that he had left the key to the code in Philadelphia, so all the Jefferson letters he received at Montpelier were incomprehensible.) Their mutual concern about secrecy reached such a point that Madison felt the need to have someone else copy all his essays for the *National Gazette* so that the printer would not recognize his handwriting. If they believed themselves to be fighting against a Federalist conspiracy, and they surely did, they felt justified in assuming the character of a conspiracy themselves, believing all the while that their own secretive tactics were fully justified to offset the tactics of their opponents.[28]

The Republican campaign against Hamilton and the bank reached a crescendo in January of 1793 when Congressman William Giles of Virginia called for an investigation of Hamilton's management of public funds. Giles was a devoted Jefferson protégé—he was even courting Jefferson's younger daughter at the time—and Jefferson himself actually drafted the indictment against Hamilton, a labor of love if there ever was one. The central charge was that Hamilton was cooking the books, shifting sums from one column to the other in order to conceal graft being dispensed to his financial cronies, the infamous "stockjobbers" and "monocrats." The goal was to force Hamilton's resignation.[29]

But contrary to Jefferson's fondest expectations, the congressional investigation ended up congratulating Hamilton on his impeccable bookkeeping and rock-ribbed integrity. Jefferson's only solace was the knowledge that he had forced his chief tormentor to spend several weeks doing the tedious work to document his accounting procedures. In Jefferson's mind, moreover, Hamilton's vindication never shook his conviction that the entire fiscal policy of the federal government was an elaborate swindle. He regarded the hard evidence produced by Hamilton as so much numerical wizardry that no one, not even Hamilton himself, could possibly understand. Instead of concluding that he had been wrong about Hamilton and his fiscal policy, Jefferson concluded that Hamilton was an even craftier criminal than he had thought.[30]

Everything Jefferson saw with his eyes was filtered through the conspiratorial categories he stored in his head, which then bent the perceptions to fit the preordained conclusions. Given the certainty and clarity of his vision, he was effectively immune to evidence that might complicate the purity of his mental categories. In a sense this immunity made him the ideal party leader, not just because he would never waiver in his devotion to the cause, but also because the cause itself transcended any mere squabble about loaves and fishes, was not just a partisan campaign for votes and power. It was a much more ennobling crusade for the rescue of republican principles from the abyss into which the Federalists were taking them. Serving as a party leader, then, was a necessary role to play in order to reach the higher calling of American redeemer. It was a vision that verged on the spiritual.

THE FRENCH CONNECTION

THUS FAR THE AGENDA of the Republican Party—a term that both Jefferson and Madison began to use—had taken shape in response to Federalist domestic policy, chiefly Hamilton's financial plan. In its most fanatical, quasi-paranoid version, the Federalists were regarded as the second coming of the British ministry on American soil, the stalking horse for a putative American monarchy and hereditary aristocracy. In its more sober-minded version, the Republicans were insisting upon a renegotiation of the constitutional settlement of 1787–88, or perhaps a stricter interpretation of federal jurisdiction that gave new life to the old Antifederalist apprehensions about centralized power. As we have seen, beneath both versions of the Republican agenda there lurked sectional interests of the Virginia-writ-large sort, meaning a palpable fear that the commercial north was replacing the agrarian south as the dominant power broker, and the overlapping fear that any recognition of federal jurisdiction over domestic policy placed slavery at risk.

Jefferson's special genius as a party leader was to deny, in all sincerity, that he was such a partisan creature, and to mask the sectional interests of the Republican cause behind the more uplifting rhetoric inspired by the revolutionary melodies of 1776. Where strategy ended and sincerity began is impossible to know. And the line between them within Jefferson's mind was just as ambiguous and ever-shifting as the line between federal and state sovereignty in the Constitution.

The Republicans opened a new angle of attack on the foreign policy front early in 1793. The immediate precipitant was the outbreak of war between France and Great Britain, news of which reached the United States in April. Washington immediately recognized this development as a shift in the diplomatic landscape and convened his cabinet to discuss the American response. Given the controversy soon to ensue, it is interesting to note the unanimous consensus within the cabinet that the United States must not be drawn into this European war.

The problem was the Franco-American alliance of 1778, which had done so much to provide the money and manpower essential for the American victory in the War for Independence. No man alive understood the essential contribution the French had made in making American independence possible more than Washington. But that was then and this was now, so Washington, an unalloyed foreign policy realist, never hesitated in issuing the Proclamation of Neutrality in late April of 1793, which effectively repudiated the French alliance.[31]

Ever resourceful, Hamilton sprang into print with a series of essays defending Washington's decision, written under the pseudonym "Pacificus." His chief argument was that the Franco-American treaty was a dead letter because Louis XVI, who signed it, was no more, having recently suffered the indignity of being beheaded. In the cabinet deliberations Jefferson opposed this interpretation, arguing that the Franco-American treaty was a contract between nations rather than governments, a wholly sensible and ultimately successful argument that made outright rejection of the French alliance impossible.

In the meantime, however, Jefferson worried that Hamilton's essays would work their customary magic and prejudice the citizenry against the French connection. Jefferson implored Madison to answer him: "For god's sake, my dear Sir, take up your pen, select his most striking heresies, and cut him to pieces in the face of the public. There is nobody else who can and will enter the lists with him." Madison did his duty in a series of essays under the pseudonym "Helvidius," complaining all the while to Jefferson that foreign policy was not his proper bailiwick. His major contribution, in fact, was to raise a constitutional question: Unless Washington regarded himself as a monarch, where did he derive the authority to issue a proclamation?[32]

Jefferson had not objected when Washington issued the Proclamation of New York in 1790, endorsing the treaty with the Creeks. But that particular proclamation had predated the emergence of the Republican Party. His somewhat strained argument in this case was that because the Constitution required a vote of Congress to go to war, it also required a vote of Congress *not* to go to war. Although this argument lost out in the cabinet deliberations, it remained a useful weapon in the Republican ideological arsenal, reinforcing the claim that the Federalists harbored monarchical tendencies. And by 1793 both Jefferson and Madison were looking for any weapon they could find to wound the Federalist opposition on the foreign policy front.

It soon dawned on Jefferson that Washington's decision to steer a neutral course in foreign policy provided a heaven-sent opportunity to inflict just such a wound: "The war between France and England seems to be producing an effect not contemplated," he explained to Monroe. "All the old spirit of 1776 is rekindling." By that he meant that American popular opinion remained resolutely pro-French, in part because of the invaluable assistance provided in the late war, in part because the French Revolution was initially perceived as a glorious extension of "the spirit of '76" onto the European continent.[33]

From a diplomatic point of view Washington's insistence on American neutrality was unquestionably correct. Indeed, it was the landmark statement of what would become the core principle of American policy toward Europe for the next century and beyond. From a political point of view, however, American neutrality ran against the grain of the decidedly pro-French sentiment in the nation at large. And Jefferson was eager to exploit that sentiment for partisan purposes.

To be sure, Jefferson was a sincere aficionado of all things Gallic, from French cooking to Parisian architecture to revolutionary politics. On the latter score, he remained wedded to his original conviction that the French Jacobins, the radical party, would conduct themselves responsibly. "I begin to consider them the true revolutionary spirit of the whole nation," he apprised Madison, "and as carrying the nation with them." Since the Jacobins were, at the very moment he wrote these words, guillotining many of his French friends, this was another case where inconvenient evidence was not allowed to penetrate those interior chambers where Jefferson stored his deepest ideals.

When his former secretary, William Short, wrote him several letters from Paris describing the mass executions and severed heads being rolled down the streets, Jefferson told him he preferred not to hear such stories: "The tone of your letters had for some time given me pain," he chided Short. "My own affections have been deeply wounded by some of the martyrs to this cause, but rather than it should have failed I would have seen half the earth desolated. Were there but an Adam and Eve left in every country, and left free, it would be better than it is now." If any of his Federalist foes had seen this letter, it would have been recycled countless times to document the charge that Jefferson was one of the most dangerous men in America.[34]

The arrival of Edmond-Charles Genet in May of 1793 as the new French minister to the United States provided the occasion for the simultaneous release of Jefferson's two most potent passions—his romantic attachment to the French Revolution and his realistic, indeed quite calculated, desire to inflict maximum damage on the Federalists. Styled Citizen Genet as a statement of his revolutionary credentials, the minister was initially received with an orgy of toasts and pro-French demonstrations. All this confirmed Jefferson's estimate that the Proclamation of Neutrality did not reflect American popular opinion, which was decidedly, and in some places deliriously, wedded to France.[35]

How Genet somehow managed to transform his status as a foreign celebrity into that of an insufferable pariah within a few short months has always seemed almost inexplicable. The most accepted explanation is that he misread his initial reception, overplayed his hand, and thereby laid the groundwork for his utter ruin. We know for a fact that he made several outrageous statements, to include authorizing American privateers to capture British ships on the high seas and claiming that Washington's Proclamation of Neutrality violated the fraternal bond with the French nation and should be studiously ignored by all liberty-loving American citizens. He seemed to believe that he could speak more credibly for the interests of the American people than its elected government. This combination of arrogance and ignorance did him in by August of 1793, when the Federalist administration, with Jefferson assenting, demanded his recall.[36]

It seems quite likely, however, that Genet's brazen behavior flowed at least in part from several conversations he had with Jefferson. These conversations were confidential and unrecorded, but Genet's later recollections make it abundantly clear that Jefferson shared with him his most sweeping Republican vision: Washington was under the influence of the pro-British Hamilton, but that cabal would prove short-lived because the vast majority of the American electorate felt a deep allegiance to the French Revolution; the Federalists were an elite minority that had temporarily captured the government, but only managed to retain power because of the immense prestige of Washington, now a pale replica of his former greatness; the assertion of American neutrality was therefore a misrepresentative statement by an illegitimate faction that did not speak for the will of the American people.

Given the fact that Jefferson was officially a member of the Federalist administration, his remarks to Genet constituted, at the very least, a serious breach of political integrity. But two years earlier Hamilton had shared his own prejudices with the British ambassador, George Hammond, in equivalently semi-treasonable fashion. (A republican government was still such a novel creation that the rules of the game remained murky.) Genet's self-inflicted demise came about, at least in part, because he felt free to act upon in public the highly partisan advice that Jefferson had shared with him in private.[37]

From Jefferson's perspective as the titular leader of the Republican

Party, Genet's behavior transformed him from a potent weapon to a dangerous liability. As he wrote in code to Madison: "We have decided unanimously [in the cabinet] to require the recall of Genet. He will sink the Republican interest if they do not abandon him." Jefferson managed to combine an ideological vision of the inevitable Republican triumph with a wholly tactical sense of when to cut his losses. As he wrote to Madison:

> I believe that it will be true wisdom in the Republican party to approve unequivocally of a state of neutrality, to avoid little cavils about who should declare it, to abandon G. [Genet] entirely. . . . In this way we shall keep the people on our side by keeping ourselves in the right. . . . I adhered to him as long as I could have hope of getting him right. . . . Finding at length that the man was absolutely incorrigible, I saw the necessity of quitting a wreck which could not but sink all who cling to it.[38]

In other words, the campaign to discredit the Federalist embrace of neutrality had backfired. Genet's extreme pronouncements had managed to transform popular opinion so that it now rallied behind the Proclamation of Neutrality. The Republicans needed to bend with this political wind rather than break in gallant but futile resistance. Jefferson's letter to Madison ended with the following postscript: "The President is extremely anxious to know your sentiments on the Proclamation. He has asked me several times. I tell him you are so absorbed in farming that you write to me always about plows, rotations, etc." Most of Madison's letters at the time, in truth, dealt with his "Helvidius" essays, which criticized the neutrality policy and Washington's authority to proclaim it. Best to spare the president such unwelcomed news.[39]

BACK AT HEADQUARTERS

IF ONE WERE KEEPING score in the party wars, by the summer of 1793 the Republicans had lost every major battle: Hamilton's fiscal program, topped off by the National Bank, was now riveted in place;

Washington's neutrality proclamation was the accepted foundation for American foreign policy; the Genet fiasco had undermined Republican efforts to mobilize public opinion in support of a French-leaning version of neutrality. As Jefferson looked back on this moment a few years later, he cringed at the memory of cabinet meetings that forced him, as he described it, "to descend daily into the arena like a gladiator to suffer martyrdom in every conflict." The string of defeats was especially frustrating to Jefferson because it flew in the face of his conviction that the vast majority of American citizens—at one point he described the breakdown as five hundred to one—was staunchly Republican. The winds of history were supposed to be at his back, but Federalist gusts kept blowing the ship of state further out to sea. As Jefferson saw it, this defiance of the natural order only confirmed Federalist skulduggery.[40]

In June of 1793 he apprised Madison that he was simply not cut out for this kind of protracted political infighting; as he rather elegantly put it, "the motion of my blood no longer keeps time with the tumult of the world." Though willing to stay on as secretary of state until a suitable replacement could be found, he told several friends that his soul was back at Monticello, already "liberated from the hated occupation of politics," eager to remain "in the bosom of my family, my farm, and my books." Monticello had always been his preferred destination in life, the place where the bucolic rhythms matched his own pulse. "I hope to spend the remainder of my days," he explained, "in occupations infinitely more pleasing than those to which I have sacrificed 18 years of the prime of my life."[41]

Incantations of virtuous retirement to rural solitude were a familiar and even formulaic refrain, especially within the planter aristocracy of Virginia. The classical models of Cicero and Cincinnatus provided the script, which Jefferson's principled withdrawal from the hurly-burly of politics to the pastoral serenity of Monticello fit perfectly. John Adams had witnessed this retirement scenario on several occasions, and while he did not doubt Jefferson's sincerity in the Ciceronian role, he suspected that, whether he knew it or not, Jefferson was merely going home to lick his wounds in seclusion and eventually launch his campaign for the presidency. "It is marvelous," he wrote to Abigail, "how political plants grow in the shade."[42]

As events were soon to demonstrate, Adams understood Jefferson's deepest impulses better than Jefferson himself, whose correspondence throughout most of 1794 suggests a man, as he put it, "totally absorbed in my rural occupations," unwilling to subscribe to any newspapers, obsessed with plans for the rotation of crops rather than the rotation of political power. What he could not acknowledge, and Adams had shrewdly predicted, was that he remained, alongside Madison, the co-leader of the Republican Party, not so much retired as on sabbatical.[43]

In effect, Jefferson and Madison had switched roles, with Madison now reentering the House to assume tactical control of the party battles after a brief retreat to Montpelier, and Jefferson leaving the battlefield to establish strategic headquarters for the Republican Party at Monticello. As it turned out, this was a more suitable arrangement, since Madison was better at the day-by-day infighting and Jefferson better at formulating grand strategy from afar. If there was any doubt who was in charge, Madison resolved it in a letter in the fall of 1794. "I shall always receive your commands with pleasure," Madison wrote, "and continue to drop you a line as decisions come up." The Federalists were now correct to regard Madison as "the General" and Jefferson as "the Generalissimo" of the Republican Party.[44]

During what proved to be Jefferson's three-year interlude at Monticello, the muscles and ligaments of an organized opposition calling itself the Republican Party grew in strength, chiefly by developing candidate slates at the state level and feeling freer to operate in the open as a viable and more confidently legitimate alternative to the Federalists. It helped that Jefferson was no longer inside the tent, an awkward location that had made a covert style almost mandatory. Freneau's *National Gazette* was replaced as the main Republican newspaper by Benjamin Franklin Bache's *Aurora*, which enjoyed a larger circulation and a more flamboyantly partisan editorial policy that went so far on one occasion as to accuse Washington of being a would-be Benedict Arnold during the War for Independence.

During this extended moment, when the very idea of a party system was evolving toward grudging acceptance, if for no other reason than the political culture of the infant republic could find no more palatable way to create an outlet for controversy, three political crises rocked the national government. Although the Republicans, once again, ended up losing each of the arguments, the Federalists paid a price for each of their victories, and the deeper issues separating the two sides became considerably clearer.

The first crisis, which crested in the spring of 1794, came when the British navy began scooping up American merchant ships on the high seas as a part of its naval blockade of France. This posed a dilemma for the government that would recur in 1812, then again in 1916. To wit, when Europe is at war and the United States declares its diplomatic neutrality, how can she sustain commercial relationships with the warring nations without being drawn into the European conflict? As it turned out, this was an inherently insoluble problem, and the Federalists implicitly acknowledged that frustrating fact by offering no workable solution other than hollow protests against British policy.[45]

The Republicans, on the other hand, thought they had a solution. Madison was the chief architect of the plan, which was to declare an embargo on all trade with Britain and France. Looking backward, this represented a new version of the old nonimportation policy of the 1760s and 1770s. Looking forward, it represented an early version of the Embargo Act of 1807. The core idea in all instances was to use America's economic leverage to starve the European powers, most especially Great Britain, into submission. The chief flaw in the plan, which Hamilton was at pains to point out, was that the United States lacked the economic leverage to make it work. Over 75 percent of American trade was with Great Britain, but less than 10 percent of British trade was with America. Moreover, 90 percent of the revenues flowing into the Treasury Department came from customs duties, the vast majority from British imports. Therefore, an embargo was likely to bankrupt the American treasury while having only a minimal impact on the British economy.[46]

That fate was avoided in 1794, because Madison's embargo bill could not make it through the Senate. In the course of the debate, however, two underlying reasons for the party split became clearer: first, Hamilton's British-leaning version of neutrality was rooted in the recognition that the entire American economy depended on sustaining trade with Great Britain, and he was tone-deaf to any political arguments that threatened that connection; second, the Republican French-leaning version of neutrality was rooted in political and ideological affinities with the principles of the French Revolution, and Madison was equivalently tone-deaf to the disastrous economic implications of that preference. Conspicuous by his absence in this unresolved debate was Jefferson, who genuinely relished being embargoed at Monticello, where the rattle of political gunfire in Philadelphia remained a distant echo. A severe attack of rheumatism even forced him to be carried to his harvest fields in a wheelbarrow pushed by two of his most trusted slaves—not just a retired but a temporarily incapacitated Republican warrior.[47]

The second crisis was the so-called Whiskey Rebellion, which played out in the late summer and early fall of 1794. The source of the trouble was an excise tax on whiskey passed by the Congress to help pay off the federal deficit created by the assumption of the state debts. The tax fell most heavily on the farmers of western Pennsylvania, who transported and sold their grain crop in the liquefied form of whiskey to eastern markets. Their representatives in Congress had all voted against the tax, but it had passed the House by an easy majority. This raised an intriguing question: What happens when a regional minority, outvoted at the national level, refuses to recognize the legitimacy of that outcome and challenges the authority of the federal government to enforce the law?[48]

The rebels portrayed themselves as an updated version of the Sons of Liberty, protesting a tax just as vile as the Stamp Act. They also claimed fraternal ties with the French Jacobins, even setting up a mock guillotine at a rally outside Pittsburgh and warning that the leaders of any federal force that came after them would be executed as would-be aristocrats. The ideological breeding ground for the rebellion was a series of local organizations styling themselves the Democratic-Republican Societies, all of which declared their allegiance to the Republican Party, indeed regarded themselves as the militant cutting edge of the reborn revolutionary ethos that the Republicans claimed to represent.[49]

Washington ordered the suppression of the rebels by an enormous demonstration of federal power, in this case twelve thousand militia that Washington himself led westward from Philadelphia, the only occasion in American history when a sitting president commanded troops in the field. The mere approach of such a formidable force crushed the rebellion in an essentially bloodless campaign that enjoyed overwhelming popular support in the nation at large. Washington's report to the Congress was greeted with thunderous applause, to include his reference to "the self-created societies" that wrapped themselves in patriotic rhetoric while, in truth, advocating treason.

For the Republicans it was a repetition of the Genet disaster on a larger scale. From Madison's perspective the entire episode should have been seen as a flagrant display of military coercion reminiscent of British travesties in the 1760s and 1770s, with the rebels cast in the role of American patriots. Instead, another version of the American Revolution had prevailed, with Washington and the militia regarded as the second coming of the Continental Army and the rebels regarded as traitorous Tories. As Jefferson had done in the Genet affair, Madison did not allow his Republican convictions to prevent a thoroughly realistic calculation of Republican interests, which in this case meant quitting the wreck that was the rebel cause before it dragged the Republicans to the bottom.

Down at Monticello, Jefferson's immersion in pastoral serenity allowed him to view this recent defeat with equanimity as another mere way station on the road to inevitable Republican ascendancy. "The time is coming," he comforted Madison, "when we shall fetch up the lee-way of our vessel." In the meantime, the only kind of thinking that captured his attention was his new crop rotation system and the splendid "almost tropical winter" in which there was less snow and ice "as would cool a bottle of wine."[50]

Madison needed to accept the fact that, as Jefferson told him, he was now the designated leader of the Republican interest—Jefferson first wrote "the Southern interest," then crossed it out and changed "Southern" to "Republican"—because there was absolutely no chance he would exchange the splendor of Monticello for the "splendid misery" of Philadelphia: "The little spice of ambition, which I had in my younger days," explained Jefferson, "has long since evaporated. . . . The question is forever closed to me."[51]

The third crisis, greater than the other two combined, accompanied the debate over the Jay Treaty in 1795–96. This proved to be a landmark decision in the history of American foreign policy and an equivalently significant precedent in clarifying the respective roles of the executive branch and the Congress in approving treaties. In the long run most historians have concluded that it was an extremely shrewd decision, for it created a British-leaning version of American neutrality that correctly foresaw the hegemony of the second British Empire and opted for the economic advantages of an Anglo-American alliance instead of the sentimental attachment to France.

Lacking our advantage of hindsight, however, public reaction to the Jay Treaty at the time was overwhelmingly negative. Jay later claimed that he could walk the entire eastern coast of the United States with his way lighted by his own burning effigies. A bit of historical background is necessary to understand the electromagnetic character of the controversy, its role in defining the sides of the party wars, and its influence in bringing Jefferson out of sanctuary at Monticello as the standard-bearer of the Republican Party.[52]

Briefly, late in 1794 Washington appointed Chief Justice John Jay to negotiate a treaty with Great Britain that had three objectives: to avoid the outbreak of war, which was looming because of Britain's confiscation of American ships and seamen; to restore trade with Britain, which was a vital lifeline of the American economy and the chief source of revenue for the federal government; and to settle the outstanding provisions of the Treaty of Paris (1783), to include the removal of British troops from the northwestern frontier and the payment of debts to British creditors, about £2 million, mostly owed by Virginia planters.

Jay returned with a treaty in 1795 that achieved all these objectives, but at the price of endorsing a pro-English version of American neutrality, effectively acknowledging England's naval and economic supremacy in return for the resumption of trade and the avoidance of war. The Americans promised to pay their outstanding debts in return for British evacuation of forts on the frontier. (The Tidewater planters, who preferred to finesse the whole debt issue, regarded this compromise as a betrayal.) Jay probably got the best deal possible, subsequently judged by most scholars as a noble bargain that kept us out of war and worked wonders for the American economy. But the treaty was initially perceived by most citizens as a cowardly condescension to British power and an embarrassing acceptance of neocolonial status within the reconfigured British Empire.

For our purposes, the diplomatic intricacies of the treaty are less important than the political debate it generated between the Federalists and Republicans. After suffering humiliation in the wake of the Whiskey Rebellion, the Republicans were looking for a winning issue, and the unpopularity of the Jay Treaty seemed like the ideal vehicle. They smelled a political opportunity even before Jay was appointed, when Hamilton was being considered as the choice and Republican opposition to the most hated Federalist of all persuaded Washington to go with Jay. An editorial in the *Aurora* then suggested, quite preposterously, that Jay was chosen because Washington wanted the chief justice abroad in order to prevent his own impeachment.

It bears noting, however, that apart from such brazenly partisan arguments on the Republican side, Jefferson honestly believed that America was betting on the wrong horse in the European conflict. "I am convinced they [the French] will triumph completely," Jefferson prophesied, citing the liberating values of the French Revolution as invincible. History proved him wrong on this score, and Jefferson subsequently edited his correspondence to conceal his misjudgment for posterity, but in the crucible of the moment he sincerely believed that the Jay Treaty put the United States on the wrong side of history. His motives for opposing the Jay Treaty were more principled than partisan, though that distinction suggests a clear line in Jefferson's mind that did not exist.[53]

But his arguments against the treaty were partisan in the extreme. Because the Federalists enjoyed a two-to-one advantage in the Senate, Jefferson developed the exotic argument that ultimate authority over all treaties actually resided in the House because it was the most representative branch of the government. The Constitution, of course, said nothing of the sort, but Jefferson apparently believed it *ought* to say that. He predicted that "the popular branch" of Congress was empowered "to rid us of this infamous act, which is really nothing more than a treaty of alliance between England and the Anglomen of this country against the legislature and people of the United States." The more he thought about it, the more Jefferson concluded that presidential authority over foreign policy was inherently monarchical, so the proper remedy lay, as he put it, "in annihilating the whole treaty making power [of the executive branch], except as to making peace."[54]

Whatever one thinks of Jefferson's highly imaginative reading of the Constitution, the heated controversy over the Jay Treaty drew him out of his retirement mode. In late December of 1795 he took out a subscription to the *Aurora*, the main Republican newspaper, in order to follow the debate and began firing off letters to Madison, ordering him to respond to Hamilton's defense of the treaty in the press. The "Generalissimo" was back in charge.[55]

This allowed Madison to assume his more comfortable role as tactician to Jefferson's strategist. Jefferson's imaginative constitutional interpretation required some serious tweaking, and no man on the planet was better at this than Madison. What Jefferson really wanted to say, Madison suggested, was not that all treaty-making power resided in the House, but rather that House control over all money bills allowed it to block all treaty provisions requiring federal funding. This was a more indirect but elegant way of achieving the same end, and it became the Republican strategy throughout the spring of 1796. A milestone in the history of political parties occurred in March, when the Republican members of the House met in caucus for the first time, thus making official and explicit what had previously been surreptitious and covert.[56]

Back at Republican headquarters at Monticello, Jefferson, now fully engaged, claimed that he had "never known the public pulse beat so full and in such universal union on any subject since the declaration of Independence." Unlike the Genet fiasco and the Whiskey Rebellion conflict, this was a debate the Republicans could not lose, in part because the vast majority of the American people clearly opposed the Jay Treaty, in part because the Republicans had the votes in the House to kill it. But April lived up to its later reputation as the cruelest month, at least for the Republicans, most especially Madison, who was leading the floor fight in the House. On April 18 he informed Jefferson that "our majority has melted." The vote was going to be extremely close because the "monocrats," "Tories," "monarchists," and "fiscal party" were practicing their political witchcraft to cast a spell over "the people."[57]

On May 1, 1796, Madison wrote Jefferson to deliver the dreadful news that the Jay Treaty had passed by a narrow majority (51–48). From a Republican point of view it was incomprehensible, and Madison, on the front lines throughout the debate, acknowledged that "this business throughout has to me been the most worrying and vexatious that I have ever encountered." In fact, the defeat was so humiliating that Madison, like Jefferson before him, resolved to retire from the party wars and seek the solace of the bucolic life at Montpelier. "A crisis, which ought to have been managed as to fortify the Republican cause," Madison lamented, "has left it in a very crippled condition."[58]

Further removed from the political battlefield, and therefore more capable of detachment, Jefferson saw a silver lining in this dark cloud: "The Anglomen have at length got their treaty through," he observed, "and so far have triumphed over the cause of republicanism. Yet it has been to them a dear bought victory." Passage of the Jay Treaty would remain a liability for the Federalists for the simple reason that the vast majority of the citizenry despised the English. Whatever strategic calculation Hamilton and the Federalists made to justify an Anglo-American partnership, no matter how shrewd for long-range economic reasons it might become, any treaty with the British leviathan ran against the American grain.

Moreover, in this particular case it was abundantly clear that the Federalists had triumphed against the popular will for one reason. It all came down to one man: "They see that nothing can support them but the Colossus of the President's merits with the people, and the moment he retires, that his successor, if a Monocrat, will be overborne by the republican sense. . . . In the meantime, patience." Instead of panicking, all true Republicans needed to wait for Washington's imminent retirement, which would then allow the natural forces to flow freely without his massive reputation to deflect them. "In the meantime," Jefferson advised, "Republicanism must lie on its oars."[59]

Madison recognized this as excellent advice, all the more persuasive because the bruising and losing battle over the Jay Treaty had left him so fatigued that any recommendation of rest had the immediate ring of truth. But before he retreated to Montpelier, he felt obliged to dispense one piece of advice of his own to Jefferson. It was the kind of intimate message best delivered in person, or "best reserved for some other occasion, perhaps for the latitude of a free conversation." But whenever the proper occasion presented itself, "you ought to be preparing yourself," he wrote Jefferson, "to hear truths which no inflexibility will be able to withstand." The inescapable truth was that, whether he liked it or not, the Republicans fully intended to make him their candidate for the presidency the following fall.[60]

A FORTUNATE FALL

MULTIPLE CONVERSATIONS, all unrecorded, had obviously been occurring within the Republican camp throughout the spring of 1796. Even earlier, during the preceding fall, Aaron Burr had visited Jefferson at Monticello to discuss New York's electoral votes in the next presidential election. But while the competition between two political parties was now taken for granted, none of the institutionalized hallmarks of a modern two-party system—political primaries, nominating conventions, orchestrated campaigns—had yet been born. So the manner in which Jefferson's candidacy had been decided—perhaps "decided" is not quite the correct word, for it more accurately "happened"—is just as impossible to recover as all those unrecorded conversations that produced it.

The selection of Adams on the Federalist side had long been a foregone conclusion, since he had been waiting in the wings as vice president, at times somewhat impatiently, for eight years. According to Madison, Jefferson's selection on the Republican side was just as foreordained despite his Ciceronian vows of retirement. He was universally regarded as the titular leader of the Republican Party, so obviously that no votes needed to be taken. He also possessed impeccable revolutionary credentials, still an essential prerequisite that Adams could claim with equivalent luster. So in this highly improvisational and rather surreptitious fashion, by the summer of 1796 all the newspapers concurred that the successor to the irreplaceable Washington was going to be either Adams or Jefferson.

One of the beauties of what we might call stealth-styled politics is that it never required Jefferson to acknowledge his candidacy to others or even to himself. All his statements, in fact, reiterated his deep distaste for the slings and arrows of political life: "I have no ambition to govern men," he declared, "no passion which would lead me to delight to ride in a storm." He was in a kind of Jeffersonian zone, denying any interest in public office, refusing to acknowledge that Madison was promoting his candidacy and counting electoral votes on a state-by-state basis.

Madison recognized this denial mechanism right away, and decided not to have any direct contact with Jefferson throughout the summer of 1796 in order to avoid a conversation that might confront Jefferson with the political facts. "I have not seen Jefferson," Madison explained, "and have thought it best to present him no opportunity of protesting to his friend against being embarked in this contest." Madison's calculated discretion allowed Jefferson to claim with total sincerity (e.g., "On my salvation I declare it") that he was utterly oblivious to the campaign being mounted on his behalf.[61]

As bizarre as such behavior might seem to us, at the time it represented only a slight extension of long-standing political etiquette. Washington had engaged in similar denials in the first presidential election. Anyone who actively campaigned for political office in the late eighteenth century was considered unworthy to serve, because the act of promoting oneself was regarded as a statement of personal ambition at odds with the qualities required for public service. To be sure, Jefferson carried this etiquette to a new level of purity by refusing even to recognize his own candidacy. (Washington had refused to talk about it, but never claimed he was unaware of it.)

While in part a function of the multitracked Jefferson psyche, the denial syndrome also reflected the prevailing unease with the partisan

character of a two-party system, which defied the entire classical tradition of political leadership, which was resolutely bipartisan. In that sense
Jefferson's psychic agility during the summer of 1796 was symptomatic of
a larger form of evasiveness, since party politics retained the stigma of
moral failure and could flourish only in a political atmosphere where no
one candidly acknowledged what they were doing.

While Jefferson focused on his drainage ditches and vetch crop at
Monticello, Madison was in regular contact with Republican operatives
in each state, focusing primarily on the key states of New York, Pennsylvania, and South Carolina, counting the prospective electoral votes. As
the voting proceeded and the returns began to come in, Madison wrote
in code to Jefferson, predicting a very close contest that Adams would
win by a whisker: "You must reconcile yourself to the secondary as well
as the primary station, if that should be your lot." (In an electoral system
that did not foresee political parties, voters chose two candidates rather
than a party ticket of two candidates, and the runner-up became vice
president.) Madison apparently worried that Jefferson might reject the
vice presidency, sending another coded letter pleading, "You must not
refuse the station which is likely to be your lot. . . . You must not with-
draw yourself."[62]

Jefferson's response seemed to confirm that his Ciceronian pose of
political indifference was more than just a pose. "I am unable to decide
in my own mind whether I had rather have it or not have it," he confessed to Madison about the vice presidency. But if there should be a tie,
he wanted it known that Adams deserved to win: "I am his junior in life,
was his junior in Congress, his junior in the diplomatic line, his junior
lately in the civil government." He wrote Adams in the same vein,
acknowledging his superior claim to the presidency by right of seniority
and reiterating his lack of political ambition: "I have no ambition to
govern men," he explained. "It is a painful and thankless task." If he had
to serve, and he preferred not to do so, the vice presidency was actually
preferable because it would allow him to spend more time back at
Monticello. In the meantime, he would brush up on his knowledge of
parliamentary procedure so as to perform his inconsequential duties as
president pro tem of the Senate.[63]

This was a classic Jeffersonian assertion, simultaneously sincere and misleading. For beneath the heartfelt expressions of generosity toward Adams, Jefferson harbored a calculated and ultimately correct diagnosis of the impossible burdens that would befall anyone who succeeded Washington, who enjoyed his customary good fortune, as Jefferson put it, "to get off just as the bubble was bursting, leaving others to hold the bag." When the Adams electoral victory became official (72–69), Jefferson expressed relief: "I know well that no man will ever bring out of that office the reputation which carries him into it. . . . This is certainly not a moment to covet the helm." Given the cascade of domestic and foreign problems sure to land on Washington's successor, best to let Adams and the Federalists bear the brunt of the inevitable political fallout. The Republicans, in effect, had been lucky to lose.[64]

Jefferson was thinking like a savvy party leader at this propitious moment, but Adams, who fully recognized what might be called "the shadow of Washington" problem, was still thinking in bipartisan terms. He sent out feelers indicating his instinct to appoint Madison as the American ambassador to France, a bipartisan gesture that Madison regarded as disingenuous, claiming Adams must have known that he would decline the offer. Ultimately the post went to another staunch Republican, James Monroe, who conducted himself accordingly as a kind of American version of Genet in Paris, urging opposition to all the Adams efforts at neutrality.

But the biggest bipartisan effort was aimed at Jefferson. Through several intermediaries Adams let it be known that he wished to give Jefferson full cabinet status, an equal say in foreign policy, and enhanced political status just short of co-president. By bringing the chief Republican leader into the councils of power, Adams hoped to end the partisan warfare and put together a political coalition that stood at least a fighting chance to replace the irreplaceable Washington.[65]

Jefferson's first reaction was conciliatory. He drafted a poignant letter to Adams, recalling their previous battles against British tyranny, reiterating his honest conviction that Adams deserved the presidency more than he. This left the door open for an Adams-Jefferson coalition presidency. But before he sent the letter he decided to run it past Madison, who advised that Jefferson's long-standing friendship with Adams must not take precedence over the long-term interests of the Republican Party. "Considering the probability that Mr. A's course of administration may force our opposition to it from the Republican quarter," Madison wrote, "there may be real embarrassments from giving written possession to him, of the degree of compliment and confidence which your personal delicacy and friendship have suggested."[66]

Madison was telling Jefferson that he had to choose between his affection for Adams and his loyalty to the Republican agenda. This was not an easy choice for Jefferson, who reminded Madison that "Mr. A. and myself were cordial friends from the beginning of the revolution." Even though they found themselves on different sides in the party wars of the 1790s, Jefferson never doubted Adams's integrity. He also wanted Adams to know that he was genuinely relieved when Adams won the election, "and have not a wish that he stands in the way of." But he agreed with Madison that sending the letter to Adams would be a political mistake. His ultimate allegiance must be to the Republican cause, which must oppose every Adams policy from outside rather than attempt to influence it from the inside.[67]

THE ELECTION OF 1796 is a fitting end point for our telling of the story—if not quite the beginning of the end, at least the end of the beginning. The process that began in 1791 with the "botanical excursion" up the Hudson by Jefferson and Madison might be regarded as the conception, and the election of 1796 as the birth of an opposition party with an alternative political agenda, a different understanding of what the American Revolution meant, a viable candidate for the presidency, and a conviction that partisan politics was an unavoidable and even essential ingredient in America's republican experiment. Though Adams never grasped the point, and his resistance was a noble but naive refusal to abandon the classical model that proved suicidal for his presidency, Jefferson was clairvoyant when he predicted that, from this time forward, "the president of the United States will only be the president of a party." In effect, the party pattern was set.[68]

Finally, there is an admittedly idiosyncratic but particularly poignant reason for selecting this moment to end our story. On the evening before the Adams inauguration, Adams and Jefferson joined Washington at the presidential mansion, then walked down Market Street together. By then Jefferson had made it clear that he was unwilling to work alongside Adams in a coalition presidency. And Adams had learned that his entire cabinet threatened to resign if Jefferson were included in their deliberations. They parted company at Market and Fifth, only a few blocks from the apartment where Jefferson had drafted the Declaration of Independence that Adams had so eloquently defended in the Continental Congress. As Jefferson recalled it, "We took leave and he never after that said one word to me or ever consulted me as to any measure of the government." It was the end of an era.[69]

The era destined to replace it made partisanship, as embodied in rival parties, the new norm, and the bipartisan ideal of Washington and Adams became a political relic to be saluted and celebrated, but only as a nostalgic irrelevancy. Unlike Washington and Adams, Jefferson understood where history was headed, though even he found it difficult to acknowledge his de facto role as a party leader. The binary categories through which he filtered experience remained defiantly moralistic— Whig versus Tory, good versus evil, white versus black. And within that scheme the Federalists remained the evil empire that he hoped "to sink . . . into an abyss from which there shall be no resurrection of it." In that sense, Jefferson took party politics to the doorway of modernity, but he himself could not walk through it.[70]

CHAPTER SIX

{ The Purchase }

T HE STORY OF the Louisiana Purchase has as many twists and turns as the Mississippi itself, and the biggest challenge in retelling it is to avoid getting caught in the diplomatic backwaters, where clerks chatter endlessly about minutiae. But just as sure as the Gulf of Mexico is the final destination of the Mississippi, the story of the Purchase flows inevitably toward a providential sense of American destiny as a continental empire, what Jefferson, with unintentional irony, called "an empire of liberty."[1]

Even the all-time American champion of historical irony, Henry Adams, acknowledged that the Louisiana Purchase, in the end, was a triumph on a par with the winning of independence and the adoption of the Constitution. Frederick Jackson Turner, the founding father of western history, also described the Purchase as the formative event in the national narrative: "Having taken the decisive stride across the Mississippi, the United States enlarged the horizon of her views, and marched steadily forward to the possession of the Pacific Ocean. From this event dates the rise of the United States into a position of world power."[2]

At least on the face of it, this triumphal tone seems wholly justified. For $15 million—the rough equivalent of $260 million today—the United States doubled its size, adding what is now the American midwest to the national domain, all the land from the Mississippi to the Rocky Mountains and the Canadian border to the Gulf of Mexico. At less than 4 cents an acre, the Purchase became the most lucrative real estate transaction in American history, easily besting the purchase of Manhattan for $24. Without quite knowing it, the United States had acquired the most fertile tract of land of its size on the planet, making it self-sufficient in food in the nineteenth century and the agrarian super-power in the twentieth.[3]

There was more. Politically, the Louisiana Purchase was the most consequential executive decision in American history, rivaled only by Harry Truman's decision to drop the atomic bomb in 1945. The fact that the man who made the decision, Thomas Jefferson, was on record as believing that any energetic projection of executive power was a monarchical act only enhanced the irony. Strategically, the Purchase opened a new chapter in American national security by removing, in one fell swoop, all British and French imperial ambitions in North America.

Spain remained the only European power blocking American expansion to the Pacific, and Spain was not so much a threatening power as a convenient presence, in effect a holding company awaiting an American takeover at the appropriate time. Although the term "manifest destiny" had not yet been coined, the Purchase made the idea itself another one of those self-evident Jeffersonian truths. A colossal and fully continental American empire was now almost inevitable. If the Mississippi ends at New Orleans and the Gulf of Mexico, the story of the Purchase (at least its triumphal version) ends at the Pacific.[4]

As befits an epic, there is an all-star international cast. On the American side, there are Thomas Jefferson and James Madison, working their collaborative magic again, this time on the foreign policy front. The Parisian delegation is headed by James Monroe, perhaps the most loyal Jefferson protégé of all, and Robert Livingston, a member of New York's baronial elite who actually sealed the deal. On the French side, no less a star than Napoleon Bonaparte heads the bill, already the most famous and feared man in the world, described by Henry Adams as "Milton's Satan on his throne of state." His supporting cast is led by Charles-Maurice de Talleyrand-Périgord, simultaneously the most brilliant and unscrupulous diplomat in Europe, the kind of man who considered

Machiavelli naive. Finally, the supporting cast includes the greatest black leader of the age, Toussaint L'Ouverture, the ex-slave turned "black Spartacus" of Santo Domingo, without whom the Purchase would never have happened.[5]

Unfortunately, the various versions of the story have all been driven by the simplistic urge to assign credit to one person or another. Most of Jefferson's biographers describe his management of the diplomacy as a tour de force, on a par with his inspirational role as author of the magic words of the Declaration of Independence. Other historians claim that Napoleon was the major player, that he, rather impetuously, "threw the province" at Jefferson and the American negotiators, that they "caught it and held it, and share between them equally—whatever credit there was." Alexander Hamilton, not one disposed to acknowledge Jefferson's brilliance, insisted that the story of the Purchase was really a tale about dumb luck. "Every man possessed of the least candor and reflection," observed Hamilton, "will readily acknowledge that the acquisition has been solely owing to the fortuitous concurrence of unforeseen and unexpected circumstances, and not to any wise or vigorous measures on the part of the American government."[6]

Though blatantly partisan, Hamilton's assessment does have the virtue of its anti-Jefferson prejudices, for it calls attention to the multiple ingredients in the diplomatic equation beyond any single player's control. In that sense the Louisiana Purchase was like the perfect storm in which European clouds, Caribbean winds, and North America's prevailing westerlies converged in one place at one time. Jefferson's genius was to seize that time, to recognize that acquiring an empire required an imperial president. Given the peaceful way the Purchase occurred, it might be more accurate to think of it as the perfect calm, and of Jefferson's greatest diplomatic talent as the patience to stand still while history formed around him.

Given the triumphal tone of most histories of the Purchase, and the somewhat silly scramble to assign credit for the triumph, it is curious that Jefferson himself made a point of not listing it on his tombstone as one of his proudest achievements. Nor did he list his presidency, in which the Purchase was unquestionably his singular accomplishment. As we shall see, there were several reasons for this omission, and modesty was not one of them.

Perhaps the best way to put it is that there is a tragic as well as triumphal version of the story. As one version moved gloriously and inexorably toward the Pacific, the other moved ominously and just as inexorably toward the Civil War, whose immediate cause was the debate over slavery in the territory Jefferson had done so much to acquire. Indeed, the tragedy was double-barreled, since the Louisiana Purchase also proved to be the death knell for any Indian presence east of the Mississippi. And since the failure to end slavery and the failure to preserve and protect the indigenous peoples of North America were the two great stains on the legacy of the founding generation, the fact that the Purchase locked these failures into place was not an achievement Jefferson wished to advertise.

We could begin the story around 15,000 B.C., with the retreat of the glacial ice that formed the Mississippi Valley. But since we are doing history rather than geology, a more appropriate starting line is March 6, 1801, as Jefferson ascended to the presidency after one of the most controversial elections in American history. In his inaugural address, destined to become one of the best in the genre, he outlined the principles that would guide him, which were essentially the same principles that had shaped the agenda of the Republican Party over the past decade: "A wise and frugal government which . . . shall not take from the mouth of labour the bread it has earned"; a reduction of the national debt, made possible by a slashing of all federal budgets and a transfer of all domestic policies to the states; an innocuous and almost invisible executive branch, rendered even more inconspicuous by Jefferson's decision to file all presidential correspondence with the relevant cabinet officers in order to eliminate even a presidential paper trail. These were "the ancient Whig principles," the values of "pure republicanism" that the Federalists had betrayed, what Henry Adams called "the strange hymn" that Americans "had learned to chant with their chief." These were the cherished principles Jefferson proclaimed. He was about to violate every one of them.[7]

JEFFERSONIAN VISTAS

ALTHOUGH JEFFERSON never traveled further west than the Natural Bridge in the Shenandoah Valley, he shared with most Virginians, including Washington, the keen sense that Europe was the past and the American west was the future. The portico at Monticello faced west, just as the piazza at Mount Vernon faced the Potomac, which both men misguidedly believed to be the providentially placed water route over the Alleghenies into the interior, linking with the Ohio and then flowing into the Mississippi Valley. (The Mississippi, of course, was the mother lode, as Madison once put it, "the Hudson, the Delaware, the Potomac, and all the navigable rivers of the Atlantic states, formed into one stream.") This early version of "Potomac fever" proved to be a hallucination—providence had somehow failed to provide a navigable water route from the Atlantic coast to the interior—but this inconvenient fact did little to deflect the westward flow of Jefferson's thinking, which, as it turned out, was even more grandiose than Washington's.[8]

A few months after he took office, Jefferson shared his vision with James Monroe, then serving as governor of Virginia: "It is impossible not to look forward to distant times," Jefferson observed, "when our rapid multiplication will . . . cover the whole northern, if not the southern continent with a people speaking the same language, governed in similar forms, and by similar laws; nor can we contemplate with satisfaction either blot or mixture on that surface." By "blot or mixture" Jefferson did not mean Native Americans, who could be assimilated if only they abandoned their tribal mores for the more confined space required by farming. (If they refused to do so, well, that was their choice, for which they must suffer the tragic consequences.) The prospective blots were the blacks, who could not be assimilated and must be shipped back to Africa or to some location in the West Indies, where, in Jefferson's view, "nature seems to have formed these islands, to become the receptacle of the blacks transplanted into this hemisphere." It seems safe to say, then, that Jefferson's pre-Purchase view of the American west was breathtakingly bold, presumptively imperialistic, and thoroughly racist.[9]

This Jeffersonian vision depended upon two crucial assumptions. At the time of his election, the census of 1800 revealed a total population of slightly more than five million, with about 500,000 residing west of the Alleghenies. Jefferson assumed that the western population would steadily swell and move the frontier gradually but inexorably forward to the Mississippi and beyond. Unlike Washington, he did not believe that this wave of settlers could or should be managed by the federal government. It was like a force of nature that must be allowed its own momentum. The lands to the west did not need to be conquered by armies, but rather occupied by settlers. In that sense, it was demography that made American destiny so manifest. The only role for government was to stay out of the way and allow the wave to roll westward.[10]

The second assumption was that the only European power with a substantial presence on the North American continent would be Spain. A map of the Spanish Empire in the Western Hemisphere in 1800 made Spain's colonial empire appear gigantic, including Florida, the Gulf Coast, and all the land west of the Mississippi to the Pacific, not to mention Mexico and much of South America. But the map was deceptive in its grandeur because Spain was a hollowed-out imperial power, in decline since the defeat of the Spanish Armada in 1588.

By 1800 the treasury in Madrid was empty, the Spanish army and navy were harmless pretenders, and the once proud diplomatic corps was adept only at posturing. "Spain is the most proper European nation," observed one American diplomat, "to possess a great empire with insignificance." Jefferson concurred: "We consider her possession of the adjacent country as the most favorable to our interests," he remarked, "and should see with extreme pain any other nation substituted for them." His only fear was that the Spanish Empire was so weak that it would abandon its American colonies "before our population can be sufficiently advanced to gain it from them piece by piece." Spain was like an elderly mother hen, sitting the nest until the Americans arrived to relieve her.[11]

Jefferson's continental calculus was confounded by a message he received from Secretary of State Madison only three weeks after the inauguration. The American ambassador to Great Britain, Rufus King, reported reliable rumors circulating in London that Spain had signed a secret treaty, ceding fully half of her North American colonies to France. If true, this transformed the entire strategic chemistry in North America by replacing the most feeble European nation with what had become under Napoleon the most potent military power on earth. For several months Jefferson monitored reports from Europe, most of which tended to confirm that Napoleon fully intended to reestablish the French Empire in America. Jefferson could only hope they were untrue. "I am willing to hope," Jefferson sighed, "as long as anybody will hope with me."[12]

By the spring of 1803, all such hoping had become a sentimental extravagance, since the secret treaty ceding Louisiana to France had become the worst-kept secret in Europe. (Talleyrand, true to his duty and his reputation for duplicity, denied all the rumors as outrageous fabrications.) By April of 1803 Jefferson had decided that the time for hoping had ended and the time for action had begun.

Pushing the quite capable Madison aside, Jefferson chose to become his own secretary of state. "I cannot forbear recurring to it personally," he explained to Robert Livingston, the American minister in Paris, "so deep is the impression it makes on my mind." For the simple truth was that the French occupation of Louisiana would be an unmitigated calamity for the United States, constituting the greatest threat to American destiny since the Revolutionary War: "It completely reverses all the political relations of the United States and will form a new epoch in our political course. . . . There is on the globe one single spot, the possessor of which is our natural and habitual enemy. It is New Orleans." Spanish control of New Orleans was not threatening, since—Spain being Spain— the outcome of a conflict was certain. But French possession was another matter altogether. "From that moment," wrote Jefferson, "we must marry ourselves to the British fleet and nation."[13]

This was an extraordinary statement coming from Jefferson, whose entire career as minister to France, secretary of state, and leader of the Republican opposition to the Jay Treaty had consistently favored France over Great Britain as America's most reliable European ally. But he was prepared to reverse himself once France became a threatening presence on the North American continent and a formidable challenge to America's demographic destiny.

Jefferson then made an extremely shrewd observation. On the face of it, a war with France was a suicidal venture, given the enormous discrepancy in military and economic resources. But all such assessments were irrelevant and misleading, "for however greater her force is than ours, compared in the abstract, it is nothing compared to ours, when to be exerted on our own soil." If Napoleon attempted to establish a French Empire in America by force of arms, he would encounter the same dilemma as the British in the War for Independence, marching hither and yon among a hostile population over a space even more immense. Livingston was instructed to apprise the French that if they attempted to occupy the Louisiana Territory, they would suffer the same fate as the British, for space and numbers were both on the American side.[14]

Any European nation that threatened Napoleon in this fashion usually found itself defeated and occupied. But space—both the Atlantic Ocean and the sheer vastness of the American interior—was a priceless strategic asset that no European nation could match. (The only exception was Russia, as Napoleon would discover at considerable cost a decade later.) Jefferson practiced what has come to be called "back-channel diplomacy" by soliciting the assistance of a prominent French aristocrat, Pierre Samuel Du Pont de Nemours, to carry Livingston's instructions back to Paris and then to quietly disseminate within the corridors of power the same threatening message conveyed to Livingston. "If France proceeds to possess New Orleans," Jefferson told Du Pont, "we must marry ourselves to the British fleet and nation." Though this had the clear ring of an ultimatum, Jefferson wanted Du Pont—and eventually Napoleon—to know that he regarded war with France as a last resort. "You know how much I value peace," he explained, "and how unwillingly I should see any event take place that would render war a necessary recourse."[15]

Jefferson was utterly sincere on this score, since war, even a successful war, would completely destroy his domestic agenda of debt reduction and minimalist government. And an alliance with Great Britain would contradict every foreign policy principle he had ever championed. (It did not help that he regarded the entire British nation as the epicenter for global tyranny.) Indeed, it is entirely possible that Jefferson's war threat was actually a bold bluff. (We can never know, because Napoleon never called it.) The preferred alternative for both sides, Jefferson informed Du Pont and Livingston, was a diplomatic resolution of the crisis. The United States was prepared to offer $6 million for the purchase of New Orleans and West Florida (the Gulf Coast from modern-day Pensacola to New Orleans). If Napoleon accepted this offer, the United States was, albeit reluctantly, prepared to accept French possession of the entire Louisiana Territory west of the Mississippi.

This was a huge concession. It is likely, though not certain, that Jefferson regarded any French presence in Louisiana as temporary. Once the advancing wave of American population reached the Mississippi, or, as Jefferson put it, "once we have planted such a population on the Mississippi as will be able to do their own business," the French position would become untenable because the Americans could mobilize an overwhelming force "without the necessity of marching men from the shores of the Atlantic 1500 or 2000 miles hither." Again, space, and more specifically space that was "peopled," was a unique and incalculable strategic advantage that Jefferson was prepared to exploit. But such scenarios all lay in the future. For now, the immediate crisis required a peaceful resolution. It was now in the hands of our man in Paris, Robert Livingston.[16]

NAPOLEONIC VISIONS

WHEN LIVINGSTON presented his credentials to the French court, he was asked if he had ever been to Europe. He responded that he had not, and Napoleon purportedly said, "You have come to a very corrupt world." As a five-year veteran of the Parisian court scene, Jefferson worried that Livingston would come off as the innocent American, lost within the intrigues of the French salon set and the sinister plottings of the inscrutable Talleyrand. "Any American contending by stratagem against those exercised in it from the cradle," Jefferson worried, "would undoubtedly be outwitted by them." For nearly a year Jefferson and Madison kept fretting that the entire future of the American republic rested in the hands of an inexperienced diplomat, a man whose confidential correspondence was often incomprehensible because of his improper use of the cipher and who carried the final burden of not being a Virginian.[17]

They need not have worried. It was true that Livingston was no confidence man in the European diplomatic mode, but he was a man of supreme confidence who could more than hold his own in sessions with Talleyrand, who found him strangely immune to duplicity, the kind of animal who could not be trapped because he always kept himself out of range. Throughout his career, Livingston had demonstrated a surprising knack for showing up where history was happening: serving with Jefferson on the committee that drafted the Declaration of Independence; delivering the oath of office to Washington in his capacity as chancellor of New York; and now representing the United States at a moment when and in a place where the destiny of the infant nation for the foreseeable future would be decided. His baronial estate on the Hudson, called Clermont—Robert Fulton named the first steamboat after it— gave him an aristocratic pedigree as secure as any Virginia grandee, and his survival within the clannish politics of New York gave him an innate sense of political agility. In retrospect, when all was said and done, it is difficult to imagine anyone better equipped or anyone who could have performed his duties more adroitly.[18]

Livingston's first achievement was to confirm that the rumors were in fact true, that Spain had signed a secret treaty ceding the Louisiana Territory to France in return for several duchies in northern Italy, including Parma and Tuscany. (The more precise term is "retrocede," since France had once claimed the territory and even named it after the French king.) Talleyrand was the mastermind of the deal, which envisioned the recovery of the French Empire in North America, a place where French debtors, criminals, and derelicts could be shipped, much like Great Britain subsequently regarded Australia, and a permanent barrier, what Talleyrand called "a wall of brass," to block American expansion or any British effort at reestablishing a dominant presence on the American continent. Finally, Louisiana would become the granary or breadbasket for the highly lucrative French colonies in the Caribbean, chiefly Santo Domingo and Guadeloupe.[19]

It was a vision of Gallic grandeur in the Western Hemisphere appropriately Napoleonic in scope. But in order for the vision to be realized, Livingston reported, the French plan for its implementation needed to work like clockwork. The first ingredient in the plan, maintaining secrecy about the treaty, had already proven impossible. The second ingredient called for the dispatch of a massive French expeditionary force of over 25,000 troops to Santo Domingo, where they would crush the ongoing slave insurrection under the charismatic ex-slave Toussaint L'Ouverture and restore slavery to the island. Then, the third ingredient: the French troops would sail to New Orleans, garrison the city, occupy the west bank of the Mississippi, and present the Americans with a military fait accompli before they had time to mobilize. The man entrusted with the command of the expeditionary force was Charles Leclerc, one of France's ablest officers, who also happened to be Napoleon's brother-in-law. All this Livingston reported in code to Madison and Jefferson two months before Leclerc departed France.[20]

One might think that, upon hearing such news, Jefferson would have called for a substantial increase in the American army and a mobilization of the state militias. But he did neither. In fact, his budget requests for 1803 called for a *reduction* in the size of the army. He was prepared to run a high-stakes gamble against the odds that the French troops would get mired down in Santo Domingo and never make it to New Orleans. "What has been called a surrender of Toussaint to Leclerc," he predicted, "I suspect will in reality be a surrender of Leclerc to Toussaint." This proved to be an extraordinarily shrewd wager, but at the time it appeared to resemble a dangerous brand of wishful thinking.[21]

In the messy way that history happens, the congested diplomatic situation became even more complicated when a midlevel Spanish functionary in New Orleans declared the port closed to all American shipping. When news of this unexpected and startling development reached Washington in January of 1803, it produced a firestorm of protests against Jefferson's aversion to military action. Senator James Ross of Pennsylvania demanded a call-up of fifty thousand militia, who would then march upon and seize New Orleans. Even Jefferson's Republican supporters, not to be outdone, urged the raising of eighty thousand troops and then to "hold them in readiness to march at a moment's warning." Hamilton argued that there were two options: "Negotiate and endeavor to purchase, and if this fails, go to war, or to seize at once on the Floridas and New Orleans, and then negociate." The latter option, he believed, was demonstrably preferable, but required energy and decisiveness, and "for this, alas, Jefferson is not destined."[22]

Still regarding war as a last resort, hopeful that the French troops in Santo Domingo would never reach Louisiana, and convinced that Madrid would soon overrule the decision to close the port of New Orleans to American commerce, Jefferson refused to move. But he did budge. He announced the decision to send James Monroe as his special emissary to join Livingston in Paris. Monroe, who was a former ambassador to France, would be given complete discretionary power to negotiate the purchase of New Orleans and the Floridas. This did not satisfy the saber rattlers in Congress, but it did answer critics who charged the president with the equivalence of criminal negligence in his response to events thus far. When Monroe indicated some reticence in accepting the assignment, Jefferson effectively ordered him to depart on the next ship. "The circumstances are such as to render it impossible to decline," Jefferson observed, adding that "on the event of this mission depends the future destinies of the republic." If he failed to make headway in Paris, Monroe was to proceed across the Channel to London and negotiate an alliance with Great Britain. And those instructions should be leaked to the French press in order to enhance his diplomatic leverage with Talleyrand and Napoleon.[23]

Meanwhile, back in Paris, Livingston was busy doing some leaking of his own. He distributed a memorandum to midlevel diplomats designed to expose the ludicrous lie that no secret treaty with Spain existed. He also revealed that France's scheme to recover its North American empire was common knowledge throughout the capitals of Europe. Livingston then raised questions about the feasibility of the French plan, suggesting that it would drive the United States into the arms of Great Britain, that Louisiana would prove indefensible in the next round of the Napoleonic Wars, and instead of a strategic asset would turn out to be an economic and military albatross. Livingston's leaks received reinforcement when the French press reported the extremely bellicose debates in the United States Senate—Livingston might have leaked these too—indicating that any putative French garrison in New Orleans would be confronted with a massive American military response.[24]

This was deft diplomacy of the highest order, but for the moment it made no difference because, as Livingston explained, Talleyrand remained obstinately wedded to the fiction that there was no secret treaty with Spain, so there was really nothing to negotiate. Then there was the Napoleonic problem: "There is no people, no legislature, no counsellors. One man is everything. He seldom asks advice, and never hears it unasked." The so-called first consul of the French Republic was really the omnipotent emperor of the French Empire, a title made official one year later. Until he decided to abandon his plan for a recovery of France's empire in North America, all diplomacy was essentially meaningless.[25]

CARIBBEAN CATASTROPHE

BECAUSE THE ENTIRE plan for reestablishing France's presence in the Western Hemisphere depended upon Leclerc's success in restoring French control over Santo Domingo, Napoleon assured that Leclerc's expedition enjoyed massive military superiority—a first wave of 25,000 troops, to be followed by a second wave of the same size if necessary. Leclerc's instructions were also brutally explicit. Upon landing his force, he should proclaim his support for Toussaint L'Ouverture and the black insurrectionaries, who had managed to seize control of the island and declare their own emancipation under the banner of "Liberty, Equality, Fraternity." Once securely ensconced and once Toussaint was convinced that Leclerc was an ally, Leclerc should unleash a war of annihilation. A thousand bloodhounds from Jamaica would be provided to hunt down every black rebel, who should be hanged, drowned, decapitated, burned alive over coals, or, for ultimate dramatic effect, crammed in the backside with gunpowder and exploded. Then the infamous Code Noir, institutionalizing all these barbarities, should be restored and the entire black population returned to slavery. When this rather gory mission was accomplished—Napoleon estimated it would take six weeks—Leclerc should transport his troops to New Orleans, where he would soon be reinforced sufficiently to stave off all challenges to the French Empire in America.[26]

The first part of the scheme worked pretty much as planned. Toussaint and the rebel leaders allowed Leclerc's force to land without opposition, though there were divisions in the rebel camp about the wisdom of this act of trust. Toussaint paid the ultimate price for trusting Leclerc, captured at a supposedly secure meeting, then shipped off to a dungeon on the Swiss border, where he died from starvation and exposure within the year. Before departing Santo Domingo, Toussaint warned Leclerc that his capture would make no appreciable difference in the outcome, because the French had no idea what they were up against.

Events soon proved Toussaint's point. Once the black population of Santo Domingo realized that Napoleon's plan called for their reenslavement, Leclerc's mission became impossible. It was a matter of numbers. The black population, two-thirds of African birth and all former slaves, totaled 500,000. (There were another 30,000 mulattoes and 30,000 whites.) This meant that Leclerc's army, even at its high point of nearly 40,000 troops, was outnumbered more than ten to one. Leclerc could not believe it when hundreds of black prisoners strangled themselves to death rather than return to slavery. Women and children laughed at their executioners as they burned to death. Meanwhile, Leclerc's army was virtually annihilated by a combination of black reprisals, yellow fever, and malaria. In his last dispatch to Napoleon before his own death, Leclerc minced no words: "This colony is lost and you will never regain it. . . . My letter will surprise you, but what general could calculate on the mortality of four-fifths of his army." It was a catastrophe for the French army, which kept pouring troops into the breach and eventually suffered over 60,000 casualties. For obvious reasons, no French expeditionary force ever made it to New Orleans.[27]

As the earthly embodiment of the all-or-nothing style, Napoleon immediately recognized that the debacle in Santo Domingo changed everything. In April of 1803 he apprised Talleyrand of his intention to sell the entire Louisiana Territory: "I renounce Louisiana," he declared.

"It is not only New Orleans that I will cede, it is the whole colony without any reservation. I know the price of what I abandon. . . . I renounce it with the greatest regret. But to attempt obstinately to retain it would be folly." When warned by his advisors that his decision was likely to establish the foundation for a rising American empire, Napoleon dismissed the warning as too farsighted: "In two or three centuries the Americans may be found too powerful for Europe . . . but my foresight does not embrace such remote fears." His immediate problem was gearing up for war with the current colossus, Great Britain.[28]

There was then the famous bath scene, where Napoleon lay in his tub, the water sprinkled with cologne, when his two brothers came in and accused him of impetuosity in deciding to sell all Louisiana. He lacked the authority to make such a huge decision without consulting the elected representatives of the legislature, they insisted, and when the debate in the legislature began, they intended to side with the opposition. "You will have no need to lead the opposition," Napoleon replied, "for I repeat there will be no debate, for the reason that the project . . . conceived by me, negotiated by me, shall be ratified and executed by me, alone. Do you comprehend me?" The big decision had been made, and the only question that remained, best left to the diplomatic accountants, was how much money could be extracted from the Americans. Napoleon indicated that he would be satisfied with 50 million livres, or $12.5 million.[29]

Livingston was the only American in Paris who could make the big decision for the United States. Monroe had just landed in France, carrying full diplomatic authority, but it would take him several days to reach Paris, so Livingston decided to act on his own before Napoleon changed his mind. "The field open to us is infinitely larger than our instructions contemplated," he wrote to Madison, but the opportunity "must not be missed." Although the ultimate cost was sure to be much larger than he was authorized to spend, Livingston presumed that the sale of western land would yield revenues that more than made up the difference. He had to either exceed his instructions or allow the opportunity to pass. By the time Monroe arrived in Paris, Livingston had already committed the United States. All that remained was haggling over the price. On May 5,

1803, both sides agreed to the sale of the entire Louisiana Territory for 80 million francs, or $15 million. Napoleon got more than he expected and the Americans got an unexpected empire. Word of the Purchase reached Washington on July 3, 1803, so the celebration the following day coincided with the anniversary of American independence, thereby enhancing the prevalent sense of destiny in the air.[30]

A NOBLE BARGAIN

IN WHAT AMOUNTED to an eerily prescient act of anticipation, Jefferson had already decided to find out what lay within the immense region west of the Mississippi months before he bought it or even knew it was for sale. In January of 1803, as part of an innocuous bill establishing trading posts with Indian tribes on the Mississippi, he requested that Congress include a secret provision authorizing him to dispatch "an intelligent officer with ten or twelve chosen men" into the North American version of outer space. What became justifiably famous as the Lewis and Clark expedition, perhaps the greatest exploratory adventure in American history, actually began as a covert intelligence operation of dubious legality. Jefferson chose Meriwether Lewis, his private secretary, to lead the mission, which was described as "a literary and scientific pursuit" in order to conceal its real purpose: "The idea that you are going to explore the Mississippi has been generally given out," Jefferson explained to Lewis. "It satisfies public curiosity and masks sufficiently the real destination," which was in fact the Pacific Ocean. (In a far western version of his Potomac dream, Jefferson believed that providence must have placed a river route across the continent that Lewis could discover.) Lewis was already launched when Jefferson apprised him that he would now be exploring land that the United States actually owned.[31]

In August Jefferson retired for two months to Monticello, where his library contained more reliable maps of the American west than were available in the capital. As he hunched over these maps, it soon became apparent to him that locating the borders of the Purchase was an interpretive act. Back in Paris, Livingston was also looking at maps and conferring with Talleyrand about the boundaries of what he had just bought: "I can give you no direction," Talleyrand said. "You have made a noble bargain for yourselves, and I suppose you will make the most of it."[32]

Jefferson proceeded to do just that. His highly creative reading revealed that the eastern border of Louisiana was the Perdido River (near present-day Pensacola), so the United States had purchased West Florida (the current Gulf Coast). This imaginative interpretation later prompted Henry Adams to observe that Jefferson "was forced at last to maintain that Spain had retroceded West Florida to France without knowing it, that France had sold it to the United States without suspecting it, that the United States had bought it without paying for it, and that neither France nor Spain, although the original contracting parties, were competent to decide the meaning of their own contract." Once unleashed, Jefferson's expansive instincts roamed southwest to the Rio Grande, where he discovered that the Purchase included all of modern-day Texas.[33]

The Spanish, of course, regarded all such claims as outrageous. Indeed, the Spanish ambassador apprised Madison that the entire Purchase was illegal, since Napoleon and Talleyrand had offered their personal word to the Spanish king that they would never sell Louisiana to another country. This was unquestionably true, Madison replied, but wholly irrelevant from the American perspective, and he might have added that trusting the word of Napoleon or Talleyrand was the diplomatic version of believing in miracles. The deeper truth was that Spain was experiencing the frustrating fate that befalls a once great empire in decline, helplessly watching itself be dismembered.

The question of West Florida lingered on for months, eventually years, but from the very start Jefferson had decided that there was no need to risk war with Spain in pushing the American claims, because Spain's inherent weakness assured that both of the Floridas and Texas would eventually, like ripe fruit, fall into the American lap, as he put it, "all in good time." And though it took longer than Jefferson estimated, that is pretty much what happened.[34]

There is no evidence that Jefferson hunched over the Constitution with the same intensity that he hunched over maps, but there is considerable evidence that constitutional issues weighed heavily on his mind during the summer of 1803. Throughout the 1790s he had labeled the Federalists "monarchists" and insisted that any energetic projection of executive power violated republican principles. Now he had just performed the most aggressive executive action ever by an American president, a projection of executive authority that would stand the test of time as perhaps the boldest in American history. If one wished to acquire an empire, it turned out, one had to become an imperial president.

But Jefferson was extremely uncomfortable in any role that required him to exercise power conspicuously, no matter how worthy the cause. "The Executive," he lamented, "in seizing the fugitive occurrence which so much advances the good of the country, have done an act beyond the Constitution." He compared himself to the guardian of a young ward, in this case the infant American republic. "I thought it my duty to risk myself for you," he explained, in effect placing his custodial duties above his own political principles.[35]

This was a plausibly pragmatic rationale, and one would be hard-pressed to find a single American historian over the next two hundred years who argued that Jefferson should have refused to seize the opportunity that Napoleon presented because of constitutional scruples. In fact, both Madison and Albert Gallatin, his extremely competent secretary of the treasury, tried to convince Jefferson that the Purchase fell within the treaty-making powers of the presidency, which meant it would be completely constitutional once ratified by three-fifths of the Senate. But Jefferson regarded that rationale as a vile Federalist doctrine that he and all devout Republicans, Madison included, had staunchly opposed when Hamilton deployed it to justify the Jay Treaty. For Jefferson, much more than a constitutional scruple was at stake. Limited executive power was the keystone of the entire republican (and Republican) edifice, the central tenet of his political religion. No matter how much grace his executive action conferred upon posterity, there was no getting around the blatant fact that it was a violation of his political creed, in effect a sin.

If we had taken Jefferson aside at this supercharged moment, we could have offered him a measure of consolation based on the advantages of hindsight. First, Jefferson's political faith had taken shape as the ideology of an opposition party. As a weapon to wield against the Federalists, it enjoyed all the advantages that the American revolutionaries enjoyed in discrediting British authority in the 1770s. But once Jefferson and the Republicans rose to power the weapon became a liability, because it effectively rendered the federal government powerless in the domestic sphere and the executive branch the puppet of Congress in foreign policy. Jefferson was loath to face this fact, but republican government at the national level simply could not function if Republican political values were strictly enforced.

Second, looking forward instead of backward, Jefferson's dilemma at the time of the Louisiana Purchase was a preview of coming attractions, most famously Abraham Lincoln's expansion of executive authority during the Civil War and Franklin Roosevelt's bold initiatives during the Great Depression. One of the beauties of the inherently ambiguous definition of executive power in the Constitution was that it could expand or contract like an accordion, making the music required in different historical contexts. Indeed, without the capacity to enlarge presidential power toward monarchical levels of authority, it is difficult to understand how republican government could effectively respond to any genuine crisis. In that sense, Jefferson might have seen himself as a political pioneer, the first but hardly the last president to exploit the ill-defined powers of his office when history required it.

However therapeutic such observations might have proved, they were obviously unavailable to Jefferson at the time. In between his expansive reading of the relevant maps, he devoted himself to the composition of a constitutional amendment, which he considered a somewhat clumsy but utterly essential companion to the treaty itself, indeed the only way to prevent the Louisiana Purchase from becoming a precedent for the kind of unfettered executive and federal power he had spent his whole career opposing. He went back and forth with Madison revising the drafts—and back and forth in his own mind about whether the constitutional amendment had to be ratified before the vote on the treaty or could come afterward. Gallatin tried to persuade him, again, that the cumbersome and time-consuming procedure for ratifying a constitutional amendment was unnecessary, and that the delay it entailed might put the entire Purchase at risk. But Jefferson remained adamant: "I think it will be safer not to permit the enlargement of the Union but by amendment of the Constitution."[36]

The final draft of the amendment Jefferson submitted looks strange to modern eyes, because it did not propose any new legal or constitutional provisions at all. Instead, it merely reiterated that the Louisiana Territory, and Florida "whenever it shall be rightfully obtained," could become parts of the national domain. But from Jefferson's perspective, insistence on a constitutional amendment effectively laundered the Purchase through the ratification process, which required approval by two-thirds of both branches of Congress and three-fourths of the state legislatures. The first part of the ratification process, requiring approval by supermajorities in both houses of Congress, transformed the Purchase from an executive action into a joint executive and congressional action. The second part recognized the sovereignty of the states as equal partners in the Purchase, thereby preserving Jefferson's compact theory of the Constitution.[37]

But Jefferson's best-laid plans fell victim to dispatches from Livingston, who warned that Napoleon was having second thoughts about the treaty and that any delay on the American side would offer him the opportunity to back out. If forced to choose between losing Louisiana or abandoning his constitutional principles, Jefferson never hesitated. "I infer that the less we say about constitutional difficulties respecting Louisiana the better," he wrote Madison, "and that what is necessary for surmounting them must be done sub silentio." This meant moving the treaty through the Congress as quickly as possible, abandoning the idea of a constitutional amendment, and remaining silent about his constitutional reservations. "To lose our country by a scrupulous adherence to written laws," he later observed, "would be to lose the law itself."[38]

More accurately, it would have meant losing Louisiana itself. Always an optimist about the future and the judgment of "the people," Jefferson consoled himself that "the good sense of our country will correct the evil of construction when it shall produce evil effects," meaning the constitutional precedent he was setting would not become a precedent at all, a prediction that proved wrong.[39]

Ratification by the Senate was a foregone conclusion. Once that body was called into special session on October 17, the final vote (21–7) took only three days, and it probably would have occurred even sooner if procedural rules did not require three separate readings for any proposed treaty. Senator William Plumer of New Hampshire, who voted with the minority, somewhat caustically claimed that the treaty received less critical attention "than the most trivial Indian contract." The debate, such as it was, took place under the shadow of doubt about Napoleon's prospective change of mind. (Over in Paris, Monroe made a major contribution by ordering the transfer of $2 million of American stock to France, a down payment that rendered Napoleon's withdrawal less likely.) Given the extraordinary opportunity to double the size of the nation, haggling over details seemed like negotiating with Saint Peter at the pearly gates after God had already admitted you to heaven.[40]

Though perfunctory, the debate was revealing in two senses. First, the New England Federalists, who opposed the treaty, questioned its constitutionality on the same strict-construction grounds that the Republicans had used against the National Bank and the Jay Treaty. And the Republicans, defending it, embraced the more expansive doctrine of implied powers (i.e., the "necessary and proper" clause) that the Federalists had deployed in those earlier controversies. In effect, both sides switched, suggesting that how one interpreted the Constitution was less a matter of principle than a function of one's location in or out of power. Oddly, Jefferson actually agreed with the Federalists, but remained true to his vow of silence.[41]

Second, beyond the shifting sands of the constitutional terrain, the main Federalist argument was that this immense prize was in fact too immense. As Fisher Ames, the philosopher-king of New England federalism, so graphically put it, the great space to the west was really "a great waste, a wilderness unpeopled with any beings except wolves and wandering Indians." Attempting to occupy it was "like sending a comet into infinite space." New England's apprehension, to be sure, was rooted in the fear that its own political influence would dwindle as the union expanded westward. But another part derived from its doubt that the United States could absorb such a massive area without overloading the still fragile republic beyond its capacity to govern, that the union itself would explode as it expanded.[42]

Jefferson dismissed such concerns as splendid examples of the pessimistic temperament one might expect from a region reared on the dark doctrines of Calvin. As he saw it, size was an American asset, not a liability: "The larger our association," he argued, "the less will it be shaken by local passions; and in any view, is it not better that the opposite bank of the Mississippi should be settled by our own brethren and children, than by strangers from another family?" And why was the preservation of the union such an unquestioned priority anyway? "Whether we remain in one confederacy, or form into Atlantic and Mississippi confederacies, I believe not very important to the happiness of either part. Those of the western confederacy will be as much our children and decedents as those of the eastern, and I feel myself as much identified with that country in future time, as with this."[43]

This was an astonishing statement, suggesting as it did that Jefferson did not worry about the assimilation of the Louisiana Territory into the United States because he thought about the process more dynamically, as part of a mutual transformation. The United States would not just integrate the west into the union; instead, the west would integrate the older states into a newer version of America. "By enlarging the empire of liberty," Jefferson wrote, "we multiply its auxiliaries, and provide new sources of renovation, should its principles at any time degenerate in those portions of our country which gave them birth." This was a truly inspirational way of thinking about the American west, and nearly a century later Frederick Jackson Turner would make it the centerpiece of his landmark interpretation of the transformative role of the frontier in American history.[44]

In 1803, however, Jefferson's main goal was to disarm his Federalist critics by challenging their dreary depiction of the Louisiana Territory as some morbid combination of a monstrous weight and the forbidden fruit. It was, he insisted, a beckoning sky under which untold generations would keep rediscovering their own version of the American promise, the geographic equivalent of the Fountain of Youth.

AN IMPERIAL REPUBLIC

IN JEFFERSON'S pre-Purchase view of American westward expansion, the wave of settlers would move gradually but steadily across the continent, reach the Mississippi River in another one or two generations, then continue its march toward the Pacific, a process of "peopling" the far west that would probably take another century. The beauty of this gradualist vision was that demography would do all the work. The process did not need to be managed by government, which needed only to harvest the fruits of inevitable American occupation. Once the population of the new territories reached the requisite size, the Constitution specified that Congress could approve their admission as new states in the union on a par with all the existent states.

The Purchase altered these expectations by replacing a series of small sips with one gigantic gulp. And it suddenly presented the federal government with a massive management problem that could not await the arrival of a somewhat distant demographic wave. The questions were daunting: How should Louisiana be carved up? Who already lived there? What form of government should be installed in the new territories? How should the resident Indian tribes be treated? Most ominously of all, should slavery be permitted or prohibited? Some guidance was provided by Article III of the treaty, drafted by Livingston and Monroe: "The inhabitants of the ceded territory shall be incorporated in the Union of the United States and admitted as soon as possible according to the principles of the Federal Constitution to the enjoyment of all the rights, advantages and immunities of Citizens of the United States, and in the meantime they shall be maintained and protected in the free enjoyment of their liberty, property and the Religion they profess."[45]

This seemed clear enough, and was obviously intended to preclude the possibility that Louisiana should be regarded as an American colony whose residents would be treated as subjects rather than fellow citizens.

France, Spain, and Great Britain could have colonies, but the American republic, by definition, could not. This in turn meant that if the annexation of Louisiana created an American empire, as it quite clearly did, it was a highly unusual and historically unprecedented kind of empire. Jefferson's rather poetical resolution of the nomenclature problem was to coin the term "empire of liberty." This solved everything verbally but nothing politically.

The response of Congress to all the nettlesome questions posed by the Purchase was more prosaic. What was termed "enabling legislation," passed in November of 1803, delegated all responsibility for federal policy in the Louisiana Territory to the president. If Jefferson was troubled by the constitutional implications of his executive action to make the Purchase, he should have been apoplectic about the unlimited authority granted him to implement it. John Quincy Adams, who was the only New England Federalist to vote for the Purchase, led the opposition— feeble as it was—against what he described as Congress's abdication of responsibility, arguing that Jefferson was being granted more arbitrary power than George III ever enjoyed over the American colonies. Adams was always his most eloquent in lost causes, and he thoroughly relished the opportunity to propose that whatever Jefferson should decide for the current residents of Louisiana, it must be specified that they could not be taxed without their consent.

"With more boldness than wisdom," Jefferson confessed, he had decided to draft the new constitution for the Louisiana Territory himself. He wished that fact kept confidential, he informed John Breckenridge of Kentucky, "because you know with what bloody teeth and fangs the federalists will attack any sentiment or principle known to come from me, and what black guardisms and personalities they make it the occasion of vomiting forth." Jefferson was absolutely right to keep his authorship a secret, because his draft constitution proposed a wholly autocratic government and made Louisiana a de facto American colony. (The Federalist press would have had a field day quoting Jefferson's own words in the Declaration back at him.) Even Madison acknowledged that "it will leave the people of that District for a while without the organization of power dictated by the Republican theory."[46]

The entire government would consist of presidential appointees, a governor and a thirteen-person council, which Jefferson suggested be called "the Assembly of Notables" to provide an air of familiarity for the French-speaking residents nostalgic for the ancien régime. A year later, in November of 1804, a delegation from the Louisiana Territory traveled to Washington and presented a remonstrance, protesting their colonial status and lack of any voice in their own government. "Do the political axioms on the Atlantic become problems when transplanted to the Mississippi?" they asked rhetorically. Jefferson never responded, indeed refused even to meet with them. He confided to friends that it was an awkward situation, but the unvarnished truth was that "our new fellow citizens are yet as incapable of self-government as children."[47]

Why Jefferson believed that is an interesting question. In a variety of other contexts, he had reiterated his faith in the capacity of ordinary Americans to understand their political interest more sensibly than their wealthier and better-educated superiors. Jefferson truly believed in the integrity of the ordinary citizenry, and in the inherent fraudulence of all political systems that arbitrarily relegated the common man to inferior status. Why, then, did he regard the roughly fifty thousand non-Indian occupants of the Louisiana Territory, most living in and around New Orleans, as unprepared for citizenship?

One rather revealing clue about his thinking on the score is the insertion of a single word in his proposed constitutional amendment for Louisiana that effectively amended Article III of the treaty. The treaty described the full range of rights enjoyed by "the inhabitants of the ceded territory." Jefferson changed it to "the white inhabitants." Strangely, no one in the Congress or the press remarked on the change at the time, so Jefferson was never forced to explain it. But it does seem plausible, indeed probable, that the Creole character of the residential population—blood mixed for generations among Spanish, French, African, and Native American residents—did not match the picture of American settlers that Jefferson saw in his mind's eye. New Orleans was more like an extension of the Caribbean than a western outpost of the Atlantic coast, especially the black and mulatto population, some of whom were wealthy and socially prominent local leaders, and the mixed bloods that defied clear racial categories. Jefferson preferred binary racial distinctions: blacks and whites. New Orleans confounded his categories. It also did not help that the bulk of the residents—white, black, and mixed—spoke French.[48]

From the very start, Jefferson had envisioned the vast tract north of the Arkansas River all the way to the Canadian border as a huge Indian reservation that would, at least for the foreseeable future, be blocked from white settlement. At first glance, this had the look of an enlightened effort to protect Native American culture along the lines of the Knox-Washington initiative over a decade earlier. But Jefferson was not thinking primarily about creating an enclave for Indian tribes across the Mississippi. (Until Lewis and Clark returned from their exploratory adventure, neither Jefferson nor anyone else was quite sure about the size and location of the trans-Mississippi Indian tribes.) Instead, he envisioned the land north of the Arkansas River as a depository for the tribes of the Ohio Valley and southward, who were currently being overwhelmed by the demographic wave rolling over them.[49]

What came to be called Indian removal could be imagined before the Louisiana Purchase, but it could not be seriously contemplated, for the simple reason that there was no place where the eastern tribes could be relocated. Now there was. Even before the Purchase was finalized, Jefferson had urged governors and military commanders in the Ohio Valley and Mississippi Territory to sign supply contracts designed to drive the Indian tribes into debt in order to accelerate the pace of their impoverishment and desperation, thereby speeding their extinction or removal. "Should any tribe be foolhardy enough to take up the hatchet," he instructed, their behavior should be used as a rationale "to seize the whole country of the tribe, driving them across the Mississippi as an example to others, and a furtherance of our final consolidation."[50]

As a general rule, Jefferson seldom used the word "consolidation" positively. He customarily used it as an epithet to criticize the concentration of political power by the federal government under the Federalists. In this case, however, it referred to the establishment of complete white dominance east of the Mississippi, an inevitability that Jefferson could claim he did not cause, only facilitated.

The Indian homeland west of the Mississippi needed to be huge, because it would eventually have to accommodate all the eastern tribes. Jefferson preferred "Indian exchange" to "Indian removal," arguing against all evidence that the eastern tribes "will be glad to cede us their country here for an equivalent there." The American government could then sell off the vacated Indian land in parcels and "pay the whole debt contracted [to France] before it becomes due." It was almost too good to be true. The Purchase had made Indian removal possible, and Indian removal would provide the revenue required to pay off the Purchase. From the Indian perspective, however, it was too true to be good, for the Louisiana Purchase sealed their doom east of the Mississippi. It is difficult to avoid the conclusion that Jefferson's poetic phrase, like his draft of the Louisiana constitution, required amending. He had indeed created an "empire of liberty," but for whites only.[51]

The triumphal and the tragic versions of the Louisiana Purchase were, therefore, joined at the hip from the very start. Or perhaps it is more accurate to say that they were linked together seamlessly in the depths and shallows of Jefferson's famously elusive mind. The depths were truly and impressively deep: the strategic recognition of America's demographic advantage over the major European powers on the North American continent; the parallel recognition that expanded executive power, despite his long-standing hostility toward its monarchical implications, was a latent constitutional weapon of incalculable value in a national crisis; the ability to move decisively when the shifting weather conditions in the diplomatic world presented a momentary once-in-a-lifetime opportunity.

On the shallow side, however, the list is also depressingly long: the inability to think about any racially mixed presence on the continent as anything other than a blot; the failure to recognize the opportunity presented by the Purchase to revisit the Native American question so as to avoid removal, rather than to exploit it in order to hasten it; the unwillingness to use this extraordinary occasion to promote the possibility of prohibiting the expansion of slavery into the Louisiana Territory. To be sure, it would have required an act of incredible leadership to have raised the forbidden question of slavery, leadership on a par with that demonstrated by Jefferson and the other founders in 1776 and 1787. Though it is somewhat difficult to believe, and the Virginia code of silence about "that species of property" meant that private thoughts and conversations on the subject never found their way into the written record, the evidence that has survived suggests that Jefferson never gave the matter any thought. If true, this was his greatest failure of all, and the tragedy that would come back to haunt his triumph with a vengeance.

THE MISSOURI EPILOGUE

HINDSIGHT HISTORY, sometimes called counterfactual history, is usually not history at all, but most often a condescending game of one-upmanship in which the living play political tricks on the dead, who are not around to defend themselves. At least on the face of it, to accuse Jefferson of failure in refusing to place the abolition of slavery in Louisiana on the political agenda would seem to commit the presentist fallacy in its most blatant form, imposing our own hindsight wisdom on a president trapped in his own time and no more capable of envisioning the Civil War than we are of predicting the effects of global warming.

Except that he was. Jefferson's long-standing position was that slavery was incompatible with the republican values on which the American nation was based, a conviction of considerable credibility since he had composed the most lyrical and memorable statement of what those values were. During his brief time as a delegate to the Confederation Congress, he had proposed a bill, which lost by only one vote, for prohibiting the extension of slavery into *all* the territories, not just the Northwest Territory. And throughout his retirement years at Monticello, he repeatedly condemned slavery as a moral travesty, a violation of all that the American Revolution stood for, the one issue capable of destroying the republican experiment that he and his fellow founders had sacrificed so much to launch. In short, when it comes to the intrinsic evil of slavery, we are not imposing our superior modern sensibilities on an oblivious or time-bound and morally challenged predecessor. Jefferson understood just as fully as we do, indeed *perhaps more so,* that slavery was wrong as well as a permanent stain on the legacy of the entire revolutionary generation.[52]

Once we are absolved of the charge of judging him unfairly against our own superior standards, two questions present themselves: First, what opportunities did the Louisiana Purchase present to put slavery in the United States on the road to extinction? Second, why was Jefferson incapable of seizing those opportunities?

The answer to the first question is reasonably clear. The Louisiana Purchase provided the last realistic opportunity for the United States to implement a policy of gradual emancipation. Two things needed to happen: first, slavery in the Louisiana Territory must be prohibited and abolition made a condition for admission into the union; second, a portion of the enormous revenues destined to accrue to the federal government from the sale of western land must be set aside in a fund for the compensation of slave-owners south of the Potomac and east of the Mississippi, who would free their slaves on an agreed-upon schedule. Many freed slaves would probably remain as hired laborers, so the exploitation of a black underclass would not be ended by this policy. But slavery would. To the extent that ending slavery was primarily an economic problem, the Louisiana Purchase offered a viable solution.[53]

The answer to the second question is more complicated. Part of the explanation is that Jefferson came under no pressure from the Federalist opposition to make slavery in the Louisiana Territory an issue. It never came up in the admittedly perfunctory congressional debate over the treaty, and then the delegation of all authority over Louisiana to the executive branch short-circuited any subsequent debate at the federal level. The Federalist press did sustain its criticism of Jefferson on the racial front, recycling his remarks in *Notes on the State of Virginia* about black biological inferiority, gossiping about his putative sexual relationship with Sally Hemings, charging him with being "the Negro president" because the three-fifths clause had provided him with the electoral votes needed to win. But instead of making slavery in the Louisiana Territory a major item in their opposition, the Federalists opted to plot a secession of the northeastern states from the now vastly expanded union, a fateful and ultimately suicidal decision that left Jefferson free to act toward Louisiana with impunity while the Federalists self-destructed.[54]

We can be absolutely certain how Jefferson himself would have explained his refusal to block the spread of slavery into the trans-Mississippi territories because the issue eventually surfaced in 1819, when Missouri became the first territory acquired in the Purchase to petition for statehood, and Jefferson spelled out his position in considerable detail.

What came to be called the Missouri Question was triggered by an amendment to the bill admitting Missouri into the union that made the prohibition of slavery a condition of statehood. The question, of course, was hardly new; it had been lurking in the political shadows ever since the Louisiana Purchase. Jefferson's position was that the issue ought to remain in the shadows or, shifting his metaphors, should be allowed to pass "like waves in a storm pass under the ship." But as the debate in Congress heated up, and it became clear that this particular wave possessed the potential to capsize the entire ship of state, Jefferson unburdened himself. An old colleague from presidential days who visited him at Monticello described Jefferson as obsessed with the Missouri Question, gesturing dramatically as he walked his fields, warning that this was the one issue that could lead to civil war, the end of the republican experiment with self-government, eventually to "a war of extermination toward the African in our land."[55]

In a justifiably famous letter to John Holmes, a congressman from Massachusetts, Jefferson claimed that the Missouri Question had aroused him "like a fire bell in the night, awakened and filled me with terror." No man on earth wished an end to slavery more than he did, Jefferson insisted, and banishing slavery from the entire United States "would not cost me a second thought, if, in that way a general emancipation and *expatriation* could be affected," meaning a removal of the freed black population back to Africa or some location in the Caribbean. But until a realistic plan to compensate slave-owners and remove the black population could be devised, to raise the slavery question was a treasonable act. At the moment, "we have the wolf by the ears, and we can neither hold him, nor safely let him go." It was a deplorable and, at least as Jefferson saw it, an insoluble dilemma in which "justice is on one scale and self-preservation the other." He concluded his letter to Holmes with the most pessimistic remark about America he ever made: "I regret that I am now to die in the belief, that the useless sacrifice of themselves by the generation of 1776 . . . is to be thrown away by the unwise and unworthy passions of their sons, and that my only consolation is to be, that I shall not live to weep over it."[56]

Biographers of Jefferson and historians of the period have frequently misread this letter, thinking that the "fire bell in the night" for Jefferson was slavery, when in fact it was the act of talking publicly about slavery. In our search for an answer to the question about Jefferson's failure to prohibit the expansion of slavery into the Louisiana Territory, it seems clear that a big part of the answer is that Jefferson believed that doing so would provoke a debate akin to the debate over the Missouri Question, a destructive debate that might lead to civil war. He wished to extend the Virginia code of silence over the entire nation.

In that sense, Jefferson's failure in 1803 to assume a leadership position on the issue of slavery in the territories was not an inadvertent act of negligence, but rather a conscious decision to avoid placing the nation on a road that he firmly believed led to the dismemberment of the union. Fifty years later, when Abraham Lincoln, rather ironically and misguidedly citing Jefferson as his role model, decided to go down the same road, the result was the Civil War, just as Jefferson had predicted.

There are two more pieces to the puzzle that the Missouri Crisis, like a flare in the night, helps to illuminate. As we have seen, Jefferson did not believe that he possessed the constitutional authority to make the Louisiana Purchase, but concluded that the opportunity was too extraordinary to miss merely because of constitutional niceties. Just as he had feared, however, the Purchase became the constitutional precedent for federal sovereignty over the territories, to include the question of slavery. When the southern delegates in Congress challenged the authority of the federal government to impose its will on Missouri, their opponents cited the precedent of the Purchase. John Adams, long retired at Quincy, relished the irony of it all: "That the purchase of Louisiana was unconstitutional or extra Constitutional I never had a doubt," he remarked with bemused satisfaction, "but I think the Southern gentlemen who thought it Constitutional then ought not to think it constitutional to restrain the extension of slavery now."[57]

If anyone had dared to ask Jefferson why he refrained from prohibiting slavery in the Louisiana Territory, he would have claimed that he lacked the constitutional authority to do so. But, and this was the rub that the Missouri Crisis rendered raw, he had exercised that very authority he disclaimed in making the Purchase itself. Like any successful political leader, indeed more than most, Jefferson was accustomed to having it both ways, and when his constitutional inconsistency was tossed back at him, he took refuge in his time-honored charge that the whole Missouri debate was a Federalist plot concocted by New Englanders, who cared not a whit about slavery or slaves but only about eviscerating him.

In an extremely revealing letter to Albert Gallatin in 1820, he simultaneously railed against this Federalist plot and confessed his utter dread at the constitutional precedent he had somehow set establishing federal control over slavery in both the territories and the states: "For if Congress once goes out of the Constitution to arrogate a right of regulating the conditions of the inhabitants of the States," he warned, "its majority may, and probably will, next declare that the condition of all men in the United States shall be that of freedom; in which case all the whites south of the Potomac and Ohio must evacuate their States, and most fortunate those who can do it first."[58]

This apocalyptic prophecy exposed the unspoken reason why Jefferson regarded any extension of federal authority over the states or territories as calamitous, for it would eventually lead to emancipation, which would then lead to racial war. No gradual emancipation plan, to include a plan that prohibited slavery in the territories, could proceed until arrangements were made to deport the free black population elsewhere, because Jefferson did not believe that blacks and whites could coexist peacefully. His most thorough assessment, made in 1824, estimated the total cost of relocating the 1.5 million slaves at $900 million, which was exactly sixty times the cost of Louisiana. This number was so daunting that, as Jefferson himself acknowledged, once you looked at it squarely, it was unnecessary to look at the emancipation question ever again. By his lights, then, there was no political solution to the slavery problem in the United States. And the ultimate reason why he did not step forward in 1803 to provide moral leadership, despite his rhetorical condemnations of slavery as a despicable disease, was that Jefferson believed that it was akin to an inoperable cancer, and that any effort by government to remove it would only end up killing the patient.[59]

The national debate over Missouri, especially the fact that he had established the constitutional precedent for federal action, deeply irritated Jefferson, and the fact that the debate also exposed the inherent hypocrisy of his own oft-stated desire to see slavery ended only made matters worse. Perhaps that is the best explanation for his final utterance on the issue, which was the bizarre claim that allowing slavery to spread into the territories was the best way to extinguish it. He called this idea "diffusion," arguing that "diffusion over a greater surface would make them [slaves] individually happier, and proportionally facilitate the accomplishment of their emancipation." When Adams learned that his old friend and rival had embraced the doctrine of diffusion, he observed that Jefferson had temporarily lost his mind, since he had somehow convinced himself that allowing a cancer to spread through the body politic would diminish its lethality. There is no rational way to explain Jefferson's belief in diffusion, except as the desperate effort to put a good face on his failure, or perhaps as a romantic hope that slavery would migrate to the west, then simply disappear in the vastness of boundless space.[60]

It is a sad, even pathetic, end to the story of the Louisiana Purchase, which explains why Jefferson never wanted it placed on his tombstone. There were, it turned out, some self-evident truths of the darker sort that Jefferson had neglected to mention in the Declaration of Independence. One was that blacks and whites could never live together in harmony. Another was that the way of life of the Native Americans was doomed to extinction. Yet another was that slavery defied resolution and any effort to do so would lead to a very bloody civil war. These were not the kind of convictions calculated to buoy the spirits. Tragedy trumped triumph in the story of the Purchase for several reasons, but mostly because race more than space defined the outer limits of Jefferson's political imagination.

AFTERWORD

The American founding lasted for twenty-eight years, from 1775 to 1803. During that time the United States declared and won its independence, a gradual revolution in the social landscape was begun that, truth be told, has yet to run its course, the political architecture for a viable nation-state was invented and implemented, a dialogue was institutionalized about how best to live within that architecture, and the prospects for a truly continental empire were rendered plausible. These were all precedent-setting triumphs.

On the tragic side, slavery south of the Potomac became a deeply embedded presence, now spreading relentlessly westward. And a vital Native American existence east of the Mississippi was put on the road to extinction. On the one hand, an enduring American republic, previously regarded as either improbable or impossible, now appeared quite likely. On the other hand, the prospects for a sectional battle over the preservation of slavery appeared inevitable. Both the seminal achievements and enduring failures of the American founding were now locked in place.

If the stories told in the preceding pages are essentially correct, then one venerable interpretation of the founding era, namely that it was a clash between "democracy" and "aristocracy," is fatally flawed, since none of the founders, to include Jefferson, regarded democracy as a goal of the American Revolution. Throughout the founding era, the term "democracy" remained an epithet, used to tar an opponent with the charge of demagogy or popular pandering. Those founders who lived long enough to experience the early manifestations of a democratic culture—Adams, Jefferson, and Madison—all expressed the same baffled disappointment that their hard-won republic was being corrupted by an alien force.

The core question posed at the founding was not whether the United States should become a democracy, but whether it should become a viable nation-state. And the chief difference of opinion was not a clash between elitists and egalitarians—both the Federalists and the Republicans were elitists—but between those favoring a wholly sovereign federal government and those anxious to preserve state sovereignty over all domestic policy. The triumph of the latter perspective with Jefferson's election in 1800 did have some democratic implications, chiefly by limiting the authority of the federal government over individual lives. But it also eliminated any chance of providing a political solution to slavery, the most conspicuously undemocratic feature of the founding, which required precisely the kind of robust federal power that the Jeffersonians viewed as a betrayal of their principles. It also, not so incidentally, made a moral resolution of the Native American problem politically impossible.

Throughout the founding era space proved the most indispensable American asset, and recognition of that elemental advantage afforded the occasion for three of the most creative moments: Washington's decision to forgo a conventional clash of armies in favor of a protracted struggle that placed impossible demands on the occupying British army; Madison's counterintuitive argument that a large republic would prove more stable than a small one; and Jefferson's recognition that, despite Napoleon's military prowess, no French army could prevent American settlement of the Louisiana Territory, and that the annexation of such a huge area would prove Madison's point about the viability of an extended republic.

Equally creative, though not so much a decision as the realization that one was not necessary, was the willingness to blur the question of political sovereignty. The unresolvable issue of the founding era was federal versus state sovereignty. Any effort to enforce an unambiguous answer to that question would probably have killed the infant American republic in the cradle. By avoiding that decision and allowing competing answers to coexist, the very purpose of government was subtly transformed from an ultimate arbiter to a framework for ongoing argument. The partisan bickering that ensued throughout the 1790s suggests that none of the founders, with the possible exception of Madison, fully fathomed the modern argumentative context they had created.

The founding succeeded in the elemental sense that the American republic survived its most vulnerable phase of development. Against all odds, the most liberal nation-state in the history of Western Civilization was now firmly embedded in the most extensive and richly endowed plot of ground on the planet. The plot itself was providential, a function of geographic and chronological good fortune. The political shape of the emerging American nation was a more human creation, flawed as all human creations must be, most notably in its prevailing racial prejudices and its inability to envision the multicultural ideal we now take for granted.

But the design of the political foundation was ingenious in its combination of stability and agility, most especially its prudent placement of an expanding liberal mandate at the start that left room, up ahead, for an Abraham Lincoln and a Martin Luther King to join the list of founders. In that sense, perhaps the most creative act of the founding era was to make time as well as space an indispensable ally, in effect extending the founding moment everlastingly into the future.

NOTES

ABBREVIATIONS

AD   Lyman H. Butterfield et al., eds., *Diary and Autobiography of John Adams*, 4 vols. (Cambridge, Mass., 1961).

AFC   Lyman H. Butterfield et al., eds., *Adams Family Correspondence* (Cambridge, Mass., 1963–93).

AIUS   Wilcomb E. Washburn, ed., *The American Indian and the United States: A Documentary History*, 4 vols. (New York, 1973).

AP   Robert J. Taylor et al., eds., *The Papers of John Adams* (Cambridge, Mass., 1977–).

DHFC   Linda Grant De Pauw, ed., *Documentary History of the First Federal Congress of the United States of America*, 15 vols. (Baltimore, 1972–76).

DHR   John P. Kaminski and Gaspar J. Saladino, eds., *The Documentary History of the Ratification of the Constitution*, 10 vols. (Madison, 1980–90).

HP   Harold C. Syrett and Jacob E. Cooke, eds., *The Papers of Alexander Hamilton*, 26 vols. (New York, 1961–79).

JCC   W. C. Ford et al., eds., *Journals of the Continental Congress*, 24 vols. (Washington, D.C., 1904–37).

JMP   James Morton Smith, ed., *The Republic of Letters: The Correspondence Between Thomas Jefferson and James Madison, 1776–1826*, 3 vols. (New York, 1995).

JP   Julian P. Boyd et al., eds., *The Papers of Thomas Jefferson* (Princeton, 1950–).

JPF   Paul Leicester Ford, ed., *The Writings of Thomas Jefferson*, 10 vols. (New York, 1892–99).

MP   William T. Hutchinson et al., eds., *The Papers of James Madison* (Chicago and Charlottesville, 1962–).

PWCF W. W. Abbot and Dorothy Twohig, eds., *The Papers of George Washington: Colonial Series*, 6 vols. (Charlottesville, 1992–97).

PWP W. W. Abbot and Dorothy Twohig, eds., *The Papers of George Washington: Presidential Series* (Charlottesville, 1987–).

PWR W. W. Abbot, Dorothy Twohig, and Philander D. Chase, eds., *The Papers of George Washington: Revolutionary War Series* (Charlottesville, 1985–).

PWRT W. W. Abbot, ed., *The Papers of George Washington: Retirement Series*, 4 vols. (Charlottesville, 1998–99).

WMQ *William and Mary Quarterly,* 3rd series.

WW John C. Fitzpatrick, ed., *Writings of George Washington,* 39 vols. (Washington, D.C., 1931–39).

PROLOGUE: THE FOUNDING

1. The seminal statement of this interpretation of liberal hegemony is Francis Fukuyama, *The End of History and the Last Man* (New York, 1993).

2. Circular to the States, 8 June 1783, *WW* 26:483–96.

3. Another way to think about the political challenge facing the founding generation is to distinguish between the long-term potential of a continental republic, which dazzled and terrified most European observers, and the short-term danger of dissolution, which these same observers regarded as likely. In order to get from the short term to the long term, the decisions by men (i.e., "agency") would be crucial. See Joseph J. Ellis, *Founding Brothers: The Revolutionary Generation* (New York, 2000), 3–19.

4. John A. Schutz and Douglass Adair, eds., *The Spur of Fame: Dialogues of John Adams and Benjamin Rush, 1805–1813* (San Marino, Calif., 1966).

5. Benjamin Rush to John Adams, 13 July 1808, Adams to Benjamin Rush, 14 March 1809, Schutz and Adair, *The Spur of Fame,* 111–12, 135; Adams to Benjamin Waterhouse, 16 August 1812, Worthington C. Ford, ed., *Statesman and Friend: Correspondence of John Adams with Benjamin Waterhouse, 1784–1822* (Boston, 1927), 81.

6. Adams to George Alexander Otis, 2 July 1820, *The Microfilm Edition of the Adams Papers,* 608 reels (Boston, 1954–59), reel 124; Adams to Benjamin Rush, 17 August 1812, Schutz and Adair, *The Spur of Fame,* 242.

7. Adams to Josiah Quincy, 9 February 1811, Charles Francis Adams, ed., *The Works of John Adams, Second President of the United States,* 10 vols. (Boston, 1850–56), 9:630. The comment by Charles Francis Adams is found in his introduction to the first volume.

8. This is my conclusion in my *Passionate Sage: The Character and Legacy of John Adams* (New York, 1991).

9. The "standing miracle" remark comes from Farewell Orders to the Armies of the United States, 2 November 1783, *WW* 27:223.

10. My own effort to imagine a viable solution to the slavery question is in Ellis, *Founding Brothers*, 81–119. A similar attempt with regard to the Native American dilemma is in Chapter 4 of this book.

11. Whitehead's remark is in Perry Miller, *Nature's Nation* (Cambridge, Mass., 1967), 3–4. Morison's assessment is in Wesley Frank Craven, *The Legend of the Founding Fathers* (Ithaca, 1956), 7.

12. Emerson's observation, actually part of a plea to the next generation to move off in their own direction, is in Edward Waldo Emerson, ed., *The Complete Works of Ralph Waldo Emerson*, 12 vols. (Boston and New York, 1903–5), 1:114.

13. Peter C. Mancall, *Valley of Opportunity: Economic Culture Along the Upper Susquehanna, 1700–1800* (Ithaca, 1991), 232. For a similar assessment of the trends within the groves of academe, see Gordon S. Wood, *Revolutionary Characters: What Made the Founders Different* (New York, 2006), 7–8, where I first encountered the stunningly ahistorical statement by Professor Mancall.

14. During the last decade eleven books on the founding or the founders have appeared on the *New York Times* best-seller list, and another six have made the expanded list. The term "founders chic" has been coined to describe the phenomenon, suggesting that it is merely a momentary fad or fashion. My own view is that it is a good deal more than that, with deep roots in a large public readership eager to learn about our origins as a nation whom current trends within the academy had previously failed to engage.

15. Douglass Adair, "Fame and the Founding Fathers," in Trevor Colbourn, ed., *Fame and the Founding Fathers: Essays by Douglass Adair* (New York, 1971), 3–26. The Adams quotation is from Adams to Francis Vanderkemp, 27 December 1816, Adams, *Works*, 10:235.

16. Wood, *Revolutionary Characters*, 3–28. The Twain quotation, originally published in *The Innocents Abroad*, is reproduced in Justin Kaplan, *Mr. Clemens and Mark Twain: A Biography* (New York, 1966), 117.

17. Bernard Bailyn, *To Begin the World Anew: The Genius and Ambiguities of the American Founders* (New York, 2003), 3–26.

18. See Ellis, *Founding Brothers*, 3–19.

CHAPTER ONE: THE YEAR

1. Three previous studies of this awkward year that strike me as first-rate are Allen French, *The First Year of the American Revolution* (Boston, 1934); Thomas Fleming, *1776: Year of Illusions* (New York, 1975); and, more recently, David McCullough, *1776* (New York, 2005).

2. *AD* 3:355.

3. The quotation is from John Adams to Benjamin Rush, 17 August 1812, John A. Schutz and Douglass Adair, eds., *The Spur of Fame: Dialogues of John Adams and Benjamin Rush, 1805–1813* (San Marino, Calif., 1966). I have assessed the

Adams posture toward all straight-line narratives of the American Revolution in *Founding Brothers: The Revolutionary Generation* (New York, 2000), 215–81. On Adams's role in the Continental Congress, the semifictional account by Catherine Drinker Bowen, *John Adams and the American Revolution* (Boston, 1950), still manages to capture the context most imaginatively.

4. Adams is almost a textbook example of the revolutionary mentality first identified by Bernard Bailyn in *The Ideological Origins of the American Revolution* (Cambridge, Mass., 1967).

5. The first historian to insist on viewing the American Revolution from the British perspective was Lawrence H. Gipson, who summarized his multivolume account in *The Coming of the Revolution, 1763–1775* (New York, 1954). The most recent version of this imperial interpretation is Theodore Draper, *A Struggle for Power: The American Revolution* (New York, 1996).

6. On the role of the colonial assemblies, the authoritative work is Jack P. Greene, *The Quest for Power: The Lower Houses of Assembly in the Southern Royal Colonies, 1689–1776* (Chapel Hill, 1963).

7. My conclusion here is harsh, but I find it inescapable. See, for example, Robert W. Tucker and David C. Hendrickson, *The Fall of the First British Empire: Origins of the War of American Independence* (Baltimore, 1982). On the British side of the story, equally derogatory, see Stanley Weintraub, *Iron Tears: America's Battle for Freedom, Britain's Quagmire, 1775–1783* (New York, 2005).

8. The authoritative study of the Continental Congress is Jack N. Rakove, *The Beginnings of National Politics: An Interpretive History of the Continental Congress* (New York, 1979). I found the official records of the congress too sprawling and inchoate to permit any accessible perspective, but the published letters of the delegates do offer periodic glimpses into deliberations. See Paul H. Smith et al., eds., *Letters of Delegates to Congress, 1774–1789*, 26 vols. (Washington, D.C., 1976–), especially vols. 2, 3, and 4.

9. *AD* 2:121, 173; Adams to James Warren, 25 June 1774, *AP* 2:99.

10. Adams to Abigail Adams, 2 July 1774, *AFC* 1:121. See also his recollection of the same letter in *AD* 3:307.

11. Adams to Moses Gill, 10 June 1775, *AP* 3:21; Adams to Abigail Adams, 15 April 1776, *AFC* 1:383.

12. Adams to Moses Gill, 10 June 1775, *AP* 3:21; Adams to James Warren, 24 July 1775, *AP* 3:89.

13. Adams to James Warren, 6 July 1775, *AP* 3:43; Adams to Moses Gill, 10 June 1775, *AP* 3:21.

14. Rakove, *The Beginnings of National Politics*, 63–68. On the creation of a navy, see *AP* 3:147–56.

15. Abigail Adams to Adams, 18 June 1775, *AFC* 1:222. On the casualties at Bunker Hill and the reaction in London, see *PWR* 1:71, 134–36, 183–84, 289–90.

16. Adams learned of the desecration of Warren's body in Benjamin Hichborn to Adams, 25 November 1775, *AP* 3:323.

17. Adams to Abigail Adams, 17 June 1775, *AFC* 1:224.

18. For the somewhat misrepresentative memory of Washington's appointment, see *AD* 3:336–40. I have discussed this moment at greater length in my *His Excellency: George Washington* (New York, 2004), 68–70.

19. The generalizations presented in these last two paragraphs represent my distilled conclusions after writing biographies of both men.

20. George Washington to Burwell Bassett, 19 June 1775, *PWR* 1:19–20. On Washington's military qualifications to head an army, see Ellis, *His Excellency*, 71–72.

21. On the tactical situation Washington encountered at Boston, see the correspondence in *PWR* 1:79–82, 134–36, 183–84. The quotation is in Washington to Joseph Reed, 1 February 1776, *PWR* 3:237–38. The "spyglasses" reference is from Peter Oliver, a prominent loyalist, quoted in McCullough, *1776*, 28.

22. General Orders, 4 July 1775, *PWR* 1:54.

23. Washington to Lund Washington, 20 August 1775, *PWR* 1:335–36. A colorful description of the New England militia units outside Boston is provided in McCullough, *1776*, 29–33.

24. General Orders, 14 and 22 August 1775, *PWR* 1:219–20, 346–48.

25. Washington to Joseph Reed, 14 January 1776, *PWR* 3:89.

26. General Orders, 3 January 1775, *PWR* 3:14.

27. Washington to Philip Schuyler, 27 January 1776, Washington to John Hancock, 4 January 1776, *PWR* 3:201–3, 19.

28. Washington to John Hancock, 9 February 1776, *PWR* 3:275.

29. Council of War, 8 October 1775, *PWR* 2:125; General Orders, 12 November 1775, *PWR* 2:354.

30. Washington to John Hancock, 31 December 1775, *PWR* 2:623.

31. On Knox, see North Callahan, *Henry Knox: General Washington's General* (New York, 1958). On Greene, there is an excellent recent biography by Terry Golway, *Washington's General: Nathanael Greene and the Triumph of the American Revolution* (New York, 2005).

32. Washington to Joseph Reed, 26 February–9 March 1776, *PWR* 3:372.

33. Council of War, 18 October 1775, Minutes of the Conference, 18–24 October 1775, *PWR* 2:183–84, 190–205; Washington to Joseph Reed, 1 April 1776, *PWR* 4:81.

34. Unknown to Adams, 9 June 1775, Humanity to Adams, 23 January 1776, *AP* 3:18–19, 411.

35. Abigail Adams to Adams, 31 March 1776, *AFC* 1:369–70.

36. Adams to Abigail Adams, 14 April 1776, Abigail Adams to Adams, 7 May 1776, *AFC* 1:382, 402.

37. *Pennsylvania Evening Post*, 14 March 1776. On the role of taverns in the politi-

cal process, see Peter Thompson, *Rum Punch and Revolution: Taverngoing and Public Life in Eighteenth-Century Philadelphia* (Philadelphia, 1999), 145–80.

38. Sullivan's original letter to Elbridge Gerry is reproduced in *AP* 4:212–13. The Adams response is in Adams to James Sullivan, 26 May 1776, *AP* 4:208–12.

39. The authoritative biography of Paine is John Keane, *Tom Paine: A Political Life* (Boston, 1995). For Paine as the ultimate advocate of the revolutionary agenda, see Harvey J. Kaye, *Thomas Paine and the Promise of America* (New York, 2005).

40. The fullest exposition of *Common Sense*, its style, message, and context, is Eric Foner, *Tom Paine and Revolutionary America* (New York, 1976).

41. Adams to William Tudor, 12 April 1776, *AP* 4:118.

42. For Paine's abolitionist credentials, see *Pennsylvania Packet*, 16 September 1775.

43. Kaye, *Thomas Paine and the Promise of America*, 34–63, makes the best case for Paine's democratic credentials and ideological clarity. The interpretation offered here does not dispute the purity of Paine's revolutionary credentials, but it does question the feasibility of his revolutionary agenda and the viability of the assumptions on which it was based.

44. Adams to John Trumbull, 13 February 1776, *AP* 4:22. On the arrival of the Prohibitory Act in the Continental Congress, see Rakove, *The Beginnings of National Politics*, 91–92.

45. Adams to James Warren, 22 April 1776, *AP* 4:135.

46. Abigail Adams to Adams, 27 November 1775, *AFC* 1:329–30.

47. Adams to Mercy Otis Warren, 16 April 1776, *AP* 4:124. The best study of the role performed by ad hoc committees is Richard Alan Ryerson, *The Revolution Is Now Begun: The Radical Committees of Philadelphia, 1765–1776* (Philadelphia, 1978).

48. *AP* 4:65–73, for the text and an editorial note on Adams's later comments on *Thoughts*.

49. *AP* 4:93; Adams to Abigail Adams, 17 May 1776, *AP* 4:10.

50. This interpretation of *Thoughts* has been inspired and influenced by Edmund S. Morgan, *Inventing the People: The Rise of Popular Sovereignty in England and America* (New York, 1988).

51. Adams to John Winthrop, 12 May 1776, *AP* 4:183–84.

52. *AP* 4:185; Adams to James Warren, 15 May 1776, *AP* 4:186.

53. The historian who has most recently called attention to these state and local manifestos is Pauline Maier, in her *American Scripture: Making the Declaration of Independence* (New York, 1997), 47–96, 217–34.

54. On this theme, see Niall Ferguson, *Empire: The Rise and Demise of the British World Order and the Lessons for Global Power* (New York, 2002), especially 73–77.

55. For a longer exegesis of this point, along with the primary sources on which it is based, see my *Passionate Sage: The Character and Legacy of John Adams* (New York, 1991), 64.

56. See Maier, *American Scripture,* 99–105, for the best synthesis of this moment.
57. Adams to Abigail Adams, 3 July 1776, *AFC* 2:30.
58. Maier, *American Scripture,* 97–153.
59. Quoted ibid., 206.
60. Those historians who believe that justice delayed is justice denied will surely find the argument offered here morally bankrupt. My only defense is to claim that it is historically, if not politically, correct, and that the decision to defer the more egalitarian implications of revolutionary ideology assured the consensus essential for the achievement of independence. In the end, I prefer prudent revolutionaries like Adams and Washington to romantic revolutionaries like Paine for reasons that are partially temperamental, and partially a response to the catastrophic consequences of the Russian and Chinese revolutions in the twentieth century. The alternative perspective has most ably and recently been provided by Gary B. Nash, *The Unknown American Revolution: The Unruly Birth of Democracy and the Struggle to Create America* (New York, 2005). The perspective offered here is most compatible with Gordon S. Wood, *The Radicalism of the American Revolution* (New York, 1992).

CHAPTER TWO: THE WINTER

1. George Washington to Nathanael Greene, 6 February 1783, *WW* 26:104.
2. Quoted in John Keegan, *Fields of Battle: The Wars for North America* (New York, 1996), 154, which provides the classic account of space, and controlling space, as the decisive factor in the two wars for North America in the late eighteenth century.
3. The most recent and most authoritative scholarly study of Valley Forge is Wayne Bodle, *The Valley Forge Winter: Civilians and Soldiers in War* (University Park, Pa., 2003).
4. Ibid., 1–29.
5. On the lower-class character of the Continental Army at Valley Forge, see Robert K. Wright, " 'Nor Is Their Standing Army to Be Despised': The Emergence of the Continental Army as a Military Institution," in Ronald Hoffman and Peter J. Albert, eds., *Arms and Independence: The Military Character of the American Revolution* (Charlottesville, 1984). See also Charles Royster, *A Revolutionary People at War: The Continental Army and American Character, 1775–1783* (Chapel Hill, 1979), 190–254, 373–78, and Robert K. Wright, *The Continental Army* (Washington, D.C., 1983), 112–42.
6. Bodle, *The Valley Forge Winter,* 15–29. See also Edward G. Lengel, *General George Washington: A Military Life* (New York, 2005), 234–45, which is the most recent synthesis of all the scholarly work on the strategic situation facing Washington at Valley Forge.
7. Albigence Waldo, "Diary of Albigence Waldo of the Connecticut Line," *Penn-*

sylvania Magazine of History and Biography 21 (1897), 306; Washington to John Bannister, 20 April 1778, *PWR* 14:577–78.

8. Editorial note, *PWR* 14:377; Benjamin Rush to Washington, 26 December 1777, *PWR* 13:7–8.

9. Washington to Henry Laurens, 23 December 1777, *PWR* 12:683; John Marshall, *The Life of George Washington*, 2 vols. (Philadelphia, 1843), 1:213–43; General Orders, 4 January 1778, *PWR* 13:137–38.

10. Editorial note, *PWR* 13:30. Greene's official appointment as quartermaster general came in General Orders, 24 March 1778, *PWR* 14:285–86.

11. The total deaths are impossible to calculate with any precision. My estimate follows Lengel, *General George Washington*, 270. See General Orders, 8 February 1778, *PWR* 13:473, for the reduction to half rations, and *PWR* 13:516, for an editorial note on the February food crisis. See Washington to Patrick Henry, 19 February 1778, *PWR* 13:591–92, for his description of the famine in camp. See Washington to Henry Laurens, 1 January 1778, *PWR* 13:103–6, for his frustration with Mifflin's incompetent replacement as quartermaster.

12. Nathanael Greene to Washington, [?] January, 1778, *PWR* 13:424–25.

13. *PWR* 13:376–409, for the final draft of the report. Washington met with the Camp Committee on a daily basis from January 28 to March 12 at Moore Hall, an estate three miles west of Valley Forge.

14. For the correspondence from all general officers to Washington containing their recommendations, see *PWR* 13:100–102, 132–36, 151–57, 524.

15. Washington to John Barrister, 21 April 1778, *PWR* 14:574, which is a more eloquent statement of the original message as articulated in *PWR* 13:377.

16. *PWR* 13:378–79, for the crucial recommendations. For the likely fate of Washington's requests within the Continental Congress, see Washington to Elbridge Gerry, 13 January 1778, *PWR* 13:220. In the end, the congress approved half pay for seven years to officers and a bonus of $80 for enlisted men who served for the duration. Although this vote took place on May 15, the money itself depended upon approval by the states, which never quite occurred. So the congress was making promises it could not keep. See Washington to Henry Laurens, 10 April 1778, *PWR* 14:459–64, for his frustration with legislative delays. On the unpopularity of the draft within the states, see Bartholomew Dandridge to Washington, 12 April 1778, *PWR* 14:484–86.

17. For the background of Steuben, see Royster, *A Revolutionary People at War*, 213–54, and Wright, *The Continental Army*, 121–52.

18. For correspondence on Steuben's drilling procedures and personality, see *PWR* 12:567; *PWR* 13:187–88, 306, 598; *PWR* 14:223–25. For the diversity of uniforms within the Continental Army, see the editorial note in *PWR* 13:306.

19. Examples of grousing about rank in the officer corps abound, but see *PWR* 13:79–81, 314–15, 494–96, 602, for an illustrative sample. See Royster, *A Revolu-*

tionary People at War, 197–210, which was the first scholarly treatment of this subject.

20. Circular to the States, 29 December 1777, *PWR* 13:36–37. See also Washington to William Livingston, 22 February 1778, *PWR* 13:644, and Washington to Board of War, 3 January 1778, *PWR* 13:111–13, for his frustration with the lack of a central government empowered to make policy.

21. The fullest expression of this nationalist sentiment from both Washington and the officer corps does not appear until the last year of the war and then the postwar period. But the initial expression began at Valley Forge because it was the time and place where the political and fiscal inadequacies of a mere confederation of states were first encountered to a degree that placed the fate of the Continental Army at risk. On Marshall's experience at Valley Forge and subsequent role as the preeminent nationalist, see Jean Edward Smith, *John Marshall: Definer of a Nation* (New York, 1996), 70–86, 417–45.

22. The best brief summaries of what became known as the Conway Cabal, a misleading label, are in Royster, *A Revolutionary People at War,* 179–89, and the editorial note in *PWR* 13:78–79.

23. Washington to William Gordon, 23 January 1778, *PWR* 13:322–23.

24. The quotation is from Lafayette to Washington, 30 December 1777, *PWR* 13:68. For the whispering campaign for and against Washington, see the following correspondence: *PWR* 13:40–41, 58, 83–84, 119, 120–22, 138–40, 150–51, 160–63, 364–66, 545–46, 609–11, 654–55; *PWR* 14:123–28, 137.

25. The quotation from Gouverneur Morris is in Paul H. Smith et al., eds., *Letters of Delegates to Congress, 1774–1789,* 26 vols. (Washington, D.C., 1976–), 9:117. Analogous comments from two general officers are in *PWR* 13:516.

26. William Stewart to Washington, 18 January 1778, *PWR* 13:276–77; William Livingston to Washington, 12 January 1778, *PWR* 13:208.

27. Lord Stirling to Washington, 26 December 1777, *PWR* 13:11, for a description of local farmers preferring the British market in Philadelphia. See also *PWR* 13:351, for similar descriptions.

28. Bodle, *The Valley Forge Winter,* 15–29, is excellent on the patchwork map of allegiances in the region.

29. Nathanael Greene to Washington, 16 and 17 February 1778, *PWR* 13:557–58, 569.

30. Editorial note, *PWR* 14:438–40.

31. See the correspondence in *PWR* 13:437, 492–93; *PWR* 14:226–28, 327. The quotation is from Washington to John Lacey, Jr., 31 March 1778, *PWR* 14:368.

32. See Washington to Nathanael Greene, 31 March 1778, *PWR* 14:367–68, for an early use of the term "cover the country." The first historian to emphasize the decisive role of the countryside in winning the war was John Shy. See his *A People Numerous and Armed: Reflections on the Military Struggle for Independence*

(New York, 1976), 193–224, and also "The American Revolution Considered as a Revolutionary War," in Stephen Kurtz and James Hutson, eds., *Essays on the American Revolution* (Chapel Hill, 1973). My emphasis here, while indebted to Shy, is somewhat different, because Shy features the militia as crucial in denying British control, whereas my argument is that Washington, who never trusted militia per se, considered the Continental Army as the crucial linchpin in the countryside around which militia could rally.

33. Washington to Henry Laurens, 24 March 1778, *PWR* 14:292.

34. See, for example, Washington to William Livingston, 25 March 1778, *PWR* 14:309, where he described the "fatal policy" of short enlistments as an "evil genius" that would eventually cast a spell that destroyed the Continental Army.

35. Washington estimated the total troop strength of the Continental Army at seventeen thousand in May of 1778, but he included the troops under Gates in the Hudson Highlands and the garrison at Rhode Island. See General Orders, 2 May 1778, *PWR* 14:641–47.

36. Washington to the General Officers, 20 April 1778, *PWR* 14:567.

37. *PWR* 14:594–99, 603–4, 605–7, 610–11, 628–32, 633–34. The last citation contains the quotation from Maxwell.

38. Steuben to Washington, 25 April 1778, *PWR* 14:636–39.

39. Antoine-Jean-Louis Duportail to Washington, 20 April 1778, *PWR* 14:559–67.

40. Nathanael Greene to Washington, 25 April 1778, *PWR* 14:621–28.

41. Washington's "Thoughts Upon a Plan of Operation for Campaign, 1778," 26–29 April 1778, *PWR* 14:641–47.

42. For Washington's response to the news of the French alliance, see Washington to Henry Laurens, 20 April 1778, *PWR* 14:570–71. For the celebration ceremony at Valley Forge, see Lengel, *General George Washington,* 269–70.

43. Washington to Henry Laurens, 18 April 1778, and Washington to John Bannister, 21 April 1778, *PWR* 14:547, 576; Henry Laurens to Washington, 24 April 1778, *PWR* 14:616.

44. The British side of this story has been most recently and engagingly told in Stanley Weintraub, *Iron Tears: America's Battle for Freedom, Britain's Quagmire, 1775–1783* (New York, 2005), 109–56. The quotation from Germain is from Lengel, *General George Washington,* 272.

45. Bodle, *The Valley Forge Winter,* 245–65, first called attention to the shape of the strategic deployment at Valley Forge and thereafter.

CHAPTER THREE: THE ARGUMENT

1. Circular to the States, 8 June 1783, *WW* 26:483–96.

2. George Washington to Lafayette, 12 October 1783, *WW* 27:185–90; Washington to Edward Newenham, 10 June 1784, *PWCF* 1:438–40.

3. Washington to James Warren, 7 October 1785, *PWCF* 3:299.

4. Richard B. Morris, *The Forging of the Union, 1781–1789* (New York, 1987), forcefully makes the nationalist argument. Merrill Jensen, *The New Nation: A History of the United States During the Confederation, 1781–1789* (New York, 1950), is the fullest argument for the confederation government. An excellent collection of scholarly articles on the subject is Herman Belz, Ronald Hoffman, and Peter Albert, eds., *To Form a More Perfect Union: The Critical Ideas of the Constitution* (Charlottesville, 1992). Gordon S. Wood, *The Creation of the American Republic, 1776–1787* (Chapel Hill, 1969), is the seminal source for the ideological issues at stake. The most comprehensive of all recent studies of the Constitution is Akhil Reed Amar, *America's Constitution: A Biography* (New York, 2005).

5. See Joseph J. Ellis, *Founding Brothers: The Revolutionary Generation* (New York, 2000), 15–16.

6. Washington to James Madison, 5 November 1786, *PWCF* 4:331–32.

7. Washington to John Jay, 15 August 1786, *PWCF* 4:212–13; Washington to James Madison, 30 November 1785, *PWCF* 3:420.

8. Many Washington letters after the war made this point. A typical and comprehensive expression is Washington to Henry Knox, 5 December 1784, *PWCF* 2:170–72.

9. David C. Hendrickson, *Peace Pact: The Lost World of the American Founding* (Lawrence, Kans., 2003), makes the most persuasive case for seeing the Confederation Congress as a diplomatic gathering of sovereign nations.

10. The fairest summary of the abiding weaknesses of the Confederation Congress remains Jack N. Rakove, *The Beginnings of National Politics: An Interpretive History of the Continental Congress* (New York, 1979), 331–59.

11. Madison to James Monroe, 9 April 1786, *MP* 9:25–26.

12. Madison to Edmund Randolph, 25 February 1787, *MP* 9:299. For the newspaper editorial, see *MP* 9:291–92.

13. All of Madison's biographers cover this crucial phase of his political evolution, but I find Jack N. Rakove, *James Madison and the Creation of the American Republic* (Glenview, Ill., 1990), 19–43, most succinct and sensible. See also Wood, *The Creation of the American Republic*, 471–73.

14. Madison to Thomas Jefferson, 12 August 1786, *MP* 9:96.

15. For correspondence on the Mississippi Question, see *MP* 9:68–71, 181–84, 309–10, 389–90, 404–6.

16. Madison's overheated remarks on Shays's Rebellion are in *MP* 9:230–31, 275–76, 314–17. Washington's reaction was equally hyperbolic. See, for example, Washington to Henry Lee, 31 October 1786, *PWCF* 4:318–19.

17. See the editorial note on the Annapolis Convention in *MP* 9:115–19.

18. Madison visited Mount Vernon on October 23–25, 1786. My informed speculation about the content of their conversations is based on the correspondence between them soon afterward.

19. The relevant correspondence is in *MP* 9:115–56, 166–67, 170–71, 199–200, 224–25. For Washington's efforts to wiggle away from Madison's entrapment, see *PWCF* 4:445, 477–81; *PWCF* 5:7–9, 95–98.

20. Madison to Washington, 24 December 1786, *MP* 9:224–25, and the accompanying editorial note that provides Randolph's letter to Washington.

21. Washington to James Madison, 31 March 1787, *PWCF* 5:116.

22. My interpretation of Madison's intellectual evolution during this crucial phase of his career is based on my reading of the primary sources with my own eyes. But it would be impossible not to be influenced by distinguished predecessors. These include the relevant pages of Rakove, *James Madison,* and Wood, *The Creation of the American Republic.* Two additional books are seminal: Marvin Meyers, ed., *The Mind of the Founder: Sources of the Political Thought of James Madison* (Hanover, N.H., 1981), and Lance Banning, *The Sacred Fire of Liberty: James Madison and the Founding of the Federal Republic* (Ithaca, 1995). Though it focuses on Madison's retirement years, Drew R. McCoy's *The Last of the Fathers: James Madison and the Republican Legacy* (Cambridge, U.K., 1989) provides backward glances of unparalleled insight. See also Gary Rosen, *American Compact: James Madison and the Problem of Founding* (New York, 2003), and, for an argument about Madison's larger consistency, the essay by Gordon S. Wood in his *Revolutionary Characters: What Made the Founders Different* (New York, 2006), 151–72.

23. See Madison to Edmund Randolph, 8 April 1787, *MP* 9:368–71, for his optimistic estimate of the delegates being chosen in several states.

24. Thomas Jefferson to Madison, 20 June 1787, *MP* 10:64; Madison to Washington, 16 April 1787, *MP* 9:382–87.

25. Madison to Edmund Randolph, 8 April 1787, *MP* 9:370–71.

26. The earliest and fullest exegesis of Madison's political agenda for the convention is provided in Madison to Jefferson, 15 March 1787, *MP* 9:317–22.

27. "Notes on Ancient and Modern Confederacies," April–June 1786, *MP* 9:3–24.

28. "Vices of the Political System of the United States," April–June 1787, *MP* 9:345–58. Wood, *The Creation of the American Republic,* 406, and Hendrickson, *Peace Pact,* 211–19, are especially good on this dimension of Madison's thinking.

29. *MP* 9:353–54.

30. *MP* 9:356–57.

31. There is an avalanche of scholarly writing on the sources of Madison's thinking about size and scale in republics, conveniently synthesized in Larry D. Kramer, "Madison's Audience," *Harvard Law Review* 112 (January 1999), 611–99. Kramer was also the first scholar to question the influence of Madison's argument on his contemporaries, a skepticism I share.

32. Editorial note on James Madison at the Federal Convention, 27 May–17 September 1878, *MP* 10:3–10. Three books stand out as reliable guides to the Constitutional Convention: Max Farrand, *The Framing of the Constitution of the*

United States (New Haven, 1913); Jack N. Rakove, *Original Meanings: Politics and Ideas in the Making of the Constitution* (New York, 1996); Carol Berkin, *A Brilliant Solution: Inventing the American Constitution* (New York, 2002).

33. This is my own synthesis of the specific ingredients in Madison's political agenda on the eve of the convention, developed over the previous months and documented in notes 25–30 to this chapter.

34. Washington to Jefferson, 30 May 1787, *PWCF* 5:208.

35. Virginia Plan, 29 May 1787, *MP* 10:15–17.

36. Madison to Jefferson, 6 June 1787, *MP* 10:29–30, which provides Madison's optimistic appraisal at the start of the Convention and his last substantive report on the deliberations until the Convention ended, in keeping with the vow of confidentiality all delegates adopted.

37. Madison's speech of June 6 on an extended republic is reproduced in *MP* 10:32–34; his reply to the New Jersey Plan on June 19 is in *MP* 10:55–63.

38. Washington to Alexander Hamilton, 10 July 1787, *PWCF* 5:2457.

39. Madison to Jefferson, 6 September 1787, *MP* 10:163–64.

40. Washington to Lafayette, 18 September 1787, *PWCF* 5:334; also Washington to Henry Knox, 19 August 1787, *PWCF* 5:297.

41. Madison to Jefferson, 24 October 1787, *MP* 10:205–20.

42. *MP* 10:212–13.

43. *MP* 10:214.

44. Washington to Edward Newenham, 29 August 1788, *PWCF* 6:488. The best collection of documents on the broad-ranging debate is Bernard Bailyn, ed., *The Debate on the Constitution*, 2 vols. (New York, 1993). The best collection on the ratifying conventions is Michael A. Gillespie and Michael Lienesch, eds., *Ratifying the Constitution* (Lawrence, Kans., 1989). Two books on the Antifederalist side of the debate are especially important: Saul Cornell, *The Other Founders: Anti-Federalism and the Dissenting Tradition in America, 1788–1828* (Chapel Hill, 1999), and Herbert J. Storing, *What the Anti-Federalists Were For* (Chicago, 1981).

45. Madison to Edmund Pendleton, 21 February 1788, *MP* 10:532–33.

46. Madison to Edmund Pendleton, 28 October 1787, *MP* 10:224.

47. Cecilia Kenyon, "Men of Little Faith: The Anti-Federalists on the Nature of Representative Government," *WMQ* 12 (January 1953), 3–43.

48. Marshall's belief that the Antifederalists enjoyed a comfortable popular majority in Virginia is in Jean Edward Smith, *John Marshall: Definer of a Nation* (New York, 1996), 119.

49. Washington to Alexander Hamilton, 25 August 1788, *PWCF* 6:481. See also the editorial note in *MP* 10:259–63 on the detective work, chiefly by Douglass Adair, to determine the authorship of the different essays in *The Federalist*.

50. See Kramer, "Madison's Audience," 664–65, for the limited distribution and influence of *The Federalist* on the ratifying conventions.

51. See *MP* 10:263–70, 284–90, 299–305, 305–9, 320–24, 377–82.

52. *MP* 10:423–28, 428–32, 438–44, 448–54.

53. Madison's correspondence on the voter count in each ratifying state was extensive and remarkably accurate. See *MP* 10:255–57, 289–90, 296–97, 310, 325–26, 346–47, 357–58, 376, 399, 411, 455, 464–65.

54. Madison to Washington, 18 March 1786, *PWCF* 5:94–95. The authoritative Henry biography of our time is Henry Mayer, *A Son of Thunder: Patrick Henry and the American Republic* (New York, 1986).

55. Jefferson's quote is in Joseph J. Ellis, *American Sphinx: The Character of Thomas Jefferson* (New York, 1996), 38.

56. Marshall's quote is in Smith, *John Marshall,* 123. On the Virginia Convention and Madison's role therein, see editorial note, Virginia Convention, 2–27 June 1788, *MP* 11:72–76.

57. *DHR* 9:952–53.

58. *DHR* 9:951, 960–61.

59. *DHR* 9:959.

60. *DHR* 9:951.

61. *DHR* 9:1028–81.

62. *DHR* 9:995–96.

63. See *DHR* 9:1210, 1218, 1328–29, 1479–80, for Henry's emphasis on the absence of a Bill of Rights. See *DHR* 9:1507, for Henry's rebuttal.

64. *DHR* 9:1506, 1512–15, 1534–37, 1560–62.

65. Washington to William Tudor, 18 August 1788, *PWCF* 6:465–66; Washington to John Armstrong, 25 April 1788, *PWCF* 6:224–25.

CHAPTER FOUR: THE TREATY

1. Bernard W. Sheehan, "Indian-White Relations in Early America: A Review Essay," *WMQ* 26 (April 1969), 267–86. See also Frederick E. Hoxie, Ronald Hoffman, and Peter J. Albert, eds., *Native Americans and the Early Republic* (Charlottesville, 1999).

2. Daniel K. Richter, *Facing East from Indian Country: A Native History of Early America* (Cambridge, Mass., 2001). The Indian quotation is from editorial note, *PWP* 10:190–94.

3. Henry Knox to George Washington, 15 June 1789, *PWP* 2:489–95.

4. Henry Knox to Washington, 4 January 1790, *PWP* 4:529–36.

5. The two standard works are Francis P. Prucha, *American Indian Policy in the Formative Years: The Indian Trade and Intercourse Acts, 1790–1834* (Cambridge, Mass., 1962), and Reginald Horsman, *Expansion and American Indian Policy, 1783–1812* (East Lansing, Mich., 1967).

6. For the treaties, see *AIUS* 4:2267–77.

7. Horsman, *Expansion and American Indian Policy,* 22.

8. Philip Schuyler to President of Congress, 29 July 1783, *JCC* 3:601–7. Washington endorsed the Schuyler strategy in Washington to James Duane, 7 September 1783, *WW* 27:133–40.

9. Benjamin Hawkins to Thomas Jefferson, 15 October 1786, *JP* 9:640–42. The Cherokee quotation is from Cherokee Chiefs to Washington, 19 May 1789, *PWP* 2:325–26.

10. *AIUS* 2:2140–43. See also Prucha, *American Indian Policy*, 36–39.

11. *AIUS* 2:2144–50.

12. Henry Knox to Washington, 7 July 1789, *PWP* 3:134–38; Prucha, *American Indian Policy*, 41–42.

13. Henry Knox to Washington, 7 July 1789, *PWP* 3:138–40.

14. *PWP* 3:141.

15. Arthur St. Clair to Washington, 2 May 1789, *PWP* 2:198–200.

16. See Henry Knox to Washington, 23 May 1789, *PWP* 2:488–95, for Knox's review of past policies and his opinion of their illegality.

17. Though somewhat dated, the authoritative biography is North Callahan, *Henry Knox: General Washington's General* (New York, 1958). Knox deserves a modern biographer.

18. Henry Knox to Washington, 15 June 1789, *PWP* 2:494. See also Horsman, *Expansion and American Indian Policy*, 53–65, and Prucha, *American Indian Policy*, 44–46.

19. Henry Knox to Washington, 28 July 1789, *PWP* 3:337–38.

20. Henry Knox to Washington, 15 June 1789, *PWP* 2:494.

21. *DHFC* 2:31–36.

22. *DHFC* 9:128–32.

23. *PWP* 3:551–64.

24. John W. Caughey, *McGillivray of the Creeks* (Norman, 1931), 3–57, which is an introductory essay followed by McGillivray's correspondence.

25. See letter of 10 July 1785 in Caughey, *McGillivray*, 90–91.

26. Caughey, *McGillivray*, 61, 128, 294. The quotation is from a letter of 10 July 1785, ibid., 92.

27. David Humphreys to Washington, 26 September 1789, *PWP* 4:86–89; McGillivray letter of 8 October 1789 in Caughey, *McGillivray*, 251–54.

28. *PWP* 4:86–89, note 3.

29. David Humphreys to Washington, 27 September 1789, *PWP* 4:91–95.

30. Letter of 12 October 1780 in Caughey, *McGillivray*, 255.

31. Henry Knox to Washington, 27 October 1789, *PWP* 4:248.

32. Washington's Memoranda on Indian Affairs, December 1789, *PWP* 4:468–94.

33. Henry Knox to Washington, 15 February 1790, *PWP* 5:140–47.

34. On McGillivray's efforts to form an alliance with the northern tribes, see letter of 20 June 1787 in Caughey, *McGillivray*, 153.

35. For the most recent synthesis of the Yazoo claims, see Richter, *Facing East from Indian Country*, 226–28.

36. See letter of 8 May 1790 in Caughey, *McGillivray*, 259–62.

37. See letter of 20 May 1790, ibid., 263.

38. See letter of 6 March 1790, ibid., 256–58.

39. See letter of 8 May 1790, ibid., 261.

40. *New York Daily Gazette*, 3, 17, 19, 21, and 22 July 1790.

41. For McGillivray's statements of confidence in his Creek warriors and the inherent fragility of the American republic, see Caughey, *McGillivray*, 130–32, 172–74, 182.

42. See *PWP* 6:104, note 2, for the episode with the Trumbull painting.

43. For the most penetrating study of the subject, see Anthony F. C. Wallace, *Jefferson and the Indians: The Tragic Fate of the First Americans* (Cambridge, Mass., 1999).

44. Opinion of Certain Georgia Land Grants, 3 May 1790, *JP* 17:288–91.

45. Merrill D. Peterson, ed., *The Portable Thomas Jefferson* (New York, 1975), 23–232, provides the most accessible edition of *Notes*. The discussion of Indians is found ibid., 93–103, 133–50.

46. Ibid., 96–99.

47. Caughey, *McGillivray*, 46. See also the letter of 26 February 1791, ibid., 288–89, where McGillivray reiterated his focus on the Yazoo threat.

48. Washington to United States Senate, 7 August 1790, *PWP* 6:213–14; Caughey, *McGillivray*, 45, for Jackson's remarks.

49. *AIUS* 4:2206–88.

50. *AIUS* 4:2290.

51. *AIUS* 4:2288.

52. Washington to United States Senate, 4 August 1790, *PWP* 6:188–96.

53. *National Advertiser* and *Gazette of the United States*, 14 August 1790. See also *PWP* 6:253–54, and Caughey, *McGillivray*, 278–79.

54. Washington to Tobias Lear, 3 April 1791, and Washington to Alexander Hamilton, 4 April 1791, *PWP* 8:49, 57–58. For the "Chinese wall" reference, see Washington to Secretary of State, 1 July 1796, *WW* 35:112.

55. See letters of 11 August 1790, 6 September 1790, and 16 October 1790 in Caughey, *McGillivray*, 273–77, 279–80, 285–86.

56. See letters of 6 July 1792, 22 July 1792, and 15 November 1792 in Caughey, *McGillivray*, 329–30, 332–37, 345.

57. Caughey, *McGillivray*, 345, 362.

58. Adam Rothman, *Slave Country: American Expansion and the Origins of the Deep South* (Cambridge, Mass., 2005).

59. For troop estimates necessary to control the frontier, see *PWP* 6:362–65, 668–70; *PWP* 8:200–225; *PWP* 9:37–41, 158–68.

CHAPTER FIVE: THE CONSPIRACY

1. Thomas Jefferson to Francis Hopkinson, 13 March 1789, *JP* 14:650; Richard Hofstadter, *The Idea of a Party System: The Rise of Legitimate Opposition in the United States, 1780–1840* (Berkeley, 1970).

2. Hofstadter, *The Idea of a Party System*, 1–40. See also W. N. Chambers and W. D. Burnham, eds., *The American Party Systems: Stages of Political Development* (New York, 1967). On political parties in the revolutionary era, see Joseph Charles, *The Origins of the American Party System* (New York, 1961); Noble Cunningham, Jr., *The Jeffersonian Republicans: The Formation of Party Organization, 1789–1801* (Chapel Hill, 1957); and the relevant chapters of Stanley Elkins and Eric McKitrick, *The Age of Federalism: The Early American Republic, 1788–1800* (New York, 1993).

3. Bolingbroke's *The Idea of a Patriot King* (London, 1749) is more conveniently available in a revised edition published in London in 1965.

4. Dumas Malone, *Thomas Jefferson as Political Leader* (Westport, Conn., 1963), 2; Dumas Malone, *Jefferson and His Time*, 6 vols. (Boston, 1948–81), 2:370.

5. Charles Francis Adams, ed., *The Works of John Adams, Second President of the United States,* 10 vols. (Boston, 1850–56), 1:616.

6. Henry Adams, *History of the United States During the Administration of Thomas Jefferson*, 2 vols. (New York, 1986; originally published 1888–91), 1:188.

7. See the excellent introduction to the correspondence during this moment by James Morton Smith in *JMP* 2:663–72.

8. James Madison to Jefferson, 1 May 1791, 10 July 1791, 21 July 1791, 24 July 1791, *JMP* 2:685, 695–96, 698–99. The classic account of the Jefferson-Madison partnership, which I find both wonderful and misguided, is Adrienne Koch, *Jefferson and Madison: The Great Collaboration* (New York, 1950).

9. Jefferson to Madison, 21 July 1791, *JMP* 2:698.

10. The best general account of this mentality is Richard Hofstadter, *The Paranoid Style in American Politics and Other Essays* (New York, 1965). The most persuasive scholarly account that explains the credibility of the Republican perspective is Gordon S. Wood, "Conspiracy and the Paranoid Style: Causality and Deceit in the Eighteenth Century," *WMQ* 39 (July 1982), 401–41. See also Lance Banning, *The Jeffersonian Persuasion: Evolution of a Party Ideology* (Ithaca, 1978), which finesses the questions raised in this paragraph.

11. See Banning, *The Jeffersonian Persuasion,* which ignores the differences between American indictments of British imperialism and the Republican indictment of Federalist policy.

12. *JPF* 1:165; Jefferson to William Short, 8 January 1825, *JPF* 1:333.

13. Norman K. Risjord and Gordon DenBoer, "The Evolution of Political Parties in Virginia, 1782–1800," *Journal of American History* 60 (March 1974), 225–62. On the economic decline of Virginia, see the recent book by Susan Dunn, *Dominion of Memories: Jefferson, Madison, and the Decline of Virginia* (New York, 2007).

14. *JMP* 1:2.
15. Macon is quoted in Peter S. Onuf, ed., *Jeffersonian Legacies* (Charlottesville, 1993), 363, from a letter in 1818 opposing federal control over internal improvements because of the constitutional precedent it set for slavery.
16. I have discussed this congressional debate at greater length in my *Founding Brothers: The Revolutionary Generation* (New York, 2000), 81–119.
17. For an excellent editorial note on the bank, see *HP* 7:236–56. Hamilton's opinion on the constitutionality of the bank is in *HP* 8:97–134. The best secondary account, which describes the embarrassment produced by Madison's essay in *Federalist 44*, is in Elkins and McKitrick, *The Age of Federalism*, 226–34.
18. The Madison essays, published between November 1791 and December 1792, are reprinted in *MP* 14:117–22, 137–39, 170, 178–79, 191–92, 197–98, 201–2, 206–8, 217–18, 233–34, 244–46, 257–59, 266–68, 274–75, 370–72, 426–27.
19. *MP* 14:197–98.
20. *MP* 14:370–72.
21. *MP* 14:371–72.
22. Though there are several fine biographies of Alexander Hamilton, they are all eclipsed by Ron Chernow's *Alexander Hamilton* (New York, 2004). In a more succinct mode, the sketch of Hamilton in Elkins and McKitrick, *The Age of Federalism*, 92–114, is without peer.
23. The "Catullus" series is in *HP* 12:379–85, 393–401, 498–506, 578–87. It ran from September to December 1792.
24. See Malone, *Jefferson and His Time*, 3:470–73, for a convenient review of the anti-Jefferson literature.
25. Jefferson to Madison, 9 June 1783, *JMP* 2:782.
26. Jefferson to Washington, 9 September 1782, *JP* 24:351–59; Jefferson to George Washington, 23 May 1792, *JMP* 2:728, note; Record of Conversation with President Washington, 6 August 1783, *JMP* 2:805–7.
27. Jefferson to Madison, 1 October 1792, *JMP* 2:740–44.
28. See the exchange of letters between Jefferson and Madison during the summer of 1793 in *JMP* 2:795–801.
29. For Jefferson's drafts of the Giles Resolutions, see *JMP* 2:760–64. A brilliant piece of detective work exposed Jefferson's authorship two hundred years later. See Eugene R. Sheridan, "Thomas Jefferson and the Giles Resolutions," *WMQ* 49 (October 1992), 589–608.
30. Jefferson to Madison, 6 March 1796, *JMP* 2:922.
31. *JMP* 2:744–60 offers an elegant summary of the foreign and domestic issues at stake. The authoritative secondary account is Elkins and McKitrick, *The Age of Federalism*, 366–84.
32. Jefferson to Madison, 7 July 1793, *JMP* 2:792; Madison to Jefferson, 2 September 1793, *JMP* 2:815–17. Hamilton's Pacificus essays are in *HP* 15:145–228.
33. Jefferson to James Monroe, 5 May 1793, *JMP* 2:771–72.

34. Jefferson to Madison, 29 June 1792, *JMP* 2:735–36; Jefferson to William Short, 3 January 1793, *JPF* 6:153–57.

35. The standard secondary account of Genet is Harry Ammon, *The Genet Mission* (New York, 1973). Elkins and McKitrick, *The Age of Federalism*, 330–65, tells the story with typical flair and wit.

36. On the cabinet's decision to revoke Genet's credentials, see Jefferson to Madison, 3 August 1793, *JMP* 2:798.

37. Genet's correspondence, reporting to his superiors in France of Jefferson's covert assurances, is conveniently available in Elkins and McKitrick, *The Age of Federalism*, 344–45, and in the corresponding endnotes.

38. Jefferson to Madison, 3 August 1793, 11 August 1793, *JMP* 2:798, 802–5.

39. Postscript in Jefferson to Madison, 11 August 1793, *JMP* 2:805.

40. Jefferson to Madison, 22 January 1797, *JMP* 2:960.

41. Jefferson to Madison, 9 June 1793, *JMP* 2:780–81; Jefferson to Mrs. Church, 27 November 1793, *JPF* 6:455; Jefferson to Enoch Edwards, 30 December 1793, *JPF* 6:495.

42. For the Adams comment (in fact, made later in reference to Madison's retirement), see Joseph J. Ellis, *American Sphinx: The Character of Thomas Jefferson* (New York, 1996), 119.

43. See Jefferson to Adams, 25 April 1794, *JPF* 7:118, for Jefferson's claim that he was in full Ciceronian mode and relished the fact that he did not need to read newspapers.

44. Madison to Jefferson, 5 October 1794, *JMP* 2:857.

45. Madison to Jefferson, 12 and 14 March 1794, *JMP* 2:835–36, where Madison describes the Federalist dilemma somewhat gleefully as an opportunity for the Republicans.

46. See Elkins and McKitrick, *The Age of Federalism*, 357–406, which is excellent at describing the idealistic intentions of Madison's plan to avoid war and his complete blindness to the economic realities.

47. See Ellis, *American Sphinx*, 120, for the debilitating effects of Jefferson's rheumatism during the summer of 1794.

48. The most recent secondary account is Thomas P. Slaughter, *The Whiskey Rebellion: Frontier Epilogue to the American Revolution* (New York, 1986). But the older account, Leland D. Baldwin, *Whiskey Rebels: The Story of a Frontier Uprising* (Pittsburgh, 1939), is still most reliable.

49. Philip S. Foner, ed., *The Democratic-Republican Societies, 1790–1800* (Westport, Conn., 1976). Foner adopts a quasi-Marxist posture toward the Whiskey Rebellion that I regard as naive and ahistorical.

50. Madison to Jefferson, 21 December 1793, and Jefferson to Madison, 28 December 1794, *JMP* 2:865–68.

51. Jefferson to Madison, 27 April 1795, *JMP* 2:877.

52. Jerald Combs, *The Jay Treaty: Political Battleground of the Founding Fathers*

(Berkeley, 1970), is the standard account. Again, Elkins and McKitrick, *The Age of Federalism*, 406–50, provides a sure-handed story of the diplomatic twists and turns.

53. Jefferson to Tench Coxe, 1 May 1794, *JPF* 6:507–8.

54. Jefferson to Edward Rutledge, 30 November 1793, *JPF* 7:40; Jefferson to James Monroe, 21 March 1796, *JPF* 7:67. See also Jefferson to Madison, 21 March 1796, *JPF* 7:68.

55. Jefferson to Madison, 21 September 1795, *JMP* 2:897–98; see also Jefferson to Monroe, 6 September 1795, *JPF* 7:27.

56. Madison to Jefferson, 13 March 1796, *JMP* 2:926. The first Republican caucus is reported in *JMP* 2:892.

57. Jefferson to Monroe, 2 March 1796, *JPF* 7:58–61; Madison to Jefferson, 18 April 1796, *JMP* 2:933–35.

58. Madison to Jefferson, 1 May 1796, *JMP* 2:936–37; see also Madison to Jefferson, 22 May 1796, *JMP* 2:938.

59. Jefferson to Monroe, 10 July 1796, *JPF* 7:89; Jefferson to Monroe, 12 June 1796, *JPF* 7:80.

60. Madison to Jefferson, 23 March 1795, *JMP* 2:875–76.

61. Jefferson to Edward Rutledge, 17 December 1796, *JPF* 7:98; Madison to Monroe, 29 September 1796, *MP* 16:404; Jefferson to Archibald Stuart, 4 January 1797, *JPF* 7:103.

62. Madison to Jefferson, 10 and 19 December 1796, *JMP* 2:949, 950–51.

63. Jefferson to Madison, 1 January 1797, *JMP* 2:952–55; Jefferson to Adams, 28 December 1796, *JPF* 7:96; Jefferson to Madison, 17 December 1796, *JMP* 2:949.

64. Jefferson to Madison, 8 January 1797, *JMP* 2:955; Jefferson to Edward Rutledge, 27 December 1796, *JPF* 7:93.

65. Jefferson to Madison, 22 January 1797, *JMP* 2:959–60, where the Adams coalition initiative is first considered.

66. Jefferson to Madison, 28 December 1796; Madison to Jefferson, 15 January 1797, *JMP* 2:954–58.

67. Jefferson to Madison, 30 January 1797, *JMP* 2:962.

68. Merrill D. Peterson, ed., *Visitors to Monticello* (Charlottesville, 1989), 31.

69. The quotation is Jefferson's recollection many years later and leaves unsaid that he was the one to reject Adams's bipartisan overture. See *JPF* 1:273.

70. Jefferson to Levi Lincoln, 25 October 1802, *JPF* 8:175–76.

CHAPTER SIX: THE PURCHASE

1. The standard history for many years was Alexander DeConde, *This Affair of Louisiana* (New York, 1976). It has been replaced by Jon Kukla, *A Wilderness So Immense: The Louisiana Purchase and the Destiny of America* (New York, 2003),

which is now the fullest, and surely the best-written, account. See also Peter Onuf, *Jefferson's Empire: The Language of American Nationhood* (Charlottesville, 2000).

2. Henry Adams, *History of the United States During the Administration of Thomas Jefferson*, 2 vols. (New York, 1986; originally published 1888–91), 1:227–392; Frederick Jackson Turner, *The Frontier in American History* (New York, 1920), 100.

3. When the border questions were eventually resolved in 1819, the Purchase totaled 529,402,880 acres.

4. Robert W. Tucker and David C. Hendrickson, *Empire of Liberty: The Statecraft of Thomas Jefferson* (New York, 1990), 87–171, which replicates the ironic wisdom of Henry Adams with all the modern accoutrements and has established itself as the authoritative work on Jefferson's foreign policy.

5. The quotation on Napoleon is from Adams, *History*, 1:227.

6. Edward Channing, *A History of the United States*, 6 vols. (New York, 1905–25), 4:319; Douglass Adair, "Hamilton on the Louisiana Purchase," *WMQ* 12 (April 1955), 273–74. See also Kukla, *A Wilderness So Immense*, 290–91.

7. *JPF* 8:1–6; Adams, *History*, 122–23; Thomas Jefferson to James Madison, 29 December 1801, *JMP* 2:1211–12.

8. Madison to Robert Livingston, 1 May 1802, *JMP* 3:1254–55.

9. Jefferson to James Monroe, 24 November 1801, *JPF* 8:105–6.

10. On the demographic situation in the United States in 1800, see the justifiably celebrated account in Adams, *History*, 1:5–14.

11. For Jefferson's view of Spain as the perfect European power to occupy North America, see Jefferson to Archibald Stuart, 25–26 January 1786, *JP* 9:215–22, and Jefferson to William C. Claiborne, 13 July 1801, *JPF* 8:71–72.

12. Rufus King to Madison, 29 March 1801, *MP* (State) 1:55–56; Jefferson to Thomas Cooper, 29 November 1802, *JPF* 8:177.

13. Jefferson to Robert Livingston, 18 April 1802, *JPF* 8:143–47.

14. Ibid., 8:146–47.

15. Jefferson to Pierre Samuel Du Pont de Nemours, 25 April 1802, Dumas Malone, ed., *Correspondence Between Thomas Jefferson and Pierre Samuel Du Pont de Nemours, 1798–1817* (Boston, 1930), 46–48.

16. Jefferson to John Bacon, 30 April 1803, *JPF* 8:228–29.

17. George Dangerfield, *Chancellor Robert R. Livingston of New York, 1746–1813* (New York, 1960), 309–11, for the Napoleon remark; Jefferson to Madison, 19 March 1803, *JMP* 2:1265–66, for Jefferson's concerns about Livingston's innocence.

18. This sketch is based on Dangerfield, *Chancellor Robert R. Livingston;* the profiles in Adams, *History*, 1:76–77, 322–23; and Kukla, *A Wilderness So Immense*, 235–38.

19. The Talleyrand quotation is from Adams, *History*, 1:241.

20. Robert Livingston to Madison, 20 December 1802, *MP* (State) 4:203–5.

21. Jefferson to Thomas McKean, 14 June 1802, quoted in Adams, *History,* 1:279. See also Jefferson to Robert Livingston, 18 March 1802, *JPF* 9:363–68. The requested budget cuts are in Second Annual Message, 15 December 1802, *JPF* 8:181–87.

22. Kukla, *A Wilderness So Immense,* 267; Adams, *History,* 1:291. The Hamilton quotation is in *HP* 26:83, which reprints Hamilton's editorial of 8 February 1803 from the *New York Evening Post.*

23. Jefferson to James Monroe, 10 and 13 January 1803, *JPF* 8:188, 192. See also Jefferson to Madison, 22 February 1803, *JMP* 2:1262.

24. The text of the Livingston memorandum, questioning the wisdom of French ownership of Louisiana, is described in Robert Livingston to Madison, 18 March 1803, *MP* (State) 4:431–32.

25. Livingston quoted in Joseph J. Ellis, *American Sphinx: The Character of Thomas Jefferson* (New York, 1996), 207. Jefferson acknowledged the accuracy of Livingston's assessment of Napoleon in Jefferson to Madison, 18 August 1803, *JMP* 2:1279.

26. Napoleon's instructions to Leclerc are quoted in Kukla, *A Wilderness So Immense,* 221–22. Three books provide the detailed and complicated context of the situation in Santo Domingo: C. L. R. James, *The Black Jacobins: Toussaint L'Ouverture and the San Domingo Revolution* (New York, 1963); Thomas O. Ott, *The Haitian Revolution, 1789–1804* (Knoxville, Tenn., 1973); Carolyn E. Fick, *The Making of Haiti: The Saint Domingue Revolution from Below* (Knoxville, Tenn., 1990). More recently, see Lester Langley, *The Americas in the Age of Revolution, 1750–1850* (New Haven, 1996), 130–33.

27. Charles Leclerc to Napoleon, 6 and 9 August 1802, quoted in James, *The Black Jacobins,* 343–45.

28. François Barbé-Marbois, *The History of Louisiana, Particularly of the Cession of the Colony to the United States of America* (Philadelphia, 1830; reprint, Baton Rouge, 1977), 274–76.

29. Ibid., 263. See also Adams, *History,* 1:328, and Kukla, *A Wilderness So Immense,* 252–54.

30. Robert Livingston to Madison, 17 April 1803, *MP* (State) 4:524–26.

31. Confidential Message on Expedition to the Pacific, 18 January 1803, *JPF* 8:192–93; Jefferson to Meriwether Lewis, 27 April 1803, *JPF* 8:193–94; Jefferson to Meriwether Lewis, 15 July 1803, *JPF* 8:199–200.

32. Quoted in *JMP* 2:1291.

33. Adams, *History,* 1:350–51. Livingston and Monroe concurred with Jefferson's expansive interpretation of the borders question, especially regarding West Florida. See Robert Livingston and James Monroe to Madison, 7 June 1803, *MP* (State) 5:72–77.

34. Jefferson to John Breckenridge, 12 August 1803, *JPF* 8:243. See also Jefferson to James Monroe, 17 July 1803, *JMP* 2:1272–73.

35. Draft of an Amendment to the Constitution, [July 1803], *JPF* 8:241–49; Jefferson to Albert Gallatin, 15 January 1803, *JPF* 8:242; Jefferson to John Breckenridge, 12 August 1803, *JPF* 8:244.

36. Jefferson to Albert Gallatin, 13 January 1803, Henry Adams, ed., *The Writings of Albert Gallatin,* 3 vols. (Philadelphia, 1879), 1:111–15.

37. Revised Draft of Jefferson's Proposed Constitutional Amendment on Louisiana, 24 August 1803, *JMP* 2:1270–71.

38. Jefferson to Madison, 18 August 1803, *JMP* 2:1278; also, on the same day, Jefferson to Thomas Paine, *JPF* 8:245. The last quotation is from Jefferson to John Colvin, 20 September 1810, *JPF* 9:46.

39. Jefferson to Wilson Cary Nicholas, 7 September 1803, *JPF* 8:247–48.

40. Plumer's comment is in *JMP* 2:1290–91.

41. Given his predilection for irony, the fact that Henry Adams lingered over this constitutional version of musical chairs is not surprising. See Adams, *History,* 1:360–63.

42. See Kukla, *A Wilderness So Immense,* 292–94, for a convenient summary of Ames's position.

43. Second Inaugural, 5 March 1805, *JPF* 8:344; Jefferson to Joseph Priestley, 29 January 1805, *JPF* 8:295.

44. *JMP* 2:1287, which was Jefferson's first use of the phrase "empire of liberty."

45. Kukla, *A Wilderness So Immense,* 350–53, which reproduces the entire treaty, to include Article III.

46. Jefferson to John Breckenridge, 24 November 1803, *JPF* 8:279–81; Madison to Robert Livingston, 31 January 1804, *MP* (State) 6:239.

47. Ellis, *American Sphinx,* 211; Jefferson to De Witt Clinton, 2 December 1803, *JPF* 8:232–83.

48. Revised Draft of Jefferson's Proposed Constitutional Amendment on Louisiana, 24 August 1803, *JMP* 2:1270.

49. Jefferson to Horatio Gates, 11 July 1803, *JPF* 8:251.

50. Jefferson to William Henry Harrison, 27 February 1803, and Jefferson to William C. C. Claiborne, 24 May 1803, quoted in Christian B. Keller, "Philanthropy Betrayed: Thomas Jefferson, the Louisiana Purchase, and the Origins of Federal Indian Removal Policy," *Proceedings of the American Philosophical Society* 144 (2000), 39–58.

51. Jefferson to John Dickinson, 9 August 1803, *JPF* 8:262–63. See also Jefferson to Horatio Gates, 11 July 1803, *JPF* 8:251. The best account of Jefferson's Indian policy during his presidency is Anthony F. C. Wallace, *Jefferson and the Indians: The Tragic Fate of the First Americans* (Cambridge, Mass., 1999), 206–75.

52. More has been written on Jefferson and slavery in recent years than on any

other topic in the Jefferson corpus. My own effort to contribute to the ongoing debate, along with references to the major scholarship on the subject, can be found in *American Sphinx,* 134–52. On the subject of Jefferson, slavery, and the Purchase, see Roger G. Kennedy, *Mr. Jefferson's Lost Cause: Land, Farmers, Slavery, and the Louisiana Purchase* (New York, 2003).

53. The outline of the gradual emancipation scheme proposed here was debated in the spring of 1790 by the House of Representatives. I tell that story in my *Founding Brothers: The Revolutionary Generation* (New York, 2000), 81–119. My point here is that the acquisition of the Louisiana Territory presented a unique opportunity to face the slavery question squarely before the Cotton Kingdom was fully established and the number of slaves multiplied to the millions. It also provided the source of revenue required to make gradual emancipation economically feasible.

54. Adams, *History,* 1:366–79, for the Federalist ad hominem attacks on Jefferson, and Kukla, *A Wilderness So Immense,* 295–300, for their secessionist response to the Purchase.

55. Merrill D. Peterson, ed., *Visitors to Monticello* (Charlottesville, 1989), 90–91. For similar sentiments, see Jefferson to Hugh Nelson, 7 February and 12 March 1820, *JPF* 10:156–57.

56. Jefferson to John Holmes, 22 April 1820, *JPF* 10:157–58. Donald E. Fehrenbacher, "The Missouri Controversy and the Sources of Southern Separation," *Southern Review* 14 (1978), 653–67, still seems to me the wisest historical commentary on the mentality that Jefferson brought to the Missouri Question.

57. Adams to Louisa Catherine Adams, 29 January 1820, quoted in Ellis, *American Sphinx,* 266.

58. Jefferson to Albert Gallatin, 26 December 1820, *JPF* 10:175–78.

59. Jefferson to David Bailey Warden, 26 December 1820, *JPF* 10:173; Jefferson to Jared Sparks, 4 February 1824, *JPF* 10:289–93.

60. Jefferson to Albert Gallatin, 26 December 1820, and Jefferson to Henry Dearborn, 7 August 1821, *JPF* 10:175–78, 191–92.

ACKNOWLEDGMENTS

My ineptitude at managing research assistants has become legendary, so I have long since given up the practice altogether. All the research for this book was done by me alone, with one exception. Cyrus Moshiri, a precocious senior at Deerfield Academy, double-checked my reading of the congressional debates over the Louisiana Purchase.

Over the years, I have developed the habit of sending draft chapters to scholarly friends with expertise in the relevant topics. And so Douglas Wilson at the Lincoln Center and Tara Fitzpatrick of Mount Holyoke read "The Year," Don Higginbotham at Chapel Hill read "The Winter," Jack Rakove at Stanford read "The Argument," and Pauline Maier at MIT read "The Conspiracy." Christopher Benfey, my colleague at Mount Holyoke, read "The Treaty." None of these readers agreed completely with my interpretation of these founding moments, and none should be held accountable for my inevitable gaffes. A former student, Carin Peller, made stylistic suggestions about several early chapters.

I asked three long-standing scholarly colleagues to read the entire manuscript. Edmund Morgan, my former mentor at Yale, made shrewd suggestions that confirmed his reputation as the best in the business. Robert Dalzell of Williams emboldened me to have the courage of my convictions. Stephen Smith, formerly editor of *U.S. News & World Report,* enhanced his standing as the sharpest editorial eye inside the Beltway. I also asked one of my current students at Mount Holyoke,

Zoë Gibbons, to read the final draft, and she responded with five hand-written pages of critical commentary that I could not afford to ignore.

The manuscript was handwritten, not with a quill, but with a medium-point rollerball pen, in black ink. Deciphering my scrawl fell to Holly Sharac, my accomplice on three previous books, who has become an editor as well as a typist.

My agent, Ike Williams, provided encouraging words as each chapter dribbled forth. During dry spells, we talked about the Boston Red Sox and the New England Patriots. My editor, Ashbel Green, solidified his reputation as the salt of the earth and the world's greatest expert on adjectives and titles. His able assistant, Sara Sherbill, ushered the manuscript through the publishing process with uncommon competence and grace and never put me on hold. My wife, Ellen Wilkins Ellis, put up with my vacant stares at dinner when my mind was back there in the eighteenth century, and displayed great grace in listening to readings of the day's work.

An early and much shorter version of the chapter entitled "The Treaty" originally appeared in a collection of essays edited by Byron Hollinshead, *I Wish I'd Been There* (New York, 2006).

The historian who most influenced me as I scribbled my words was Henry Adams. His monumental account of the Jefferson and Madison presidencies focuses on a slightly later era, but his seamless combination of style and irony became my model for the story I tried to tell.

The dedication is to my youngest son, a sixteen-year-old lad who claims he can write better than his father and that this dedication is long overdue.

Joseph J. Ellis
Amherst, Massachusetts

INDEX

271

A NOTE ABOUT THE AUTHOR

Joseph J. Ellis is Ford Foundation Professor of History at Mount Holyoke College. Educated at the College of William and Mary and Yale University, he was dean of the faculty at Mount Holyoke for ten years. His *Founding Brothers: The Revolutionary Generation* won the Pulitzer Prize in 2001, and *American Sphinx: The Character of Thomas Jefferson* earned the 1997 National Book Award. He has three sons and lives in Amherst, Massachusetts, with his wife, Ellen.

A NOTE ON THE TYPE

This book was set in Adobe Garamond. Designed for the Adobe Corporation by Robert Slimbach, the fonts are based on types first cut by Claude Garamond (c. 1480–1561). Garamond was a pupil of Geoffroy Tory and is believed to have followed the Venetian models, although he introduced a number of important differences, and it is to him that we owe the letter we now know as "old style." He gave to his letters a certain elegance and feeling of movement that won their creator an immediate reputation and the patronage of Francis I of France.

COMPOSED BY CREATIVE GRAPHICS,
ALLENTOWN, PENNSYLVANIA

BOOK DESIGN BY ROBERT C. OLSSON

Marian Burros, the nationally-known Food Editor for the Washington Post, broadcasts regular consumer features for NBC-TV.

PURE & SIMPLE
Delicious Recipes for Additive-free Cooking

An Elegant & Easy Cookbook
with Up-To-Date Advice on
Avoiding Ingredients that Contain
Chemicals & Preservatives

MARIAN BURROS

BERKLEY BOOKS, NEW YORK

PURE & SIMPLE

A Berkley Book / published by arrangement with
William Morrow and Company, Inc.

PRINTING HISTORY
William Morrow edition published 1978
Berkley edition / September 1979
Berkley trade paperback edition / September 1982

ISBN: 0-425-05643-0

A BERKLEY BOOK ® TM 757,375
Berkley Books are published by Berkley Publishing Corporation,
200 Madison Avenue, New York, New York 10016.
The name "BERKLEY" and the stylized "B" with design are
trademarks belonging to Berkley Publishing Corporation.
PRINTED IN THE UNITED STATES OF AMERICA

ACKNOWLEDGMENTS

F PEOPLE FIND *Pure & Simple* useful, it will be thanks to the efforts of a lot of people. Credit for the accuracy and clarity of the information, and the workability of the recipes, is shared by many, some of whom prefer anonymity!

Among those willing to be counted, I want to especially thank my husband, Donald. In addition to being the best chopper and slicer any cook can have, he is the taster par excellence. His approval or disapproval of a newly created recipe determined whether or not anyone else ever got to taste it.

My daughter, Ann, who helped me prove an important point about the inconvenience of convenience foods, as recounted elsewhere in the book, is also an excellent critic of taste.

My son, Michael, tested several recipes, contributed a few new ones and raised my consciousness about vegetarian dishes.

Over the years Shang Patterson has tested hundreds of recipes for me in my work as a newspaper food editor. She did yeoman's service on the book, especially in the convenience-food section.

My dear friend Sherley Koteen graciously agreed to read the manuscript to make sure it was intelligible to lay persons.

Joan Dye Gussow, chairman of the program in nutrition education at Columbia University Teachers College, read the first chapter as a nutrition educator and professional editor. Her help was invaluable. It is because of such a good friend and colleague that I haven't put my foot in my mouth.

If the book works, my friends and family deserve a lot of the credit; if it doesn't, blame me.

M.F.B.

Bethesda, Maryland
September, 1977

CONTENTS

INTRODUCTION

Sugar, hydrogenated coconut and soybean oils, propylene glycol, mono-stearate (emulsifier for uniform blending of oils), corn syrup solids, sodium caseinate (a protein), whey solids, sodium silico aluminate (prevents caking), hydroxylated soybean lecithin and acetylated mono-glycerides (emulsifiers), artificial flavor and color, BHA (a preservative).

THAT LIST OF UNRECOGNIZABLE, UNPRONOUNCEABLE INGREDIENTS produces fake whipped cream, found frequently on top of a chocolate mousse, spread over pumpkin pie or as a garnish for an ice cream parfait. You can recognize the product by its unreal whiteness and oily aftertaste.

Have you ever wondered how much this ersatz cream costs compared to genuine heavy whipping cream?

Have you ever wondered what all those ingredients might be?

In the late Fifties and early Sixties I never gave such questions a thought. Like the vast majority of other Americans I couldn't wait to try the newest convenience product. Advertising had conned me into believing, just as it had almost everyone else, that what came out of the laboratories of the big food companies tasted better, was cheaper than anything I could make at home and would save me hours of drudgery in the kitchen.

But I was lucky. I was exposed to some of the finest cooking in the world through travel to France and Italy. And by one of those strange twists of fate, just as I was beginning to question the taste of the highly processed foods, I began to get little hints that some of the things being put into them might not be safe either. Eventually it dawned on me that in addition to a lack of taste and the questions of safety, I was paying too much for these foods which were also short on nutrition.

So over the years I have moved away from highly processed or so-called convenience foods. This chapter, I hope, explains why.

PROCESSED FOOD: WHAT IT MEANS

By the time any food arrives at the supermarket it has been processed in some way, but there are degrees, from the simplest defuzzing of peaches and the more complex cutting up of a steer into family-size portions, to the kind of processing that produces fake whipped cream.

Sometimes the processing yields products that imitate natural foods—albeit poorly—with combinations of chemicals that never quite make it on the taste scale and definitely don't make it when it comes to providing various micronutrients and trace minerals found in real foods.

Frequently technology destroys the integrity of the natural product by removing most of the nutrients; it often adulterates the raw material by adding a variety of additives. Some additives provide longer shelf life or keep ingredients from separating. Others offer bright new colors, change the flavor or texture. Still others replace the expensive valuable nutrients with cheap ones to increase profitability. Almost without exception, these highly processed foods are far more costly than what is made at home from scratch.

After all, when you prepare food at home, no one is paying you factory labor rates to add a pat of butter to a pot of peas or put the peas-in-butter-sauce into one of those plastic pouches, which also take a tremendous amount of fossil fuel energy to produce. This makes the peas-in-butter-sauce in the boil-in-the-bag pouch in the coated-paper carton cost 20 cents more than the ingredients are actually worth. But the greatest profitability for the food manufacturer is in the highly processed foods, and they often turn out to be those with the least nutritional value. They certainly are the ones with the most food additives.

PROCESSED FOODS: THE COST FACTOR

The purchase of most highly processed foods such as sauce mixes, Hamburger Helper, orange juice substitutes and vegetable dishes with sauce usually does mean overpayment. We have been conned by advertising into believing that we not only don't want to take the time to make these seemingly complicated dishes with dozens of unpronounceable ingredients, but we really aren't capable. Besides, don't cake mixes taste just as good, even better, than homemade cakes? Aren't soups made from a chemical feast just as good as Grandma's? (Only if Grandma was a food technologist in a white lab coat.) How about those seasonings for ground beef that are supposed to put from-scratch creations to shame in half the time?.

The answer is a resounding "No!" But if we are unable to make cakes from scratch, part of the problem may be that no one has ever taught us. Many home-economics classes in school show students only how to open a box, pour the contents into a bowl, and add an egg and some water.

Of course, someone at home should be doing the teaching, and probably anyone who has gotten this far in the book isn't letting his or her children grow up ignorant of the fact that warm mixtures must be added slowly to uncooked eggs; that flour can't be added to liquid without making a paste first; that real food tastes better than fake.

Another sad and ironic point is that in most cases convenience foods aren't that convenient. Hamburger Helper is a wonderful example. So are salad-dressing mixes, pancake mixes, flavored rice—the list is endless.

We did a time-and-motion study with Hamburger Helper once, just for fun. The anchorman on the evening news at WRC-TV, NBC's Washington station where I work, pooh-poohed a piece I did that explained why it is cheaper and quicker and better to make Hamburger Helper from scratch. I challenged him to a Hamburger Helper cookoff with my thirteen-year-old daughter.

I taught her the basic elements that give flavor to one of the Hamburger Helper varieties, minus all the unnecessary chemicals. With or without the box, you still have to supply the meat and brown it and cook the noodles. My daughter, Ann, cooked her from-scratch version in under five minutes; the anchorman, Jim Vance, took over eight. He was convinced, especially after he tasted hers and liked the flavor better! Moreover, the cost factor put a double whammy on the whole game. At the time a box of Hamburger Helper cost 69 cents, but with noodles from a box, a can of tomato sauce and the seasonings, the from-scratch version cost only 45 cents.

PROCESSED FOODS: THE SAFETY FACTOR

With the banning of certain additives over the last several years you must have wondered about the safety of those still in the food.

If you have, you probably dismissed such questions as unimportant, because, after all, the store wouldn't sell you anything that wasn't safe to eat. Right?

Wrong!

You were right to wonder but wrong to assume that everything added to food is safe and throughly tested.

Perhaps you react as the First Lady, Rosalynn Carter, told me she did when she used to do her own grocery shopping. In October, 1976, Mrs. Carter said she was concerned about the additives put in food. "It bothers me a little. I do try to read ingredients but I haven't had time to become really concerned, because I do so little cooking now and I use so few of those things.

"I know how distressed I get in the grocery store [when something isn't labeled]. You have to know what you're eating."

The Food and Drug Administration, which is supposed to oversee the safety of what may be put into food, has an extremely difficult job. There are several reasons for this. The nature of the federal bureaucracy is to leave things as they are, not to rock the boat. In addition, the pressures brought by special-interest groups such as the food industry, which want to conduct business with as little government intervention as possible, are extremely powerful. And the countervailing force—you and me, the consumer—is pitifully small and weak in comparison.

It doesn't help that many of the important officials in the FDA have worked for the food industry which they are supposed to be regulating, or plan to join the industry when they leave the FDA. Such regulators do not regulate with the kind of impartiality and steely-eyed objectivity needed. Though the FDA Commissioner appointed by President Carter, Dr. Donald Kennedy, has no such ties and has earned high marks from consumer advocates for some of his actions, there is a long way to go. So many additives in use have never been tested properly. And the process of testing them is lengthy.

Thus the safety of food additives is not what it should be. Every year brings the banning or petition for banning of another chemical that has been added to food for decades. In 1976 Red Number 2 and Red Number 4 food colors were finally banished from foods. That same year the FDA was petitioned to ban all of the other coal-tar-based dyes along with sodium nitrite, found in most processed meats. The attempt by the FDA to ban saccharin made headlines in March, 1977. And the governmental group studying food additives already in use put out a report that said there might be problems with BHT, an additive used to prevent oils from turning rancid. BHT has been removed from the GRAS (Generally Recognized As Safe) list and placed in an interim category which permits continued use while further testing is conducted. In the meantime a petition to ban BHT has been presented to the FDA. The same government-appointed group studying additives also said that hydrolized vegetable protein (HVP) should be taken out of baby food. Generally, the public is not even aware that questions of safety have arisen about a food additive until something drastic, such as a ban, is imminent.

In 1976 it became abundantly clear that some tests of safety submitted to the FDA by a manufacturer wishing to market a new additive had been rigged. Companies have juggled statistical results to prove safety; the records kept on test animals have been sloppy or, worse, altered. (The FDA is investigating some of these companies and tests now.) So it's a little difficult to have faith in the safety of the food supply, particularly the safety of processed foods.

The food industry argues that there are many hazardous substances occurring *naturally* in foods. And they are right. There are many hazardous substances which make their way into food, not just from pesticides, fungicides and herbicides, but from the water, air and earth itself: DDT, PBB's, PCB's end up in food and then in us—unintentionally, of course. This fact leads some people to conclude that if an additive is not absolutely safe, what difference does it make? Of course! But why make matters worse? As Dr. Jean Mayer, formerly professor of nutrition at Harvard University and now president of Tufts University, wrote in the introduction to *Eater's Digest: A Consumer's Factbook of Food Additives*, "any added chemical of necessity increases the risk, albeit by a small amount." If you keep adding up these small amounts, pretty soon the amount isn't so small anymore. And there is no way to know how much of such potentially dangerous substances are needed to cause birth defects or cancer.

Cancer experts say there is no known level at which a carcinogen (cancer-causing agent) can be considered safe. One then has to decide whether or not it is worth taking the risk. Do the benefits of eating bacon or ham cured with sodium nitrite, or beef liver contaminated with traces of diethylstilbestrol (DES), outweigh the risks? What about saccharin? It is considered a weak carcinogen, but that does not mean that you would have to drink eight hundred bottles of diet soda a day to get cancer, as the diet industry would have you believe. It simply means that it takes more of a weak carcinogen than of a strong one to cause cancer; it takes longer for tumors to develop and fewer people in the population will be stricken.

Is using saccharin worth the risk? Maybe, if you are diabetic, though many doctors who specialize in the treatment of diabetes say it is not essential, that desire for sweet things should be satisfied with naturally sweet foods such as fruits.

Most saccharin, however, is not used by diabetics. It is used by soda-pop drinkers, especially teen-agers and young adults. Unfortunately, this puts those believed to be at greatest risk—unborn children—at the mercy of what the mother-to-be has been drinking. In the famous Canadian rat study on which the proposed saccharin ban is based, the greatest number of malignant tumors occurred in the animals whose mothers had been fed saccharin while they were carrying the fetuses.

Do the benefits—so far undetermined—outweigh the risks? Only if you are in the business of selling diet sodas, it seems to me!

Mrs. Carter told me in an interview with her before she became First Lady that her gut reaction to potential hazards in the food supply is "remove it. Find out if it is safe and then put it back on the market. We ought not wait until after it's tested," she said. "I don't think we should suffer until we find out."

The benefits of food additives are often benefits for food manufacturers. For example, by adding BHT to a box of its product, a cereal company can give it a shelf life of two years. But who keeps cereal at home for two years?

Certainly the artificial red coloring and artificial strawberry flavoring in most strawberry ice cream does nothing for the consumer. But by adding red coloring and artificial flavor the producer doesn't have to put in very many strawberries, if any! Sure, this is cheaper than naturally colored and flavored ice cream; but when you compare the taste and quality, no matter how cheap the artificial product is, it isn't worth the price. You know how true that is if you have ever left cheap ice cream on the drainboard overnight and returned the next morning to find a gummy mass where there had once been a great big half-gallon. What happened? In addition to the synthetic ingredients in the cheap ice cream, so much air has been beaten into it that when it melts, there's very little real substance left.

Since artificial colors are under a deep cloud of suspicion as potentially dangerous and certainly insufficiently tested, why eat them? Because through conditioning we have come to expect our food to look a certain way.

Ruth Winter, author of *A Consumer's Dictionary of Food Additives*, thinks she knows what happened:

> We want enhanced food because all of our lives we have been subjected to beautiful pictures of foods in our magazines and on television. We have come to expect an advertiser's concept of perfection in color and texture, even though Mother Nature may not turn out all her products that way. As a result the skin of the oranges we eat are dyed bright orange to match our mental image of an ideal orange.

A Swedish journalist, visiting here several summers ago, brought the point home very quickly. She made short shrift of the introductory pleasantries when we met. What she really wanted to know was why our cheeses were such a funny color. In Sweden, she said, they didn't have artificially colored cheeses, and orange seemed a peculiar shade! Orange Cheddar cheese doesn't taste any different from natural creamy-colored Cheddar, but some people think orange cheese means expensive aged cheese. It doesn't. Bright-orange Cheddar cheese versus naturally colored cheese appears to be a matter of economic deception. This is certainly the case with the orange color in orange breakfast drinks. Such drinks are colored orange to make them look like orange juice. They are flavored to make them taste a little like orange juice and even have a few of the nutrients found in the real thing. But they don't contain the trace nutrients found in real oranges which are essential to health. And clearly they don't taste like the real thing!

LABEL LANGUAGE: WHAT IT MEANS

How many times have you looked at a label on a can or box and seen words such as "enriched" or "fortified" or even "antioxidant" and wondered exactly what those terms meant? Probably many times! I've tried here to provide a working knowledge of a few of the more commonly used terms.

Enrichment

Are all the chemical additives risky? Certainly the ones which have been singled out here are: sodium nitrite, saccharin, DES, artificial colors and BHT. But some additives actually do relatively good things. In certain foods some, but not all, of the vitamins and minerals which had been stripped away in the processing are re-added. In this case additives are good, or at least harmless. The process of re-adding vitamins and minerals is called *enrichment* and is used for such foods as breads, white rice, and cereals.

Fortification

Fortification, or adding nutrients to foods that didn't have them even before processing, is another relatively beneficial process. However, no amount of fortifying with a few nutrients is going to turn junk food into good food.

Those dreadful "fortified" cupcakes, sometimes served as part of the school-breakfast program in some places, are a perfect example. (The Department of Agriculture, under Secretary Bob Bergland, proposed removing them from the program in 1977.) Even if such a cupcake had 100 percent of the Recommended Daily Allowance of the eight vitamins and minerals used in nutrition labeling, it would still be totally unsuitable for breakfast, as are breakfast bars and other candies, cookies and fortified sweets. They contain too much sugar, too much fat and, in certain cases, undesirable additives such as artificial color.

Vitamins and minerals, of course, are good guys, and their addition to food is not all bad. The iron used to fortify bread and the iodine added to salt are examples of beneficial fortification. But for the most part it's better to obtain nutrients directly from their natural source.

Flavor Enhancers

Flavor enhancers are used to bring out the flavor in foods but, in fact, reduce the amount of natural (and more expensive) ingredients needed in food. The ubiquitous monosodium glutamate (MSG) is such a product. It's hard to find any prepared products for entrees and side dishes without it.

Besides the fact that MSG makes manufactured chicken soup seem as if it contains a lot of chicken when it may contain very little or none, MSG has an unpleasant, allergic effect on many, many people. MSG causes what is known as the Chinese Restaurant Syndrome because the reaction was discovered by a doctor after he ate Chinese food. Symptoms include tightness in the neck, base of the skull, head and chest, as well as dizziness. The reaction passes within a few hours, fortunately.

Thickening Agents and Stabilizers

Thickening agents and stabilizers are needed when inferior ingredients or poor manufacturing practices are used which might result in a watery or lumpy product. Thickening agents, such as modified food starch, are used in cheap yogurt to give it the same consistency as properly made yogurt.

Preservatives and Antioxidants

Preservatives and antioxidants prevent spoilage, but often they are not necessary except to give the product an extremely long shelf life or to cover up poor manufacturing practices.

The best-known preservatives are sodium nitrite and sodium nitrate (nitrates convert to nitrites). Sodium nitrite is used in almost all processed meats; sodium nitrate in a few. In the stomachs of test animals nitrites combine with substances called amines, found in other foods, drugs and tobacco smoke, to form potent carcinogens called nitrosamines. In bacon, however, nitrosamines are formed when the product is fried.

Sodium nitrite is also a flavor enhancer and a coloring agent. (It makes processed meats pink.) It also is used to prevent the formation of the botulism toxins, which can be fatal. However, there are other methods to ensure the safety of processed meats. The old-fashioned long curing of bacon and ham produces not only the same result, but provides what some consider a superior taste. To preserve other processed meats without nitrites, such as bologna, salami, liverwurst, hot dogs, turkey ham, chicken hot dogs, freezing is safe and effective.

There are alternatives to nitrites, but the large manufacturers aren't listening. In September, 1977, the U. S. Department of Agriculture and the FDA told manufacturers of processed meats that they would have to prove specifically that nitrosamines did not form in their products before they hit the stomach and that their use of sodium nitrite was not only essential but safe. The saga of sodium nitrite has been unfolding for many years, but with increased intensity since 1973. A resolution to the problem may be a long way off.

Probably less hazardous but totally unnecessary are the antioxidants BHA (butylated hydroxyanisole) and its close relative BHT (butylated hydroxymethylphenol). Some potato-chip manufacturers don't find it necessary to use either chemical, so obviously they aren't essential, but most potato, corn and tortilla chips contain BHA and/or BHT. Some salad oils and shortening contain one or both chemicals; some don't. This is true for cereals, too. The so-called natural cereals use neither chemical yet they last on the grocers' shelves for nine months or longer. You must read the label to find out where these antioxidants are.

Artificial Colors

Artificial colors, which are purely cosmetic, may be on their way out over the next ten years or so. Either the coal-tar-based dyes have been poorly tested or tests have shown potential hazards. These artificial colors also may cause hyperactivity in some children.

Food colorings can be listed simply as "artificial color" or "FD&C certified coloring," which refers to an FDA food, drug and cosmetic regulation. There is no way to know what such colors are.

Yellow Number 5, also called tartrazine, is a special case because many people are allergic to it. The FDA has proposed that foods containing Yellow Number 5 indicate the presence of the color on the label.

Since artificial colors are potentially hazardous and unnecessary, why eat anything in which they are found? There has been a move toward the use of "natural" food colorings recently, primarily because one by one, artificial colors are being banned. When a label reads "natural color," the coloring agent might be something harmless such as paprika, turmeric or grape skins. But it does not mean the color of the product is its natural color.

A former Commissioner of the FDA, Dr. Alexander Schmidt, said:

> When we take luxury versus necessity into consideration, we begin to move solidly into the area of foods. Certain substances with which we deal, cosmetics for example . . . are not essential to support life, and

therefore should present no risk whatsoever. I have yet to see a really convincing, comprehensive, and quantitative analysis of the benefits of food additives. . . . Some must be described as cosmetic. And we've already established that cosmetics should be without risk.

Artificial Flavors

No matter the flavor, food technologists would have you believe that it is impossible to tell the difference between natural and artificial flavors. But if you have a fairly well developed palate, you can. The artificial flavor often leaves a strange aftertaste; sometimes it doesn't have any recognizable taste at all.

Have you ever tasted an artificially flavored product blindfolded? It's often impossible to tell what the flavor is without a clue from the name or picture. With sweets the overriding taste is usually not flavor, but sweetness.

Meat Analogs

Imitation meat is made of processed soy protein, which has an appearance, texture and nutritive value something like meat. It is used extensively in prepared beef stews, ground-meat products such as spaghetti sauces, and even prepared fish products. It is very cheap and is listed on the label as textured vegetable protein (TVP), textured soy protein or isolated soy protein. But if you want a substitute for meat, you're better off with complementary proteins such as beans and rice, or milk products, even eggs.

LABEL READING: HOW TO DO IT; PACKAGING: WHAT TO LOOK FOR

And *you* can do something about all the other additives, too. If you don't like being ripped off, if you care about how things taste, if you worry about polluting your body with untested or poorly tested substances, you can move away from highly processed foods. You have to learn how to read labels and you have to be selective about raw ingredients.

After January 1, 1978, if all went according to government plan, it should have become a bit easier to find out what is in most processed foods. As of that date, only the following foods still were not required to list all ingredients: cocoa products, macaroni and noodle products, milk and cream, natural cheeses (as opposed to processed cheeses, which are required to list ingredients), food flavorings, mayonnaise and salad dressings, some canned fruits, fruit juices and vegetables, bread, butter and ice cream. By July 1, 1979, ice cream is supposed to carry ingredient labeling. Some food products, such as mayonnaise and salad dressing, appear to be listing all ingredients now, but that is not necessarily the case.

Ingredients are listed in order of predominance, so if water is the first ingredient there is more water in the product than anything else.

The use of additives in unprocessed foods is a little trickier. There are some fruits and vegetables which don't have to indicate the presence of artificial color: Florida oranges, which are dyed during certain months (but not those from California or Arizona); red potatoes; some sweet potatoes.

Much of the produce in the supermarkets is waxed: apples, tomatoes, cucumbers, potatoes, cantaloupes, oranges, bell peppers, lemons, pears, grapefruits, plums, yams. The box in the back room may indicate the presence of wax, but nothing at the point of sale does. You must either peel these fruits and vegetables or wash them thoroughly. Some people go so far as to use Ivory soap to wash them.

Then, of course, there are the *hidden* additives. Keep in mind that many of the chemical residues which are polluting our world end up in the fat of animals. This and the other unhealthful aspects of eating too much fat are excellent reasons for sticking with lean meats and cutting away excess fat.

Most processed meats are also loaded with fat, so they are a very expensive source of protein. You'd have to eat ten slices of bacon or six slices of bologna to get the same amount of protein found in one three-ounce hamburger. Three ounces of hamburger cost about 22 cents; ten slices of bacon cost $1.15; six slices of bologna are 56 cents.

The excessive fat, the high price and the sodium nitrite are enough reasons to scratch such foods from your regular menu. Occasionally, when you may want a bacon or ham flavor, you can seek out those made without sodium nitrite. And that's one place where label reading becomes important.

Most processed products containing sodium nitrite will list the additive on the label, but not if the product has been repackaged at the store or if it has not been sold in interstate commerce. It's reasonable to assume that in the absence of an ingredient statement to the contrary, all of the following contain sodium nitrite: bacon, ham, hot dogs, bologna, salami, liverwurst, luncheon meats, beef jerky, chicken hot dogs, turkey ham, pastrami, corned beef, smoked and pickled tongue, cured sausage, some fresh sausage, smoked fish such as lox, Nova Scotia salmon, whitefish and sturgeon, salt pork.

And don't be fooled if a sign says these meats contain no sodium nitrate (with an *a*). Few processed meats do anymore, but they still contain the nitrites (with an *i*). Nevertheless, each year it becomes easier to find nitrite-free products. Three years ago there was only one place to buy nitrite-free bacon in Washington, D.C. Now there are a dozen or more. And anyone can purchase nitrite-free country ham from the Prospect Store, 10312 U. S. Highway 42, Prospect, Kentucky 40059, and Kites in Wolftown, Virginia 22748.

DES is still permitted as a growth stimulant in cattle, even though in large amounts it has caused a rare form of cancer in some female offspring, and infertility in some male offspring, of women who took it during pregnancy. You have three alternatives: avoid beef entirely and stick to chicken and fish; buy organically grown beef; stay away from beef liver, where most chemical residues end up.

If you don't want to eat ice cream or yogurt with artificial ingredients, there are more choices on the market today than a few years ago. Yogurt and frozen yogurt must list their ingredients on the label. Soon ice cream will have an ingredient statement, too, with one ridiculous exception. Because of the powerful dairy lobby, ice cream, along with butter and natural cheese, does not have to list the presence of artificial coloring. The new FDA regulation that is scheduled to take effect July 1, 1979, requiring ingredient labeling for ice cream, will not change that fact. The FDA has told ice cream manufacturers that they ought to disclose the source of the coloring, but the agency can't force them to do so.

With as many chemicals as most commercial ice creams contain, it hardly seems newsworthy that manufacturers wanted to degrade the product further. But their desire to do away with one of the few natural ingredients left in ice cream—milk!—made headlines across the country. The manufacturers wanted to substitute casein, a chemically derived milk protein, because it would have saved them about 2½ percent in costs. Would the people who buy ice cream ever see these savings? Even the International Association of Ice Cream Manufacturers says it's "doubtful." And don't be taken in by the ice cream label that trumpets "All natural flavor." That doesn't make the rest of the ice cream natural.

On the subject of flavors, a product can call itself "strawberry" ice cream or "orange" drink if it is flavored naturally. If it contains more natural than artificial flavor, it must say "strawberry flavored" ice cream. If it contains more artificial than natural flavor, then it must say "artificially flavored strawberry" ice cream.

But be on your guard for another trend to the "natural" bandwagon. Many products are calling themselves "natural" because the additives they contain come from natural sources: guar gum, locust bean, hydrolized cereal solids.

I have just one simple rule of thumb for determining the naturalness of a product. If I can't make it in my kitchen, it doesn't fit my idea of natural.

Just as it's easier these days to buy more natural ice cream, there are a lot more whole-grain breads available with natural ingredients. No, they won't last in the bread box for three weeks, like white so-called bread that makes better spitballs than sandwiches. But you can keep them for many days in the refrigerator (toast to freshen when the bread gets firm) and much longer in the freezer. Usually it's impossible to tell by looking if the product is 100 percent whole grain or just colored with caramel to make you think so. But the list of ingredients will tell you. If any ingredient listed is "white flour," "enriched flour," "wheat flour," or "sprouted wheat," the bread is *not* whole grain.

That phrase "wheat flour" has been turning up more and more on bread products and it's easy to believe the term is meant to confuse you into thinking the bread is whole wheat. A whole-grain bread will have only whole grains in it. For 100 percent whole-wheat bread, look for "*whole*-wheat flour."

Since ingredients are listed in order of predominance, if the package lists "wheat flour" and then "whole-wheat flour," there is more wheat (white) flour in the product than whole-wheat flour.

With the rage for fiber in the diet, whole-grain breads are a good way to add it, but breads containing powdered cellulose are not. The source of powdered cellulose is likely to be ground-up trees, or wood pulp, which has been chemically treated. The best-known "bread product," touted as high in fiber, is ITT Continental Baking Company's Fresh Horizons Special Formula bread.

The company insists that powdered cellulose is not wood pulp, or, as Senator George McGovern called it during a Senate hearing, "sawdust." But all of ITT's protestations will not change the fact that the powdered cellulose in the bread product started out as a tree. And there are no scientific studies that demonstrate the safety of eating large amounts of wood pulp over a long period of time.

When I wrote a story in *The Washington Post* in 1976 which explained that the powdered cellulose in Fresh Horizons once grew in a forest, ITT threatened legal action, claiming inaccuracies in the story, a threat they never carried out.

When Dr. Art Ulene and I repeated similar information on his "Feeling Fine" segment of the "Today" show the following summer, ITT made the same charges and asked for an opportunity to appear on the show. Dr. Ulene agreed and said he would include some film showing how a loaf of Fresh Horizons was made, from tree to finished product. At first ITT said OK, but the company changed its mind just as the film crew was about to shoot the mixing of the ingredients in the bakery.

Fresh Horizons, which costs 10 cents more per loaf than ordinary bread, must call itself "Special Formula bread" because it is not really bread according to FDA standards. Fresh Horizons is 46 percent water and 7.5 percent wood pulp. Regular bread contains between 35 and 36 percent water and, of course, no wood pulp.

Don't buy breads containing "powdered cellulose." When you want to add fiber to your diet, eat whole grains, fruits and vegetables.

Label reading is also crucial when you approach the cheese display. It is also confusing and time-consuming. But reading labels is the only way you won't have a fast one put over on you, unless you stick with natural cheeses.

The best, and supposedly most expensive, is natural cheese. It has the highest content of dairy product, often called milk fat, and the least amount of moisture (water). You are most likely to find uncolored cheese in this category. Almost without exception all processed cheeses are artificially colored whether or not the label says so.

Pasteurized processed cheese comes next, with a lower milk-fat content and more water. Then pasteurized processed cheese *food* with even less milk fat and even more water. Finally, pasteurized processed cheese *spread* has the least milk fat of the four and the greatest amount of water.

There is one additional class of cheese products called "imitation." This includes diet cheeses and filled cheeses, the latter containing no milk products.

Since milk fat is the costliest ingredient in cheese, the most expensive cheeses should be the natural ones, but that is definitely not the case. The price of processed cheeses is directly related to the amount of packaging, shaping or cutting. Things such as Cheez Kisses, which are made of cheese spread, cost over 50 cents more per pound than a natural aged sharp Cheddar. If your store has unit pricing, so that you can compare the cost per pound, you will spot that in a minute.

As for those individually wrapped cheese slices (most of which are artificially colored anyway), once again you are paying someone to do the wrapping. Almost any time someone else does the slicing, chunking, shaping, cutting or separating, it will cost more.

Aside from all thought of value, price and artificial color, there is not a single processed cheese that can hold a candle to a natural cheese when it comes to taste.

A package of chicken parts—breasts, wings, drumsticks, etc.—is far more expensive than a whole chicken. Even a cut-up chicken, which usually costs a few cents more per pound than a whole chicken, is a better buy than chicken parts. Watch out for those "family packs" and other combinations that have more necks and backs than any normal chicken. They are not good buys.

And when it comes to another kind of poultry—turkey—read labels. Butterball turkeys contain no butter, just cheap vegetable oil. The best buy in turkeys is frozen, plain. The best-tasting are fresh; they cost more but are well worth it.

There are some rare exceptions to the cost of parts versus the whole: pieces of canned fruits, vegetables and nuts are cheaper than the whole. In other words, whole peaches, even peach halves, cost more than peach slices; whole green beans are more expensive than cut; walnut chips are cheaper than walnut halves.

And don't ignore the volume-versus-weight game in the produce section. A lot of produce is sold by the piece, not the pound. Some pieces weigh as much as a pound more than others, but cost the same. So take the time to weigh several heads of cauliflower or baskets of cherry tomatoes if they are sold by volume, to find the best buy.

If supermarkets insist on packaging produce and you find that the apples come only six or more to the package, but all you need is three, either open the package and take out what you want, or ask the produce man to do it for you. If the produce department frowns on this, take it up with the store manager. You might remind him or her that the store is in business to serve customers, not to make them buy more than they can use. If none of these techniques works, take your business elsewhere.

If you don't know what an ingredient is in the prepared foods you wish to buy, you have two choices: leave the product on the shelf or write the manufacturer and ask him. If he doesn't respond, drop the product like a hot potato. What does the company have to hide?

SUPERMARKET ALTERNATIVES

You may have better luck understanding labels in a natural-food store, but you also may be paying a stiff price for some products that are exactly the same as those in the ordinary supermarket. Do some comparative shopping. There are even some instances where the natural-food store offers a better buy. At the one in which I shop, powdered yeast, free of BHT, and unprocessed bran are much, much cheaper. So are some of the grains such as buckwheat groats and bulgur, as well as sunflower seeds, which come unsalted as do all the nuts. (Toasted, unsalted sunflower seeds are a delicious snack!)

Often the natural-food stores are the only source of nitrite-free processed meats in a city, and if you like those foods it's worth the extra money.

Another alternative to supermarket shopping is the farmer's market or roadside truck. These are wonderful places to buy fresh produce from nearby fields and orchards. They help keep local farmers in business and provide city dwellers with the taste of real food, sometimes at savings, seldom for more than the going supermarket price.

These markets are doing extremely well for the same reason people are turning away from convenience foods. Two surveys conducted by both ends of the food chain, a farmers' group and a supermarket industry organization, show this very clearly.

Food Marketing Institute, the trade association for the supermarket industry, has been studying shoppers' habits since 1974. Every six months one of the questions its asks shoppers is whether they have cut down on the amount of convenience foods they have purchased. The numbers who have cut down have been increasing.

The Agriculture Council of America asked shoppers if they were satisfied or dissatisfied with the quality and nutritional value of the food they bought. Fifty percent said they were *not* satisfied. Eighty-six percent said they would prefer less convenience packaging and would welcome the opportunity to buy more in bulk. Eighty-nine percent would like to see more direct farmer-to-consumer marketing. Most people think this will save money; some would prefer it because they could get better quality.

In a 1976 survey of the shopping habits of working versus nonworking women, one of the most interesting statistics of all turned up. More working than nonworking women said they "never" bought frozen TV dinners, prepared main-dish entrees, vegetables, dessert or instant coffee. Apparently, no one has ever been able to sell them a bill of goods about the convenience of convenience foods.

Working and nonworking women alike who did not use such products said:

"If I relied on convenience foods I couldn't afford it."

"I don't like the way they taste."

"They aren't good for you."

"There are too many additives, so I avoid them."

"They all taste alike."

DIETARY GOALS

When you consider the chemicals fed to animals, the pesticides sprayed on the produce, you understand the subtitle of the book: Cooking with the "most" natural, additive-free ingredients you can buy. Nothing is really "pure and simple." And if you are like me, you do the best you can. You get rid of as many hazards as you do not care to live with. You make some compromises.

I use sugar for special-occasion desserts because I still believe there is room for a moderate amount of it in the diet. I also think there is room for an occasional fried dish, but not for lunch every day, or even once a week.

I guess I probably subscribe to the general outline of the Senate Nutrition Committee's report "Dietary Goals for the United States." The report was made public in January, 1977, and has become extremely controversial because it recommends drastic changes in dietary habits in this country. Almost every special-interest group has attacked it: the cattlemen, the sugar association, egg producers, dairy industry, fruit and vegetable canners and the American Medical Association. Why? Because the recommendations call for a drop in the consumption of beef, eggs, sugar, dairy products (particularly those high in fat), canned fruits and vegetables.

How did the AMA get into the act? It's hard to say, except that the association strongly suggests in its critique of "Dietary Goals" that disease should be cured, not prevented.

While I do not agree completely with the Nutrition Committee's dietary recommendations, they provide the most comprehensive guide to eating better for a longer and healthier life ever put out by the federal government. The Committee had no ax to grind.

These are the six goals outlined by the Nutrition Committee report:

1. An increase in consumption of complex carbohydrates so they account for 55 to 60 percent of the caloric intake.
2. Reduction in sugar consumption by 40 percent so that it accounts for about 15 percent of total caloric intake.
3. Reduction in overall fat consumption by 10 percent so that it accounts for about 30 percent of total calories.
4. Reduction in saturated-fat consumption to account for about 10 percent of total calories; and balance that with polyunsaturated and monosaturated fats, which should account for about 10 percent of the calories each.
5. Reduction in cholesterol consumption to about 300 milligrams a day.
6. Reduction in salt consumption by 50 to 85 percent.

Since diet-related illness—heart disease, certain forms of cancer, diabetes and obesity—is believed to be the major cause of death and disability in the United States, Americans have to start changing their eating habits. Moderation is the key, so I would be the first to say that many of the recipes in the book are not appropriate as a steady diet.

But for festive or important occasions, for parties and celebrations, why not? If you eat fruit for dessert five nights a week, there's nothing wrong with a mousse or a cake on Saturday. If you have plain broiled entrees at family meals every weekday night, a casserole of chicken, sour cream and wine for Sunday dinner is just fine.

Well-prepared basic ingredients are far more satisfying than the highly processed foods so you tend to eat less of them. Psychologically, it is because you are satisfied by them. Physiologically, foods high in complex carbohydrates—fruits, vegetables, whole grains—add more bulk to your diet than refined carbohydrates—candy, cookies and other sweets—so you are more quickly satiated.

Ironically, using natural or barely processed ingredients (frozen plain vegetables) does not cost more than using highly processed foods.

NEW TRENDS IN COOKING

Along with the turning away from factory-produced convenience is an increase in the purchase of kitchen equipment designed to make cooking from scratch quicker and easier. From the costly food processors which make short work of onion chopping, meat grinding, etc., to the slow cookers which make it possible to simmer a stew all day while you are at work, sales have increased dramatically.

Attendance at cooking schools is high. Men are going more often, too, as young households share more of the kitchen chores.

Frankly, it had never occurred to me to combine the serious aspects of my work as food editor of *The Washington Post* and reporter for WRC-TV—economics, safety and health—with my love of well-prepared foods and good cooking. It was my agent's idea!

This chapter is the serious part. Doubtless it will anger some people. There will be attempts to discredit it, but I'll stick with erring on the side of safety. And anyone who can argue that factory-prepared food tastes as good as what you make at home with the best ingredients either was born without taste buds or has had them numbed by countless encounters with the technological marvels of laboratory-created foods.

For those who like the ready-when-you-need-it quality of some convenience foods, a chapter has been included on making your own. These recipes are as convenient as anything you can buy, are practically free of additives and always cost less than those you buy readymade when comparable ingredients are used. You can make them when you have the time and put them away to use when you are in a hurry.

Some of the convenience-food recipes are included not only for convenience but also to show you how easy it is to make certain foods at home such as your own meat sauce, frozen yogurt, mincemeat with real meat, flavored gelatins, and beef and chicken stock or broth (the words are interchangeable). Most of the recipes in this chapter are for family meals when you are in a rush, though some of them certainly fit properly into entertaining menus. There is a chapter on meatless main dishes, making it easier to entertain your lacto-ovo vegetarian (those who eat egg and milk products but not meats) friends and relatives. Everyone seems to have at least one these days. Dozens of recipes in other chapters are meatless as well.

These recipes are an eclectic collection of dishes with which I have been experimenting and entertaining for the last five years. There has been no particular effort to include "one of each kind." Rather, there is an almost visible thread running through them which traces my interest in new ethnic foods—Chinese, particularly Szechuan, Middle Eastern and Mexican—and my increasing reliance on vegetables and fruits.

In other words, the recipes are simply those I have served that our guests have enjoyed. Coming to dinner at our house involves being a guinea pig most of the time. So far no complaints.

In my metamorphosis from user of convenience foods to lover of the basics, I have learned many new things. They include changes and substitutions that must be made in order to convert ingredients in the following recipes:

- Substitute brown rice for white-brown rice. It takes 45 minutes to cook brown rice, so just start it earlier. When cooked, it has a nut-like flavor and doesn't look much browner than white rice.
- Substitute honey or molasses for sugar. It does not work for everything, and certainly not in a light cake. Honey and molasses give a moister, chewier, heavier texture and also may cause excessive browning.

  For every 1¼ cups sugar, use 1 cup honey and decrease liquid by ¼ cup. If there is no liquid in the recipe, add ¼ cup of flour. Unless sour cream or sour milk is used in the recipe, add a pinch of baking soda.

  For every ¾ cup sugar, use 1 cup unsulfured molasses. Decrease liquid by ¼ cup for each cup of molasses, omit any baking powder and add ½ teaspoon baking soda.

- Substitute unbleached white flour for bleached all-purpose on a one-to-one ratio.
- Substitute whole-wheat for white all-purpose flour. For every cup of white use ¾ cup whole-wheat. Reduce shortening by using two tablespoons for every three called for. Add a tablespoon or two of liquid for cakes, slightly more for breads.
- Substitute fresh herbs for dried. Use three times as much fresh. If a recipe calls for 1 tablespoon of dried dill, use 3 tablespoons fresh. This is just a guide because the amount you use will depend in part on the age, and therefore potency, of the dried herbs with which you usually cook.
- Use fresh ginger. When you find it buy a large piece; and after you have used what you need, freeze the rest. When you need fresh ginger, thin slices can be cut quite easily from the frozen piece.
- Use Chinese or Japanese soy sauce. Use the Chinese light (unless the recipe directs otherwise) if you can get it. If not, use the Japanese brand found in most supermarkets. *Don't* use the American brand; it has more "junk" than the others and is much saltier.
- Substitute pasteurized heavy cream for ultrapasteurized heavy cream. The dairy industry has figured out a way to make heavy cream last four times as long as any self-respecting cream should through ultrapasteurization. Also, many people complain that ultrapasteurized cream does not whip properly.
- Substitute unsalted for salted butter. First, it is less likely to be colored. Then it is more likely to be fresh. Unsalted butter is made from fresh cream instead of cream that has turned. Salt helps to disguise the soured taste.
- Learn to use less salt. While some recipes call for a specific amount of salt, less can be used, or it can be eliminated entirely except where it performs a specific function, such as in the recipe for making gravlax (marinated salmon).

To make it easier to entertain without the use of convenience foods, most of the recipes in the book can be prepared ahead of time and

REMEMBER THE CODE
BY THE RECIPE TITLES . . .

F   means the dish may be frozen.

R   means it may be made ahead and refrigerated; the number tells you for how many days.

For instance: F / R2—the dish may be either frozen or refrigerated for two days.

either frozen weeks in advance or refrigerated for one or more days before serving.

While freezing does not improve the flavor of anything, there are many dishes whose quality is not noticeably affected. Cooking ahead and refrigerating most dishes will not affect their taste or texture. Dishes which may be frozen are marked with an *F*; dishes which may be refrigerated are marked with an *R* plus a figure (*1, 2, 3*) indicating the number of days ahead they may be prepared and refrigerated.

Even in the recipes which require last-minute work, there are often steps that can be done ahead: washing, chopping, preparation of the sauce, braising or initial sautéing.

I have always found it immensely helpful to program the preparation of a party. First I work out the menu so that very few, possibly even none, of the dishes are last-minute. Then comes a cooking schedule since I must fit it in on nights and weekends.

I make two, sometimes three, grocery lists. One is for the ingredients which are bought well in advance, either because they won't spoil or because they will be used in recipes that are prepared ahead. That list includes the wine for dinner and cocktails. Before dinner we serve as much wine as hard liquor, white wine being the great favorite. The second list is for ingredients that may be bought the day before the party. The final one is for those ingredients that will suffer if they are even one day old.

Then I write a list of all the dishes and serving pieces that will be needed. It's much easier than standing at the drawer and scratching my head, wondering what I ought to serve the mousse on!

I also make note of when things must be defrosted and when they must go in the oven.

I tend to get so interested in conversations at parties that without my lists the food might never make it to the table. The trick still is getting it all there at the same time, and my time and temperature information keeps me out of trouble.

I find it rather exciting that cooking this way means not only less expensive but more nutritious and better-tasting food. But maybe the greatest thrill of all is knowing that even if I haven't beaten the system, at least we are on an equal footing.

I

A FEW "CONVENIENCE" RECIPES

ᴇ

BREAKFAST NOG

2 servings

2 ripe bananas
1½ cups milk

2 eggs
1 teaspoon vanilla

Cut banana in quarters and place in electric blender with remaining ingredients. Cover and blend until smooth.

ᴇ

INSTANT BREAKFAST

1 serving

1 cup cold milk
1 egg

3 tablespoons undiluted orange juice concentrate

Place ingredients in blender and blend at high speed until frothy. Serve immediately.

(Including froth, this makes 2 cups.)

ᴇ

INSTANT COCOA

Makes 6 cups of mix

4 cups instant nonfat dry milk
¾ cup unsweetened cocoa powder

1¼ cups or more sugar
⅛ teaspoon salt

Combine ingredients and stir well. Store in tightly covered container in cool, dry place. To make instant cocoa, stir mixture. Place

3½ tablespoons of mix in cup and pour in a little of 1 cup boiling water, stirring well to dissolve mixture. Continue pouring water and stirring. Serve immediately.

❧

HOT MOCHA MIX

Makes approximately 6 cups of mix

1 cup unsweetened cocoa
2 cups sugar
4 cups nonfat dry milk powder

¾ cup instant coffee powder
1 vanilla bean or 3 tablespoons dried orange peel

Combine all ingredients and mix well. Store in airtight container for at least a week before using so that flavors can blend.

To serve, stir mix well. Place 3 tablespoons of mix in cup. Pour in a little of 6 ounces of boiling water and stir well to dissolve mix. Continue pouring in water and stirring and serve immediately.

❧

CINNAMON SUGAR

2 tablespoons cinnamon

1 cup sugar

Mix and store tightly covered. Use for toast, etc.

❧

SEASONED SALT

Makes approximately 1 cup

1 cup salt
2½ teaspoons paprika
2 teaspoons dry mustard
1½ teaspoons oregano

1 teaspoon garlic powder
(or to taste)
½ teaspoon onion powder

Mix together and store in airtight container. Use to season oil and vinegar dressing, meats, fish and vegetables.

❧

CURRY POWDER

So many different spices can go into a curry powder: ginger, coriander, cayenne, cumin, cardamom, chiles, cinnamon, fennel, mace, black pepper, mustard and of course turmeric, which gives curry the golden color, are some of them. Here is one suggestion for a curry powder, not particularly fiery, but it can be heated up with cayenne.

    2 tablespoons each ground coriander, black pepper, cumin, *chile* *
        and turmeric
1¼ teaspoons ground ginger

Mix well and store in airtight container away from light.
Always bring the full flavor of the curry out by cooking it in the dish. It is not enough just to stir it in.

❧

FIVE SPICE POWDER

This is a Chinese seasoning which differs in content, depending on the cookbook. If you cannot purchase it, you can make your own by mixing equal parts of:

Anise	Cinnamon	Clove
Fennel	Black Pepper	

Since some of these spices are not available ground, you may have to grind them yourself. A pepper mill will work, but it's a bit slow. An electric grinder makes it a little easier.

---

* This is pure *chile* (with an *e*) powder found in Spanish grocery stores. Chili (with an *i*) powder is a mixture of several spices.

❧

R3

FIVE SPICE DIP

Makes approximately 3 cups

The unusual ingredient is the Five Spice Powder, a Chinese mixture.

2 cups sour cream
½ teaspoon Five Spice Powder
  (page 39)

½ cup peanuts, chopped
  coarsely
½ cup chopped chutney
1 tablespoon chopped onion

If serving immediately, combine all ingredients. Otherwise, combine all ingredients but peanuts. Just before serving, add peanuts. Serve with an assortment of raw vegetables. Will keep a week.

❧

GRANOLA

Makes about 10 cups

Grains, nuts, seeds and dried fruits, sweetened with honey or molasses, are called granola when the grains are toasted before the other ingredients are added. Granolas are rich in protein, iron and *calories*. They will keep for weeks when stored in the refrigerator.

3 cups rolled oats
1½ cups wheat germ
½ cup dry skim-milk powder
1 cup slivered or coarsely
  chopped almonds
½ cup sesame seeds

1 cup hulled sunflower seeds
½ cup vegetable oil
¼ to ½ cup honey
1 cup raisins
½ cup dried apricots, cut up

Toast the oats in a shallow pan at 300 degrees for 15 minutes. In a large bowl combine the wheat germ, skim-milk powder, almonds, sesame and sunflower seeds. Heat the oil and honey just until warm. Combine with mixture in the bowl. Combine contents of bowl with toasted oats and spread in several shallow pans in thin layer. Continue toasting, stirring occasionally, for 15 minutes more, or until ingredients are toasted. Spoon into large container; add raisins and apricots. Cool and store in tightly covered container in the refrigerator. Serve with milk or yogurt.

NOTE: My son likes this granola better with roasted, unsalted peanuts. You can vary it any way that suits your taste.

❧

R / F

GARLIC BUTTER

This will keep as long as butter keeps in the refrigerator. It can be cut into individual portions and frozen for several months.

½ cup (¼ pound) butter, softened
2 to 3 cloves garlic, minced or put through garlic press
2 tablespoons minced parsley

Combine ingredients and beat until fluffy. Cover tightly and refrigerate or freeze. Use for garlic bread or on vegetables, or over broiled fish or beef.

❧

R

HONEY BUTTER

Makes 1 cup

½ cup honey   ½ cup soft butter

Blend honey and butter. Store in refrigerator. Serve with hot biscuits or pancakes.

🍱

R

BLENDER MAYONNAISE

Makes approximately 1¾ cups

If you want to make mayonnaise at home and have a blender, it is quick work indeed. It is not quite as good as the mayonnaise beaten by hand, but much better than the sweetened, chemically preserved, commercial product. This will keep 2 or 3 weeks, well covered, in the refrigerator.

1 egg	1¼ cups salad oil, or combination of salad and olive oil
1 teaspoon dry mustard	
½ teaspoon salt (scant)	2 tablespoons lemon juice, or half lemon juice and half white wine vinegar
Dash cayenne pepper	

Place the egg, mustard, salt, cayenne and ¼ cup oil in blender. Blend at high speed until completely mixed. With blender still running, take off center of cover or cover itself and slowly pour in ½ cup of oil. After it is completely blended (it may be necessary to turn off motor and mix mayonnaise a little with scraper), blend in lemon juice thoroughly. Then slowly add remaining oil, turning motor off and on as necessary to blend completely.

NOTE: Tarragon vinegar may also be used.

🍱

R

INSTANT CHEESE SAUCE

1½ pounds Gruyère cheese, finely grated	¾ cup sour cream
	Salt to taste

Mix cheese and sour cream; season to taste with salt. Pack in tightly covered container and refrigerate.

To use, spread mixture on broiled fish run under broiler to melt cheese, or spoon into piping hot split baked potatoes, or mix with hot mashed potatoes, or spread on toasted bread and broil until cheese melts, or spoon over scrambled eggs or into omelet before folding, or spoon over hot vegetables.

This will keep as long as the sour cream keeps. Check the carton for the expiration date.

❧

R/F

CREAM SAUCE MIX FOR VEGETABLES

Makes 2 cups

½ cup butter	2 tablespoons onion powder
½ cup flour	2 teaspoons salt
½ cup nonfat dry milk powder	¼ teaspoon pepper

Cut the butter into the flour along with remaining ingredients, until mixture is very crumbly. Refrigerate or, if desired, keep in the freezer along with frozen vegetables with which the mixture is used.

To use: combine 2 cups of vegetables with ½ cup water and bring to boil. Cover pan and cook vegetables until they are tender but still crisp. Length of time will depend on the vegetables. Stir in 3 tablespoons of sauce mix and cook, stirring until sauce thickens. Season to taste with salt. Serve.

Vegetables and sauce can be seasoned with herbs: peas with oregano; green beans with basil; carrots with dill. Allow ¾ teaspoon dried herb for each 2 cups of vegetables; 2 to 2½ teaspoons fresh herbs.

ᴈᴂ

R

THOUSAND ISLAND DRESSING

Makes 1½ cups

1 cup Mayonnaise (page 42)   1 tablespoon pickle relish
½ cup chili sauce

Combine ingredients and store in refrigerator indefinitely. For variation, add finely chopped green olives, grated onion or minced green pepper.

ᴈᴂ

CHEESE SALAD SEASONING

Makes approximately 8 tablespoons

¼ cup dry grated cheese (Parmesan, Romano, Cheddar)   ¼ teaspoon black pepper
2 tablespoons sesame seeds   2 teaspoons paprika
2 teaspoons salt   1 teaspoon celery seed
    ½ teaspoon garlic powder

Combine ingredients and mix well. Store in airtight container. To use, sprinkle on salads or mix with salad dressing, about 2 teaspoons to a cup of dressing.

ᴈᴂ

SALAD DRESSING MIX

Enough for 8 cups liquid

2 to 4 teaspoons salt   1 teaspoon black pepper
1 teaspoon dried minced garlic   1 teaspoon sugar
4 teaspoons instant minced onion   1 teaspoon paprika

Combine ingredients and store, tightly covered, in cool, dry place. To use, combine 2 tablespoons water with ¼ cup vinegar. Stir in 1½ teaspoons season mix and then ⅔ cup salad oil. Beat well or shake in tightly covered bottle. Makes 1 cup salad dressing.

❦

FRENCH DRESSING MIX

Enough for 8 cups dressing

2 to 4 teaspoons salt
1 tablespoon plus 1 teaspoon
 paprika

1 tablespoon plus 1 teaspoon
 dry mustard
½ teaspoon black pepper

Combine ingredients and store in tightly covered container at room temperature.

To make French dressing: combine 1 tablespoon of mix with ¼ cup vinegar or lemon juice and ¾ cup salad oil.

Variations:

For garlic French dressing, add 1 crushed clove garlic.
For curry French dressing, add ¼ to ½ teaspoon curry powder.
For blue cheese dressing, stir in 2 teaspoons water with ¾ cup crumbled blue cheese.

❦

VINAIGRETTE DRESSING

Makes 1 cup

1 tablespoon French Dressing
 Mix (above)
¾ cup salad oil
¼ cup vinegar

2 tablespoons finely chopped
 dill pickle
2 teaspoons chopped chives
1 hard-cooked egg, chopped

Combine oil and vinegar with mix and shake well. Add remaining ingredients and shake again.

~

MIXED PICKLING SPICE

Makes 2/3 cup

4 cinnamon sticks, each about 3 inches long
1 piece dried ginger root, 1 inch long
2 tablespoons mustard seed
2 teaspoons whole allspice
2 teaspoons whole black peppercorns

2 teaspoons whole cloves
2 teaspoons dill seed
2 teaspoons coriander seed
2 teaspoons whole mace, crumbled
8 bay leaves, crumbled
1 whole dried red pepper, 1½ inches long, chopped

Wrap cinnamon sticks and ginger root in clean cloth. Pound with a mallet or hammer until finely crumbled; discard stringy part of ginger. Add to the remaining ingredients and stir well. Store in airtight container.

~

POULTRY SEASONING

Makes scant 1/2 cup

2 tablespoons dried marjoram
2 tablespoons dried parsley
2 tablespoons dried savory

1 tablespoon dried sage
1½ teaspoons dried thyme

Combine ingredients and store in airtight container. Use as you would any commercially prepared poultry seasoning.

❦

SHAKE IT AND BAKE IT

Enough for 6 pounds of chicken

1 cup flour
2 teaspoons salt
1 teaspoon pepper
½ cup cracker crumbs

1 teaspoon herbs (thyme,
   oregano, basil or a mixture)
Milk or water

Combine dry ingredients, stirring to mix. Use half the mixture for 3 pounds of chicken. Reserve remainder in a tightly covered container. Moisten the chicken with milk or water. Shake chicken pieces with mix, a few at a time, in paper bag. Bake in greased shallow pan at 350 degrees for 45 minutes to 1 hour.

❦

R / F

ITALIAN COATING MIX

1 quart fine bread crumbs
½ cup finely grated Romano or
   Cheddar cheese
3 small cloves garlic, crushed

½ cup vegetable oil
1 cup fresh parsley, chopped
1 teaspoon salt
1 teaspoon pepper

Combine all ingredients and mix thoroughly; freeze. Spoon out amount needed to pat on chicken pieces. Place a single layer of coated food in shallow pan; cover with foil and bake at 350 degrees 45 to 60 minutes. Five minutes before baking time is up, remove foil and brown.

This mixture keeps for a week in the refrigerator; in the freezer it does not become solid, but remains spoonable.

Can be used to coat fish, veal and chicken.

❦

HELP FOR HAMBURGERS

Five 1-cup servings

This is Oriental-style.

1 pound ground beef
3⅓ cups hot water
2¼ cups instant rice

2 tablespoons instant minced
  onion
¼ cup soy sauce
Salt to taste

Brown meat in skillet; drain off fat. Add hot water, rice, onion and soy sauce. Mix well and bring to boiling point. Cook over medium-high heat until most of liquid has evaporated, 10 to 15 minutes. Season to taste with salt, if desired.

❦

INSTANT STUFFING

4 servings

Makes use of leftover bread ends, stale slices and crust.

4 cups large bread crumbs or
  cubes
1 teaspoon dried minced onion
1 teaspoon dried parsley

½ teaspoon thyme
Dash sage
3 tablespoons butter
½ cup Chicken or Beef Stock
  (pages 89, 90)

Place bread crumbs or cubes on a baking sheet and heat at 350 degrees for 5 to 10 minutes, until dry. Place in tightly covered container. When you have 4 cups of crumbs, stir in onion, parsley, thyme and sage. Cover and store in cupboard; it will keep for weeks.

To make stuffing, melt butter; add crumb mixture and toss to coat.

Slowly add stock and mix gently but well. Cook over low heat until hot, or place in baking dish and bake at 350 degrees for 30 minutes. If mixture is too dry, add more stock or water. Season with salt and pepper and serve.

NOTE: If you prefer to use freshly chopped onion and parsley, add them when you combine stuffing mixture with butter. For 2 cups of crumbs, allow 1 tablespoon chopped onion and 1 tablespoon chopped parsley.

R / F

MEAT SAUCE

One-third of recipe serves 4 to 6 people

3 pounds ground beef	3 (8-ounce) cans tomato sauce
3 large onions, chopped	Salt and pepper to taste
3 green peppers, seeded and chopped	1 tablespoon oregano
	1½ teaspoons basil
6 cloves garlic, finely chopped	6 tablespoons coffee
3 (1-pound) cans tomatoes	1½ cups dry red wine
3 (6-ounce) cans tomato paste	

Brown meat in skillet, stirring to break up pieces. Push meat to side and sauté onion, peppers and garlic until onion is soft. Add remaining ingredients and simmer for 1½ hours, or until mixture is thick.

Serve over spaghetti or your favorite pasta. One third of recipe is enough for 1 pound of spaghetti.

The rest of the sauce can be frozen in portions suitable for your family's use in other recipes.

To make sloppy joes:

Combine 2 cups of meat sauce with one teaspoon Worcestershire sauce and hot pepper sauce to taste. Serve over buns.

To make chili:

Combine 2 cups meat sauce with a 15-ounce can of kidney beans and 1 tablespoon chili powder.

❦

OATMEAL COOKIE MIX

8 dozen

3 cups sifted flour	2 teaspoons salt
2½ cups sugar	1 cup shortening
1 teaspoon baking soda	3 cups rolled oats
1 teaspoon baking powder	

Sift together flour, sugar, soda, baking powder and salt. Cut in shortening until mix resembles cornmeal. Add rolled oats and mix well. Store in tightly covered container at room temperature.

To make 2 to 2½ dozen cookies:

2 cups oatmeal cookie mix	1 tablespoon milk
1 egg	1 teaspoon vanilla

Place mix in bowl, add egg, milk and vanilla. Mix well. Drop from teaspoon onto greased baking sheets. Bake at 375 degrees for 12 to 15 minutes, until golden. Remove from sheet and store.

Variations:

½ cup chopped nuts, or	½ cup chopped dates
½ cup raisins, or	

❧

R / F

SLICE AND BAKE COOKIES
Approximately 4 dozen

½ cup sugar
½ cup shortening
1 egg yolk
1½ teaspoons vanilla extract
1½ cups sifted flour

¼ teaspoon salt
½ teaspoon baking powder
3 tablespoons milk
1-ounce square unsweetened
   chocolate, melted

Cream sugar and shortening. Stir in yolk and vanilla. Combine flour, salt and baking powder. Stir alternately with milk into sugar mixture to make soft dough.

Divide dough in half. Add chocolate to one half; mix thoroughly. On wax paper roll out each half into rectangles ⅛ inch thick. Turn white dough onto chocolate dough with chocolate dough extending ½ inch beyond white dough along edge toward which you will roll. Remove wax paper; roll up like jelly roll.

Wrap in wax paper; refrigerate or freeze, if desired. To finish cookies, cut roll into thin slices, ⅛ to ¼ inch thick. Bake at 375 degrees for 8 to 10 minutes, depending on thickness of cookies.

Dough keeps indefinitely in the freezer and for a couple of weeks in refrigerator.

❧

R

BRAN OATMEAL MUFFIN MIX
8 dozen medium muffins

2 cups boiling water
2 cups 100 percent bran
1 cup shortening
3 cups sugar (white or brown or
   mixed)
4 eggs

1 quart buttermilk
5 cups flour
1 teaspoon salt
5 teaspoons baking soda
4 cups uncooked oatmeal

Pour boiling water over the bran and set aside while mixing the rest of the ingredients. Cream sugar and shortening. Add eggs, buttermilk, flour, salt and soda. Add cereals last. Use some of mix if desired, refrigerate remainder. Pour into well-greased medium muffin tins until ¾ full. Bake 15 to 20 minutes in a preheated 375-degree oven. For batter just out of the refrigerator, bake 20 to 25 minutes at the same temperature.

Raisins, nuts or dates can be added, but just before baking only. This can be refrigerated up to 3 months.

❧

MASTER BAKING MIX

Makes 7 cups

6 cups unbleached flour
2½ tablespoons double-action baking powder
1½ teaspoons salt
¾ cup vegetable shortening *

Sift dry ingredients together. Cut in shortening until mixture is crumbly. Store in tightly covered container in cupboard.

❧

MARMALADE NUT BREAD

1 loaf

3 cups Master Baking Mix (above)
½ cup sugar
½ cup chopped nuts
1 egg, well beaten
1 cup milk
½ cup orange marmalade

Combine mix with sugar and nuts. Combine egg, milk and marmalade and blend. Add gradually to dry mixture, mixing only until flour

---

* If butter is used instead, mix must be stored in refrigerator.

is moistened. Turn into greased 9-x-5-x-3-inch loaf pan and bake at 350 degrees for 45 to 50 minutes. Cool in pan.

When cool, wrap bread in aluminum foil and allow to mellow at room temperature one day before slicing.

ಀ

DATE NUT MUFFINS

1 dozen

2 cups Master Baking Mix (page 52)
½ cup chopped pitted dates
¼ cup chopped nuts

1 egg, well beaten
½ to 1 tablespoon sugar
⅔ cup milk

Stir dates and nuts into mix. Stir egg, sugar and milk together. Add, all at once, to dry mixture. Stir only until flour is moistened—the batter will be lumpy. Fill medium-size greased muffin tins ⅔ full. Bake at 425 degrees for 15 to 18 minutes.

ಀ

BISCUIT MIX

Makes 13 cups

This can be used for waffles, pancakes, biscuits, and as a coating for chicken. Use it for anything for which you use packaged biscuit mix.

9 cups sifted flour
⅓ cup baking powder
1 cup plus 2 tablespoons nonfat milk solids

4 teaspoons salt
1¾ cups vegetable shortening

Sift all dry ingredients. Cut shortening into flour until mixture resembles coarse cornmeal. Store, well covered, in cool, dry place.

❧

PANCAKES

Approximately twelve 4-inch pancakes

2 cups Biscuit Mix (page 53)   1 cup milk
2 eggs

Combine and beat until smooth. Bake pancakes on hot greased griddle until golden on both sides.

NOTE: To make fruit pancakes, add 1 cup blueberries, sliced strawberries, diced bananas or diced peaches to batter after it has been beaten.

❧

WAFFLES

Three 9-inch waffles

2 cups Biscuit Mix (page 53)   1 egg
2 tablespoons oil   1½ cups milk

Combine ingredients and beat until smooth. Bake according to directions on waffle maker.

❧

WRAP FOR HOT DOGS

Enough for 10 nitrite-free hot dogs, bratwurst or sausages

1 cup Biscuit Mix (page 53)   ¼ cup cold water

For onion flavor:

Mix 1½ teaspoons dried minced onion with water and allow to sit for a minute or two, then mix with Biscuit Mix. Form into ball. Knead a few times and roll out into 7½-×-8-inch rectangle. Cut into 10 rectangles.

For barbecue flavor:

Brush 2 tablespoons barbecue sauce over rolled-out dough.

For pizza flavor:

Combine ⅛ teaspoon garlic powder, 1½ teaspoons dried minced onion, ⅛ teaspoon oregano and 1 teaspoon dried parsley. Add to water and allow to sit for a minute or two.

For cheese flavor:

Sprinkle ½ cup grated cheese over rolled-out dough.

ℰ

PASTRY MIX

Makes 8 to 9 cups

6 cups sifted flour
1 tablespoon salt

1 (1-pound) can vegetable
shortening (about 2½ cups)

Mix flour and salt in large bowl. Cut in shortening until mixture resembles coarse meal. Cover and store mix in cool place (it does not require refrigeration).

ℰ

PIE CRUSTS

For a 1-crust pie, use 2 to 4 tablespoons cold water and:

1¼ cups mix for 8-inch pie
1½ cups mix for 9-inch pie

1¾ cups mix for 10-inch pie

For a 2-crust pie, use ¼ to ⅓ cup cold water and:

2 to 2¼ cups mix for 8-inch pie

2½ to 2¾ cups mix for 10-inch pie

2¼ to 2½ cups mix for 9-inch pie

Measure mix into bowl; sprinkle on water, a little at a time, mixing quickly and evenly with fork until dough just holds together in a ball. Roll out as you would any pie crust.

ꞔ

PUDDING AND PIE FILLING

Makes 10 cups

In earlier times these were known as cornstarch puddings. But that isn't a particularly appealing name.

3½ cups instant nonfat dry milk

¾ cup sugar
¾ cup cornstarch

Combine ingredients and store in tightly covered container in cool, dry place.

To make vanilla-flavored pudding: Stir the basic mix thoroughly and measure out 1 cup. Gradually add 2 cups of cold water; bring mixture to boil, stirring, over low heat. Mixture is boiling when it bubbles and plops. Add 1 teaspoon butter and ½ teaspoon vanilla. Stir until butter melts; pour into serving dishes and refrigerate. Makes four ½-cup servings.

For chocolate pudding: Combine mix and water as directed above. Stir in either one ounce of unsweetened chocolate or 4 tablespoons unsweetened cocoa and ½ teaspoon vanilla. Stir to mix well and pour into serving dishes. Refrigerate until set.

✑

R4

CRÈME FRAÎCHE

Makes approximately 1 pint

1 pint heavy cream for whipping *

2 tablespoons buttermilk

Pour cream into a jar. Stir in buttermilk. Cover loosely. Leave in a warm place, such as on top of stove, until cream thickens like yogurt. This can take as long as 4 days. Store in refrigerator for up to one week.

✑

F / R

MARY HUMELSINE'S MINCEMEAT

Makes approximately 7 quarts

This mincemeat, which Mary Humelsine makes every year for Christmas, is the real thing . . . it has meat in it. Mary's husband, Carl, is chairman of the board of Colonial Williamsburg.

2 pounds lean beef cubes
1 pound beef suet
5 pounds apples, peeled and cored and cut in quarters
2½ pounds raisins
2 pounds currants
½ pound citron, finely chopped

2 pounds brown sugar
3 pints apple cider
2 tablespoons cinnamon
1 tablespoon nutmeg
1 tablespoon ground cloves
1 tablespoon allspice
Salt to taste

---

* Do not use ultrapasteurized cream.

Cook the beef in water to cover until tender. Put cooked beef, suet and apples through coarse blade of meat grinder. Mix all ingredients together and pack tightly in sterilized jars (some liquid may be left over). Will keep indefinitely in refrigerator, up to a year, or can be frozen. Use in any recipe calling for mincemeat.

❦

F

FROZEN YOGURT

2 or 3 servings

This does not look like the frozen soft yogurts so popular right now, but it is delicious, contains much less sugar than the commercially produced brands, and it is all natural.

1 envelope unflavored gelatin
1 tablespoon lemon juice
2 tablespoons water

1 cup strawberries, blueberries, raspberries, cut-up peaches or nectarines, or 1 small cut-up banana
1 tablespoon sugar
1 cup plain yogurt

Soften gelatin in lemon juice and water. Heat either over hot water or over very low heat, stirring just until gelatin dissolves. Remove from heat. Add fruit, yogurt and sugar and mix lightly. Pour into blender and blend until mixture is fairly smooth. Little pieces of fruit are fine. They add bits of color and texture.

Pour mixture into mixing bowl and freeze solid. When ready to serve, remove bowl from freezer and allow mixture to soften just enough so that it can be beaten with an electric mixer. Beat until creamy but still quite thick and frozen. Serve immediately.

❦

R2
LEMON GELATIN
4 servings

1 envelope unflavored gelatin	⅛ teaspoon salt
½ cup cold water	1 cup boiling water
⅓ cup sugar	¼ cup lemon juice

Soften gelatin in cold water. Add sugar, salt and boiling water and stir until dissolved. Add lemon juice; stir well and pour into individual serving dishes or a 2-cup mold. Chill for several hours.

For orange gelatin:

Use ¼ cup cold water, 1 tablespoon lemon juice, ¼ cup sugar along with gelatin, salt, boiling water and ½ cup orange juice; follow directions above.

❦

R2
FRUIT GELATINS
4 servings

With natural ingredients, it is possible to make almost any fruit-flavored gelatin.

1 tablespoon unflavored gelatin	1 cup fruit juice
¼ cup cold water	Sugar
¾ cup boiling water	¼ teaspoon salt

Soak the gelatin in the cold water to soften. Dissolve in boiling water, stirring. Add 1 cup of the following fruit juices: orange, apricot, grapefruit, cranberry, grape, canned or cooked pineapple,* peach, etc. Stir in salt. If not sweet enough, add sugar to taste. Chill until mixture is set in mold which has been rinsed in cold water.

If desired, diced fruit may be added after gelatin has become the consistency of unbeaten egg whites.

NOTE: Sherry and other wines can be used for some or all of the fruit juice. Strong coffee can be substituted entirely to make coffee-flavored gelatin.

---

* Fresh pineapple juice contains an enzyme which prevents gelatin from setting.

II

APPETIZERS

ೞ

F / R3

CAPONATA

2 medium eggplants
½ to ¾ cup olive oil
1 cup chopped celery
2 medium onions, chopped
1 cup coarsely chopped
  tomatoes

¼ cup capers, drained
¼ cup wine vinegar
1 tablespoon sugar
1 tablespoon pignoli (pine nuts)
Freshly ground black pepper to
  taste

Peel eggplant and cut into ¾-inch cubes. Heat oil in large skillet and cook eggplant in it over high heat until it is lightly browned, about 10 minutes. Stir often. Remove eggplant with slotted spoon. Place celery and onion in remaining oil in skillet; lower heat and cook until celery is tender. Add tomatoes, cover and continue to cook for 10 minutes longer, stirring occasionally. Add eggplant, capers, vinegar, sugar, nuts and pepper to taste and simmer over low heat for 5 minutes. Chill and serve cold with black bread.

Freeze, if desired.

ೞ

R1

CHICKEN LIVER PÂTÉ IN ASPIC

Makes 5 cups

1 cup plus 2 tablespoons
  chicken broth
2 envelopes unflavored gelatin
3 tablespoons chopped green
  onion
½ cup Madeira or medium-dry
  sherry
3 tablespoons chicken fat

1 pound chicken livers
¼ cup chopped green onion
Salt and freshly ground black
  pepper to taste
¼ teaspoon nutmeg
½ teaspoon anchovy paste
  (optional)
Watercress for garnish

Sprinkle gelatin on chicken broth to soften. Cook over low heat, stirring, until gelatin is completely dissolved. Remove from heat and stir in ¼ cup Madeira and 3 tablespoons green onion.

Pour into 6-cup mold and chill until firm.

Meanwhile, sauté the livers and green onions in chicken fat until livers are tender and pink. Blend livers in blender with remaining Madeira until smooth. Add salt, pepper, nutmeg and anchovy paste; blend thoroughly. Spoon mixture in mold; cover and refrigerate overnight, or until firm. Unmold onto plate, garnish with watercress and serve with crackers.

ም

R3

CLAM AND CHUTNEY DIP

Makes approximately 3 cups

1 pint sour cream
2 tablespoons chopped
 chutney
Few dashes hot pepper sauce

¼ teaspoon or more Curry
 Powder (page 39)
1 (7-ounce) can minced clams,
 drained

Combine all ingredients and mix well. Chill. Serve with crackers or raw vegetables.

ም

R3

CURRIED CHEDDAR SNACKS

64 pieces

1 cup chopped black olives
½ cup chopped green onion
1½ cups shredded Cheddar
 cheese
½ cup Mayonnaise (page 42)

1 teaspoon or more Curry
 Powder (page 39)
Salt to taste
64 squares thinly sliced dark
 bread

Combine all of ingredients except bread. Refrigerate, if desired. To serve, spread on bread and broil until cheese melts.

℘

F / R2

CURRIED MUSHROOM STRUDELS

Approximately 60

1 pound fresh mushrooms, finely chopped	½ cup sour cream
¼ cup butter	1 teaspoon salt
1 teaspoon Curry Powder (page 39)	Freshly ground black pepper
2 tablespoons lemon juice	½ cup additional melted butter
	½ pound *phyllo*

Sauté mushrooms in butter with curry and lemon juice. Stir in sour cream, salt, pepper. Cool mixture and prepare *phyllo*. Keep *phyllo* covered with wax paper and damp towel while working with it. Cut each sheet into strips 3 inches wide. Working quickly, brush a strip with melted butter. Fold over ¼ inch of bottom edge. Put ½ teaspoon mushroom filling near folded edge and fold *phyllo* over filling so that bottom of dough meets side to form triangle, folding as you would

Phyllo completely folded!

fold the American flag. Place seam side down on baking sheet. Brush tops with melted butter and bake at 400 degrees for about 15 minutes, until golden. Serve warm.

To make ahead, bake and freeze with layers of wax paper between triangles. To serve, defrost and bake at 350 degrees for about 15 minutes, until strudels are puffed and bubbly.

NOTE: *Phyllo*, paper-thin sheets of dough used extensively in Middle Eastern cooking, are best if purchased fresh but, if fresh ones are unavailable, they can be purchased frozen.

ℰ

R3 TO 4

GRAVLAX (MARINATED SALMON)

10 servings

Ulla Wachtmeister, wife of the Swedish Ambassador to the United States, sets one of the finest tables in Washington. She is an excellent cook and serves Swedish food. This is Countess Wachtmeister's recipe.

2 pounds center-cut fresh
 salmon
1 tablespoon sugar
1 tablespoon salt

1⅓ tablespoons coarsely ground
 black pepper
1 large bunch dill, coarsely cut
Mustard Sauce (below)

Split fish into 2 halves. Remove all the bones. Wash and wipe skin. Combine the sugar, salt and pepper and sprinkle over halves of flesh. Sprinkle on the dill and place two salmon halves flesh side together. Place in enamel or glass container and cover tightly. Place brick or other heavy weight on top of salmon and refrigerate for 3 to 4 days, turning salmon occasionally. Remove the dill and scrape off seasonings. Slice salmon thinly and garnish with fresh dill and lemon and serve with Mustard Sauce.

ℰ

MUSTARD SAUCE

2 tablespoons Dijon mustard
1 tablespoon sugar
2 tablespoons vinegar

6 tablespoons oil
1 heaping tablespoon chopped
 dill

Mix mustard with sugar and vinegar; add oil slowly, beating as you add. Stir in chopped dill and serve with Gravlax. Swedish mustard will make a much sweeter sauce.

❧

HORSERADISH SAUCE

Enough for one recipe of Gravlax (page 66), or serve with smoked salmon.

3 heaping tablespoons prepared white horseradish with liquid thoroughly squeezed out
1 tablespoon powdered sugar

½ teaspoon dry mustard
2 tablespoons white wine vinegar
Salt and pepper to taste
1 cup heavy cream, whipped

Mix horseradish with sugar, mustard, vinegar, salt and pepper. Gradually add to whipped cream. Chill sauce for several hours before serving.

❧

R3

HERB CHEESE

This is an inexpensive imitation of the French triple-cream Boursin.

2 large cloves garlic
8 ounces cream cheese (fresh, without gum if possible), softened
4 ounces farmer cheese

½ cup finely minced chives
½ cup finely minced parsley
Salt to taste
Freshly ground black pepper

Mash garlic; add with chives and parsley to cheeses. Beat well. Season with a little salt and a lot of pepper. Chill.

❧

R1

HERB-CHEESE STUFFED MUSHROOMS

Makes 36

This is the homemade version of mushrooms stuffed with the famous French triple-cream cheese called Boursin.

36 medium-sized fresh mushrooms
8 ounces Herb Cheese (page 67)
Parsley

Remove the stems from the mushrooms by breaking off where they join the cap. Rinse the caps and drain well to dry. Wipe with paper towel, if necessary. Reserve stems for other use. Fill each mushroom cap generously with the cheese. Refrigerate, if desired. To serve, decorate each stuffed mushroom with a small piece of parsley.

❧

F / R3

HERBED CHEDDAR CHEESE

Makes 1 cup

1 cup sharp Cheddar cheese, finely grated	½ teaspoon tarragon, rubbed fine
½ teaspoon sage	½ teaspoon chervil
½ teaspoon fennel seeds, crushed	1 tablespoon chopped fresh chives, or 1 teaspoon dried
½ teaspoon dill seeds, crushed	

Combine grated cheese with herbs and blend them in well. Place mixture in 1-cup mold to shape, if desired. Refrigerate or freeze. To serve, return to room temperature. Serve with bland crackers or raw vegetables.

ॐ

R7

PIMIENTO CHEESE SPREAD

4-ounce jar pimientos, drained   1 teaspoon dry mustard
½ pound grated sharp Cheddar   2 tablespoons Mayonnaise
   cheese   (page 42)

Chop drained pimientos and mix with cheese, mustard and mayonnaise until mixture is well mixed and moistened. Allow mixture to sit at room temperature for half an hour so flavors have a chance to blend.

Use as you would any cheese spread.

This will keep a week or longer in the refrigerator.

ॐ

HOT BRIE

1 large Brie, about 2¼ pounds
Slivered toasted almonds

Remove the center of the chalky white substance from the top of the Brie, leaving about an inch border and cutting about ⅛ inch or less deep.

Put Brie back into wooden box, which has been wrapped in heavy-duty aluminum foil.

Roast almonds at 400 degrees about 10 minutes, or until browned. Sprinkle toasted almonds in cutout section of Brie.

If you can put the cheese 8 to 10 inches from broiler, place Brie under broiler and heat until cheese becomes runny. But be careful it doesn't get too runny or it will fall apart. Watch carefully. Check after 8 to 10 minutes.

If you cannot get enough distance between heat and Brie, then put in 450-degree oven until Brie is runny.

Serve with unsalted crackers or French bread.

༒

F / R3

INDIAN CHEESE SPREAD

Makes 1¼ cups

This deliciously spicy recipe can be served with crackers or with raw
vegetables as a dip.

2 tablespoons chutney
1½ to 2 teaspoons Curry Powder
(page 39)
2 tablespoons English mustard

10 ounces finely grated sharp
Cheddar cheese, at room
temperature
4 tablespoons milk
2 tablespoons lemon juice

Cut chutney up finely and mix with curry. Work in remaining ingredients and chill before serving.

༒

F / R3

LIPTAUER CHEESE

Makes 1½ cups

A Middle European dish, it was originally made with Liptauer, a
goat's milk pot cheese.

4 ounces pot cheese or small-curd
dry cottage cheese
4 ounces cream cheese, softened
4 ounces butter, softened (1 stick)
1 tablespoon grated onion

½ teaspoon caraway seeds
1 teaspoon anchovy paste
1 teaspoon Dijon mustard
1 teaspoon paprika

Combine all ingredients and blend thoroughly. Freeze, or refrigerate up to a week. To serve, bring to room temperature and blend until quite smooth. Serve with black bread.

✌

R1

MARINATED TOMATOES AND OLIVES

Makes 4 cups

1 cup salad oil
1 cup cider vinegar
2 teaspoons salt
2 teaspoons sugar
1 teaspoon freshly ground
black pepper

1 bay leaf
1 medium clove garlic, minced
1 pint cherry tomatoes
2 (16-ounce) cans pitted ripe
olives, drained

Mix together first 7 ingredients and beat well. With fork, pierce each tomato once; add to marinade. Add well-drained olives. Cover and refrigerate, stirring occasionally. To serve, remove tomatoes and olives with slotted spoon from marinade. Serve with cocktail picks.

NOTE: The liquid can be used again as a marinade or salad dressing.

✌

R1

MUSHROOMS STUFFED WITH MUSHROOMS

3 to 3½ dozen

½ pound fresh mushrooms,
finely chopped *
¼ cup butter
3 tablespoons flour
¾ teaspoon salt

1 cup light cream
2 teaspoons minced chives
1 teaspoon lemon juice
36 to 42 large mushrooms,
cleaned and stems removed

---

* Stems from the large mushrooms can be used as part of the ½ pound of finely chopped mushrooms.

Sauté chopped mushrooms in butter; blend in flour and salt. Stir in cream and cook until thick. Add chives and lemon juice. Cool. Stuff large mushroom caps with mixture. Heat mushrooms at 400 degrees for about 12 to 15 minutes, until filling begins to bubble and mushrooms begin to soften.

ༀ

R1

MUSSELS À LA VIVAROIS

48 mussels; enough for
8 servings as first course;
about 16 as hors d'oeuvres

Adapted from the three-star Parisian restaurant Vivarois

4 dozen mussels, thoroughly cleaned	4 sprigs parsley
2 medium onions, minced	1 teaspoon thyme
4 teaspoons peppercorns	3 cups white wine
	Garlic-Butter Mixture (page 73)

In advance, clean mussels thoroughly by scrubbing with a stiff brush and rinsing several times in cold water. Combine the next five ingredients in large pot with cover and cook over medium heat for 5 minutes.

Add the mussels; cover and cook for about 10 minutes, until mussels open. Remove mussels from liquid and leave mussels on one half-shell. Place a generous dab of Garlic-Butter Mixture in each mussel. Refrigerate, if desired. To serve, bake at 400 degrees for 10 minutes, until butter mixture is bubbly.

ꝫ

F / R3
GARLIC-BUTTER MIXTURE

¾ cup butter, creamed
6 tablespoons finely minced shallots
3 cloves garlic, crushed
6 tablespoons minced parsley

4 anchovy fillets, pounded to a paste
4 teaspoons anisette
2 teaspoons lemon juice

Combine creamed butter with remaining ingredients and blend thoroughly.

This mixture can be used with snails, too.

ꝫ

R1
MUSSELS RAVIGOTE

16 as hors d'oeuvres; 8 as first course

50 mussels, thoroughly scrubbed and soaked in cold water
½ cup dry white wine
1 shallot, halved

1 sprig parsley
4 peppercorns
Parsley for garnish

Sauce:

2 small shallots
2 tablespoons wine vinegar
2 tablespoons white wine
1½ teaspoons finely minced fresh tarragon, or ½ teaspoon dried
¾ cup mayonnaise
1½ teaspoons drained capers

1½ teaspoons finely minced parsley
1½ teaspoons finely minced chives
Freshly ground black pepper
1 teaspoon Dijon mustard
Salt, if necessary

Combine the mussels, wine, shallot, parsley and peppercorns in heavy pot. Cover and cook until mussels open, 10 to 15 minutes. Discard any mussels that do not open. When they are cool enough to handle, open mussels and discard one shell half. Loosen mussels from remaining half and put back on half.

While mussels are cooking, combine shallots, vinegar, wine and tarragon in small pot. Cook over high heat until liquid evaporates completely. Combine this mixture with remaining sauce ingredients. Adjust seasoning, adding salt if necessary. Decorate mussels with a dab of mayonnaise mixture and a sprig of parsley and refrigerate until serving time. Serve cold.

ᖗ

F / Rl

NACHOS

Approximately 8 dozen pieces

From the Land of Tex-Mex

1 dozen corn tortillas (if frozen, defrost)
Oil for frying

8 ounces Cheddar cheese, sliced (approximately)
1 (3-ounce) can jalapeño peppers

Cut each tortilla into 8 wedge-shaped pieces. Fry in hot oil until lightly golden. Cut wedge-shape pieces of cheese just a little narrower than tortilla wedges and place on top of tortillas. Place thin slivers of jalapeños on top of wedges. Freeze, if desired. To serve, defrost and place under broiler until cheese melts. Serve hot.

❧

F / R2

1, 2, 3 HORS D'OEUVRES

*Approximately 70 pieces,
between the size of a quarter
and a half-dollar*

A favorite from Betty Talmadge of Georgia

1 pound combination of hot and mild bulk pork sausage, or all hot
2 cups finely grated sharp Cheddar cheese
3 cups Biscuit Mix (page 53)

Combine sausage, cheese and Biscuit Mix; roll into balls the size of a marble. Freeze or refrigerate, if desired. To serve, bring to room temperature and bake in shallow pan at 350 degrees for 15 to 20 minutes, until golden brown on bottom.

❧

R3

POOR MAN'S CAVIAR

Makes approximately 4 cups

A Russian zakuska, or hors d'oeuvre

2 large eggplants
2 tablespoons olive oil
2 large onions, chopped fine
2 cloves garlic, minced
2 medium green peppers, chopped fine

2 (6-ounce) cans tomato paste
2 teaspoons white vinegar
Salt and freshly ground pepper to taste

Bake eggplants whole at 425 degrees on rack in center of oven for about one hour, turning a couple of times until soft and skin is charred and blistered. Remove skin from eggplant and chop meat fine. Heat 2 tablespoons of oil and cook onions, garlic and green pepper in oil until soft but not brown. Add tomato paste and simmer for 3 to 5 minutes. Stir in vinegar, salt and pepper and chopped eggplant and cook slowly for 30 minutes in skillet. Cool and serve thoroughly chilled as appetizer with thin slices of pumpernickel.

ꙮ

R2

ROQUEFORT CHEESE MOLD

3-cup mold

1 package unflavored gelatin
½ cup dry white wine
1 cup boiling water
2 tablespoons sugar
2 tablespoons lemon juice
½ cup sour cream
1 tablespoon minced parsley
½ teaspoon Worcestershire sauce

Salt to taste
1½ teaspoons vinegar
4 ounces Roquefort cheese, crumbled
½ cup broken walnut meats
Watercress or cherry tomatoes for garnish

Soften gelatin in wine. Dissolve in boiling water with sugar and lemon juice. Blend in sour cream, parsley, Worcestershire, salt and vinegar. Chill until mixture is syrupy. Stir in crumbled cheese and nuts. Turn into 3-cup mold and chill until firm. Unmold to serve. Fill center with watercress or cherry tomatoes; place crackers around the outside of mold.

ॐ

F / R1

SEAFOOD-STUFFED *PHYLLO*

30 to 35 pastries

1 tablespoon butter	1 cup crab meat or cooked
1 tablespoon flour	shrimp
½ cup milk	1 beaten egg yolk
Salt to taste	1 teaspoon lemon juice
3 shallots, finely chopped	Nutmeg and white pepper
1½ tablespoons butter	5 sheets 12-inch-wide *phyllo*
	⅛ to ¼ pound butter, melted

Prepare a béchamel sauce: Melt 1 tablespoon butter. Remove from heat and stir in flour. Carefully stir in milk and cook, stirring, until smooth and thick. Season with salt.

Sauté shallots in 1½ tablespoons butter. Add crab meat. To the béchamel sauce, add the beaten yolk, lemon juice, nutmeg and white pepper to taste. Gently stir in crab-meat mixture. Cool.

Keep *phyllo* covered with wax paper and damp towel while working with it. Cut each sheet into strips 2 inches wide. Working quickly, brush a strip with melted butter. Fold over ¼ inch of bottom edge. Put a teaspoon of filling near folded edge and fold *phyllo* over filling so that bottom of dough meets side, to form triangle, folding as you would fold the American flag (page 65). Place seam side down on baking sheet. Brush tops with melted butter and bake at 400 degrees for about 15 minutes, until triangles are golden. Serve warm.

To make ahead, bake and freeze with layers of wax paper between triangles. To serve, defrost and bake at 350 degrees about 15 minutes, until *phyllo* are puffed and bubbly.

❧

R1

SNAIL-STUFFED MUSHROOMS

3 per person as appetizer or first course

⅔ cup soft butter
1½ teaspoons finely minced
  shallots
2 large cloves garlic, crushed
1½ tablespoons minced parsley

½ teaspoon salt
Freshly ground black pepper
18 snails
18 large mushroom caps, cleaned

Cream together the butter, shallots, garlic, parsley, salt and a few grinds of black pepper. Drain and rinse the snails. Put a little of butter mixture into each mushroom cap. Place snail on top of butter mixture; top with a little more butter. Let stand out for 2 or 3 hours, or refrigerate overnight. Bake at 400 degrees for 15 minutes, until bubbly and hot.

❧

R3

SOUR CREAM HORSERADISH SAUCE

Makes 1 cup

2 tablespoons finely minced
  shallots or green onions
1 tablespoon chopped fresh dill

¾ cup sour cream
2 tablespoons white horseradish
1 tablespoon Mayonnaise
  (page 42)

Combine ingredients and mix well. Use with any kind of marinated fish, or add 1 can rinsed and well-drained tuna which has been broken up into fine pieces. Serve with dark bread, such as pumpernickel or rye.

ᨑ

F / R2

TIROPETAS

150 pastries

A Greek specialty

½ pound feta cheese
1 pint large-curd cottage
    cheese
12 ounces cream cheese
3 eggs

2 tablespoons finely chopped
    parsley
Dash pepper
⅛ teaspoon nutmeg
¾ pound *phyllo*
1 cup butter, melted

With fork, cream together until smooth the feta, cottage cheese and cream cheese. Add the eggs, one at a time, beating until smooth. Mix in the parsley, pepper and nutmeg. Lay out *phyllo* one sheet at a time (keep remaining covered with damp cloth) and cut into strips 1¾ inches wide. Brush each strip with melted butter. Fold over bottom edge ¼ inch. Place less than a teaspoon of filling on that end of pastry strip and fold over one corner to make a triangle; continue folding pastry from side to side in the shape of a triangle (like folding the American flag; page 65). Place seam side down on baking sheet. Continue in this manner until each baking sheet is filled. Then brush tops of pastries with melted butter and bake at 375 degrees for 15 to 18 minutes, until golden brown. Repeat this operation until all filling is used.

Refrigerate or freeze, if desired. To serve, if frozen, place directly from freezer in oven at 350 degrees and bake for about 15 minutes, or until heated through and butter is bubbling. If refrigerated, bake at 350 degrees about 10 minutes.

❧

R2

WALNUT BOURBON PÂTÉ

Makes approximately 5 cups

¼ pound butter
1 small onion, coarsely
 chopped
1 pound chicken livers
1½ cups chicken broth
2 tablespoons dry sherry
½ teaspoon paprika
¼ teaspoon allspice
¼ teaspoon ginger

⅛ teaspoon hot pepper sauce
Salt to taste
1 clove garlic, crushed
½ cup bourbon
1 envelope unflavored gelatin
1 cup chopped walnuts
Parsley and cherry tomatoes
 for garnish

Melt butter and add onion and livers. Cook about 10 minutes, until onion softens and becomes translucent. Add ¾ cup broth, sherry and seasonings. Continue to cook 5 minutes longer. Remove from heat and add bourbon. Sprinkle gelatin over remaining ¾ cup broth. Dissolve by heating broth over low heat. Place chicken liver mixture in blender and blend until smooth. Add broth mixture and walnuts. Spoon mixture into 5- or 6-cup mold and chill overnight. To serve, unmold and garnish with parsley and cherry tomatoes. Serve with dark bread or crackers.

III

SOUPS

🐝

F / R2

AVOCADO CURRY SOUP

4 or 5 servings

1 tablespoon butter	1 cup light cream
1 to 2 teaspoons Curry Powder (page 39)	1 slightly beaten egg yolk
12 ounces Chicken Stock or broth (page 90)	Few dashes hot pepper sauce
	1 medium-size avocado

Melt butter; stir in curry and add stock. Bring to boil; cover and simmer 10 minutes. Combine cream with yolk and gradually stir into soup, cooking over low heat. Remove from heat. Mash half of avocado and dice the other half; add both to soup. Refrigerate or freeze, if desired. To serve hot, reheat, stirring constantly. To serve cold, if frozen, defrost and beat vigorously to blend.

🐝

F / R3

BEEF AND BARLEY SOUP

Makes approximately 2½ quarts

2 cups canned tomatoes	½ pound green beans, tips cut off, washed and cut in half
¾ pound boneless chuck, cut into 1½-inch cubes	½ cup coarsely chopped rutabaga
Salt and pepper to taste	1½ cups coarsely chopped cabbage
Celery tops from ½ bunch	½ cup sliced carrots
2 sprigs parsley	½ cup sliced celery
¼ cup regular barley	½ cup thinly sliced onion
1 cup tomato juice	

Drain the liquid from the tomatoes and reserve. Add enough water to liquid to make 1 quart. Place in large kettle with beef, salt and pepper to taste, celery tops and parsley. Cover and cook slowly for 1 hour. Add barley. Cook 1 hour longer. Remove and discard celery tops and parsley. Add tomato juice, reserved tomatoes and remaining ingredients. Bring to a boil. Reduce heat and cook about 45 minutes. Serve immediately, refrigerate or freeze. To serve, reheat.

◆

BERMUDA FISH CHOWDER

Eight to ten 2-cup servings

3 pounds rockfish or sea bass	1 (28-ounce) can tomatoes
2 pounds any other fish fillets	1 (8-ounce) can tomato sauce
1 teaspoon salt	2 tablespoons chopped parsley
1½ teaspoons dried leaf thyme	¾ teaspoon Worcestershire
½ teaspoon ground cloves	sauce
1 bay leaf	¼ teaspoon hot pepper sauce
¼ cup butter or margarine	¼ teaspoon Curry Powder
2 onions, chopped	(page 39)
6 ribs celery, chopped	Lemon wedges
1 green pepper, chopped	Dark rum and sherry

Remove heads and tails of rockfish or sea bass. Discard tails. Place heads, fish bodies and fillets in large kettle. Add water just to cover, salt, thyme, cloves and bay leaf. Cover and simmer 15 minutes. Strain, reserving stock. Discard heads; remove skin and bone from fish and flake the fish. In large kettle melt butter; add onions, celery and green pepper. Cook until tender. Add tomatoes, tomato sauce, parsley, Worcestershire sauce, hot pepper sauce and curry powder. Simmer, uncovered, for 15 minutes. Add reserved fish stock and flaked fish. Simmer 15 minutes. Serve in heated soup bowls, adding a squeeze of lemon juice, a dash or two each of rum and sherry and additional hot pepper sauce to taste to each serving. Serve with warm crusty bread and butter.

❧

R1

BLOODY MARY SOUP

6 servings

1 medium onion, sliced
3 stalks celery, diced
2 tablespoons butter
2 tablespoons tomato puree
5 cups tomato juice

2 teaspoons Worcestershire
  sauce
Salt and pepper to taste
1 tablespoon lemon juice
½ cup vodka

Sauté onion and celery in butter until golden. Add puree. Cook 1 minute. Add tomato juice and simmer 10 minutes. Add remaining ingredients; cook 1 minute longer; strain. Return to heat; bring to boil. Refrigerate at least 4 hours, or overnight. Serve ice-cold.

❧

R1

BLUEBERRY SOUP

Makes approximately 5 cups

Fruit soups come from Scandinavia. They are served at the end of a meal, but they can be served at the beginning, too. They are not too sweet and, with a dollop of sour cream on top, become both tart and sweet. Peaches, sweet or sour cherries, and plums all make good fruit soups. If you use sweet cherries, you can substitute port wine for the vermouth. Incidentally, the port wine goes well with the blueberries, too.

1 pound fresh blueberries
  (1 pint), washed and drained
4 cups water
Peel of 1 lemon
½ cup dry vermouth

1 stick cinnamon
6 to 8 tablespoons sugar
3 cloves, whole
¼ cup fresh orange juice
1 cup sour cream

Place all ingredients, except the sour cream, in a saucepan and cook over medium heat until mixture begins to boil and berries begin to burst and turn soft. Remove cloves, lemon peel and cinnamon. Puree mixture, about 1 cup at a time, in blender. Chill thoroughly, preferably overnight, and serve with dollops of sour cream.

NOTE: To serve for dessert, top with dollops of whipped cream, accompanied by thin butter cookies.

⁓

CLAM AND OYSTER BROTH

Makes 5 cups

1 pint oysters
2 pints clams
5 cups water
1 teaspoon Worcestershire
  sauce

¼ teaspoon celery seed
Salt and pepper to taste
4 tablespoons butter

Drain the liquor from the oysters; reserve. Combine the clams with their liquor, the oyster liquor, water, Worcestershire sauce, celery seed and salt and pepper to taste. Bring to a boil. Sauté oysters in butter just until edges curl. Do not overcook. Just before serving, drop sautéed oysters in broth.

⁓

R1

COLD SPINACH SOUP

8 servings

2 (10-ounce) packages fresh
  spinach, washed and tough
  stems removed
½ cup freshly minced onion
2 cups light cream

2 cups Chicken Stock (page 90)
¼ cup dry vermouth
1 teaspoon grated lemon rind
½ teaspoon mace
2 hard-cooked eggs, chopped

Cook the spinach in its own moisture with the onion until spinach is tender, about 3 to 5 minutes. Place in blender with some of the light cream and blend until smooth. Place the rest of the cream and the stock with the blended spinach in a pot and cook just until flavors are blended. Stir in vermouth, lemon rind and mace and chill thoroughly. Serve topped with chopped eggs.

᪐

R2

IRANIAN CUCUMBER SOUP

6 servings

The yogurt base makes this Middle Eastern dish an extremely refreshing soup.

3 cups plain yogurt	¾ cup finely chopped walnuts
1½ cups grated cucumber	1 clove garlic, minced
½ cup seedless raisins	½ teaspoon salt
¾ cup cold water	¼ teaspoon white pepper
1 tablespoon minced fresh dill	

Beat yogurt in electric mixer or with rotary beater. Add cucumber and raisins. Blend in cold water. Add the remaining ingredients; blend well and chill thoroughly. Serve.

᪐

R1

MO'S CLAM CHOWDER

12 to 14 very generous servings

1 pound nitrite-free bacon, diced	6 cups minced clams, drained
¼ pound nitrite-free smoked ham, diced	6 cups milk
6 cups chopped onion	Salt and freshly ground black pepper to taste
¼ cup flour	Butter
12 cups diced potatoes	Paprika

Sauté the bacon and ham until bacon is brown. Drain off the fat. Add the onion and sauté until it is limp. Stir in the flour. Add the potatoes and clams and cook about 15 minutes, until potatoes are very soft. Add the milk and season to taste with salt and pepper.

Serve hot with a dollop of butter and a sprinkling of paprika on top of each serving.

Can be reheated.

ও

R1

SHERLEY'S VICHY-SQUASH

4 servings

Since the first cookbook, my dear friend and longtime cooking companion, Sherley Koteen, has always had a recipe in each one.

1 zucchini, the size of a large cucumber	3 tablespoons finely chopped onion
2 tablespoons snipped fresh dill, or 2 teaspoons dried dill	1 small garlic clove, chopped
10 sprigs watercress, including stems	¾ to 1 teaspoon Curry Powder (page 39)
3 ounces cream cheese	2 teaspoons lemon juice
1 cup low-fat milk	¼ teaspoon ginger
1 tablespoon olive oil	Salt and pepper to taste

Combine all ingredients in blender and blend until mixture is smooth. Chill thoroughly and serve ice-cold, garnished with sprigs of watercress.

᭍

R1

STRACIATELLI

6 servings

3 large eggs
4 heaping tablespoons freshly
   grated Parmesan cheese

2 tablespoons finely minced
   parsley
6 cups Chicken Stock (page 90)

Beat eggs until frothy. Stir in cheese and parsley. The egg mixture can be combined the day before. The soup stock can be made well ahead and frozen.

Bring broth to rolling boil. Pour beaten-egg mixture slowly into soup, stirring constantly until egg sets. Serve hot.

᭍

F / R2

BEEF STOCK

Makes 8 or more cups of stock

3 pounds beef flanken
1 pound shinbone
1 knuckle
8 cups water

3 carrots, scraped and halved
1 onion, quartered
2 ribs celery, cut in half
Salt and pepper to taste

Place the beef plus shinbone and knuckle in pot with water. Bring to boil over medium heat. Skim off surface scum just before water boils. Add remaining ingredients; bring to boil again. Cover and lower heat so liquid simmers. Simmer for 2½ to 3 hours, until meat is so tender it almost falls apart. Strain stock. Cool stock and remove fat.

Freeze whatever stock is not used immediately in portions suitable for use in other recipes.

NOTE: Beef is delicious served cold with Horseradish Sauce (page 67).

ꝑ

F / R2

CHICKEN STOCK

Makes 7 cups of stock

5 pounds chicken, cut up
2 quarts water
3 carrots, scraped and halved
1 onion, quartered

2 ribs celery, cut in half
1 tablespoon salt
½ teaspoon pepper

Combine ingredients in a large pot, cover and bring to boil. Reduce heat to simmer and cook for 30 to 40 minutes, until chicken is just tender. Strain stock. Cool stock and remove fat. Freeze whatever stock is not used immediately.

Use cold chicken for salads or casseroles.

ꝑ

F / R3

FISH STOCK

Makes 3 quarts

3 pounds fish bones, heads and trimmings
4 quarts water
3 small bay leaves
8 peppercorns
1 teaspoon dried thyme

2 onions, chopped coarsely
2 carrots, scraped and chopped coarsely
2 celery stalks with leaves
Salt to taste

Wash the fish well. Place in pot with water and remaining ingredients. Bring to a boil and simmer 30 minutes. Strain. Refrigerate or freeze and use as needed.

Dry white wine may be added, from ½ cup to 2 cups, and cooked with the rest of the ingredients.

❧ IV ❧

POULTRY

᠌

R1
BARBECUED HONEY CHICKEN
4 servings

½ cup dry sherry
2½ teaspoons cinnamon
⅓ cup honey
2 tablespoons lime juice

1 small clove garlic, crushed
Salt and pepper to taste
3- to 3½-pound chicken,
   cut in serving pieces

Mix together sherry, cinnamon, honey, lime juice, garlic and salt and pepper. Pour this mixture over chicken, turning pieces to coat well. Refrigerate overnight, or longer if desired. Remove and broil chicken over charcoal, basting with marinade, turning frequently.

᠌

R1
CARRIE LEE NELSON'S PEKING CHICKEN
4 servings

Mrs. Gaylord Nelson is the wife of the Wisconsin Senator. She is one of the finest non-Chinese Chinese cooks. This recipe is much like Peking duck, but a lot less expensive.

1½ tablespoons Chinese
   peppercorns
1½ tablespoons salt
1 (3½-pound) frying chicken
½ cup light Chinese soy sauce,
   or Japanese soy sauce
2 tablespoons dry sherry
5 cups water
2 green onions, cut in 2-inch
   sections

3 slices fresh ginger,
   cut ⅓ inch thick
1 tablespoon star anise
3 tablespoons flour
3 tablespoons black tea
3 tablespoons brown sugar
8 *moo shi* wraplings (doilies)
8 green onion "brushes"
Hoisin sauce

Combine the peppercorns and salt. Fry over low heat in frying pan until salt is brown and peppercorns are dark and have taken on a distinctive aroma. Rub this mixture inside and outside of chicken and place in refrigerator overnight.

Combine soy sauce, sherry, water, green onions, ginger and star anise. Bring to boil; place chicken in boiling mixture and turn heat to medium. Cover and cook chicken 10 minutes on one side; turn and cook 10 minutes on second side. Turn off heat and let chicken cool in sauce with cover on for 20 minutes.

When ready to serve, prepare bed of charcoal in grill. Charcoal is ready when gray ash has formed on coals. Make a tray out of aluminum foil. Combine flour, black tea and brown sugar and sprinkle on tray. Place tray directly on charcoal. Place grill racks over charcoal and put chicken on rack. Cover grill with hood; be sure all vents are closed. Smoke chicken for 20 minutes. Chicken should be well browned.

Serve warm or cold, but not hot. Remove chicken from bone, but leave skin intact in large pieces. Serve pieces with wraplings which have been steamed to warm, accompanied by "brushes" and hoisin sauce.

The brushes are made by cutting the green from the white of the scallion. With knife, cut off root from white part of scallion, then slash end lengthwise to make brushlike appearance.

Each wrapling is spread with hoisin sauce, then a piece of chicken and scallion brush are enclosed in it. It is eaten with the fingers.

NOTE: To make this dish, a source of Chinese groceries is necessary.

ᔓ

R1

CHICKEN IN RUM

3 or 4 servings

This recipe is adapted from one that is sold by Joyce Berthould in a farmers' market in Bethesda, Maryland.

Salt and pepper to taste
2 teaspoons Worcestershire
sauce
1 tablespoon soy sauce
¼ cup Jamaican golden rum
2 cloves garlic, minced
½ cup minced chives

1 (3½- to 4-pound) chicken,
cut in small pieces
4 tablespoons vegetable oil
3 tablespoons brown sugar
1 cup minced onion
¼ pound mushrooms, sliced
½ cup water
2 pimientos, sliced

Combine salt, pepper, Worcestershire, soy sauce, rum, garlic and chives to make a marinade. Marinate chicken in mixture for 4 or 5 hours, or overnight. Remove chicken from marinade and reserve the liquid.

Heat oil in heavy skillet. When it is very hot, add brown sugar. When sugar has melted and turned dark brown, add chicken. Cook 8 minutes, turning chicken occasionally until it has browned. Add onion and marinade; cook 5 minutes over high heat. Add mushrooms and ½ cup water; cover. Cook over medium to low heat for 30 minutes. Decorate with pimientos.

༜

F / R2

CHICKEN PROVENÇAL

4 servings

2 large cloves garlic,
minced
2 anchovy fillets
1 (2-pound, 3-ounce)
can tomatoes, well drained
¼ cup dry white wine
½ teaspoon dried thyme
½ teaspoon dried marjoram

1¼ teaspoons dried basil
Salt and pepper
1 (3- to 3½-pound) chicken,
cut in serving pieces
Lemon juice
Flour
¼ cup olive oil
¾ cup chopped black olives

Combine garlic, anchovies, tomatoes, wine and seasonings together in a saucepan and cook over low heat for 1 hour, until thickened.

Brush skin of chicken with lemon juice and dust with flour which has been seasoned with salt and pepper. Brown on both sides in olive oil. Arrange chicken pieces in bottom of shallow casserole. Pour tomato sauce over the chicken. Sprinkle chopped olives on top. Refrigerate or freeze, if desired. To serve, return to room temperature and bake at 350 degrees for 40 to 50 minutes.

ᶜᵒ

R1

CHICKEN, ROMAN STYLE

4 servings

5 pounds chicken, cut in serving pieces
¼ cup flour
2 teaspoons salt
½ teaspoon freshly ground black pepper
6 tablespoons or more butter
½ cup finely chopped onion
¼ cup nitrite-free ham, cut in julienne strips

½ cup dry white wine
¼ teaspoon dried rosemary
1½ cups fresh or canned tomatoes, well drained
2 green peppers, sliced
2 medium cloves garlic, minced
2 tablespoons olive oil

Rub chicken pieces with mixture of flour, salt and pepper. Melt 4 tablespoons butter in skillet and brown chicken in it. Use more butter, if needed. Remove chicken. Melt 2 tablespoons butter and sauté onion and ham for 5 minutes. Return chicken to skillet and add wine and rosemary; cook over low heat until wine is absorbed. Add tomatoes. Cover and bake at 350 degrees for about 1 hour, or until chicken is done.

Meanwhile, sauté green pepper and garlic in hot olive oil. Fifteen minutes before chicken is done, add to chicken. Taste for seasoning and serve.

If desired, dish can be prepared to the point just before baking, and refrigerated. When you are ready to serve it, return it to room temperature and continue with directions.

꿍

CHICKEN WITH EGGPLANT

6 servings

8 cups eggplant, peeled and cut
  in shoestring strips
1 pound uncooked white chicken
  meat, cut in shoestring strips
2 tablespoons cornstarch
4 tablespoons dark Chinese soy
  sauce, or Japanese soy sauce
2 tablespoons dry sherry

½ cup peanut oil
10 dried hot red peppers (or
  fewer), finely chopped
2 cloves garlic, minced
2 tablespoons finely chopped
  fresh ginger
Salt to taste
1 cup Chicken Stock (page 90)

Cover eggplant with boiling water; let stand 5 minutes; drain well. Dredge the chicken meat in a mixture of cornstarch, soy sauce and sherry.

In large skillet or wok heat the oil; sauté the peppers until they take on a brownish-red color. Remove them from the pan. In the same pan sauté the chicken for about 2 minutes, until it is done. Add the eggplant, garlic, sautéed peppers, ginger, salt and chicken stock. Heat through and serve.

NOTE: When working with hot peppers, discard the seeds; they are the hottest part of the pepper. Do not touch your face with your hands while you are preparing the peppers as they are likely to cause a burning sensation. Wash your hands thoroughly with soap and water after working with the peppers.

꿍

Rl

CHINESE BARBECUED CHICKEN

4 servings

Remember Alice from the song "Alice's Restaurant"? This is a recipe adapted from one of Alice's.

Marinade:

1 cup light Chinese soy sauce, or Japanese soy sauce
1 cup dry sherry

2 large cloves garlic, minced
2 teaspoons fresh ginger, minced
4 pounds cut-up chicken

Sauce:

½ cup hoisin sauce
1 cup dry sherry
½ cup catsup

¼ cup brown sugar
1 clove garlic, minced

Combine marinade ingredients and pour over chicken pieces in shallow pan. Marinate overnight, turning occasionally if pieces are not completely covered. Combine sauce ingredients and set aside. To serve, remove chicken pieces from marinade. Place in shallow pan and cover with sauce. Bake at 350 degrees for 45 minutes, turning once, or until chicken is done. Baste several times.

ॐ

CHINESE CHICKEN AND WALNUTS

8 to 10 servings

6 tablespoons peanut oil
2 cups bamboo shoots, cut in julienne strips
4 cups Chinese cabbage, cut in julienne strips
2 cups celery, cut in julienne strips
2 cups onions, cut in julienne strips
16 water chestnuts, sliced paper-thin
3 cups walnuts

1½ teaspoons salt
4 tablespoons cornstarch
2 teaspoons sugar
4 tablespoons light Chinese soy sauce, or Japanese soy sauce
4 tablespoons dry sherry
3 pounds uncooked white meat of chicken, cut in julienne strips
1 cup Chicken Stock or broth (page 90)

In a large skillet or wok heat 3 tablespoons of the oil. Lightly sauté bamboo shoots, cabbage, celery, onions and water chestnuts, cooking only until crisp-tender. Remove. Brown walnuts in same oil. Drain. Combine salt, cornstarch, sugar, soy sauce and sherry. Dredge chicken in this mixture. Heat remaining 3 tablespoons oil in skillet and quickly sauté the chicken in the hot oil until tender. Add the stock to the chicken; heat. Add the vegetables and nuts and heat through.

Serve with rice.

NOTE: For ease of preparation, have ready bamboo shoots, cabbage, celery, onions, water chestnuts and chicken. Combine salt, soy sauce, sherry, sugar and cornstarch; dredge chicken in it.

ꗞ

F / R2

MEXICAN CHICKEN

6 servings

2 (2½-pound) chickens, cut up	½ to ¾ teaspoon cumin
2 cups dry white wine	½ teaspoon coriander
2 cups water	1 cup chopped onion
1 onion, cut in quarters	1 clove garlic, minced
1 tablespoon salt	8 ounces corn tortillas
1½ cups tomato puree	Oil for frying
1 cup sour cream	½ cup pitted ripe olives, halved
½ teaspoon *chile* powder	1¼ cups grated Cheddar cheese
2 tablespoons finely chopped canned, or fresh, hot green *chiles*	

Place chicken in large kettle with wine, water, onion and salt. Cover and simmer until meat is tender, about 45 minutes to 1 hour. Cool chicken, remove bones and skin and keep chicken in large pieces. Blend together tomato puree, sour cream, *chile* powder, green *chiles*, cumin, coriander, chopped onion, garlic. Cut each tortilla into 8 wedges and cook quickly in hot oil on both sides, until crisp, adding oil as needed. Drain thoroughly on paper. Layer chicken, sauce, tortillas, olives and cheese in 1½-quart casserole, reserving some cheese for top. Freeze, if desired. To serve, return to room temperature and bake at 350 degrees until hot and bubbly, about 25 to 30 minutes. Five minutes before finished, sprinkle on remaining cheese and cook until cheese melts.

☙

R1

STUFFED CHICKEN BREASTS

4 to 6 servings

3 whole chicken breasts, boned, skinned and halved
Salt and pepper to taste
6 thin slices nitrite-free country ham
¼ cup freshly grated Parmesan cheese

¾ cup chopped parsley
½ cup blanched slivered almonds
4 tablespoons butter
½ cup dry vermouth
2 tablespoons brandy
4 tablespoons Chicken Stock or broth (page 90)

Cut a pocket in each chicken breast very carefully. It doesn't need to be very big, but try not to have any tears or holes in it. Sprinkle with salt and pepper. Line pockets with ham. Combine cheese, parsley, and almonds and stuff each pocket with some of mixture. Heat butter in large skillet. Sauté breasts 8 to 10 minutes per side, or until golden. Start with pocket side down and cook slowly so very little stuffing comes out (some will). Turn carefully. Add vermouth and brandy. At this point dish may be refrigerated until serving time. To serve, cover skillet and bring liquid to boil; simmer gently for 10 to 15 minutes. Remove breasts to warm platter. Add stock to skillet; stir and heat through. Then pour liquid from skillet over chicken breasts and serve.

☙

ROAST GOOSE

If goose is frozen, thaw as you would a turkey (page 104). Remove excess fat from body cavity and neck skin. Fat may be rendered and used in other cooking. Rinse bird and drain. Salt cavity.

Fill neck and body cavity loosely with stuffing; or do not stuff, and put quartered onion and cut-up stalk of celery in cavity. Fasten neck skin back with skewer. Tie legs together or tuck in band of skin at tail, if present. Tie wings flat against body.

Place goose, breast side up, on rack in shallow roasting pan. Salt well. Prick all over with fork. If meat thermometer is used, insert deep into inside thigh muscle. Roast at 400 degreees for 45 minutes to 1 hour, depending on size of bird. During roasting, spoon off accumulated fat.

Reduce temperature to 325 degrees and continue roasting. Thermometer should reach 180 to 190 degrees. If thermometer is not used, press meaty part of leg between protected fingers. When bird is done, it should feel soft. Prick thigh with fork. Juices should run beige in color, not pink. Skin should be golden brown and crisp. See chart for roasting time.

Leftover stuffing should be removed from bird. Refrigerate separately from meat.

ROASTING TIMETABLE
(STUFFED WHOLE GOOSE)

READY-TO-COOK WEIGHT (POUNDS)	TIME AT 400 DEGREES F.	PLUS TIME AT 325 DEGREES F. (HOURS)	TOTAL ROASTING TIME (HOURS)
6 to 8	45 minutes	1 to 1½	1¾ to 2¼
8 to 10	1 hour	1¼ to 2	2¼ to 3
10 to 12	1 hour	2 to 2½	3 to 3½
12 to 14	1 hour	2½ to 2¾	3½ to 3¾

For unstuffed goose:
  8-pound goose, deduct 20 minutes
  9-pound goose, deduct 25 minutes
  10-pound goose, deduct 30 minutes

ROAST TURKEY

Allow at least ¾ pound per serving for turkeys under 12 pounds. Allow ½ to ¾ pound for turkeys over 12 pounds.

Fresh turkeys should be washed, dried and allowed to come to room temperature before being stuffed and cooked. Stuffing should never be placed in bird until just before cooking. Turkeys should never be cooked overnight at a low temperature. In both cases the idea is to prevent spoilage, for bacteria will multiply rapidly under such conditions.

Frozen unstuffed turkeys may be brought to room temperature by two different methods. Thaw the bird in its wrapper on a tray in the refrigerator. Allow 1 to 2 days if under 12 pounds; 2 to 3 days if between 12 and 20 pounds; and up to 4 days if over 20 pounds.

To hasten the process, thaw a turkey under 12 pounds at room temperature for 6 hours and return to the refrigerator for 12 hours. Allow 8 hours out and 12 in for birds 12 to 18 pounds, and 10 hours plus 12 hours for those larger.

Generally, the stuffed and trussed bird is placed on the rack breast up. Oil or butter is rubbed over the skin of the bird, which is then basted every 20 minutes or so.

Aluminum foil may be used as a tent over the bird or applied in the later stages over breast and drumsticks to keep browned skin from burning.

Allow about ½ hour after the bird comes from the oven before carving. This allows the juices to "set," meaning moister meat, and carving becomes easier.

Times for roasting are indicated in the accompanying table.

TIMETABLE FOR ROASTING TURKEY

Internal Temperature 185 Degrees

READY-TO-COOK WEIGHT	APPROXIMATE TOTAL COOKING TIME
6 to 8 pounds	3 to 3½ hours
8 to 12 pounds	3½ to 4½ hours
12 to 16 pounds	4½ to 5½ hours
16 to 20 pounds	5½ to 6½ hours
20 to 26 pounds	6½ to 7 hours

This timetable is based on chilled or completely thawed turkeys at a temperature of about 40 degrees and placed in preheated (325 degrees) oven. For unstuffed turkeys reduce roasting time by 5 minutes per pound.

If a thermometer is not used, test for doneness about 30 minutes before timetable so indicates. Move drumstick up and down—if done, the joint should give readily or break. Or press drumstick meat between fingers; the meat should be very soft.

COOKING TURKEY IN FOIL

Prepare turkey as directed for roast turkey. To wrap, place turkey breast side up in middle of large sheet of heavy-duty aluminum foil. (For larger birds, join 2 widths of foil.)

Brush with shortening, oil or butter. Place small pieces of aluminum foil over the ends of legs, tail and wing tips to prevent puncture. Bring long ends of aluminum foil up over the breast of turkey and overlap 3 inches. Close open ends by folding up foil so drippings will not run into pan. Wrap loosely and do not seal airtight.

Place wrapped turkey breast up in open shallow roasting pan in oven at 450 degrees. Follow timetable for approximate time. Open foil once or twice during cooking to judge doneness. When thigh joint and breast meat begin to soften, fold back foil completely to brown turkey and crisp skin.

TIMETABLE FOR COOKING IN FOIL

Internal Temperature 185 Degrees

READY-TO-COOK WEIGHT	APPROXIMATE TOTAL COOKING TIME
7 to 9 pounds	2¼ to 2½ hours
10 to 13 pounds	2¾ to 3 hours
14 to 17 pounds	3½ to 4 hours
18 to 21 pounds	4½ to 5½ hours

❧

R1

PRUNE TURKEY STUFFING

Enough for 20- to 26-pound bird

1½ cups snipped pitted prunes
⅔ cup orange juice
½ cup melted butter
8 cups toasted diced bread
1 cup peeled, diced apple
⅔ cup minced celery

⅓ cup minced onion
2 eggs, slightly beaten
Salt and pepper to taste
Dash cayenne
1 teaspoon ginger

Soak prunes in orange juice for 1 hour. Mix bread with remaining ingredients, including prunes. Refrigerate, if desired.

Stuff turkey lightly, allowing for expansion. Roast turkey as directed.

❧

R1

VICTORIAN STUFFED TURKEY

Enough for 10- to 13-pound turkey

1-pound loaf unsliced white
   bread
½ of 1-pound loaf egg bread,
   unsliced
¾ cup rye bread, torn in bits
¼ pound butter
3 onions, finely chopped
½ of large bunch of celery,
   including leaves, chopped
3 ounces fresh mushrooms,
   sliced

½ of 12-ounce can chestnuts,
   drained and broken in small
   pieces
½ pound fresh sausage
Turkey liver, diced
Salt and pepper to taste
Sage and thyme to taste
2 eggs
3½ to 4 cups Chicken Stock
   (page 90)
1 pint oysters and liquid,
   optional

Cube bread in ½-inch cubes. Add rye. Place in large roasting pan in 275-degree oven and bake until dry, like Melba toast; turn often. Melt butter; add onions and celery. Cover and cook until onions are slightly golden. Add mushrooms and cook, covered, for 10 to 15 minutes.

Add onion mixture to bread with chestnuts. Fry sausage until brown; drain off fat, reserving a little of the fat in which to cook the turkey liver. Cook turkey liver. Add sausage to stuffing mixture. Add turkey liver. Season with salt, pepper, sage and thyme. Beat eggs well; add. Carefully stir in chicken broth. If oysters are used, poach them in their own liquor until edges curl; cut them in half and add to stuffing. Adjust seasoning and stuff turkey cavity and neck.

ᔒ

HICKORY-SMOKED TURKEY

10 to 12 servings

Just as delicious as the very expensive kind you buy in the fancy delicatessen

10- to 12-pound ready-to-cook turkey
Salt

½ pound butter, flavored with Seasoned Salt (page 38)

You will need an outdoor grill with a hood and a motor-driven spit.

Wash turkey and rub cavities with salt. Place turkey on the spit, putting spit in on the diagonal to keep turkey balanced. Skewer in place and then truss so that wings and other appendages do not fly around.

Have very slow coals in the back of the firebox, a drip pan under the bird as it revolves on the spit. Place a small pan of water at one end of the firebox for moisture.

Roast, hood down, basting every half-hour with butter mixture. Toss damp hickory chips on coals. Every 30 minutes or so, check the fire, adding water and hickory chips when they have disappeared. Empty the drip pan several times so fire cannot start from the collected grease.

Although most directions say to roast for 4½ to 5 hours, turkeys are often done in 3¼ to 3½ hours. Watch the bird carefully. The skin will turn black; this is natural.

Test turkey for doneness (see directions under Roast Turkey, page 105). Remove from spit and allow to sit for 30 minutes before carving.

Some people will like the burnt skin, others will not. Slice as you would any turkey and serve warm or cold.

V

FISH

❧

EGG FOO YONG

3 servings

6 eggs
2 cups bean sprouts, washed and drained
2 tablespoons finely chopped onion
1 teaspoon salt
Pepper to taste
1 cup crab meat, cooked shrimp or other fish

Salad oil
1 tablespoon sugar
1 tablespoon cornstarch
3 tablespoons light Chinese soy sauce, or Japanese soy sauce
1½ cups water

The batter can be made ahead. Beat eggs. Add bean sprouts, onion, salt, pepper and crab meat. Refrigerate, if desired. To serve, beat to mix again. Grease skillet with a little salad oil. Cook 6 separate pancakes on both sides until golden brown. Keep them warm as they are done.

Make a sauce as follows, preparing mixture ahead of time: Mix sugar and cornstarch. Add soy sauce and water. When ready to serve, cook mixture until thickened, stirring occasionally. Serve hot with hot pancakes.

❧

GRILLED ROCKFISH WITH FENNEL

6 servings

This is the American version of a famous Mediterranean dish, *loup de mer* with dried fennel. *Loup de mer* is unavailable here, and even a whole rockfish isn't easy to come by, although you can usually find fillets. Dried fennel is found in a few specialty shops, so . . .

1 whole rockfish (striped bass) weighing about 6 pounds, or 2 bass fillets weighing 3 pounds each	1 teaspoon salt
	Freshly ground black pepper to taste
1 tablespoon fennel seed	¼ cup olive oil
	1 tablespoon brandy

Rinse the fish and dry on paper towels. If you are using a whole fish, have the head and tail removed and the inside cleaned. Cut 3 or 4 slashes in the skin of the whole fish or fillets, but not all the way through. Place the fillets together, sandwich-style.

Crush the fennel seeds either by placing them between 2 sheets of wax paper and using a rolling pin, or with a mortar and pestle. Combine the crushed fennel with the salt, pepper, oil and brandy.

Beat the mixture well and brush over the skin of the fish on both sides, being sure extra amounts are put in the slashes. Place the whole fish, or the fillets (laid together flesh to flesh), in a hinged grill and cook over medium charcoal fire about 5 inches from coals for about 8 minutes on each side, until the skin is crisp and well browned and flesh flakes easily with fork.

Remove fish from grill and remove bones from whole fish. Slice into 6 servings and serve with lemon wedges.

❧

KOULIBIAC

10 servings

A glorious Russian dish

2 pounds fresh salmon	5 tablespoons chopped fresh parsley
7 tablespoons butter	
½ pound mushrooms, chopped	3 tablespoons chopped fresh dill weed
1 cup chopped onion	
5 hard-cooked eggs, coarsely chopped	Salt and freshly ground black pepper
1½ cups cooked rice	1 pint sour cream, optional

Cut salmon into thin slices and sauté in 4 tablespoons butter until cooked. Sauté mushrooms and onions in 3 tablespoons butter. Combine with eggs, rice, parsley and dill and mix well. Carefully mix in salmon. Season with salt and pepper. Chill until ready to make *koulibiac*.

Pastry *for* koulibiac:

4 cups unbleached flour
1 cup unsalted butter, chilled and cut in small pieces

2 tablespoons rum
¾ cup ice water, approximately
1 egg, beaten

Combine flour and butter and work in butter with fingertips until mixture resembles coarse cornmeal. Add rum with water and mix. Toss together. If dough is crumbly, add more water. Dough should be stiff. Divide dough in half and wrap well; refrigerate for several hours (it can be refrigerated for several days as well).

Place one ball of dough on floured board and roll into rectangle about ⅛ inch thick, brushing with more flour if needed. Trim into a rectangle about 10 x 17 inches. Place dough on greased cookie sheet and place filling on dough, leaving an inch border all the way around. Brush border with beaten egg. Roll remaining ball into rectangle 8 x 15 inches. Drape over rolling pin and place over filling. Seal bottom edges of pastry border over top, using fingers, and flute edges as for a pie.

Top can be decorated by rolling out remaining scraps cut into shapes. Brush top of pastry with beaten yolk; decorate with cutouts, if desired.

The *koulibiac* can be put together several hours ahead. Remove from refrigerator 1 hour before baking. Bake at 400 degrees for 30 minutes; reduce heat and bake at 350 degrees for 30 minutes longer, until golden brown. If pastry becomes too brown, cover lightly with aluminum foil while baking. Serve at once with sour cream, if desired.

If the *koulibiac* is to be baked as soon as it is assembled, refrigerate it for 20 minutes first.

ᛩ

R1

MO'S SEAFOOD IN CHEESE SAUCE

8 to 10 servings

Mo runs the best seafood joint on the Oregon coast, in the town of Newport Beach.

½ cup butter
½ cup flour
4 cups milk
2 teaspoons salt
¼ pound mushrooms, sliced
1½ teaspoons chopped green pepper
⅓ cup chopped green onion

½ cup chopped black olives
1½ teaspoons chopped pimiento
1 pound cooked shrimp
1 pound crab meat
2 teaspoons Worcestershire sauce
4 cups grated sharp Cheddar cheese

Melt the butter; stir in the flour. Off the heat, add the milk and stir to make smooth mixture. Return to heat and cook until smooth and thickened. Season with salt and add the mushrooms, green pepper, green onion, olives, pimiento and Worcestershire. Mix well. Stir in shrimp and crab and 3 cups of cheese. Cook over very low heat until cheese is melted. Turn into shallow casserole and sprinkle top with remaining cup of cheese.

Refrigerate, if desired, until serving time. To serve, bake at 350 degrees for 25 to 30 minutes, until the dish is heated through and cheese is melted.

✌

MOULES MARINIÈRE

4 servings

With crusty bread and a salad, enough for a complete meal

4 pounds mussels
2 medium onions, minced
4 teaspoons peppercorns
4 sprigs parsley

1 teaspoon thyme
3 cups white wine
6 tablespoons butter
2 tablespoons minced parsley

Wash mussels in several changes of cold water, scrubbing thoroughly. In large pot with cover, combine onion, peppercorns, parsley sprigs, thyme and wine. Cook for 5 minutes. Add mussels; cover and cook 10 minutes, until shells open. Discard any which do not open. Keep mussels hot. Strain pan juices through fine sieve or triple layer of cheesecloth. Reduce pan liquid by half over high heat. Remove from heat; stir in butter and minced parsley. Pour over mussels and serve.

✌

OVEN-TOASTED SHAD ROE

4 servings

1½ pounds shad roe
½ tablespoon prepared mustard
1 teaspoon anchovy paste
1 tablespoon Worcestershire sauce

Pinch of cayenne
Pinch of rosemary
1 tablespoon butter
3 tablespoons dry sherry
3 drops bitters
4 slices hot buttered toast
1 lemon, sliced

Place roe in saucepan; cover with boiling water; reduce heat immediately and simmer roe gently for 15 minutes. Drain. Cut roe into

1-inch pieces. While roe is simmering, blend mustard, anchovy paste, Worcestershire, cayenne, rosemary, butter, sherry and bitters. When roe is done, dip drained pieces in mustard mixture until well coated; arrange on hot buttered toast and bake at 400 degrees for 5 minutes. Garnish with lemon slices.

ଏ

REPUFFABLE SHRIMP OR TUNA SOUFFLÉ

4 to 6 servings

3 tablespoons butter	1 cup finely chopped cooked
2 tablespoons cornstarch	shrimp, or well-drained canned
½ teaspoon salt	tuna
¼ teaspoon pepper	4 egg yolks
1 cup milk	5 egg whites

Have ready a buttered 2-quart soufflé dish.

Melt butter over low heat. Remove from heat and blend in cornstarch and seasonings. Slowly stir in milk until mixture is smooth. Cook and stir over medium heat until sauce boils and thickens, 5 to 6 minutes. Add shrimp or tuna. Remove from heat. Cool for 5 minutes. Beat egg yolks well. Slowly stir a little of cooled shrimp mixture into yolks, beating vigorously. Return yolk mixture to shrimp mixture and mix well. Beat whites until stiff but not dry. Fold into shrimp base. Pour into soufflé dish and set in shallow pan containing an inch of hot water. Bake at 350 degrees for 1 to 1¼ hours.

To repuff, leave in soufflé dish; set dish in shallow pan with 1 inch of hot water. Reheat at 350 degrees until puffed, about 25 to 30 minutes.

NOTE: You can substitute 1 cup finely cut-up cooked chicken or turkey, cooked vegetables, ham or pork.

ℛ1

SALMON CUCUMBER SOUFFLÉ

8 to 10 servings

2 envelopes unflavored gelatin	2 tablespoons vinegar
½ cup cold water	2 pounds boneless salmon,
½ cup Chicken Stock (page 90)	cooked, or 2 (1-pound) cans red
1 cup Mayonnaise (page 42)	salmon, drained and flaked
2 teaspoons Worcestershire	3 cups peeled, diced cucumber
sauce	1 cup heavy cream, whipped stiff
1 teaspoon salt	3 egg whites, beaten stiff
½ teaspoon pepper	Cucumber slices
2 tablespoons grated onion	French Dressing (page 45)

In large bowl sprinkle gelatin on cold water to soften. Heat stock to boiling; stir into softened gelatin until dissolved; cool. When cool, add mayonnaise, Worcestershire, salt, pepper, onion and vinegar, beating until smooth. Refrigerate, stirring occasionally, until mixture mounds when dropped from spoon.

Meanwhile, fold a 30-inch length of foil, 12 inches wide, in half lengthwise. Wrap around outside of a 2-quart soufflé dish so collar stands 3 inches above rim. Fasten with tape.

Beat mayonnaise mixture with eggbeater until light and fluffy. Fold in salmon, cucumber, whipped cream and beaten egg whites. Turn into prepared soufflé dish and refrigerate until firm.

To serve, remove foil collar; garnish with cucumber slices that have been marinated in French Dressing.

༜

SALMON IN PARCHMENT

4 servings

2 shallots, minced
8 mushrooms, sliced
2 tomatoes, peeled, seeded and diced
1 cup dry white wine

Salt and white pepper
4 (4 to 6 ounces) salmon or rock-fish fillets
1 cup heavy cream

Combine the shallots, mushrooms, tomatoes, wine, salt and pepper and spoon into shallow baking dish. Place salmon fillets on the mixture, cover and simmer on top of stove about 5 to 7 minutes, until the salmon is half done. Drain salmon thoroughly and remove to platter. Continue to drain liquid as it accumulates. Boil the sauce until there is almost no liquid left; add the cream and stir. Cook slowly for 1 hour, or until mixture is quite thick. It can be done ahead of time and sauce refrigerated, the salmon refrigerated separately.

Fold 4 sheets of parchment paper in half crosswise. Cut into heart shapes, as large as possible. Open and butter lightly. Place the thoroughly drained fish on one half of heart; top with sauce and fold other half of heart over. Seal by folding the two edges together all the way around to make a pleat. The point of the heart can be held in place with a straight pin. The recipe can be prepared up to an hour ahead at this point.

Bake at 400 degrees for 12 to 15 minutes. Serve fish in parchment.

༜

SALMON WITH SORREL

4 servings

From former White House chef René Verdon, who now owns Le Trianon Restaurant in San Francisco.

½ cup dry white wine
1 cup dry vermouth
2 shallots, minced
Few dashes lemon juice
Salt and freshly ground white
    pepper

32 leaves fresh sorrel, stems re-
    moved, steamed until limp
    and then shredded
6 (6-ounce) salmon or rockfish
    (striped bass) fillets
1 cup heavy cream

Combine wine, vermouth, shallots, lemon juice, salt, pepper and shredded sorrel. Place in shallow baking dish. Place fish fillets on top; cover and simmer on top of stove 10 to 15 minutes, until fish is cooked. Remove fish to platter; drain and keep warm. Boil liquid until it is reduced by half. Add cream and cook until mixture thickens. Serve over fish.

ೆ

WHOLE GRILLED FISH

8 servings

12 slices nitrite-free bacon
10 sprigs parsley
Salt and white pepper to taste
1½ to 2 cups dry white wine

6 to 8 pounds whole fish (salmon,
    striped bass, etc.), slit, cleaned,
    head and tail removed after
    weighing

Lay 8 slices of bacon and the parsley inside the fish. Season inside and out with salt and pepper. Lay 4 slices of bacon on top of fish. Place fish on double thickness of heavy-duty aluminum foil with enough additional foil to make tight package. Shape foil so that it will hold the wine. Pour wine over fish. Secure package tightly and place 4 to 5 inches from medium hot coals. Cook for 45 minutes to 1 hour, or until fish flakes easily when tested. Remove foil, bacon and parsley. Remove bones and serve.

NOTE: Three pounds of salmon fillets (2 fillets put together) will cook in 30 minutes, using half of the other ingredients. Will serve 6.

❧ VI ❧

MEATS

⮜⮞

F / R2

ANISE BEEF

4 servings

Made with chuck beef, this is a very reasonably priced Chinese dish, but a lot of fat must be cut away; other cuts of braising beef will require less trimming.

2 pounds beef chuck	1 teaspoon salt
1 clove garlic	1 tablespoon dry sherry
2 tablespoons peanut oil	Dash pepper
3 tablespoons dark Chinese soy sauce, or Japanese soy sauce	2 cloves star anise *
1 tablespoon water	1 teaspoon sugar

Trim as much fat as possible from beef. Crush garlic. Heat oil in heavy pan; brown beef quickly on all sides. Add garlic, soy sauce, water, salt, sherry, pepper, star anise and sugar. Cover and simmer for 1 hour. Turn meat and simmer 1 hour longer. Cook longer, if necessary, until tender. Slice meat thinly and serve hot. If desired, refrigerate or freeze after slicing. To serve, return to room temperature; skim off excess fat and heat through at 350 degrees for 15 minutes.

⮜⮞

R1

BEEF ROLL-UP

6 servings

1½ pounds ground beef	½ teaspoon caraway seeds
½ cup caraway rye bread crumbs	1 tablespoon Worcestershire sauce
1 egg	Salt and pepper to taste
½ cup chopped onion	1¾ cups sauerkraut, well drained
¼ cup sweet pickle relish	1½ cups grated Gruyère cheese
¼ cup Thousand Island Dressing (page 44)	

* If star anise is unobtainable, use anise extract, but only a few drops.

Combine meat, bread crumbs, egg, onion, and all seasonings in large bowl. Work mixture thoroughly with hands. On sheet of wax paper, shape the mixture into a rectangle about 7 x 15 inches. Sprinkle with sauerkraut and grated cheese, leaving a 1-inch border around all edges. Starting with narrow end, carefully roll up mixture, like a jelly roll. The wax paper acts as a guide only; don't roll up the paper inside the beef. Refrigerate, if desired. To serve, return to room temperature and place on shallow baking dish. Bake at 350 degrees for 30 to 45 minutes.

ဢ

F / R2

BRACIOLE

4 to 6 servings

These are Italian meat rolls.

1 tablespoon finely chopped parsley
1 teaspoon minced garlic
¼ teaspoon dried sage
1½ pounds beef bottom round
¾ cup ground or finely chopped cooked beef and nitrite-free ham
16 julienne strips of nitrite-free country ham

2 hard-cooked eggs, quartered
2 slices provolone cheese, cut into 4 strips each
Salt and pepper to taste
Olive oil
1½ cups chopped onion
1 cup dry red wine
8 large fresh mushrooms, sliced
¾ cup tomato sauce

Combine parsley, garlic and sage. Cut the bottom round into 8 slices and pound flat (sometimes you can get the butcher to slice it for you, and then it is thin enough so that it doesn't have to be pounded). At the narrow end of each piece of beef, place 1½ tablespoons ground meat, 2 pieces ham, ¼ egg, 1 strip provolone, parsley mixture, salt and pepper to taste. Roll up and fold in sides. Secure with toothpick. Repeat until all meat is used.

Roll *braciole* in oil, salt and pepper. Pour a little oil into heavy skillet and brown *braciole* on all sides. Add the onion and brown. Add the wine and cook quicky over high heat. Add mushrooms and tomato sauce. Place meat and sauce in covered baking dish. At this point the dish can be refrigerated or frozen, if desired. To serve, return to room temperature and bake at 350 degrees for 45 to 60 minutes. If top rolls seem to be drying out, spoon sauce over and continue baking.

❧

R2

CHINESE POT ROAST

4 servings

2 (10-ounce) packages fresh
  spinach
2 tablespoons peanut oil
1 clove garlic
One 4- to 6-pound brisket of beef,
  trimmed of fat, or fresh picnic
  ham skinned and trimmed
  of fat

Pepper to taste
½ cup dry white wine
 2 cups light Chinese soy sauce,
  or Japanese soy sauce
½ cup sugar
 1 teaspoon Five Spice Powder
  (page 39)

Clean spinach and set aside. Heat oil in heavy pot; add garlic and meat. Brown meat on all sides. Pour off fat. Add pepper, white wine, soy sauce, sugar and spices and 4 cups water. Cover and bring to boil. Reduce heat and simmer for 2 to 3 hours, until meat is tender. When meat is cooked, remove from pot and slice. Arrange sliced meat on serving platter and keep warm.

Skim as much fat as possible from cooking liquid and place spinach in liquid in pot. Turn heat to high for 2 to 3 minutes and cook spinach, stirring constantly. Remove. Trim meat platter with spinach and serve.

❧

R3
CORNED BEEF
8 servings

1 (4-pound) beef brisket, fat removed	2 bay leaves
4 quarts hot water	12 peppercorns
1½ pounds salt, plus salt for coating	2 cloves garlic, cut in half
	4 teaspoons Mixed Pickling Spice (page 46)

Wash and dry beef. Rub with 3 to 4 tablespoons salt. Dissolve 1½ pounds salt in hot water. Place beef in an enameled or glass pot or stone crock and pour salted water over it. Cool. Stir in a bay leaf, half the peppercorns, 1 clove garlic and half the pickling spices. Weight meat with plate, brick or other heavy object, if necessary, so that meat is completely covered with liquid. Cover pot. Allow to sit at room temperature for 48 hours. (Meat will not be pink, because it has no sodium nitrite in it.)

To cook, wash meat to remove brine. Place in pot with boiling water to cover, remaining peppercorns, garlic clove and pickling spice. Cover and simmer for 4 hours, or until fork-tender.

Serve as you would any corned beef, warm or cold, thinly sliced.

❧

F / R2
KESHY YENA
8 servings

Keshy Yena comes from the word in Spanish for cheese, *queso*, and the word for filled, *llena*. Spanish is one of the several languages that go into making up the language spoken on the Dutch island of Curaçao —Spanish, Dutch and English, with a smattering of Portuguese, French and African. Originally, *Keshy Yena* was served in a scooped-out Edam cheese, but the Edam is so expensive that, while the dish is not as handsome this way, it is considerably less expensive. We've made some of our own adjustments, too.

2 pounds round steak, cut into strips as thin as possible
¼ cup flour
Salt and freshly ground black pepper to taste
½ cup vegetable oil
½ cup dry red wine
2 green peppers, coarsely chopped
½ cup finely chopped onion
½ pound fresh mushrooms, sliced

2 medium tomatoes, coarsely chopped
¼ teaspoon cayenne pepper
1 tablespoon finely chopped sour pickle
3 tablespoons seedless raisins, or chopped prunes
6 small pimiento-stuffed olives, drained and finely chopped
1¼ cups Beef Stock (page 89)
1 pound Edam or Gouda cheese

Dredge beef strips in flour with salt and pepper. Heat ¼ cup oil in heavy pan and cook beef strips in it until browned. Add the wine and cook 1 or 2 minutes, then remove from heat and set aside.

Heat remaining oil and cook green peppers, onion and mushrooms in it until soft but not brown. Add tomatoes and cayenne and cook briskly until most of liquid in pan has evaporated. Remove from heat. Stir in pickle, raisins or prunes, and olives. Combine vegetable mixture with beef. Blend well and add beef stock.

Line a 3-quart casserole with round slices of cheese ⅛ inch thick. Reserve some of cheese for top. Spoon mixture into casserole and top with remaining cheese slices. Bake at 350 degrees for 20 to 30 minutes, or until cheese is brown and bubbly.

If prepared ahead, refrigerate or freeze. To serve, return to room temperature and bake as directed for 30 minutes.

❧

F / R2

PASTICHIO

6 to 8 servings

It is an interesting thing about this Greek dish—the natives serve it at
room temperature, but Americans prefer it hot.

Meat Sauce:

1 tablespoon butter
1 onion, finely chopped
1 pound lean ground beef
1 teaspoon salt
1/4 teaspoon pepper
1/2 teaspoon nutmeg
1/4 teaspoon cloves

1/4 teaspoon cinnamon
1/2 cup dry white wine or beef
stock
3/4 cup tomato sauce
1/4 cup grated *kefalotyri* cheese
(or Parmesan)

In heavy skillet melt butter; sauté onion a few minutes, then add
meat. Break up meat with fork; drain off fat; add salt, pepper, spices
and wine or beef stock. Cover and simmer 5 minutes. Stir in tomato
sauce; cover and simmer 45 minutes. Stir in cheese and mix well. Set
aside.

Macaroni:

1/2 pound large elbow macaroni
3 quarts boiling water
1 tablespoon salt
1/4 cup butter

2 eggs, slightly beaten
1/2 cup grated *kefalotyri* cheese
(or Parmesan)

Cook macaroni in boiling salted water until not quite tender. Drain;
rinse pan to wash away starch and melt butter in same pan. Return
drained macaroni and stir to mix in butter. Add eggs and cheese and
stir until mixed. Set aside.

Cream Sauce:

¼ cup butter
1 tablespoon flour
4 cups milk
1 teaspoon salt

¼ teaspoon nutmeg
3 whole eggs plus 3 yolks
¼ cup grated *kefalotyri* cheese
(or Parmesan)

Melt butter. Stir in flour. Remove from heat and add milk with salt and nutmeg. Stir and return to low heat, cooking until mixture thickens a little. Beat eggs and yolks well and add to cream sauce, beating until smooth. Add cheese and beat until smooth.

Using a buttered 8-x-8-x-2-inch pan, assemble layers as follows with ¾ cup grated *kefalotyri* cheese (or Parmesan): ½ macaroni, ¼ cup grated cheese, all the meat sauce, 4 tablespoons cream sauce, remaining macaroni, ¼ cup grated cheese, remaining cream sauce, and remaining cheese. Bake at 350 degrees for 40 minutes, or until knife inserted in center comes out clean. Let stand in warm place, until *pastichio* firms up. Return to oven to reheat before serving. If desired, freeze before baking. To bake, return to room temperature and follow directions.

ॐ

F / R2

SOUTHWESTERN POT ROAST

6 servings

One 3-pound brisket of beef, or chuck roast
Salt and freshly ground black pepper to taste
1 medium onion, sliced and separated into rings

2 cloves garlic, minced
1½ teaspoons paprika
1 tablespoon canned, or fresh, green *chile* peppers, chopped (more if you like it hotter)
1 tablespoon brown sugar

Trim off excess fat from meat. Brown it on both sides in its own fat. Season with salt and pepper. Add onion and garlic and sauté until limp. Add remaining ingredients. Cover and cook over very low heat so meat just barely simmers, turning occasionally. Cook until tender, about 3 hours.

Meat can be frozen or refrigerated. To serve, remove fat layer, return the roast to room temperature, slice and reheat slowly in its own liquid.

❧

R3

PICKLED TONGUE

6 servings

1 fresh beef tongue, about 3 pounds
1 tablespoon Mixed Pickling Spice (page 46)
1 clove garlic, peeled and halved

Cover tongue with water; add pickling spices and garlic. Cover and simmer gently for 2½ to 3 hours, until tongue is fork-tender. Drain. When it is cool enough to handle, skin and trim off gristle and small bones. Slice tongue portion; serve hot or cold.

R1

PIQUANT TONGUE

3 servings

3 cups cooked Pickled Tongue (above), cut in slivers or pieces
2 anchovy fillets, rinsed and drained
1 tablespoon pine nuts
1 clove garlic, cut up

½ teaspoon capers
½ slice white bread, soaked in water and squeezed
6 tablespoons olive oil
2 tablespoons red wine vinegar
Freshly ground black pepper

Combine anchovies, pine nuts, garlic, capers and bread. Either pound to a paste in a mortar with a pestle, puree in blender or mash with wooden spoon in wooden bowl. Add the oil and vinegar alternately to make a smooth blended paste. Season with pepper. Combine with tongue and adjust seasonings. Serve cold.

᧚

R1

ZUCCHINI BOATS

4 servings

4 medium zucchini (about 2 pounds)
½ pound spicy hot pork sausage
¼ cup chopped onion
1 clove garlic, minced
½ cup freshly grated Parmesan cheese

½ teaspoon Worcestershire sauce
¼ cup fine cracker crumbs
1 slightly beaten egg
Salt and pepper to taste
¼ teaspoon dried thyme

Cook whole zucchini in boiling salted water until barely tender, 7 to 10 minutes. Cut in half lengthwise and scoop out pulp; mash the pulp, reserving the shell.

In a skillet cook the sausage. Drain off fat and add onion and garlic to the skillet, and cook until onion is soft. Stir in drained, mashed zucchini pulp. Reserve 2 tablespoons Parmesan cheese; mix all remaining ingredients together with zucchini mixture. Spoon into zucchini shells. Place in shallow baking dish. Refrigerate, if desired. To serve, sprinkle with reserved cheese and bake at 350 degrees for 25 to 30 minutes, or until heated through.

❦

LEG OF LAMB

6 servings

If you have been thinking about serving this dish enough in advance, you can insert slivers from 4 cloves of garlic into small incisions all over the leg a day or two before roasting.

6- or 7-pound whole leg of lamb
1 carrot, scraped and cut in
   large slices
1 onion, peeled and cut in large
   slices

1 cup Beef Stock or broth
   (page 89)
4 cloves garlic

Let lamb sit at room temperature for 30 minutes before roasting. Place in roasting pan with onion and carrot and roast at 325 degrees for 2 to 2½ hours, for medium-rare. For better-done meat, allow another 30 minutes or so. When lamb is cooked, allow to sit for 20 minutes so juices will be reabsorbed. While lamb is being carved, remove as much grease as possible from the juices in the pan. Discard onion and carrot and add the broth and reduce the liquid slightly by boiling. Pass gravy separately.

❦

F / R2

BARBECUED PORK

8 servings

2 pounds boneless pork
   tenderloin, or butt
1½ tablespoons soy sauce
2½ tablespoons hoisin sauce
1 tablespoon dry sherry

1 tablespoon honey
1 teaspoon sugar
Generous pinch of Five Spice
   Powder (page 39)
Additional honey

Combine all the ingredients but the pork. Cut the pork into strips about 1½ to 2 inches wide, 2 inches thick and 3 to 5 inches long.

Rub all sides of pork strips with marinade mixture and marinate overnight, turning pork strips in marinade occasionally. Using S-curved curtain hooks, hang the strips of pork from the hooks and hang the hooks from a rack in the oven set at the highest level. (The length of the pork strips will depend on the height of your oven!) Set a pan of water in the bottom of the oven, to catch the drippings from the pork. Roast at 425 degrees for 15 minutes. Reduce heat to 325 degrees and roast for 15 to 20 minutes longer, until pork is thoroughly cooked. Immediately upon removing from oven, brush with honey. Refrigerate or freeze, if desired. If frozen or refrigerated, reheat in foil before serving.

Serve warm or at room temperature, sliced thinly against the grain. Pass remaining marinade, hot mustard, soy sauce or plum sauce separately.

ꝏ

MO SHU RO PORK

3 or 4 servings

Known as *moo shi* pork, this dish really cannot be made successfully without access to Chinese ingredients.

10 tiger-lily buds	2 tablespoons peanut oil
2 medium dried Chinese mushrooms	½ cup lean shredded pork
1 tablespoon tree ears	2 tablespoons dark Chinese soy sauce, or Japanese soy sauce
½ cup fresh bean sprouts	1 teaspoon sugar
1 scallion	6 to 8 Chinese pancakes ("doilies")
1 or 2 slices fresh ginger root	Hoisin sauce
2 eggs	

In advance soak tiger-lily buds, mushrooms and tree ears in 1 cup warm water for 20 minutes. Wash and drain. Wash and drain bean sprouts. Shred mushrooms and scallion stalk, cutting green part into

2-inch sections. Mince ginger root. Beat the eggs and stir 1 tablespoon oil into egg mixture.

When ready to serve, heat remaining oil in wok or skillet over high heat. Add ginger and cook 30 seconds. Add shredded pork and stir about 2 minutes. Add 2 tablespoons soy sauce and 1 teaspoon sugar and stir a few more times. Add ginger, tiger-lily buds, mushrooms and tree ears and mix well. Add 2 tablespoons water and bring to boil. Set aside.

Add eggs to pan. Scramble quickly. Add bean sprouts and mix thoroughly. Combine with pork mixture and serve hot with doilies.

To heat doilies, steam them.

Put filling in doilies and roll up, like cigarettes. Serve with hoisin sauce.

❧

F / R2

GUISADO

This is a Mexican stew from La Cocina in Aspen, Colorado, with a few home touches.

2 pounds diced very lean pork
Salt and freshly ground black
    pepper to taste
1 large onion, diced
2 small cloves garlic, minced
2 (28-ounce) cans tomatoes
3 tablespoons chopped green
    chiles (more if you like the
    stew hotter)
¼ cup minced parsley

2 teaspoons cumin
2 teaspoons dried oregano
1 teaspoon dried thyme
1 small hot dried red pepper,
    minced, seeds removed
2 cups Chicken Stock or
    bouillon (page 90)
5 potatoes, peeled, diced and
    cooked

Brown the meat in its own fat. Season with salt and pepper. Sauté onion and garlic in the same pan until golden. Add all of remaining ingredients but the potatoes. Cover and simmer for 2 hours. Adjust seasonings during cooking. Add potatoes during last 20 minutes of cooking. If desired, prepare ahead but do not add potatoes if freezing. To serve, if frozen, defrost, adjust seasonings; add potatoes and cook 20 minutes.

❧

R1

CHINESE BARBECUED RIBS

6 servings

¾ cup hoisin sauce
3 tablespoons yellow bean paste
1½ tablespoons black Chinese soy sauce, or Japanese soy sauce

1½ tablespoons brown sugar
1 tablespoon fresh ginger, minced
6 pounds lean spareribs

Combine all ingredients but spareribs. Place spareribs in water to cover and bring to boil; boil for 30 minutes. Drain and dry ribs. Spread ⅔ of the hoisin-paste mixture over ribs, on both sides. Allow to marinate in this paste for at least 2 hours, or overnight if desired, in the refrigerator. To serve, grill ribs 8 to 10 inches from hot coals, about 20 minutes, brushing frequently with remaining hoisin mixture. Ribs are ready when the juice between 2 ribs that have been cut runs clear. Cut ribs into serving pieces and serve with hot mustard, if desired.

VII

MEATLESS
MAIN
DISHES

❦

R1

BROCCOLI RICE CASSEROLE

10 servings

This dish was served at the Food Day celebration in 1977 at the White House. The entire meal was vegetarian, which made the beef industry so angry it fired off a telegram to President Carter, demanding that meat be included. The casserole is excellent as a combination side dish or as a main dish for a vegetarian meal. This is an adapted version.

1½ cups brown rice
Dash of salt
  2 tablespoons oil
  1 large onion, chopped
  2 large cloves garlic, minced
  ½ teaspoon dillweed
  1 teaspoon thyme
  1 teaspoon oregano
  ½ bunch parsley, chopped
  ½ pound mushrooms, sliced

  1 green pepper, sliced
  2 pounds broccoli, approximately; tough stalks removed, remainder sliced thin
  ½ cup unsalted cashews
  ½ pound Gruyère cheese, grated
  ¼ cup grated Parmesan cheese
  ½ pint sour cream

In heavy saucepan with tight-fitting lid combine rice with 3 cups water and dash of salt. Bring to boil; reduce heat and simmer for about 45 minutes, until all water is absorbed. Do not stir rice while it cooks.

Heat oil in large frying pan. Sauté onion, garlic, dill, thyme and oregano until onion starts to wilt. Then add parsley, mushrooms and green pepper. Stir 1 or 2 minutes and add broccoli. Stir often. As soon as broccoli changes color and becomes tender, but is still crisp, add nuts and remove from heat.

Spread cooked rice in 9-x-13-inch baking dish. Cover with vegetable-nut mixture, then with cheeses, and finally with sour cream. Bake for 20 minutes at 350 degrees, until mixture is bubbly and cheese has melted.

Dish can be assembled in advance and refrigerated. To serve, return to room temperature and bake about 25 or 30 minutes.

∾

F / R2

BULGUR CASSEROLE

10 or 12 servings

4 tablespoons oil
2 cups chopped onion
3 cloves garlic, finely chopped
¼ pound fresh mushrooms, chopped
1½ cups bulgur (cracked wheat)
2 cups sliced black olives

1 (1-pound, 12-ounce) can tomatoes
1 cup dry sherry
2 teaspoons oregano
Salt and pepper to taste
2 cups grated Cheddar cheese
4 tablespoons chopped parsley
Paprika

Heat oil in skillet. Sauté onion, garlic and mushrooms in hot oil until onion is golden. Add bulgur, olives, tomatoes, sherry, oregano, salt and pepper. Mix well; bring to boil and pour into 4-quart casserole. Refrigerate or freeze, if desired. When ready to serve, return to room temperature, cover and bake at 375 degrees for 20 to 30 minutes, until mixture is heated through. Uncover, sprinkle with cheese and continue baking for 15 minutes, until cheese melts. Sprinkle with parsley and paprika and serve.

NOTE: This dish can be made nonvegetarian by browning 2 pounds of ground beef in its own fat, then adding onion, mushrooms and garlic and sautéing until onions are golden.

ᕘ

R1

CHILAQUILES

8 servings

¼ pound plus 4 tablespoons butter
1 medium onion, chopped
1 medium tomato, chopped
4 cups finely chopped fresh, frozen or dried green medium-hot *chiles* *

13-ounce can evaporated milk
24 ounces sour cream
Salt to taste
2 dozen corn tortillas

Heat 4 tablespoons butter in large skillet. Add onion, tomato and *chiles*. Sauté about 10 minutes, until onion is softened. Add milk and bring to a boil. Reduce heat and stir in sour cream; do not allow to boil.

Meanwhile heat remaining butter, a few tablespoons at a time, in a large skillet. Add a few tortillas in a single layer, and allow to warm and soften on both sides. Stack tortillas until ready to use. In dish deep enough to hold tortillas stacked with *chile* sauce between them, place one tortilla, top with about 1 tablespoon *chile* mixture, and spread to cover tortilla. Top with another tortilla and then more *chile*, using up all tortillas and *chile*, ending with *chile* mixture. If served immediately, cover with foil and heat about 15 minutes at 350 degrees.

To serve the next day, refrigerate. To heat, place dish in pan of water about 1 inch deep. Bake at 250 degrees, covered, about 1 hour, until heated through.

---

* *Chiles* used in New Mexico, from where this recipe comes, are difficult to find here. They are 5 to 8 inches long, range from medium to hot in flavor and are sometimes called California *chiles*. To substitute, combine about 3 cups chopped bell peppers and one cup chopped hot *chiles*, such as jalapeños.

ೞ

ʀ1
ENCHILADAS
2 dozen

3 tablespoons oil
1 cup mild pure red *chile*
   powder *
2 tablespoons flour
4 cups water
Salt to taste
Pinch of sugar

2 dozen corn tortillas
½ cup oil
1½ cups grated Muenster or
   Monterey Jack cheese
½ cup finely chopped onion
13-ounce can evaporated milk,
   or 1½ cups sour cream

Heat 3 tablespoons oil in skillet. Combine *chile* powder and flour and stir into oil until well mixed. Remove from heat and gradually add water until mixture is smooth. Return to heat; add salt and sugar and simmer for 10 minutes.

In separate skillet heat ½ cup oil, a few tablespoons at a time. Dip tortillas into oil on both sides, just long enough to warm and soften. Drain on absorbent paper and then dip each tortilla in chili mixture and shake to drain. In center of each tortilla place 1 tablespoon cheese and 1 teaspoon onion. Roll tortillas into tube and place close together, seam side down, in shallow oblong baking dish. Combine remaining chili mixture with evaporated milk and pour over enchiladas (rolled tortillas). If served immediately, cover with foil and bake at 350 degrees for 20 to 30 minutes.

To serve the next day, refrigerate. Then bake at 250 degrees about 1 hour, or until heated through.

---

* Pure *chile* powder is available in Spanish markets. It is not the same as the chili powder found in supermarkets, which is a mixture of spices.

ॐ

FRENCH MUSHROOM TARTE

6 servings

F / R2

Tarte Pastry:

2 cups flour, sifted   1½ sticks sweet butter, softened
1 teaspoon salt   ⅓ cup ice water

Into large bowl sift flour and salt. Cut in the butter and work mixture with your fingers until it resembles cornmeal. Add the water and work to firm dough quickly. Knead slightly on floured surface. Turn out on lightly floured board and roll into ¼-inch-thick circle. Line either a 10-inch pie plate or flan ring on a cookie sheet with the pastry, making a fluted edge and cutting off the excess. Prick bottom and sides with fork. Line with a piece of buttered wax paper and weight with dry rice or beans to prevent bottom crust from puffing up. Bake at 375 degrees for 30 minutes. Remove flan ring, if used, paper and rice and bake 10 minutes more, until golden brown.

The tarte may be prepared a couple of days ahead, wrapped well after cooling, and held at room temperature until serving time; or it may be made several weeks ahead and frozen. Defrost before filling.

R1

Tarte Filling:

3 tablespoons butter   2 tablespoons shallots, finely
3 tablespoons flour   minced
¾ cup milk   2 tablespoons butter
½ cup heavy cream   1 teaspoon lemon juice
2 egg yolks, lightly beaten   1 teaspoon salt
1 pound fresh mushrooms, cut   Freshly ground pepper
   in large dice   2 cups grated Gruyère cheese

Melt the butter in saucepan; stir in flour until blended and cook over low heat for a minute or two. Remove from heat and stir in milk, blending well. Cook until mixture thickens. Stir in cream and egg yolks.

Meanwhile, sauté mushrooms and shallots in 2 tablespoons butter, cooking over high heat until liquid has evaporated. Stir in lemon juice. Add to cream sauce with salt, pepper and 1 cup cheese. Pour into tarte shell; sprinkle with remaining cheese and bake at 350 degrees for 15 to 20 minutes, until mixture bubbles and cheese begins to brown. Serve hot.

Filling may be prepared a day ahead, refrigerated and then carefully reheated before being poured into tarte shell for baking.

ข

F / Rl

ITALIAN-AMERICAN EGGPLANT

6 servings

4 tablespoons olive oil	⅔ cup water
1 large onion, finely chopped	¾ cup dry red wine
1 large clove garlic, minced	1 teaspoon basil
Salt and freshly ground pepper to taste	1 teaspoon oregano
	1 teaspoon Worcestershire sauce
1 medium eggplant, peeled and sliced	8 ounces mozzarella cheese, sliced
1 (6-ounce) can tomato paste	½ cup grated Parmesan cheese

In 2 tablespoons of oil, sauté the onion and garlic until onion is limp. Season with salt and pepper. Meanwhile, sauté eggplant slices in remaining oil on both sides, until limp and golden. Line a shallow casserole with eggplant slices.

Add the tomato paste, water, wine, basil, oregano and Worcestershire to onion mixture and stir, heating through. Spoon the mixture over the eggplant slices. Top with slices of mozzarella and sprinkle with Parmesan. Bake at 325 degrees for 20 minutes, until cheese is melted and bubbly.

Can be made ahead and refrigerated or frozen. To serve, return to room temperature and bake at 325 degrees for 30 to 40 minutes.

ᘐ

R1

KOLOKITHOPITA

Approximately 24 pieces

This is a Greek squash pie.

3 pounds zucchini or yellow squash, grated	¾ pound feta cheese, crumbled
½ teaspoon salt	1 tablespoon chopped parsley
8 eggs, lightly beaten	¼ pound butter, melted
¼ cup farina	½ pound *phyllo*
Dash of pepper	½ pound butter, melted

Scrub, dry and grate squash. Add salt. Let stand for 15 minutes, then squeeze to remove as much liquid as possible. Add eggs, farina, pepper, cheese, parsley, ¼ pound melted butter. Mix well.

Use oblong pan approximately 9-x-13 inches and at least 2 inches deep. With soft pastry brush, butter bottom and sides. Lay 1 *phyllo* at a time, buttering each well, and use 6 for the bottom. Spread the squash mixture and add 8 more *phyllo*, buttering each one as well as top one. Bake at 350 degrees for 15 minutes, lower to 325 degrees and bake for another 30 minutes, or until top is golden brown.

Allow to cool for about 5 minutes; cut into 2-inch squares and serve. If served much later or refrigerated, reheat in oven to restore crispness to pastry.

❧

R2

POLENTA WITH TOMATO SAUCE

6 servings

1½ cups salted water
1½ cups vegetable stock
1½ cups polenta, or finely
   ground yellow cornmeal
 6 tablespoons butter
 ½ cup freshly grated Parmesan
   or Romano cheese
 ½ pound fresh mushrooms,
   sliced

2 tablespoons flour
2 cups milk
Salt and pepper to taste
Pinch of nutmeg
1 cup diced canned tomatoes,
   drained
Additional Parmesan for
   topping

Bring water and stock to boil; slowly add polenta, stirring constantly with a wooden spoon until all the lumps disappear. Continue cooking over low heat for about 10 minutes, until all the moisture has evaporated and the polenta comes away from the sides of the pan. Add 2 tablespoons butter and ¼ cup cheese. Mix and spread in a 9-x-11-inch shallow buttered baking pan, so mixture is approximately ½ inch thick; cool. Sauté mushrooms in 2 tablespoons butter. In another pan, melt remaining butter; stir in flour. Stir in milk gradually with salt, pepper and nutmeg. Cook, stirring, until sauce is thickened. Add remaining cheese, mushrooms and tomatoes.

Turn polenta out of pan and slice sideways into 2 layers. Put 1 layer into a buttered pan a little larger than the polenta itself. Cover with half the sauce. Add the second layer and top with remaining sauce. Sprinkle with additional Parmesan cheese and refrigerate, if desired.

To serve, return to room temperature and bake at 375 degrees for about 20 to 25 minutes, until sauce is bubbly and cheese is browned.

❧

R1

RIGATONI WITH BROCCOLI

8 to 10 servings as pasta course, or 12 as side dish

½ pound fresh mushrooms,
    sliced
2 tablespoons butter
1½ cups light cream
1 cup cooked broccoli, finely
    chopped
1 cup canned Italian plum
    tomatoes, chopped

½ teaspoon oregano
½ teaspoon basil
1 pound rigatoni
Freshly ground black pepper
Salt to taste
¼ cup freshly grated Parmesan
    cheese

Sauté mushrooms in butter for 5 minutes. Combine them with cream, broccoli, tomatoes, oregano and basil. Cook for about 5 minutes. Refrigerate if prepared ahead.

Cook rigatoni in boiling salted water for about 18 minutes, or until just tender; drain. Place rigatoni in hot sauce. Season to taste with salt and pepper. Remove from heat and add cheese. Mix well and serve.

❧

SCRAMBLED EGG FOO YONG

6 servings

This is the kind of dish into which you can put any appropriate vegetable scraps. If you want to turn it into a meat dish, add shrimp, chicken, turkey.

10 tablespoons butter
1 large onion, chopped
3 stalks celery, chopped
¼ pound mushrooms, chopped

Salt and freshly ground black
    pepper
1 cup bean sprouts
12 eggs, beaten

Heat 6 tablespoons butter in large skillet. Sauté onion and celery in butter until almost tender. Add mushrooms and sauté a minute or two longer. Add bean sprouts. Stir cooked vegetables into beaten eggs. Add salt and pepper to taste. Heat 4 tablespoons butter in same skillet. Cook and stir egg mixture in skillet until cooked, but still moist.

℞

℞l

SEASHELLS AND EGGPLANT

4 servings as main dish; 12 as side dish

1 large eggplant, skin on, finely diced	2 tablespoons unsalted butter
1 cup minced celery	2 cups canned Italian plum tomatoes, finely diced
4 tablespoons olive oil	Salt and freshly ground black pepper to taste
1 onion, finely chopped	
1 tablespoon minced parsley	1 pound small macaroni shells
1 clove garlic, minced	Freshly grated Parmesan or Romano cheese
1 teaspoon oregano	
1 teaspoon thyme	

Soak eggplant in salt water for 1 hour. Drain thoroughly in colander. Sauté celery in 2 tablespoons oil for about 5 minutes; add onion, parsley, garlic, oregano and thyme. Cook 5 minutes more.

In another pan sauté the eggplant in remaining oil plus butter until soft. Combine all vegetables. Add the tomatoes with their juice and bring to rapid boil.

At this point the dish may be refrigerated, if desired. To serve, simmer the vegetables over low heat for about one hour. Season with salt and pepper.

Cook shells in boiling salted water as directed on package, just until tender. Drain and add to hot sauce; heat through. Serve topped with generous amounts of freshly grated cheese.

❧

R1

SPINACH TARTE

30 squares for hors d'oeuvres, or 6 to 8 as side dish

This can be served hot as a side dish, or it can be served cold or slightly warm as an hors d'oeuvre.

1 pound fresh spinach, or 1 (10-ounce) package frozen spinach, defrosted
2 tablespoons butter
1½ cups chopped onion
½ pint yogurt and ½ pint sour cream
4 ounces grated sharp Cheddar cheese

4 ounces (¼ pound) fresh mushrooms, sliced
3 eggs, lightly beaten
1 teaspoon Worcestershire sauce
⅛ teaspoon nutmeg
Salt to taste

If using fresh spinach, cook quickly in covered pot without liquid until it has wilted. Drain thoroughly to remove excess moisture. If using frozen spinach, defrost and squeeze out liquid.

In butter, sauté onions until golden. Combine all of ingredients in 9-x-12-inch baking dish.

Refrigerate if desired. To serve, return to room temperature and bake at 350 degrees for about 40 minutes, until eggs are set and mixture is firm.

Serve hot or cold.

❧

Rl

TABBOULEH

6 to 8 servings

1 cup bulgur (cracked wheat)
3 medium tomatoes, chopped
1 bunch green onions, chopped
3 cups chopped parsley
¼ cup fresh mint, chopped
½ cup olive oil

4 to 6 tablespoons lemon juice
Salt and freshly ground black
  pepper to taste
Lettuce leaves
Cinnamon

Wash the bulgur; cover with hot water and allow to stand for 30 minutes. Drain thoroughly and then squeeze dry with hands. Chop the vegetables and mint together. Beat in the oil, lemon juice, salt and pepper, and mix with bulgur until well blended. Serve in lettuce-lined salad bowl, preferably glass, sprinkled with cinnamon. Or pass cinnamon separately.

❧

Rl

TORTILLA DE SPINACA (SPINACH CASSEROLE)

12 servings as main dish

Sara Clapp made this dish for a story I was doing about her and her cooking, which is a mixture of her heritage—Greek, Sephardic Jewish, and Argentine. Note what it says for garlic: not a clove, but a whole head. You are not overwhelmed by it.

6 (10-ounce) packages fresh or frozen spinach
10 slices whole-wheat bread
1 head garlic, peeled and finely chopped
2 bunches spring onions, thinly sliced
1 pound mushrooms, chopped
3 tablespoons oil
Salt and freshly ground black pepper to taste
1 tablespoon dried dillweed, or 3 tablespoons chopped fresh dill

2½ teaspoons dried oregano
1 teaspoon nutmeg
1 teaspoon paprika
1 tablespoon dried mint leaves, or 3 tablespoons chopped fresh mint
6 eggs, slightly beaten
½ cup grated Parmesan cheese
Milk, if needed
4 tablespoons melted butter
1 cup bread crumbs

If spinach is frozen, defrost and squeeze out liquid into a measuring cup. Cook fresh spinach without adding additional water, just until it wilts. Drain, reserving liquid. Moisten bread with water; then squeeze out water. Sauté garlic, onions and mushrooms in 2 tablespoons oil until onions soften. Add the salt, pepper, dill, oregano, nutmeg, paprika and mint and mix well. Remove from pan. Heat remaining tablespoon oil and sauté spinach in it briefly. Combine spinach, bread, garlic mixture, eggs and cheese. Add enough milk to spinach juices, if necessary, to make 2 cups. Mix with spinach. Grease a 3- to 3½-quart shallow baking dish and spoon in spinach mixture. Melt 4 tablespoons butter; add bread crumbs and stir to moisten thoroughly. Sprinkle buttered crumbs over top of spinach.

Refrigerate if desired. To serve, return to room temperature and bake at 350 degrees for 45 to 60 minutes, until mixture is bubbly and hot. Cut into squares and serve.

NOTE: This dish also may be served on the side to 20 people. It can be served cold as an appetizer with feta cheese, tomatoes and onion slices, Greek olives and Greek bread.

ᔕ

RAREBIT FONDUE

Makes 2 cups

4 cups diced mild Cheddar
cheese
2 teaspoons Worcestershire sauce
2 cloves garlic, minced

1 cup tomato puree
4 tablespoons dry sherry
Cubes of French bread

In heavy saucepan combine cheese, Worcestershire, garlic and tomato puree. Cook over low heat until cheese is melted and smooth. Stir in sherry and cook until well heated. Pour into fondue pot and keep warm. Spear bread on forks and dip in fondue or serve over toast.

ᔕ

F / Rl

RICOTTA RICE

6 servings

3 cups cooked brown rice
¼ cup finely chopped green
onion
1½ cups ricotta cheese (creamed
cottage cheese if ricotta is
not available)

1 clove garlic, minced
½ pint sour cream
2 tablespoons milk
Few drops hot pepper sauce
Salt to taste
⅓ cup grated Parmesan cheese

Combine rice and onions. Blend ricotta, garlic, sour cream, milk, hot pepper sauce and salt. Stir into rice mixture. Turn into buttered 1½-quart casserole. Refrigerate or freeze, if desired. To serve, return to room temperature and sprinkle with Parmesan. Bake at 350 degrees for 25 minutes.

᭡

F

INDIVIDUAL CHEESE SOUFFLÉS

4 servings

Soufflés which can be made ahead and frozen, popped directly from freezer to oven, then served. No last minute work!

2 tablespoons butter	1 cup hot milk
4 tablespoons flour	1½ cups grated sharp cheese:
½ teaspoon salt	Cheddar or Parmesan
¼ teaspoon pepper	6 eggs, separated
¼ teaspoon dry mustard	

Have ready four 1-pint (2-cup) soufflé dishes or six ½-pint (1-cup) soufflé dishes, or a combination of those. Line the dishes with aluminum foil, fitting as snugly as possible and allowing for a 5- or 6-inch overhang, which will be used to cover the soufflé tops during freezing and then act as collars during baking.

Melt butter. Blend in flour and seasonings and cook 1 minute. Remove from heat; slowly stir in hot milk until mixture is smooth. Cook and stir over medium heat until sauce thickens. Reduce heat, add cheese and stir until cheese is melted and blended. Cool for 5 minutes. Beat yolks well. Slowly add a little of the cooled cheese mixture to yolks, stirring vigorously. Then pour the remaining egg-yolk mixture into cheese mixture and mix well.

Beat egg whites until stiff but not dry. Fold whites into cheese base. Pour into soufflé dishes and freeze (up to 4 weeks). After mixture is frozen, remove soufflé dishes and wrap soufflés in foil.

To serve, return soufflés to soufflé dishes and make a collar out of foil. Bake at 300 degrees for 50 to 60 minutes.

ᴖ

LOW-CAL LAST-MINUTE SOUFFLÉ
2 servings

4 eggs, separated
1½ cups coarsely grated sharp
    Cheddar cheese

2 tablespoons dry skim-milk
    powder
Salt and pepper to taste

Combine cheese and skim-milk powder with slightly beaten egg yolks. Season with salt and pepper. Beat whites stiffly with a pinch of salt. Fold into cheese mixture. Turn into ungreased 2-cup soufflé dish and bake at 425 degrees for 10 to 15 minutes, until soufflé is puffed and brown.

ᴖ

F / R3

PASTA WITH THREE CHEESES
6 servings

2 to 3 tablespoons fine dry
    bread crumbs
12 ounces bow-tie noodles,
    cooked with salt and drained
2 tablespoons butter

4 ounces freshly grated
    Parmesan cheese
4 ounces Gruyère cheese, diced
5 ounces diced mozzarella
    cheese

Butter a shallow 3-quart baking dish; coat with bread crumbs.

Toss noodles with butter. Add cheeses and toss lightly, reserving a little Parmesan for top.

Turn half the noodle mixture into baking dish. Top with half of white sauce (see page 155). Repeat layers. Sprinkle remaining Parmesan on top. Bake at 350 degrees for about 25 minutes, or until hot and bubbly.

If desired, freeze before baking. To serve, return to room temperature and bake as directed.

White Sauce:

3 tablespoons butter
3 tablespoons flour
3 cups milk

Salt and pepper to taste
1/8 teaspoon nutmeg

Melt butter; remove from heat and stir in flour. Gradually add milk and return to heat. Cook, stirring, until mixture thickens. Season with salt, pepper and nutmeg.

❦ VIII ❦

VEGETABLES

❧

ASPARAGUS WITH BREAD-CRUMB SAUCE

8 servings

½ cup butter
4 tablespoons bread crumbs

4 pounds asparagus, cooked and drained

Melt butter; add crumbs. Cook and stir until crumbs are browned. Serve over hot asparagus.

❧

BAKED CHEESE GRITS

8 to 10 servings

1 cup grits
½ cup butter
3 cups grated sharp Cheddar cheese

4 eggs, separated
¼ cup light cream
Dash Worcestershire sauce
Salt and pepper to taste

Cook grits until thick and smooth according to package directions. Stir in butter, 2 cups cheese, slightly beaten yolks, cream, Worcestershire and seasoning. This can be done up to an hour ahead, but don't let mixture get cold.

When ready to bake beat whites until stiff; fold into grits. Spoon into greased 2-quart casserole. Bake at 350 degrees for 30 minutes; sprinkle top with remaining cheese and bake 15 minutes longer.

❧

F / R1

BEA'S RATATOUILLE

12 servings

4 large eggplant (5 pounds), cut
  in 1-inch cubes
6 medium (5 pounds) zucchini,
  cut into 1/4-inch-thick slices
6 onions (2½ pounds), sliced
6 green peppers, cut in 1-inch
  pieces
5 cloves garlic, put through
  garlic press
15 sprigs fresh dill, or 2½ teaspoons dried dillweed

12 sprigs fresh parsley
2 teaspoons dried oregano
1 (2-pound, 3-ounce) can
  peeled Italian tomatoes
1½ tablespoons drained capers,
  optional
3 tablespoons salt
½ teaspoon freshly ground
  black pepper
¼ cup olive oil

Do not peel eggplant or zucchini. Remove tough stems from fresh
dill. Place all ingredients in 1 or 2 large pots. Mix contents of pot(s)
until they are coated well with oil and the seasonings are evenly distributed. Cover and bake at 350 degrees, stirring frequently in the
beginning until vegetables soften and juices begin to flow. After that,
stir occasionally and bake 2 hours. Leave cover off during last half-hour
of cooking.

Or cook, covered, on top of stove about 1 hour, just below a simmer.
Test for doneness. If soft, uncover, raise heat a little and simmer a
half-hour to reduce liquid.

Serve hot or cold.

❧

BRAISED ENDIVE

8 servings

8 large endives, washed and
  drained
1 medium onion, sliced
⅓ cup butter

¾ cup Beef Stock (page 89),
  Chicken Stock (page 90) or
  vegetable stock
Salt and pepper to taste

Place the endives in a saucepan with the onion. Dot with the butter and cover with the stock. Season with salt and pepper. Cover and simmer over low heat about 30 minutes, until endives are tender and liquid is absorbed.

ᛩ

BROCCOLI WITH WHITE WINE

4 servings

2 pounds fresh broccoli, tops
　only
1 large clove garlic, minced
3 tablespoons olive oil

¼ teaspoon freshly ground black
　pepper
½ teaspoon salt
1 cup dry white wine

Ahead of time cut broccoli at point where all branches meet stems. (Use stems for soup.) Break up broccoli heads into individual branches. Cook garlic in hot oil for about 30 seconds. Toss broccoli in oil until well coated. Add pepper, salt and wine. Cover and simmer about 10 minutes, until tender. Serve with liquid from pan poured over.

ᛩ

BRUSSELS SPROUTS WITH GREEN GRAPES

6 servings

1 quart Brussels sprouts
1 cup green grapes, seeded and
　halved
3 or 4 tablespoons butter

Salt and freshly ground black
　pepper to taste
½ cup heavy cream

Clean, strip off any yellow leaves and slice off ends of sprouts. Partially cook in boiling water until not quite tender, about 5 minutes. Drain. Return well-drained sprouts, grapes and 2 tablespoons butter to pan. Season with salt and pepper and heat until butter is melted and sizzling. Pour in cream; reduce heat to low and cook sprouts until cream has almost evaporated completely, about 10 minutes. Dot with 1 or 2 tablespoons more butter. Adjust seasonings and serve.

✷

F / R2

CIDER RICE PILAF

4 servings

6 tablespoons butter
1 cup brown rice
Salt and freshly ground black
  pepper to taste
1 teaspoon grated orange peel

⅓ cup chopped onion
½ cup chopped celery
¼ cup chopped parsley
⅛ teaspoon dried rosemary
2½ to 3 cups apple cider

In skillet melt the butter. Add rice and cook slowly, stirring, until rice is golden. Add salt, pepper, orange peel, onion and celery; continue sautéing for about 5 minutes. Add 3 tablespoons parsley and the rosemary.

In saucepan bring cider to boil; stir into rice. Cook rice, tightly covered, over low heat about 1 hour, or until all of liquid is absorbed and rice is tender. Serve topped with remaining parsley.

You can also refrigerate or freeze before cooking, if desired. When ready to serve, return to room temperature. Some of the liquid will be absorbed and the rice partially cooked. Continue cooking until rice is tender. Top with parsley and serve.

✷

CORN ROAST IN FOIL

10 ears

By this method it is possible to make old corn taste pretty good.

1 quart water
2 tablespoons sugar
10 ears corn

¼ pound, or more, melted
  butter
Seasoned Salt (page 38) or table
  salt

Combine water and sugar and soak corn in mixture for 15 minutes. Remove and wrap each ear, still in husks, in piece of aluminum foil.

Place foil-wrapped corn on grill and cook for 15 minutes, turning often. Remove foil, strip corn of husks (unless your hands are very tough, you will need to wear gloves) and roll corn in shallow platter of melted butter. Season with salt, if desired.

ツ

F / R1

CRACKED WHEAT (BULGUR) WITH PEACHES

6 to 8 servings

This is excellent with poultry and is enough to stuff a 10-pound goose or 2 (5-pound) chickens.

½ pound dried peaches, cut in quarters, or half dried apples and half peaches
½ cup tawny port or apple cider
1 cup cracked wheat (bulgur)
2 cups cold water
¼ cup butter

2 celery stalks, chopped
2 medium onions, chopped
⅓ cup pine nuts
1 teaspoon dried sage
Salt and freshly ground black pepper

Soak the cut-up peaches in the wine overnight. Drain and reserve any wine not absorbed. Soak the cracked wheat in the cold water for 2 hours (overnight if desired) until all the liquid is absorbed.

Melt the butter; sauté the celery and onions until tender and lightly golden. Remove from heat; add the cracked wheat, peaches, pine nuts, sage, salt and pepper. Place in a large casserole and bake at 350 degrees for 45 minutes, until heated through. Stir once or twice.

If desired, prepare ahead, refrigerate or freeze until serving time. Return to room temperature and bake as directed.

NOTE: If you are serving this dish with poultry, use the reserved port with stock to baste bird(s).

❧

DRY SAUTÉED STRING BEANS

4 servings

A wonderful Szechuan vegetable dish

2 pounds fresh beans, trimmed
Peanut or soy oil for deep frying
2 tablespoons soy oil
2 to 3 tablespoons ground pork
2 teaspoons Szechuan pickle
   (Szechuan preserved
   vegetables, finely chopped)
2 tablespoons chicken broth or
   water
2 tablespoons dry sherry

½ teaspoon ground ginger
½ teaspoon minced garlic
2 tablespoons hoisin sauce
1 tablespoon dark soy sauce
¼ teaspoon white pepper
2½ teaspoons oyster sauce
1 to 1½ teaspoons red *chile*
   paste or sauce
1 tablespoon spring onions
1 teaspoon sesame oil

Deep-fry green beans at 325 degrees for one minute in peanut or soy oil. When skins of beans get wrinkled, but before they burst, the beans are ready; drain thoroughly.

Heat 2 tablespoons soy oil in wok or heavy skillet until very hot. Add pork and pickle and stir to coat meat with oil. Add chicken broth and cook until pork browns. Then add sherry, ginger, garlic, hoisin sauce, soy, pepper, oyster sauce and *chile* paste. Stir well. Add green beans and stir. Add spring onions and sesame oil just before serving.

❧

FIDEO (VERMICELLI)

3 to 4 servings

This is a New Mexican version of a Mexican dish and will go well with any Mexican food, but is also a good accompaniment to chicken, beef or fish.

8-ounce package vermicelli (thin
  spaghetti)
2 tablespoons oil
2 small onions, chopped fine

2 small tomatoes, chopped
  fine
2 cloves garlic, minced
1½ cups Chicken Stock or broth
  (page 90)

Brown vermicelli in hot oil very slowly. Drain vermicelli on absorbent paper and place in pot with cover. Sauté onion, tomato and garlic in oil remaining in pan until onion is tender. Combine with broth and salt to taste. Pour over vermicelli. Cover and cook slowly on top of stove until all the liquid is absorbed and vermicelli is tender.

ᕫᗱ

F / R2

FRUITED BULGUR

10 servings

Very good with poultry

¼ cup butter
1 large onion, minced
¾ cup slivered blanched
  almonds
1 pound cracked wheat
  (bulgur)

4½ cups Beef Stock (page 89) or
  Chicken Stock (page 90)
¾ cup dried apricots, cut up
4 tablespoons currants

Melt the butter in a skillet. Sauté the onion and almonds in the butter until golden. Add the bulgur and cook until bulgur begins to turn golden. Add the stock, apricots and currants and place in casserole. Bake at 350 degrees for 40 to 45 minutes, until all liquid is absorbed. Serve.

You can also prepare ahead up to baking, then refrigerate or freeze. To serve, return to room temperature and bake at 350 degrees about 30 minutes, until heated through.

℞

GALUSKA

6 servings

A variation on Hungarian noodles from Paulette Fono and the restaurant, Paprikas Fono, in San Francisco she owns with her husband.

3 cups flour
2 tablespoons salt
3 whole eggs
1 cup water
1 teaspoon oil

3 quarts of water
4 tablespoons butter, melted
1 cup shredded sharp cheese, optional

Place flour and 1 tablespoon of salt into large mixing bowl and mix well with wooden spoon. Add eggs and water, using wooden spoon and a beating motion. Mix until evenly blended and no large lumps of egg and flour remain. Allow 2 minutes for mixing. Scrape off sides of bowl and pour a teaspoon of oil on top of dough to prevent from drying.

In large pot, bring 3 quarts of water and 1 tablespoon of salt to boil. Take small cutting board. Place ⅓ of dough on it. Dip knife into boiling water and cut a narrow strip of dough approximately ¼ inch wide. Lean cutting board over top of pot and cut dough quickly into 1- or 2-inch pieces, with cutting and scraping motion, scraping dough off board, directly into boiling water. Dip knife frequently into boiling water. Repeat until all dough is gone.

Wait until *galuska* come to top of water. Allow to boil briefly. Stir with slotted spoon, then take *galuska* out with this spoon and quickly wash with cold water; drain. Place in ovenproof serving dish. Dribble some melted butter on top of *galuska*. Repeat until all dough is used up. Sprinkle with cheese, if desired. Mix *galuska* thoroughly so that it is well coated with butter and cheese. Serve immediately, or refrigerate. Reheat in same dish by placing *galuska* (covered) in a 350-degree oven for 25 to 30 minutes.

꙳

GRILLED POTATO PACKAGES
4 to 6 servings

4 medium potatoes, pared and
    cut in ½-inch cubes
1 cup chopped onion
½ cup coarsely chopped green
    pepper

Salt and pepper to taste
¼ teaspoon caraway seed
¼ cup butter

Place potatoes in center of 18-x-22-inch rectangle of heavy-duty aluminum foil. Add onion and green pepper. Season with salt, pepper and caraway. Dot with butter. Seal securely. Place foil package, seam side down, on grill 5 inches from coals. Grill 20 minutes. Turn package and grill 20 minutes longer, or until potatoes are done. Toss lightly with fork and serve. (Indoors, bake in foil at 425 degrees for about 40 minutes.)

꙳

R1
HOT HERBED TOMATOES
6 servings

1½ pints cherry tomatoes
6 tablespoons finely minced
    onion
1 large clove garlic, finely
    minced
6 tablespoons chopped parsley

⅓ teaspoon dried thyme
¾ cup soft bread crumbs
¾ teaspoon salt
Dash pepper
6 tablespoons olive oil or salad
    oil

Stem tomatoes and wash; drain. Combine remaining ingredients; mix well. Arrange tomatoes in single layer in lightly oiled, shallow baking dish. Sprinkle bread-crumb mixture over tomatoes. Refrigerate, if desired. To serve, return to room temperature and bake at 425 degrees for 6 to 8 minutes, or until tomatoes are softened.

~&~

F / R2

MUENSTER-STUFFED POTATOES

12 servings

6 baking potatoes	1 cup milk
1 cup firmly packed, coarsely grated Muenster cheese	Salt and freshly ground black pepper to taste
1 clove garlic, crushed	⅓ cup fine bread crumbs
10 tablespoons melted butter	

Scrub potatoes and bake at 400 degrees for about 45 to 50 minutes, or until done. Cut potatoes in half lengthwise and scoop out potato. Reserve shells.

In a bowl, mash potatoes or press through ricer. While hot, add the cheese, garlic and 8 tablespoons (½ cup) butter. Gradually stir in milk until potatoes are light and fluffy. Season with salt and pepper. Spoon into potato shells. Combine bread crumbs with 2 tablespoons butter and pepper. Spoon mixture over potatoes, and refrigerate or freeze, if desired.

To serve, return to room temperature and bake at 350 degrees for 25 to 30 minutes.

~&~

PARSLEY NOODLES

6 servings

1 pound broad egg noodles	Salt
¼ cup butter	Freshly ground black pepper
¼ cup finely chopped parsley	

Cook noodles according to package directions. Drain thoroughly. Stir in melted butter, parsley, salt and lots of freshly ground black pepper.

✌

R1

POLENTA BEL PAESE

6 to 8 servings

3 cups boiling water
1 teaspoon salt
1 cup cornmeal
1 cup cold water

12 ounces Bel Paese (or other mild cheese such as Gouda, Colby, Muenster, Monterey Jack), grated
4 tablespoons butter

Bring 3 cups water to a boil. Combine salt, cornmeal and 1 cup cold water and mix well. Pour into boiling water and bring to boil again, stirring. Reduce heat so mixture simmers and cook for 5 minutes, or until cornmeal is thick and water has evaporated.

Turn hot cooked polenta into greased 9-x-9-inch pan and spread to make a layer about ½ inch thick. Chill an hour or two or overnight. Cut into cubes and place in greased shallow baking dish; sprinkle with grated cheese and bits of butter.

Refrigerate, if desired. To serve, return to room temperature and bake at 400 degrees until polenta is hot, bubbly and lightly browned, about 25 to 30 minutes.

✌

F / R1

RAISIN PILAF

10 servings

½ cup plus 2 tablespoons butter
2 large onions, minced
2 cloves garlic, minced
2½ cups brown rice
½ teaspoon cinnamon, heaping

Salt and pepper to taste
5 to 6 cups Chicken Broth (page 90)
¾ cup raisins
5 tablespoons chopped toasted almonds

In 6 tablespoons butter sauté onions and garlic until soft. Stir in rice and cook 5 to 6 minutes. Add cinnamon, salt and pepper and enough chicken broth to cover rice.

Refrigerate or freeze, if desired. To serve, return to room temperature, cover and simmer for 45 to 60 minutes, until rice is tender and liquid has been absorbed. Stir in remaining butter, raisins and almonds; heat and serve.

❧

F / Rl

RICE AND PECAN CASSEROLE

14 to 16 servings

½ pound butter
4 green onions, white part only, chopped
1 clove garlic, minced
1 pound mushrooms, sliced
2 cups brown rice

½ teaspoon dried thyme
¼ teaspoon turmeric
Salt and freshly ground black pepper to taste
1½ cups chopped pecans
6 cups Beef Stock (page 89)

Melt butter. Sauté onions, garlic and mushrooms in butter until onion is golden. Stir in rice and cook, stirring frequently, until rice is golden. Season with thyme, turmeric, salt and pepper. Stir in pecans. Turn into 3-quart casserole and pour over the stock.

If desired, refrigerate or freeze. To serve, return to room temperature and cover. Bake at 400 degrees for 1 hour and 20 minutes, or until liquid is absorbed.

❧

Rl

SAUCE VINAIGRETTE FOR HOT ASPARAGUS

8 servings

6 tablespoons olive oil or salad
  oil
2 tablespoons white or red wine
  vinegar

½ to 1 teaspoon salt
12 grinds of pepper mill
1 teaspoon Dijon mustard
4 pounds fresh asparagus

Blend oil and vinegar, salt and pepper. Blend in mustard. Beat with wire whisk. Refrigerate, if desired. To serve, return to room temperature and, just before pouring over asparagus, beat again with wire whisk.

To cook asparagus, break off tough ends, wash and cook over boiling water in a steamer, just until tender. Drain and pour dressing over hot asparagus. Serve immediately.

❧

Rl

STUFFED ZUCCHINI

6 servings

6 small zucchini, cut in half
  lengthwise
Olive oil
2 small cloves garlic, minced
⅓ cup bread crumbs

6 black Greek olives, chopped
1 tablespoon capers
1 tablespoon chopped parsley
6 anchovy fillets, coarsely
  chopped

Scoop out and discard seeds and a small amount of flesh from zucchini. Sauté halves quickly in olive oil. Then, in a saucepan, parboil for 5 minutes; cool. Sauté garlic and crumbs in 3 tablespoons oil for 2 minutes. Add chopped olives, capers, parsley and anchovies. Stuff zucchini with this mixture and sprinkle with additional crumbs.

Brush zucchini with oil. Arrange in baking dish and bake at 375 degrees for 20 minutes, or until tender, brushing once with oil. Chill. Serve cold. (May be served hot, as well.)

❧

R1

SWEET POTATOES AND WALNUTS

10 to 12 servings

3 pounds sweet potatoes	Salt to taste
2 tablespoons brown sugar	1 cup milk
3 tablespoons butter	½ cup brandy
½ teaspoon cinnamon	1 cup broken walnut meats
½ teaspoon nutmeg	

Cook sweet potatoes in their jackets. Drop them in boiling water to cover and cook, covered, until tender, about 25 minutes for medium. Drain; cool enough so they can be handled in order to peel. Mash while still warm.

Grease a 2-quart casserole. Combine warm mashed potatoes with remaining ingredients and turn into prepared casserole. Bake at 400 degrees for 30 minutes.

To prepare ahead, refrigerate after combining ingredients in casserole. To serve, return to room temperature and bake at 400 degrees for 30 to 45 minutes.

ᵡ

Rl

TOMATO ZUCCHINI CASSEROLE

6 to 8 servings

Butter

3 medium zucchini, scrubbed and sliced into ovals on the diagonal

1 large onion, sliced

3 large tomatoes, sliced

4 anchovy fillets, cut up

1 tablespoon capers

1 clove garlic, minced

1 teaspoon salt

Freshly ground black pepper to taste

2 teaspoons dried basil

½ cup freshly grated Parmesan cheese

Rub shallow ovenproof casserole with butter. Line dish with half of sliced zucchini, onion and tomatoes. Top with half of anchovies, capers, garlic, salt, pepper, basil and cheese. Dot with butter. Repeat layers. Dot with butter.

Refrigerate, if desired. To serve, return to room temperature and bake, uncovered, at 375 degrees for 45 minutes, or until zucchini is tender.

ᵡ

Rl

WINTER SQUASH WITH NUTS AND MADEIRA

6 servings

2 acorn squash, or 1 butternut squash, approximately 1¼ pounds (enough to make 3 cups of ¼-inch-thick slices)

2 tablespoons butter

2 tablespoons oil

1 cup heavy cream

¼ cup Madeira

Salt and freshly ground black pepper to taste

½ cup bread crumbs

½ cup walnuts or pecans, coarsely chopped

2 tablespoons melted butter

Peel, quarter and seed squash. Cut into 1/4-inch-thick slices. Sauté the slices in the butter and oil until lightly browned, about 2 to 3 minutes. Butter a 1-quart baking dish. Place half the squash in the dish. Sprinkle with salt and pepper. In a bowl combine the cream and Madeira, and pour half this mixture over the squash in the dish. Top with remaining squash; season and pour over remaining cream mixture. Combine bread crumbs and nuts with melted butter and sprinkle over the top. Bake at 325 degrees for 45 minutes, or until squash is done.

To prepare ahead, refrigerate after casserole is complete. To serve, allow to sit at room temperature for about 30 minutes and then bake as directed for 55 minutes to 60 minutes.

᭡

ZUCCHINI WITH WALNUTS

4 servings

1 pound zucchini
3 tablespoons butter
1/2 cup walnuts, coarsely chopped

1 tablespoon butter
Salt and freshly ground black pepper

Wash zucchini, remove ends and cut into slices 1 inch thick. Heat 3 tablespoons butter in frying pan and sauté zucchini until they just begin to soften.

Meanwhile, brown walnuts in 1 tablespoon butter. Combine the walnuts with the zucchini; season with salt and pepper and cook until zucchini is tender.

Walnuts can be sautéed ahead and set aside.

IX

SALADS

❧

R1

CHINESE SHREDDED CUCUMBER

8 servings

4 cucumbers
Salt
1 large clove garlic, minced
2 tablespoons light soy sauce

5 teaspoons peanut oil
1 teaspoon sesame oil
1 teaspoon sugar
1 teaspoon vinegar

Peel and shred cucumbers, reserving a section for the sliced garnish. Sprinkle well with salt. Let stand 1 to 2 hours and then drain. Combine minced garlic with soy sauce, peanut and sesame oils, sugar and vinegar. Blend well. Add to cucumbers. Toss well and refrigerate, if desired, or serve immediately. If refrigerated, when ready to serve, pour off excessive liquid. Decorate with thinly sliced cucumber.

❧

COOL GREENS

6 servings

½ cup olive oil
4 tablespoons red wine vinegar
1 clove garlic, halved
1 tablespoon chopped parsley
1 teaspoon dry mustard
1 teaspoon salt
Freshly ground black pepper
5 cups torn lettuce

5 cups torn spinach
1 small bunch watercress
2 avocados
2 large oranges, peeled, sectioned and cut in half, optional
½ red onion, thinly sliced, if available

Combine oil, vinegar, garlic, parsley, mustard, salt and pepper; chill. In advance, wash and tear up greens and remove stems from watercress. Refrigerate in plastic bags. At serving time, arrange greens in salad bowl, slice in avocado, optional oranges and onion. Remove garlic from dressing. Shake well and pour over salad. Toss gently.

ᴥ

R2

CRANBERRY SALAD MOLD

8 to 10 servings

2 packages unflavored gelatin
½ cup cold water
2½ cups orange juice
2 cups ground raw cranberries

2 oranges, seeded and ground
2 cups finely chopped celery
1 cup chopped walnuts
½ cup sugar

Soften gelatin in cold water and dissolve over low heat. Remove from heat and stir in orange juice. Chill until partially set. Combine cranberries, oranges, celery and walnuts, and stir in sugar. Add cranberry mixture to the partially set gelatin, and pour into 8-cup mold. Chill until firm. Unmold to serve.

ᴥ

R1

CUCUMBER SALAD

6 to 8 servings

3 to 4 cucumbers
1 tablespoon salt
1¼ cups water
¼ cup sugar

⅓ cup vinegar (white distilled)
1 or 2 cloves garlic, mashed
Sour cream and paprika for
    garnish

Peel cucumbers with potato peeler. Slice thinly. In mixing bowl combine salt, water, sugar, vinegar and garlic; mix well. Pour dressing over cucumbers and allow to stand for at least 1 hour in refrigerator before serving. Serve in large salad bowl (not wood) with some of dressing. Garnish with sour cream and paprika.

❦

Rl
CUCUMBER WALNUT SALAD
4 servings

8 ounces plain yogurt
1 tablespoon olive oil
1 teaspoon dry white wine
½ teaspoon salt
1 teaspoon chopped fresh dill, or ⅓ teaspoon dried dill

1 clove garlic, minced
White pepper to taste
2 large cucumbers, peeled and chopped
½ cup walnut pieces

Blend all ingredients but cucumbers and walnuts. When smooth, add cucumbers. Place in refrigerator to chill; overnight, if desired. At last minute stir in walnuts and serve.

❦

ELSA'S GREENS AND MUSHROOM SALAD
6 to 8 servings

Elsa Castro, our housekeeper, makes the best salad in town.

1 pound mixture of Boston lettuce, endive, spinach and red lettuce
¼ pound mushrooms, thinly sliced
¾ to 1 cup coarsely grated Muenster or Cheddar cheese
1 to 1¼ cups Oil and Vinegar Dressing (page 188)

Tear lettuce into bite-size pieces. Mix gently with mushrooms and cheese. Toss with dressing to serve.

❧

R1 (VEGETABLES)
R2 (MARINADE)

FRESH VEGETABLE MARINADE

12 servings

1 tablespoon dry mustard
1 tablespoon sugar
1 tablespoon salt
1 cup cider vinegar
1 teaspoon black pepper
1 cup olive oil ⎱ or use 2 cups salad oil
1 cup salad oil ⎰

1 tablespoon minced parsley
2 pounds small fresh
   mushrooms, cleaned
4 pint baskets small cherry
   tomatoes

Mix together mustard, sugar and salt. Slowly add vinegar until dry mixture is absorbed. Add oil, pepper and parsley, and stir or shake until oil and vinegar are blended. Pour over vegetables. Allow vegetables to marinate overnight. To serve, remove vegetables from marinade.

❧

R1

NECTARINE AND CUCUMBER SALAD

10 servings

2 cups plain yogurt
2 tablespoons chopped fresh
   mint, or 2 teaspoons dried
   mint
1 teaspoon salt

½ teaspoon sugar
1 large clove garlic
2½ pounds nectarines, sliced
2 cucumbers, pared and sliced
   thinly

Combine yogurt, mint, salt, sugar and garlic and mix well. Place a layer of nectarines and then a layer of cucumbers in a shallow serving dish. Spoon on some of the yogurt mixture; repeat this layering, ending with nectarines and topping with yogurt mixture. Cover and refrigerate for at least 2 hours, overnight if desired. Serve with slotted spoon.

ORANGE SPINACH SALAD

6 to 8 servings

10 ounces raw spinach, washed, drained and stems removed
¼ pound mushrooms, sliced

1 (5-ounce) can water chestnuts, drained and diced
4 oranges, peeled and diced

R1
Dressing:

¼ cup salad oil
2 tablespoons vinegar
2 tablespoons orange juice

1 tablespoon soy sauce
¼ teaspoon salt
¼ teaspoon dry mustard

Tear spinach coarsely and toss in large salad bowl with mushrooms, water chestnuts and oranges. Combine dressing ingredients thoroughly and toss with spinach mixture just before serving.

Salad dressing can be made a day ahead.

R3

PICKLED BEETS

Makes approximately 4 cups

2 pounds beets
1 cup wine vinegar
1 teaspoon salt
Pinch of sugar

5 peppercorns
4 whole cloves
½ bay leaf

Cut off tops from beets, leaving 1-inch stem. Wash. Place beets in boiling water to half-cover them. Cover and cook about 45 minutes, until tender but still firm. If necessary, add more boiling water. Drain beets, reserving 1 cup of beet liquid.

Plunge beets into cold water to stop cooking process. Drain; peel off skins and cut into slices. Place in container with tight cover. Combine reserved beet liquid with remaining ingredients in pot and bring to boil. Pour over beets; be sure they are completely covered. Cover and chill. Serve drained and chilled.

NOTE: Pickled Beets should be made several days in advance. They are a fine accompaniment to the Koulibiac (page 112).

❧

Rl

PIQUANT ZUCCHINI

8 servings

4 medium zucchini, trimmed and scrubbed	¼ teaspoon thyme
	1 teaspoon coriander
¼ cup olive oil	1 bay leaf
¼ cup lemon juice	1 clove garlic, crushed
1 teaspoon salt	2 tablespoons chopped parsley
¼ teaspoon pepper	

Slice zucchini ¼ inch thick. Combine all other ingredients in saucepan. Add zucchini. Bring to boiling. Reduce heat; simmer until zucchini is tender, about 5 to 7 minutes. Chill.

R1

POTATO SALAD

6 to 8 servings

4 cups cooked potatoes, cubed
1 small onion, minced
1 tablespoon minced fresh parsley
Salt and pepper to taste
1 teaspoon capers, drained
1½ teaspoons chopped fresh dill, or ½ teaspoon dillweed

1 egg
5 teaspoons lemon juice
1½ tablespoons wine vinegar
2 hard-cooked eggs, diced
¾ cup sour cream
¼ cup Mayonnaise (page 42)
¼ cup celery, chopped
¼ cup green pepper, chopped

In large bowl mix potatoes with onion, parsley, salt, pepper, capers and dill. Beat egg with lemon juice and vinegar; mix in diced eggs, sour cream, mayonnaise, celery and green pepper. Add to potato mixture; chill and serve.

RED AND GREEN SALAD

6 servings

3 tablespoons olive oil
2 tablespoons red wine vinegar
1½ tablespoons Dijon-style mustard
Salt and freshly ground black pepper to taste
1 large clove garlic, pressed

¼ small head red cabbage, coarsely shredded
10 raw Brussels sprouts, very thinly sliced
⅓ cup blue cheese, crumbled
2 tablespoons chopped green onion

Mix together oil, vinegar, mustard, salt, pepper and garlic. Beat or shake to blend well. (Dressing can be made ahead.) Gently stir dressing into cabbage and Brussels sprouts just before serving, along with cheese and green onion.

❦

R1

ROASTED PEPPER AND MUSHROOM SALAD

5 or 6 servings

5 green peppers
1 pound mushrooms, washed, stems removed

½ cup Oil and Vinegar Dressing (page 188)
Salt and freshly ground black pepper to taste

Roast peppers at 450 degrees for 15 to 20 minutes, until skins blister and brown. Cool; remove skin. Remove stems and seeds, and slice into ¼-inch-thick strips.

Slice mushroom caps; reserve stems for another use. Combine peppers and mushrooms and toss with dressing. Season with salt and pepper as needed. Chill.

❦

R2

SEAFOAM SALAD

6 to 8 servings

1-pound, 4-ounce can unsweetened crushed pineapple
2 packages unflavored gelatin
1 cup water
4 tablespoons lime juice

4 tablespoons sugar
¼ teaspoon salt
1 teaspoon dillweed
½ cup dry vermouth
2 cups unflavored yogurt

Drain pineapple well, reserving juices. Add juices to gelatin with water, lime juice, sugar, salt and dill. Mix well and heat to boiling, stirring to dissolve gelatin. Remove from heat and stir in vermouth. Chill until mixture is consistency of unbeaten egg white. Blend in yogurt. Stir in pineapple. Pour into 1½-quart ring or other shaped mold and chill until firm. Unmold to serve.

SPINACH SALAD WITH YOGURT DRESSING

6 servings

2 pounds fresh spinach	8 slices crisply cooked and well-drained nitrite-free bacon, crumbled
3 hard-cooked eggs, coarsely chopped	
	⅔ cup Yogurt Dressing (page 189)

Wash spinach well and dry thoroughly by draining on racks or in colander. Break into bite-size pieces and mix gently with eggs and bacon. Toss with dressing just before serving.

R2

TANGY RICE SALAD

4 to 6 servings

4 cups fluffy cooked rice	¼ teaspoon turmeric
1 tablespoon vinegar	¾ cup raisins
1 teaspoon lemon juice	⅓ cup chopped green pepper
1 tablespoon salad oil	⅔ cup yogurt or sour cream
2 teaspoons Curry Powder or more to taste (page 39)	⅔ cup Mayonnaise (page 42)

Sprinkle hot rice with vinegar, lemon juice and oil. Mix lightly; add curry and turmeric, and blend. Stir in raisins and green pepper. Add the yogurt and mayonnaise; mix well. Place in 6-cup mold and chill. Either unmold to serve or heap on lettuce-lined plate.

ℰ

R1

WHITE BEAN AND TUNA SALAD
(*FAGIOLI TOSCANI ALL' OLIO*)

6 servings

2 cups dry white kidney, marrow, Great Northern, or navy beans
2 quarts water
¼ cup olive oil
1 tablespoon lemon juice
Salt and lots of freshly ground pepper

¼ cup green onions, finely chopped
2 tablespoons parsley, finely chopped
1 (7-ounce) can tuna, preferably packed in olive oil

Combine beans with water and bring to boil. Boil briskly for 2 minutes, remove from heat and let beans soak 1 hour. Then cook them in soaking water over low heat for another 1½ hours, or until tender. Add more water if necessary. Drain.

Combine oil, lemon juice, salt and pepper, and pour over beans. Add green onions and parsley, and mix gently. Refrigerate. To serve, drain tuna, break into chunks and place on top of beans.

ᷓ

R1

WINTER SALAD

12 servings

4 large Bermuda or Spanish
  onions, sliced
2 cups milk
2 cups water
4 hard-cooked eggs, chopped
2 teaspoons prepared mustard
2 teaspoons salt

½ teaspoon pepper
1 teaspoon sugar
½ cup olive or salad oil
4 tablespoons cider vinegar
2 small bunches celery, diced
4 large beets, cooked, peeled
  and sliced

Boil onion slices in milk and water until tender. Drain and chill onions.

To make the dressing, chop eggs and mix with mustard, salt, pepper and sugar. Stir in oil, blending well. Then stir in vinegar.

Toss the onions with celery and beets; spoon dressing over and mix gently. Let stand for several hours in the refrigerator.

ᷓ

R1

ZUCCHINI SALAD

6 servings

6 small zucchini, scrubbed,
  ends cut off
1 tablespoon salt

Lettuce
Oil and Vinegar Dressing
  (page 188)

Cook zucchini in salt water until almost tender, about 5 minutes; drain. When cool, slice thinly lengthwise in about ⅓-inch-thick slices to within 1 inch of bottom, but not through skin. Refrigerate. When ready to serve, spread each zucchini out in a fan shape on lettuce-lined plate. Pour dressing over.

R1

LEMON AND OIL DRESSING

Makes 1 cup

1 small clove garlic, cut in half	2 tablespoons fresh lemon juice
¼ teaspoon dry mustard	Salt and freshly ground black
6 tablespoons olive oil	pepper to taste

In a bowl combine all ingredients and blend with a fork or wire whisk. Refrigerate. To serve, shake dressing well, remove garlic and pour over greens.

R1

OIL AND VINEGAR DRESSING

Makes approximately 1⅓ cups

⅓ cup-plus wine vinegar	¼ teaspoon paprika
1 teaspoon salt	½ teaspoon dry mustard
⅛ teaspoon pepper	1 cup olive or salad oil
½ teaspoon sugar	1 clove garlic

Mix the vinegar with the seasonings and add the oil slowly while beating.

❧

R3

ROQUEFORT SOUR CREAM DRESSING

Makes approximately 1¼ cups

1 cup sour cream
½ teaspoon dry mustard
½ teaspoon minced onion

2 ounces Roquefort or other
good blue cheese, crumbled
2 tablespoons dry white wine

Combine all ingredients and mix well. Use for sliced tomatoes or on any kind of salad, such as green or tossed.

❧

R2

YOGURT DRESSING

Makes 1 cup

1 cup plain yogurt
1 teaspoon lemon juice
½ teaspoon minced chives
½ teaspoon dry mustard

¼ teaspoon paprika
Salt and pepper to taste
1 small clove garlic, mashed

Combine ingredients thoroughly and chill. Allow to sit at least several hours for flavors to blend.

X

BREADS

℞

F / Rl

BRIOCHE

1 package yeast	¾ cup sweet butter
¼ cup lukewarm water	½ teaspoon salt
2 cups flour	1 tablespoon sugar
3 eggs plus 1 egg yolk	

Dissolve the yeast in lukewarm water. Stir in ½ cup flour until it forms a stiff ball. Turn out on lightly floured surface and knead a little to get a smooth surface. Cut a cross on the top of the ball and drop into a pitcher of lukewarm water. Let ball rise to the top (it will take 5 to 7 minutes).

Spoon 1½ cups flour onto pastry board. Make a well in the center and break in 2 eggs. Begin to knead the paste, adding the third egg little by little, to make a soft dough. Then pick up and crash down onto board about 100 times. The dough will be elastic when it detaches itself cleanly from fingers.

Knead the butter with the salt and sugar and then knead it into the dough. Mix it thoroughly but gently. Be sure not to overwork dough or it will lose its elasticity. Remove ball of sponge from water and drain on towel. Add it to dough, cutting and folding in. Form into ball and put it in floured bowl. Cover with plastic wrap and damp towel. Let it rise in warm place until double in bulk, about 2 hours. Turn the dough out onto lightly floured board and punch down. Return to bowl and chill for 6 hours, or overnight. It will rise a little. Punch down and proceed.

For individual brioches (about 8 to 10):

Place dough on lightly floured surface. Shape two-thirds of it into 2-inch balls to fit into 3-inch fluted brioche molds or muffin tins. Form an equal number of "hats," shaped something like a pear. Cut a cross in the base or make a depression and fit hat into depression. Be sure the base does not fill the mold more than half full. Cover and let rise about 30 minutes or until double in bulk. Cut around the base of the hat to keep it separate from the body during baking. Brush surface of brioche with a mixture of the egg yolk and 1 tablespoon water. Bake at 425 degrees for 15 to 20 minutes, until golden.

For one large brioche:

Fill fluted brioche mold half full and make hat with remaining dough, following procedure above.

Bake at 425 degrees for about 30 minutes, until golden.

For miniatures:

Use the smallest-size brioche molds; follow directions above and bake at 425 degrees for 7 to 10 minutes. Cool. To use for hors d'oeuvres, remove hats; hollow out brioche and dry the shell at 350 degrees for 3 to 4 minutes. Fill as desired and replace hats. Heat before serving. (Eat the insides!)

❧

F / R1

CARROT BREAD

2 loaves

4 eggs	¼ teaspoon salt
¾ cup honey	2 teaspoons cinnamon
½ cup unsulfured molasses	½ teaspoon cloves
1¼ cups salad oil	½ teaspoon nutmeg
2½ cups whole-wheat flour	2 teaspoons grated orange
2 teaspoons baking powder	peel
1½ teaspoons baking soda	2 cups grated carrots

Beat eggs in large bowl; add honey and molasses gradually and beat until thoroughly mixed. Add oil slowly and continue beating until well mixed. Stir in flour, baking powder, baking soda, salt, cinnamon, cloves, nutmeg and orange peel. Blend until mixture is smooth and stir in carrots.

Pour batter into 2 greased 9-x-5-inch loaf pans and bake at 350 degrees for 30 minutes. Reduce heat to 300 degrees and bake about 20 minutes longer, or until loaves test done. Tester should come out clean when stuck in center of bread. Cool in pans 10 minutes. Place loaves on wire racks and cool completely. Wrap in aluminum foil and store overnight before serving, or freeze. When loaves defrost, they will have mellowed.

ꞥ

F / R1

CHEESE AND APPLE BREAD

1 loaf

This tastes best the second day.

½ cup butter
2 eggs
⅔ cup sugar
2 cups flour
1½ teaspoons baking powder

½ teaspoon baking soda
1 teaspoon salt
1 cup peeled shredded apples
½ cup shredded Cheddar cheese

Combine butter, eggs and dry ingredients in large mixing bowl; blend well. Stir in apples and cheese. Turn into well-greased 9-x-5-inch loaf pan. Bake at 350 degrees, about 50 to 60 minutes, until center of loaf tests done. Cool thoroughly before removing from pan. Serve with sweet butter.

Freeze, if desired.

ซ

F / R3

GEORGIAN BREAD

Approximately 24 pieces

2 packages fresh yeast
1 tablespoon plus ½ teaspoon
sugar
1 cup warm milk

3½ cups flour, approximately
(more may be needed)
2 teaspoons salt
¼ pound butter, softened

Cheese filling:

1¼ pounds Muenster cheese,
grated

2 tablespoons butter,
softened
2 eggs

Sprinkle yeast and ½ teaspoon sugar over ½ cup warm milk. Allow to stand 2 to 3 minutes; then stir to dissolve yeast.

In warm place allow yeast to double in volume, about 8 minutes. Place flour in large bowl. Make well in center; add remaining milk, yeast mixture, 1 tablespoon sugar, salt and butter. With large spoon, blend in flour with other ingredients until too thick to stir. Then, using fingers, blend to form dough. Add more flour, if needed, to gather into ball. Knead dough on lightly floured surface for 6 to 10 minutes, until it is elastic, sprinkling on more flour as needed to keep the dough from sticking. Form into ball and place in lightly oiled bowl. Cover and allow to rise in warm place about 45 minutes, or until doubled in bulk. Punch dough down and allow to rise again for 30 minutes, until doubled in bulk again.

While dough is rising, prepare cheese filling. Combine cheese, butter and 1 egg in large bowl and beat with spoon until well blended and smooth.

Punch dough down and roll out on lightly floured board to thickness of about 1/16 inch. Cut into 4½-inch circles. On each round of dough, spread 1½ tablespoons cheese, leaving about 1½-inch border uncovered. Draw edges of dough up over filling to center, covering it and forming 6 pleats to make a hexagon-shaped pastry, or fold over sides and then fold in edges. Arrange on greased baking sheets; brush tops with remaining egg, which has been lightly beaten. Allow dough to rest 10 minutes, then bake at 375 degrees for 20 to 25 minutes, or until golden-brown. Serve warm.

These can be prepared several days ahead, refrigerated, and reheated at 350 degrees for 10 to 15 minutes. They can be prepared further in advance and frozen. To serve, defrost and reheat.

ᘛ

F

MIKE'S BREAD

4 loaves

My son, Michael, decided to contribute an original bread recipe to the book. Since he spent one summer baking bread for a living, he's well qualified to innovate. This crunchy-crusted, spongy-textured loaf with nutlike flavor was an instant success.

1 cup cornmeal, uncooked
1 cup whole-wheat cereal, uncooked
1 cup regular oatmeal, uncooked

2 tablespoons yeast
½ cup honey
2 teaspoons salt
2 cups whole-wheat flour
6 to 8 cups unbleached flour

Heat 4 cups of water to boiling. Pour boiling water over cornmeal, wheat cereal and oatmeal; cool. Meanwhile, add yeast to 1 cup warm water, and "proof." The yeast is proofed when small bubbles appear on the surface, in about 5 to 7 minutes. When water-grain mixture is cooled to about 100 degrees or so, add yeast mixture to it. Then add honey, 1 cup water and salt. Stir well. Add whole-wheat flour, ½ cup at a time, mixing well with spoon between additions. Add unbleached flour, about 1 cup at a time, mixing with spoon. When dough becomes too stiff to mix with spoon, use hands. Use only enough of the un-bleached flour to make a soft dough which will still be sticky.

Turn out on well-floured board and knead for 5 minutes. Dough will still be sticky. Place in well-greased bowl, cover with damp cloth and place in warm place to rise until doubled in bulk, or until a finger pressed into dough leaves imprint, about 1 hour.

Punch dough down; turn out on lightly floured board. Shape into 4 loaves and place in well-greased 9-x-5-inch loaf pans. Cover with wax paper and allow to rise in warm place until doubled in bulk, about 1 hour.

Bake at 350 degrees for about 65 minutes, or until loaves test done. Remove from pans and cool on wire racks before slicing.

❧

ONION POPOVERS

6 large popovers

3 eggs
1 cup milk
3 tablespoons chopped onion
¼ teaspoon salt

1 tablespoon melted shortening or oil
1 cup sifted flour

Blend together eggs, milk, onion, salt and shortening. Blend in flour until smooth, then beat at least 1 minute in electric mixer or 3 minutes with rotary beater. Fill well-greased custard cups half full. Bake at 400 degrees for 40 to 45 minutes, or until dark golden-brown and firm to the touch. Serve immediately.

❧

F / R1

PORTUGUESE SWEET BREAD

2 round loaves

2 packages yeast
¼ cup warm water
1 cup sugar
6 to 7 cups flour, approximately
1 teaspoon salt

1 cup milk, scalded and cooled to room temperature
3 eggs, room temperature
¼ pound sweet butter
1 beaten egg for glaze

In small bowl dissolve yeast in warm water. In large mixing bowl combine sugar, 4 cups flour and salt. Make a well in center of flour mixture and pour in yeast and milk. Add eggs and stir mixture until ingredients are combined. Beat in small pieces of butter. Then add more flour until dough forms soft ball. When it become difficult to stir the dough, work in flour with fingers. Turn dough out onto floured board and knead it with the heel of your hand until it is smooth and elastic.

Grease bowl and place dough in it. Cover and place in warm place to rise until double in bulk, about 1 hour. Dough is ready when a dent remains in it after it has been poked with a finger. Punch dough down; divide in half and let rest for 10 minutes.

Grease two 9-inch pie plates. Pat each half of dough into 8-inch round in each plate. Cover and place in warm place to rise again until doubled in bulk, about 40 minutes.

Brush top of each loaf with beaten egg and bake at 350 degrees for 45 to 60 minutes. Loaves are done when wooden toothpick inserted in center comes out clean. If tops brown too much before loaves are baked, cover tops lightly with aluminum foil. Cool loaves on wire rack. Serve warm with sweet butter.

Loaves freeze beautifully.

༝

SOPAIPILLAS

Approximately 20

The *sopaipillas* can be served just as a hot bread with soup or *guacamole*. In New Mexico they are always served with the meal, but with sweet toppings.

1¾ cups flour   2 tablespoons shortening
 2 teaspoons baking powder   ⅔ cup cold water
 1 teaspoon salt   Oil for deep-fat frying

Sift together dry ingredients; add shortening and cut in with pastry blender or knives. Gradually add just enough cold water to make dough of pastry consistency. Turn out on lightly floured board and knead gently until smooth. Cover dough and let rest for 5 minutes.

Roll out into even, 12-x-15-inch rectangle, about ⅛ to ¹⁄₁₆ inch thick. Cut into 2-x-3-inch pieces or 3-inch squares.

Cover dough with wax paper. Heat oil in deep pan to 375 degrees. Drop dough into very hot oil, a few at a time, turning them over 3 or 4 times so that they will puff evenly.

Allow to turn golden-brown on both sides. Serve warm with confectioners' sugar, warm honey or warm apple jelly.

✽

F / R1

STEPHANIE HARRIS'S OATMEAL-PLUS BREAD

3 loaves

Stephanie Harris, a vegetarian, puts lots of protein into this bread. It is not exactly simple, but it makes a wonderfully crunchy, thick, heavy loaf.

4½ cups water	¾ cup warm water
2 cups rolled oats, uncooked	¾ cup soy flour
1 cup high-protein cereal, uncooked *	4 cups whole-wheat flour
½ cup 12-grain cereal (or high-protein cereal) *, uncooked	1 cup triticale flour
	4 cups unbleached white flour
4½ teaspoons salt	¼ cup wheat germ
½ cup honey	½ cup nonfat-milk powder
3 tablespoons margarine	250-milligram vitamin C tablet,
3 tablespoons yeast (3 cakes)	crushed, mixed with 5 teaspoons whole-wheat flour

Combine water, cereals and salt, and boil for 1 minute. Stir in honey and margarine. While cooling, dissolve yeast in warm water. Then add

---

* These high-protein cereals are available in many natural-food stores. If only one kind is available, use 1½ cups of it.

to cooled cereal. Sift flours and add to cereals. Add milk powder and wheat germ. Crush vitamin C tablet; mix with whole-wheat flour and add 4½ teaspoons of mixture to dough. Turn out onto floured board and knead until smooth. Put in greased bowl and let rise until double in bulk, covered with damp towel. Knead again briefly and divide into 3 loaves. Place in greased 9-x-5-inch pans and let rise, covered, until doubled in bulk. Bake at 375 degrees for 40 minutes, or until well browned. Loaves freeze well.

WARM SPRINGS INDIAN FRIED BREAD

6 to 8 cakes

This recipe is from the Warm Springs Indian reservation in Oregon. Serve the bread with lots of butter.

3 cups sifted flour
2 teaspoons baking powder
1 teaspoon salt
1 teaspoon sugar

1 tablespoon butter
¾ to 1 cup warm milk
Fat for deep frying

Combine dry ingredients; cut in butter. Add enough warm milk to make a dough that is soft but easy to handle. Knead on floured board until dough is very smooth, soft but elastic. Don't use a lot of extra flour. Divide dough into 6 or 8 balls, each about the size of a lemon. Brush tops with melted butter. Cover and let stand 30 to 45 minutes.

Pat out each ball into a round 5 or 6 inches in diameter and ¼ inch thick. Fry in deep hot fat which has been heated to 365 degrees. Dough should rise to surface immediately. Cook until brown on one side; turn and brown on other side. Be careful not to pierce crust of bread in turning. Drain thoroughly on absorbent paper.

❧

F / R1

WHOLE-WHEAT BANANA BREAD

2 loaves

1⅓ cups honey	1 tablespoon baking powder
1 cup unsalted butter	½ teaspoon salt
3 large, very ripe bananas, mashed	1 teaspoon nutmeg
4 eggs	½ cup milk
3 cups whole-wheat flour	1 teaspoon vanilla

Cream honey and butter; add mashed bananas and beat well. Add eggs. Combine dry ingredients and add to batter alternately with milk, and then add vanilla. Spoon into 2 greased 9-x-5-inch loaf pans and bake at 350 degrees for 50 to 55 minutes. Cool in pans on rack for 10 minutes; remove from pans and cool completely on rack.

The bread should not be served until it has been allowed to mellow for 1 day, well wrapped in foil and left at room temperature. Alternately, the bread may be frozen; it will be ready to eat after defrosting.

❧

F / R3

ZUCCHINI WALNUT BREAD

2 loaves

2½ cups shredded, unpeeled zucchini	¾ teaspoon salt
1 cup whole-wheat flour	3 eggs
1½ cups unbleached flour	1¼ cups sugar
2 teaspoons baking powder	¾ cup vegetable oil
½ teaspoon baking soda	¼ cup honey
1 teaspoon cinnamon	½ cup raisins
½ teaspoon nutmeg	2 teaspoons grated lemon rind
½ teaspoon ground cloves	1 cup chopped walnuts

Shred zucchini and allow to sit in strainer to allow moisture to drain off. Stir together flours, baking powder, baking soda, spices and salt. Beat eggs until very light. Gradually beat in sugar, beating until mixture is light. Beat in oil until mixture is light. Blend in flour mixture with rubber spatula until smooth. Add zucchini, honey, raisins, lemon rind and nuts. Stir until well mixed. Spoon batter into 2 greased 9-x-5-inch loaf pans and bake at 350 degrees for 40 to 50 minutes, until loaves are done. Cool in pan 10 minutes. Then remove and cool on wire racks. Wrap in aluminum foil and store overnight before slicing.

Freeze, if desired.

❧ XI ❧

DESSERTS

❧

FRUIT AND CHEESE

Apples—with Camembert, Cheddar, blues, Parmesan
Bananas—with goat cheeses such as *chabichou*
Cantaloupe—with Parmesan
Cherries—with Crema Danica
Figs—with Stilton
Grapes—with Camembert; provolone; feta or other sheep cheese; Pont l'Évêque; Appenzeller
Honeydew—with Edam
Nectarines—with Brie
Oranges—with Gorgonzola
Peaches—with triple creams such as Crema Danica, Gervais, Chantilly; Gorgonzola
Pears—with Camembert, provolone, blues
Pineapple—with Camembert
Plums—purple with Stilton; red with Appenzeller
Strawberries—with triple creams

❧

R1

CHOCOLATE-DIPPED FRUITS

8 servings

36 to 40 orange segments, or 48 medium-sized strawberries with stems; or combination of both
2 (1-pound) packages semisweet chocolate squares

Wash berries and dry. Melt chocolate over hot water to a temperature of about 100 degrees. Stir occasionally. Keep over hot water, but not on the stove while dipping.

If dipping berries, hold them by the stem and swirl around in chocolate. If a berry is without a stem, use a toothpick. Use toothpicks to hold orange segments while dipping. Place dipped fruit on baking sheet which has been covered with wax paper. Cover any spots on the fruit which were missed with a little chocolate on a spoon. Chill dipped fruits until chocolate hardens and serve.

℧

R1

CHOCOLATE-WRAPPED PEARS

6 servings

1 cup sugar	6 firm, ripe pears with stems
4 cups water	4 ounces semisweet chocolate
Juice of 1 lemon	squares
2 cinnamon sticks	4 tablespoons sweet butter,
4 whole cloves	softened
2 tablespoons crème de menthe	Fresh or crystallized mint

Dissolve sugar in water. Add lemon juice, spices and crème de menthe and simmer, tightly covered, for 10 to 15 minutes. Peel the pears carefully, leaving stems intact, and cut a slice off bottoms so they will stand upright. Poach pears in gently boiling syrup until tender, 30 to 40 minutes. Cool pears in syrup and chill thoroughly, overnight.

Melt chocolate in a bowl over warm water. Add butter and stir until it is melted and mixture is smooth. Remove pears from syrup and dry carefully with paper towel. Dip pears in melted chocolate to coat evenly. Use spoon, if necessary, to fill in uncoated spots. Lift pears to drain off excess chocolate; arrange on a serving dish. Decorate top of each pear with sprig of fresh or crytallized mint. Chill until ready to serve.

❧

R1

GRAPES IN BRANDY

4 servings

¾ cup honey
6 tablespoons good brandy
1 tablespoon lemon juice

1 pound seedless grapes,
washed and drained
1 cup sour cream

Mix the honey, brandy and lemon juice thoroughly. Add the grapes to the mixture and stir gently to coat grapes completely. Chill for several hours, or overnight. Stir occasionally.

To serve, spoon into 4 individual serving dishes and top each portion with ¼ cup sour cream.

❧

MARINATED FRUIT

8 servings

⅔ cup dry vermouth or orange
juice
5 tablespoons sugar*
½ teaspoon cinnamon

1 large pineapple, cut in wedges
4 navel oranges, peeled and
sectioned
2 pears, unpeeled and diced

Combine the vermouth, sugar and cinnamon and allow to stand in the refrigerator for at least 1 hour. Strain the liquid, discarding the sugar residue. Pour liquid over prepared fruits. Marinate at least 1 hour in the refrigerator before serving.

---

* If orange juice is used, reduce sugar to 2 tablespoons.

❦

R2

BLUEBERRY KIR SAUCE

5 servings

1 tablespoon butter
1 tablespoon cornstarch
¼ cup crème de cassis
¾ cup dry white wine

1 tablespoon lemon juice
1½ cups fresh or frozen
 blueberries

Melt butter in saucepan. Combine cornstarch and cassis to make a smooth mixture. Gradually stir cassis mixture into melted butter. Add wine and lemon juice and cook, stirring, until mixture is thick. Stir in berries and cook just until they begin to burst. Chill. Serve over vanilla ice cream.

❦

R3

SAUCE FOR NECTARINES (OR PEACHES)

Makes approximately 2 cups

1½ cups sour cream
4½ tablespoons crème de cacao

4½ tablespoons Seville orange
 marmalade
Dash salt

Combine ingredients and serve with chilled, sliced nectarines (or peaches).
Makes enough for 10 to 12 pieces of fruit.

❦

R1

NECTARINES AND BRANDY
4 to 6 servings

6 medium nectarines	1½ teaspoons vanilla
¾ cup sugar	1 cup sour cream
1 cup water	1 tablespoon confectioners'
3 tablespoons brandy	sugar
	2 tablespoons brandy

Blanch and peel nectarines; pit and cut into quarters. In large sauce-pan, combine nectarines, granulated sugar and water. Bring to boil; simmer 1 minute. Stir in 3 tablespoons brandy and vanilla. Let stand until mixture reaches room temperature; then chill. Just before serv-ing, arrange fruit in 4 to 6 individual dishes. Combine sour cream, confectioners' sugar and remaining brandy; spoon over nectarines and serve.

❦

R1

ORANGES MARINATED IN LIQUEUR
4 servings

6 seedless oranges	12 tablespoons orange liqueur
	or crème de cacao

Peel oranges, removing all of white membrane.* Slice. Place oranges in individual serving dishes or one large serving dish and pour over

---

* To peel oranges easily, plunge them into boiling water and reduce heat to bare simmer. Allow oranges to heat for 3 to 4 minutes. This makes the peel easy to remove and takes most of the white pith with the skin.

I have never found out, however, if the heat destroys a lot of the vitamin C, so I recom-mend it only when there are a lot of oranges to be peeled for a party.

either orange liqueur or crème de cacao. Refrigerate for 12 to 24 hours, turning oranges occasionally so they are covered with the liqueur.

Serve chilled.

ᖇᕝ

ORANGE ICES

6 servings

2 teaspoons freshly grated
  lemon peel
2 tablespoons freshly
  squeezed lemon juice
½ pint heavy cream, whipped

1 quart orange sherbet,
  softened
¾ cup chilled dry sherry
Fruit or mint leaves for garnish

Have peel and juice prepared ahead. Whip cream.

Place sherbet in bowl with lemon peel and juice. Beat until creamy while gradually adding chilled sherry. Pour or spoon immediately into stemmed chilled glasses. Top with whipped cream and garnish as desired. Serve with straws.

ᖇᕝ

R1

PEACHES IN ORANGE LIQUEUR

6 servings

2 pounds fresh peaches
¼ cup butter
1 cup sugar

½ cup orange liqueur
  (Cointreau, Triple Sec or
  Grand Marnier)
¼ cup lemon juice
½ cup slivered almonds

Wash, halve and pit peaches. Arrange, cut side down, one layer deep, in shallow baking pan. Cream together butter and sugar; stir in orange liqueur and lemon juice. Spoon mixture over peaches and refrigerate, if desired. To serve, return to room temperature and sprinkle with almonds. Bake at 375 degrees for 35 to 40 minutes, until peaches are soft. Baste with juices once or twice. Serve warm, not hot.

ᵔᵕ

PEARS IN ZABAGLIONE

8 servings

8 firm, ripe pears with stems
1 lemon, sliced

¼ to 1 cup sugar, depending
    on ripeness of pears
Zabaglione Sauce (recipe below)

Peel pears and cut off slice at bottom so they will stand up. In water just to cover the pears, with lemon slices and sugar, cook the pears until tender. Keep water at a simmer; *do not boil*. Drain and chill pears in refrigerator for several hours, or overnight.

Zabaglione Sauce:

8 egg yolks
¼ cup sugar

1 cup Marsala wine
2 tablespoons brandy
1 tablespoon water

Combine yolks with sugar in top of double boiler. Beat well with rotary beater or wire whisk. Add wine, brandy and water and beat well. Place over hot water and continue beating until mixture thickens. Remove from heat and chill.

To serve, place pears in stemmed goblets or individual glass serving dishes, if possible. Spoon over sauce and decorate with green leaf at stems.

℞

R1

PEARS WITH GORGONZOLA

6 servings

3 pears, ripe but not mushy   5 ounces Gorgonzola cheese,
                                       softened

Wash pears, halve and remove centers with teaspoon. Also remove woody part, but leave stems intact. Into cavities, spoon the cheese. Refrigerate. It's best to serve the pears when the refrigerator chill is off, so leave them out about 15 minutes before serving.

℞

R2

RED PLUM COMPOTE

6 servings

⅔ cup sugar   3-inch stick cinnamon
1 cup dry white wine   Zest of ½ lemon
1 cup water   18 firm, ripe, red plums,
4 whole cloves   stemmed and rinsed

Combine sugar, wine, water, cloves, cinnamon and lemon in saucepan large enough to hold the plums. Bring ingredients to boil and cook, uncovered, for 5 minutes.

Add plums and bring mixture to boil; lower heat and simmer the plums 10 to 20 minutes, depending on their ripeness, until they are tender but still hold their shape.

Some plums will be ready before others. Remove them as they are. Then, when all are cooked, return all the plums to the syrup and cool. Chill plums in syrup.

This is excellent served either plain or over vanilla ice cream.

PREPARE-AHEAD CHOCOLATE SOUFFLÉ
8 servings

This is not as light as a traditional French soufflé and, because of the flour content, it can be prepared several hours ahead and baked when it is time to serve.

5 egg yolks	2 ounces unsweetened
3/4 cup. sugar	chocolate, melted
4 drops vanilla	8 egg whites
1 cup unbleached flour	Confectioners' sugar
2 cups milk	1/2 pint heavy cream, whipped

In a bowl beat yolks with 1/2 cup sugar and vanilla until light and fluffy. Gradually beat in flour until a paste is formed. Meanwhile, bring milk to a boil. Add egg mixture all at once and bring again to boil, beating vigorously with wire whisk until paste is smooth. Continue stirring with wooden spoon until mixture is thick, like a pastry cream. Add melted chocolate and stir until blended. Cool. Beat egg whites until soft peaks form; gradually beat in remaining 1/4 cup sugar until stiff peaks form. Fold egg whites into batter. Cover bowl lightly and allow to sit at room temperature for up to 4 hours before serving. To serve, spoon into 8 greased individual 2-inch soufflé dishes and bake at 350 degrees for 20 minutes. Dust with confectioners' sugar and serve with whipped cream on the side.

Rl

COLD LEMON SOUFFLÉ
10 to 12 servings

2 envelopes unflavored gelatin	2 cups sugar
1/2 cup cold water	2 teaspoons grated lemon rind
8 eggs, separated	2 cups heavy cream
1 cup fresh lemon juice	Strawberries and toasted,
1 teaspoon salt	slivered almonds for garnish

To make a collar for the soufflé dish, fold a 30-inch length of foil, 12 inches wide, in half lengthwise. Lightly butter inside of collar and wrap around outside of 2-quart soufflé dish so the collar stands above the rim by 3 inches. Fasten with tape.

Sprinkle gelatin over cold water to soften. In top of double boiler combine yolks, lemon juice, salt and 1 cup sugar. Cook over boiling water, stirring, until mixture coats the back of a spoon. Stir in gelatin and lemon rind; turn into a bowl and refrigerate until mixture is slightly thickened, stirring occasionally.

Beat whites until they hold their shape; gradually beat in 1 cup sugar; continue beating until mixture holds stiff peaks. Whip cream until stiff. Fold cream and whites gently into lemon mixture. Pour into prepared soufflé dish; refrigerate until firm, at least 3 hours.

To serve, remove soufflé collar; top with strawberries and almonds.

❧

Rl

ESPRESSO MOUSSE

12 to 15 servings

1 envelope unflavored gelatin	3 tablespoons brandy
¼ cup cold water	1 teaspoon grated lemon peel
1 cup brewed extra-strength espresso coffee	½ cup chopped toasted almonds or chopped walnuts
1 cup sugar	3 egg whites
2 cups heavy cream	¼ teaspoon salt

Sprinkle gelatin over ¼ cup cold water to soften. Heat the coffee and ¾ cup sugar in pan until sugar dissolves. Add gelatin to hot mixture and stir to dissolve gelatin; cool. Pour this mixture into a shallow dish which can go into the freezer. Freeze for 45 minutes or until mixture is solid 1 inch around edge, no more. Pour mixture into cold bowl; beat until smooth and creamy. Whip cream until soft peaks form; fold into coffee mixture with brandy, lemon peel and nuts. Beat egg whites with salt until foamy. Gradually beat in remaining ¼ cup sugar, beating until stiff peaks form. Fold into coffee mixture. Spoon into 2- or 2½-quart soufflé or similar serving dish and refrigerate for several hours or overnight, until firm.

‹◦›

F

FROZEN GRAND MARNIER SOUFFLÉ

8 servings

2 tablespoons unflavored
gelatin, soaked in ¼ cup
water
½ cup boiling water
6 egg yolks

1⅓ cups orange juice
2 cups sugar
⅔ cup Grand Marnier
1 pint heavy cream, whipped
Praline

Dissolve gelatin in boiling water. In a separate bowl beat egg yolks until light; add orange juice, sugar, Grand Marnier, and gelatin and mix until it starts to thicken. Fold in whipped cream. Pour into 7-inch soufflé dish with wax-paper collar. Freeze at least 4 hours (the soufflé will keep for a couple of weeks in freezer). Remove from freezer a half-hour before serving. Remove collar. Roll edge in ground praline.

Praline:

½ cup sugar
2 tablespoons water

½ cup slivered toasted
almonds

Boil sugar and water in heavy-bottomed saucepan until caramelized. Stir in almonds and pour on greased baking sheet. When cold and crisp, grind or pound into crumbs. This will keep indefinitely in tightly closed jar in refrigerator.

✌

F / R2

GRASSHOPPER MOLD

12 servings

2 envelopes unflavored gelatin
1 cup cold water
1 cup sugar
¼ teaspoon salt
6 eggs, separated

½ cup crème de menthe
½ cup white crème de cacao
2 cups heavy cream, whipped
Garnish: whipped cream,
　　chocolate shavings, optional

In medium saucepan sprinkle gelatin over water. Add ½ cup of the sugar, salt, and egg yolks; stir until thoroughly blended. Place over low heat; stir constantly until gelatin dissolves and mixture thickens slightly, about 5 minutes. Remove from heat; stir in crème de menthe and crème de cacao. Chill, stirring occasionally, until mixture mounds slightly when dropped from spoon.

Beat egg whites in large bowl until stiff but not dry. Gradually add remaining ½ cup sugar and beat until very stiff. Fold whites into gelatin mixture. Then fold in whipped cream. Turn into 12-cup mold. Chill until firm. If desired, garnish with additional whipped cream and chocolate shavings.

✌

F

SPOOM

6 servings

1 cup sugar
½ cup water
4 egg whites

1 quart lemon sherbet or ice,
　　softened
Dry red or rosé wine, or
　　champagne
6 large strawberries, optional

Combine sugar and water and cook over high heat until mixture reaches 238 degrees on a candy thermometer (soft-ball stage *). Beat the whites until very stiff. While syrup is still hot, pour it in a thin thread very slowly over beaten whites, beating vigorously all the time. Combine this meringue with the sherbet in champagne or other stemmed glasses or in individual sauce dishes, filling the glass three-quarters full. Freeze. This will keep for a week or so. When ready to serve, lace each serving with wine, top with strawberry and serve immediately.

ღ

R1

STRAWBERRY BAVARIAN

6 servings

1 quart strawberries, hulled	3 tablespoons cherry-flavored liqueur
2 envelopes unflavored gelatin	
¼ cup cold water	2 cups heavy cream, whipped
½ cup sugar	Whole strawberries for garnish

Puree strawberries in blender. In a saucepan soften gelatin in cold water. Add to puree with sugar. Heat and stir until gelatin is dissolved. Cool and add cherry liqueur. Chill, stirring occasionally, until mixture begins to thicken. Fold in whipped cream and spoon into 8-cup mold or serving bowl until mixture is set. To serve, unmold and top with whole berries.

---

* Soft-ball stage can be tested as follows without a thermometer: Have a cupful of cold, not ice, water ready. Drop a little of boiling syrup into the water. When the syrup can be gathered up in the fingers into a soft ball that holds its shape until pressure is removed, it has reached the soft-ball stage, 238 degrees.

❧

F

STRAWBERRY SORBET, OR MOUSSE

12 servings

3 pints strawberries, hulled and cleaned

2 cups sugar

Juice of 3 lemons

Juice of 3 oranges

½ cup orange liqueur

Combine strawberries with sugar and juices in blender and blend until smooth. Add orange liqueur and pour into refrigerator ice-cube trays for freezing. Freeze until mixture is partially frozen. Transfer to a large bowl and beat until mushy. Return to trays and freeze until firm. To serve, leave in refrigerator about 45 minutes before serving.

To make this sorbet into a mousse:

After mixture is partially frozen, beat until mushy. Fold in 1 stiffly beaten egg white and ½ cup heavy cream, whipped. Follow remaining directions. Or follow directions through first freezing and make several days ahead. Freeze until firm. Two hours before serving, allow to sit at room temperature 15 to 20 minutes. Then beat in blender until mushy and continue with directions.

❧

STRAWBERRIES WITH KIRSCH

10 servings

2 quarts strawberries

⅔ cup confectioners' sugar, or to taste

3 tablespoons kirsch (or other suitable liqueur such as Cointreau, Grand Marnier, or orange Triple Sec)

Crème Fraîche (page 57)

Wash and hull berries; place in bowl and sprinkle with sugar, then kirsch. The quantities really depend on the sweetness and flavor of the strawberries. Chill in the refrigerator for a maximum of 2 hours or the berries become too soft.

The strawberries are most attractive when served from a large glass bowl or in footed goblets. Pass Crème Fraîche separately.

ဗ

F / R3

KATE'S LEMON SQUARES

Makes approximately 100

Crust:

1 cup butter, softened
½ cup confectioners' sugar

2 cups unbleached flour
Pinch of salt

Topping:

4 eggs
2 cups granulated sugar
6 tablespoons flour

6 tablespoons fresh lemon juice
6 tablespoons lemon rind
Confectioners' sugar for topping

For crust: Combine ingredients; blend with fingers or pastry blender, then pat evenly into 10-x-15-inch jelly-roll pan. Bake at 350 degrees for 20 minutes.

Meanwhile, beat eggs slightly; stir in sugar, flour, lemon juice and rind. Mix well and spread over baked crust. Bake for 25 minutes more. When cooled, cut into squares; remove and sift with confectioners' sugar.

To freeze: bake, cut into squares and freeze. To serve, defrost and sprinkle with confectioners' sugar.

ᵠ

LEMON ICE WITH WINE

6 servings

6 generous scoops lemon ice or
lemon sherbet

½ cup white wine

2½ to 3 tablespoons orange
liqueur

Spoon the sherbet into individual serving dishes, preferably glass stemware. Combine the wine and orange liqueur and pour over the ice just before serving.

ᵠ

F / R2

ERNA'S LACE COOKIES

Makes approximately 30

⅔ cup blanched almonds
½ cup butter
Dash salt

½ cup sugar
1 tablespoon unbleached flour
2 tablespoons milk

Grind almonds. Melt butter in skillet. Add salt, sugar and flour and stir over low heat until sugar melts. Add almonds and milk and blend well, stirring until mixture thickens a little. Cool about 1 minute. Drop from a teaspoon on greased and floured cookie sheets. Leave room between them because they spread. You can get about 10 cookies per regular sheet. Bake at 350 degrees for 6 to 8 minutes, or until golden-brown. Cool only long enough for cookies to firm up so they can be removed from cookie sheet with a knife. If they set too hard return to oven briefly to soften.

These cookies can be frozen if well wrapped, or they will keep a couple of days if stored in tightly covered container and kept dry.

᷐

F / Rl

DOUBLE CHOCOLATE THREAT

12 servings

For chocaholics, this is nirvana!

Brownie Crust:

⅓ cup butter
2 squares unsweetened
  chocolate
1 cup sugar
2 eggs, well beaten
⅔ cup unbleached flour

½ teaspoon baking powder
¼ teaspoon salt
1 teaspoon vanilla
½ pint heavy cream, whipped,
  for garnish

Melt butter and chocolate over low heat or in top of double boiler over hot water. Remove from heat, add sugar and eggs and mix well. Sift together flour, baking powder and salt. Stir into chocolate mixture. Add vanilla and pour into greased and floured 8- or 9-inch-square baking pan. Bake at 350 degrees for 30 to 35 minutes, until brownies are baked but not dry. Cool. Remove from pan and cut into strips wide enough to come most of the way up the sides of a 2-quart soufflé dish or charlotte mold. Cut the strips through the center to make 2 thinner layers. Line bottom and sides of dish with brownie layers. Don't worry about piecing; it won't show.

While brownies are baking, make . . .

Filling:

1½ pounds semisweet chocolate
½ cup strong coffee
3 eggs, separated

½ cup coffee liqueur
½ cup heavy cream

Melt chocolate with coffee over low heat or in top of double boiler over hot water. Remove from heat. Beat yolks until pale in color; stir into chocolate. Stir in coffee liqueur. Cool. Beat whites until stiff but not dry. Whip cream stiff. Fold whites and cream into chocolate mixture and spoon into brownie-lined dish.

Chill overnight in refrigerator, well wrapped, or freeze. To serve, defrost if frozen. To remove from pan, loosen from sides with knife, then dip into hot water to loosen and turn out onto serving plate.

Whip ½ pint heavy cream until stiff and cover top and parts of sides with cream. Serve small slices.

℀

R7

SYLVIA'S FRUITCAKE

6 pounds

Sylvia Schur's fruitcake is like no other. It has little candied fruit, lots of dried fruit in large pieces, and lots of large pieces of nuts. There is very little cake in relation to the fruit. Don't chop nuts or cut up fruit.

½ pound shelled Brazil nuts	1 cup drained uncolored
½ pound shelled walnuts	maraschino cherries
½ pound shelled pecans	1½ cups unbleached flour
1 pound pitted dates	1 teaspoon baking powder
1 pound dried apricots	1 teaspoon salt
3 ounces pitted prunes, halved	6 eggs
1 cup diced glacéed fruit, or ½	1 cup sugar
cup diced glacéed fruit and	2 teaspoons vanilla
½ cup raisins	Nuts for garnish
	¾ cup brandy

Line a 6-cup round cake or soufflé dish with brown paper.

Combine fruits and nuts in large bowl. Sift flour and baking powder over fruits and nuts, and combine until everything is well coated. Beat salt, eggs, sugar and vanilla until foamy. Pour egg mixture over fruits and nuts and combine thoroughly but gently. Fill prepared pan to the top with batter. Press cake mixture down in pan so it will hold shape after baking. Stud cake with additional nuts. Bake at 300 degrees for 1¼ hours, or until cake tester comes out clean. Spoon half of brandy over cake as it comes from oven. When cake cools, pour rest of brandy over it.

To store, after cake cools, wrap in cheesecloth which has been soaked in brandy. Overwrap tightly with heavy-duty aluminum foil or store in airtight container. When cheesecloth dries out, resoak in brandy.

INDEX

biscuit mix for, 53
buying, 26
Carrie Lee Nelson's Peking, 95-96
Chinese
  barbecued, 99-100
  and walnuts, 100-101
with eggplant, 99
Italian coating mix, 47
Mexican, 101-102
poultry seasoning, 46
Provençal, 97-98
Roman style, 98
in rum, 96-97
shake it and bake it, 47
stock, 90
stuffed chicken breasts, 102
Chicken liver pâté
in aspic, 63-64
walnut bourbon, 80
Chilaquiles, 141
Chile powder, 39n., 142n.
Chiles, 141n.
Chili, 50
Chinese Restaurant Syndrome, 19
Chinese
  barbecued ribs, 135
  chicken
    barbecued, 99-100
    and walnuts, 100-101
  pot roast, 125
  shredded cucumber, 177
Chocolate
  double threat, 223-224
  fruits dipped in, 207-208
  pears wrapped in, 208
  prepare-ahead soufflé, 215
  pudding, 56
Chowder
  Bermuda fish, 84
  Mo's clam, 87-88
Chutney, clam dip with, 64
Cider rice pilaf, 162
Cinnamon sugar, 38
Clam
  chowder, Mo's, 87-88
  and chutney dip, 64
  and oyster broth, 86
Clapp, Sara, 150
Coal-tar-based dyes, 14, 20
Cocina, La, 134
Cocoa, instant, 37-38
Coffee gelatin, 60
Compote, red plum, 214
Consumer's Dictionary of Food Additives, A
  (Winter), 17
Convenience foods, 11-33
Convenience recipes, 37-60
Cookies
  Erna's lace, 222
  oatmeal mix, 50
  slice and bake, 51

Cooking trends, 30-33
Corn roast in foil, 162-163
Corned beef, 126
Crab meat
  egg Foo Yong, 111
  Mo's seafood in cheese sauce, 114
Cracked wheat, *see* Bulgur
Cranberry
  gelatin, 60
  salad mold, 178
Cream, heavy, 32
Cream sauce for vegetables, 43
Crème fraîche, 57
Cucumber
  salad, 178
    Chinese shredded, 177
    with nectarines, 180-181
    with walnuts, 179
  salmon soufflé with, 117
  soup, Iranian, 87
Curry (curried)
  avocado soup, 83
  Cheddar snacks, 64
  French dressing, 45
  Indian cheese spread, 70
  mushroom strudels, 65-66
Curry powder, 39

Date nut muffins, 53
Desserts, 207-225
  blueberry kir sauce, 210
  chocolate
    double threat, 223-224
    fruits dipped in, 207-208
    pears wrapped in, 208
    prepare-ahead soufflé, 215
  Erna's lace cookies, 222
  fruit
    and cheese, 207
    chocolate-dipped, 207-208
    marinated, 209
  gelatins, 59-60
  grapes in brandy, 209
  grasshopper mold, 218
  lemon ice with wine, 222
  lemon squares, Kate's, 221
  mincemeat, Mary Humelsine's, 57-58
  mousse
    espresso, 216-217
    strawberry, 220
  nectarines
    and brandy, 211
    sauce for, 210
  oranges
    ices, 212
    marinated in liqueur, 211-212
  peaches
    in orange liqueur, 212-213
    sauce for, 210
  pears
    chocolate-wrapped, 208